The Making of
the English Middle Class

The Making of
the English Middle Class

Business, Society
and Family Life
in London, 1660–1730

PETER EARLE

University of California Press
Berkeley and Los Angeles

For my father, J.B.F. Earle

First published in 1989 by Methuen and the University of California Press
Berkeley and Los Angeles
Copyright © Peter Earle 1989

Typeset by CentraCet, Cambridge
Printed in Great Britain
by Mackays of Chatham

ISBN 0-520-06826-2

Contents

Illustrations

TABLES

FIGURES

Preface

This is a book about the London middle classes in the period between 1660 and 1730. The period was chosen because of the availability of sources and also because it was the lifetime of Daniel Defoe, on whom I have written previously and whose views on a wide range of subjects will be found scattered through the pages. The subject was chosen because it seems to me an extremely important one, despite the fact that it has long been the habit of social and economic historians to be slightly embarrassed by, if not downright critical of, the rise of bourgeois society. This has led to an absurd dichotomy in the academic mind, which simultaneously welcomes a rise in the living standards of the people and sneers at the self-improving, self-serving ambitions of the middle classes which made such improvement possible.

An unhistorical distaste for the bourgeois and for profit has been paralleled by the fashion of English historians, and particularly English urban historians, to play down the significance of London and to insist on a broad development of English economy and society in which provincial enterprise is seen as equally important to that of the metropolis. This may be true of the second two-thirds of the eighteenth century, but it is certainly not true of the period covered by this book, the period which defined and created the society and economy which ushered in the modern world. In this period, London was the only real city in England, and London totally dominated English urban culture and indeed invented it, so much so that the greatest compliment that could be paid to a provincial town was to be called a little London.

The book is in three parts. Part One starts with an introduction which attempts to define what contemporaries thought of as the 'middle station' or the 'middling sort of people' and what we would think of as the middle class. There then follows a description of the London economy, with the emphasis on the opportunities which existed for the middling people to make a good living. Part Two examines the business life of Londoners, starting with apprenticeship and going on to consider the problems and potential rewards of a business career in the metropolis. Part Three looks at the family, social, political and material life of the middle-class Londoner, thus hopefully providing a well-rounded group portrait of this enterprising and ambitious sector of English society.

In the text I often use the word 'Augustan' to describe my period, an adjective borrowed from Professor Geoffrey Holmes, who like myself feels that the period has a special character in English history, but has no single word adjective like Elizabethan or Victorian to describe it. He therefore borrowed the adjective 'Augustan' from the literary historians and, since this seems rather a good word to describe the period, at once imperialistic, solid, urbane and prosperous, I have often used it myself. When I use the word 'City', i.e. with a capital, I mean the ancient area within the walls, the same area that we call the City today. When I write 'city', with a lower case c, I mean the whole built-up area, as I do when I write 'London', 'the metropolis', 'metropolitan', etc.

My thanks are due to the staffs of the London libraries and record offices where I have gathered the bulk of my material and also to those of provincial record offices who kindly replied to my enquiry regarding London material in their collections. In the end, I regret that time prevented me from making use of what sounds as though it would have been a valuable additional source for the book. I would also like to thank Steve Rappaport for advice on coding my material, Anne McGlone for advice and assistance on computing, David Hebb for telling me to cut everything I wrote by a third, Jeremy Boulton for reading the chapter on marriage, Henry Horwitz for reading the whole manuscript, members of seminars in London, Leeds and Cambridge for useful criticism of papers drawn from my material, members of my special subject and M.Sc. classes at L.S.E. for comment and discussion over the years, and my family for putting up with my obsession with my word processor and with finishing the book. I would particularly like to thank an anonymous reader for Methuen whose friendly advice has, I hope, much improved the structure of the book. I would finally like to thank two other people whom I have not met: Percival Boyd, whose Index of London Citizens in the library of the Society of Genealogists has proved invaluable, and Richard Grassby, whose articles based on the Orphans' Inventories and published in 1970 first drew my attention to the wealth of material in what has been the main source for this book.

One

Metropolitan
Economy and Society

1 The Middle Station

This book is about the men and women who occupied what Daniel Defoe called the middle station. We would call such people the middle class, a term not much used before the later eighteenth century, though it had long been apparent that a tripartite description of society was a useful one and expressions like the 'middle station' or 'the middling sort of people' were common in the late seventeenth and early eighteenth centuries.[1]

Who were these middling people? Such a question is no easier to answer than it is to define the middle classes today. There is, inevitably, so much blurring at the edges. However, in very general terms, there is no great problem. The 'upper part of mankind', the upper class in our terminology, were the gentry and aristocracy. These were men of independent means, normally but not necessarily landowners, who lived 'on Estates and without the Mechanism of Employment'. They were, in other words, men with a private income who did not have to work for a living. The 'mechanick part of mankind', the working class, were 'the meer labouring people who depend upon their hands.'[2] Between these extremes were the middling people, who worked but ideally did not get their hands dirty. The majority were commercial or industrial capitalists who had a stock of money, acquired by paternal gift, inheritance or loan, which they continually turned over to make more money. They also, together with the upper part of mankind, employed the mechanicks, who had no stock of money and so depended on others for their living.

Such a description makes the social structure of our period look superficially like that of Victorian times as described by Karl Marx, a fact which should not be surprising since Marx's society certainly grew out of the one discussed in this book.

Marx analysed society on economic lines and writers in our period were beginning to do the same, moving away from a conservative view of the world in which status, esteem and degree were the criteria for ranking the social order. Such changes in social description were necessary to take account of the changes in society brought about by economic development from the sixteenth century onwards. The growth of towns, and especially of London, the expansion of inland and foreign trade, of industry and the professions, had rapidly increased the numbers of those belonging to the urban middle station and made a nonsense of systems of social classification based on a purely rural and agricultural society. Meanwhile, the social polarization which accompanied these changes had created increasing numbers at the bottom of society who were completely divorced from ownership or use of land or any other form of capital and so were forced to be 'meer labouring people who depend on their hands'. Such, in embryo, were the proletariat who were later to be described by Marx.

Very few middling people were the sort of capitalists that Marx had in mind when he analysed the bourgeoisie. This was still a pre-industrial society in which most capital was engaged in agriculture, commerce and distribution. The days of huge concentrations of industrial capital and of a large industrial labour force were yet to come. Work was still on a small scale and few capitalists employed more than half a dozen people, a fact which makes it difficult to define the break-off point between the middle and working classes. Indeed, many people who clearly belong to the working classes, such as poor farmers and most artisans, were in a sense petty capitalists. They owned their own tools and used their own money to buy raw materials, seed and stock, and hoped to make a profit by the labour which they added to this petty capital. However, the net result of all this effort was no improvement in their lot. They continued to labour all their lives, each week hoping to make sufficient money to feed themselves and provide the capital for the next week's work. These people do not belong to the middle station.

Other petty capitalists who hardly seem to differ in kind managed to cross this barrier in society. What lifted them out of the mechanick part of mankind was the fact that their activities not only fed and clothed them but also enabled them to accumulate on a regular basis and so improve themselves. It was, then, accumulation and improvement, as well as the employment of capital and labour, which were the essential features of the middle sort of people. There might be a huge social and financial gulf between the rich Levant merchant and the small shopkeeper, but this should not disguise the fact that both men were engaged in essentially the same type of activity. They were both turning over capital for profit, even if their capitals, their turnover and their rates of profit and accumulation were very different. Both types of men will be considered in this book.

The break-off point at the top of the middle station is just as difficult to determine as that at the bottom. The first problem is where to place the professional men. Some writers thought that professionals, especially 'the Men of Letters, such as Clergy, Lawyers and Physicians', were honorary members of the gentry.[3] Some were not so sure. On the one hand, such men did not share a major characteristic of the gentleman in that they were not idle; their very profession was a 'mechanism of employment'. But they also did not share in an important feature of the lives of most middling people. They did not turn over capital to make a profit, relying for their income mainly on salaries, fees and perquisites. The professionals in fact occupied an intermediate position between the upper and middling parts of mankind. Some of them, such as bishops and most barristers and physicians, were clearly members of the upper class. Most other members of the learned professions probably thought of themselves as upper class, priding themselves on their education and often on their birth, and clinging valiantly to such labels as Esquire and gentleman. However, as will be seen when the professions are looked at more closely in Chapter 2, most of these people really belong to the middle station in terms of income and life-style, even if they do not fit too neatly into the functional definitions which have been employed here.

Another major problem was the definition of the status 'gentleman'. A gentleman was properly a man entitled to bear arms, and heralds continued to make periodical visitations to determine who was or was not fit to bear arms up to the end of the seventeenth century. However, they had no penal sanctions to enforce their decisions and many people were indifferent to their jurisdiction.[4] In reality, anyone who looked and behaved like a gentleman might be accepted as one, a point which Sir Thomas Smith had made in the sixteenth century: 'To be short, who can live idly and without manual labour, and will bear the port, charge and countenance of a gentleman, he shall be called master . . . and shall be taken for a gentleman.' Such a loose definition simply became looser as time went on. The Swiss writer, Guy Miège, wrote in 1703 that 'any one that, without a Coat of Arms, has either a liberal or genteel education, that looks gentleman-like (whether he be so or not) and has the wherewithal to live freely and handsomely, is by the courtesy of England usually called a gentleman'. The 1730 edition of Nathaniel Bailey's dictionary is freer still in its definition: 'In our days all are accounted Gentlemen that have money.'[5]

The problem had been compounded by the appearance of a new sort of gentleman on the English scene. It had once been a reasonable assumption that most gentlemen were country gentlemen who lived idly off the rents of their landed estates. But, by the seventeenth century, such an assumption was no longer tenable. More and more gentlemen were living in cities, especially in London, and more and more people living in cities were calling themselves gentlemen. When the Heralds visited London in the 1630s, they accepted the claims of 1172 Londoners to be gentlemen.[6] This in itself was a fairly high figure, over 1 per cent of the adult male population of the metropolis, but there would have been many more men whose claims to be gentlemen would have been accepted by their peers. Some of these urban gentlemen still lived off the rents of country estates, but many relied mainly on urban investments and so were difficult to distinguish from retired members of the middle station who had invested their accumulated profits in the same securities. When both types of people also shared the same metropolitan culture and were quite happy for their children to intermarry, the distinction became meaningless.

The records of the Heralds' Visitation show that 91 per cent of London gentry were younger sons of country gentry.[7] This highlights another confusing aspect of English social structure. In a period when primogeniture was becoming universal amongst the landed gentry, some means of supporting the younger sons had to be found. The obvious way was to provide them with an education and an inheritance sufficient to enable them to make their own way in the world, either in some profession or in trade. Since the best place to do this was in London, an almost impenetrable web of relationships was woven between the middling people of London and the country gentlemen. A study of Northamptonshire shows that, by 1700, most younger sons of the county's gentry families had gone either into the church or into trade in London, while the daughters had married London merchants much more frequently than the sons of local gentry families. Given the need to look outside the family estates for a living, Northamptonshire had little to offer in comparison with London.[8]

Apprenticeship records confirm this trend. Service as an apprentice was the normal route to a business career in London and, demeaning though it might seem, it was a route taken by countless younger sons of gentlemen. Apprentices were required to register their father's occupation or status and historians have discovered that in relatively prestigious London livery companies, such as the Grocers, Goldsmiths and Fishmongers, over a quarter of all apprentices described themselves as the sons of gentlemen.[9] Gentry recruitment on this scale meant that, after a few generations, there would have been few members of the London business world who were not quite closely related to county families, and few county families who did not have a relative earning a living in London. Social attitudes were bound to be modified in such circumstances and it is clear that the son of a gentleman who went into trade did not for that reason lose all his gentility, even though he was unable to be as idle as his elder brother. Such developments make it easy to understand why contemporary social commentators found it convenient to blur their descriptions of the social hierarchy.[10]

It seems clear that, in Augustan England, trade did not defile a gentleman as it had apparently done in the past, still did across the Channel, and was again to do in the England of Jane Austen. Indeed, the effects of gentry penetration of the commercial world were rather the raising of the status of trade than the lowering of that of the sons of the gentry who made a living in the city. A French memorandum of 1729 stated that 'Trade in that country [i.e. England] is upon a more honourable footing than in any other'[11] and this seems to have been true enough, though the Dutch would have been the equals of the English in this respect. Trade had become respectable, an attitude which reflected not only the gentry connection but also a general acceptance that trade was vital for the nation's prosperity.

It was, however, overseas trade which was seen to be most vital and it was the merchants who gained the greatest social benefits from any change in attitude. The stereotype of the merchant in drama and in literature written for the upper class had once been one of a money-grabbing, mean-spirited and socially inept man who could be characterized by some such name as Alderman Nincompoop or Sir Simon Scrape-all. Such stereotypes were perpetuated in Restoration comedy but attitudes were changing and, by the early eighteenth century, the merchant had become 'a responsible and sober citizen, with respectable morals and manners', in short, the next best thing to a gentleman.[12] 'Trading formerly rendered a Gentleman ignoble,' wrote Guy Miège, 'now an ignoble person makes himself by merchandizing as good as a gentleman.' 'We merchants,' says a merchant of Bristol in Steele's *Conscious Lovers* of 1722, 'we merchants are a species of gentry that have grown into the world this last century, and are as honourable and almost as useful as you landed folk, that have always thought yourselves so much above us.'[13]

The distinction between the 'upper part of mankind' and the middle station was thus becoming increasingly confused. Professional men might behave in a similar way to urban gentlemen of independent means, who in turn could be mistaken for retired members of the middle station. Add to all these, active merchants who considered themselves and were considered by others to be gentlemen and quite ordinary shopkeepers who happened to be brothers and sons of country gentlemen. Where did it stop? There was of course no clear line. If a merchant could be a gentleman, why not a rich linen-draper or a mercer? Why not a rich tavern-keeper or a coal merchant? Why not, when 'in our days all are accounted gentlemen that have money'.

It would in fact be far more likely for the coal merchant's son, rather than the successful man himself, to be accepted as a gentleman. Josiah Tucker noted that the self-made man of business 'may not always meet with respect equal to his large and acquired fortune; yet if he gives his son a liberal and accomplished education, the birth and calling of the father are sunk in the son; and the son is reputed, if his carriage is suitable, a gentleman in all companies'.[14] But, even if it might take two generations to make a real gentleman, there was still plenty of scope for social improvement within the middle station itself. Trades and occupations were actually graded by their degree of gentility, so everyone knew where they stood. Merchants and other prestigious members of the middle sort might acquire the airs and trappings of a gentleman. Lesser members of the commercial classes could ape their betters or could bring up their children to a more genteel occupation and so place them further up the ladder which led upwards through the middle station and 'out of the dross of mankind'.[15]

The social ambition and economic development of the middling sort of people attracted much comment. One writer in 1678 went so far as to assert that it was the ambition which caused the development, a hypothesis which has been taken up by modern social historians. 'There are two great Causes of Labour and Industry,' he wrote. 'Necessity for Food and Emulation. . . . Emulation provoaks a continued Industry, and will not allow no Intervals or be ever satisfied. . . . Every Neighbour and every Artist is indeavouring to outvy each other, and all men by a perpetual Industry are struling to mend their former condition: and thus the People grow rich.' This perpetual industry and desire for self-improvement was later described by a Frenchman: 'The Englishman is never satisfied with what he has obtained; his mind gets bored when in rest. The desire to increase always his property by continuous speculations destroys in him the love of tranquillity which inclines all well-to-do men towards idleness.'[16] Reading comments like this makes one wonder what has happened to the English since the eighteenth century. Have they been seduced by the idleness of their social betters?

The results of such energy could be seen in many fields of human activity. At a fairly trivial level, it was noted how the former humble dress of the shopkeeper, his furniture and his style of entertainment had been transformed by his vanity. 'Such is the expensive humour of the times', wrote Defoe, 'that not a family, no, hardly of the meanest tradesman, but treat their families with wine, or punch, or fine ale; and have their parlours set off with the tea-table and the chocolate-pot; treats and liquors all exotick, foreign and new among tradesmen, and terrible articles in their modern expense.'[17] Clothing, furniture and social behaviour were important symbols of self-confidence but cultural changes went much further than mere outward trappings. The middle classes were creating a completely new culture for themselves, a bourgeois culture that was destined to become the dominant national culture.

Some sort of middle-class culture had long existed, closely allied to the dominant culture of the gentry and aristocracy but, in our period, this culture was transformed by the ambition and thirst for knowledge of the middle station. This group was almost universally literate and their demand for self-improvement was eagerly met by the publishers. There were books on merchants' accounts and trade, geography and exploration, social etiquette and childrearing, history and law, gardening and cookery, as well as the religious books which had previously dominated the output of the press.[18] The late seventeenth century also saw an escalation in the number of pamphlets, sometimes on similar subjects to the full-length books but mainly treating the ephemeral political and economic issues of the day. From the 1690s, these were joined by an increasing number of newspapers and periodicals, which became a flood in the first decade of the eighteenth century, the period which saw the first London daily appear in 1702 and the birth in 1709 of what was to be a great favourite, the literary magazine pioneered by Addison and Steele and directed primarily to the cultural improvement of the rising middle class. And finally came the novel, often with its hero or heroine a member of the middle station, 'a literary form which treated realistically common experiences of character in the middle walks of life, supplanting, meanwhile, the romances which had detailed the exotic adventures of knights and rogues'.[19] In 1760, George Colman wrote *Polly Honeycombe*, which presents a whole range of middle-class stereotypes. Mr and Mrs Honeycombe are seen at breakfast. Honeycombe is reading the newspaper and discusses the social news with his wife, who exhorts him to drink up his tea, a nice image of the London bourgeoisie. Their daughter Polly thinks that 'a Novel is the only thing to teach a girl life and the way of the world', while her unsuccessful suitor Mr Ledger, who is mocked for his businessman's jargon, confesses that he hardly ever reads anything 'except the Daily Advertiser, or the list on Lloyd's'. The publishing industry had managed to satisfy every part of bourgeois society.

The new middle class received a mixed reception from the writers of the day. Bishop Burnet had a good word for them. 'As for the men of trade and business,' he wrote in 1708, 'they are, generally speaking, the best body in the nation, generous, sober, and charitable. . . . There may be too much of vanity, with too pompous an exterior, mixed with these in the capital city; but upon the whole they are the best we have.' Henry Fielding took a different view in 1751: 'Trade hath indeed given a new face to the whole nation . . . and hath totally changed the manners, customs, and habits of the people, more especially of the lower sort; the narrowness of their fortunes is changed into wealth; the simplicity of their manners into craft, their frugality into luxury, their humility into pride, and their subjection into equality.'[20]

Equality was a strange conceit in what was otherwise a hierarchical society, and was noticed by other writers. In 1740, a Frenchman maintained that society in London was egalitarian and so propitious to trade, 'the profession of equality'.[21] Equality, or the dream of it, produced insolence and conceit in the middle class and such attitudes were a common subject for attack. The target was often easy enough, since most tradesmen were not gentlemen and never would be despite their social pretensions. Tradesmen had different educations and value systems. They needed to work hard and they needed to save rather than spend if they were to improve themselves, so they found it difficult or even dangerous to adopt the behaviour of a class characterized by leisure and high spending.

The tradesman who tried to ape the manners of the gentleman, the 'cit' who tried to be a 'wit', was a common theme of plays performed on the London stage. Mr Jordan, the 'Citizen turn'd Gentleman' in Edward Ravenscroft's popular adaptation of Molière, was mocked because he had to learn at an advanced age how to dance and fence and talk like a gentleman. The ridicule was as much because he has given up the honourable role of citizen as because he makes such a poor gentleman. The City-wits of Thomas Shadwell's play, *The Scowrers*, are mocked because they are unable to behave as drunken hooligans with quite the style of the gentlemen scowrers of the town led by Sir William Rant. 'There's a mechanick thing!' cries Eugenia. 'There is not such an odious Creature as a City-Spark. . . . When a Man is lewd with a bon Grace; there's something in it, but a Fellow, that is aukwardly wicked, is not to be born.' Defoe was later to mirror Eugenia's city-spark when he described Moll Flanders's foolish choice of a second husband. 'I was not averse to a tradesman', she says, 'but then I would have a tradesman, forsooth, that was something of a gentleman too; that when my husband had a mind to carry me to the court, or to the play, he might become a sword, and look as like a gentleman as another man, and not like one that had the mark of his apron-strings upon his coat. . . . Well, at last, I found this amphibious creature, this land-water thing, called a gentleman-tradesman.'[22]

Defoe was warning his tradesmen readers to stick to their trades and not let the dream of gentility bankrupt them. Other writers were worried that men of the middle station were not genteel enough. Sir Richard Steele approved of the progress of the middle classes, but felt that trade itself should be conducted with dignity, decorum and a due care for the rest of society, a distinction which he illustrated by the two merchants, Paulo and Avaro. 'This Paulo grows wealthy by being a common good; Avaro, by being a general evil: Paulo has the art, Avaro the craft of trade. When Paulo gains, all men he deals with are the better: whenever Avaro profits, another certainly loses. In a word, Paulo is a citizen, and Avaro a cit.' Economic success should not be at the expense of one's fellow citizens, a theme which had provided the guiding rule in the Rev. Richard Baxter's commercial ethics: 'Do as you would be done by.' Economic success should also not entail disdain for the unsuccessful. 'Well, this thing call'd prosperity makes a man strangely insolent and forgetful,' wrote Tom Brown. 'How contemptibly a cutler looks at a poor grinder of knives, a physician in his coach at a farrier on foot, and a well-grown Paul's church-yard bookseller upon one of the trade that sells second-hand books under the trees in Moorfields.'[23]

Such contempt for the poor and unsuccessful was common enough and attracted a certain amount of spiritual sanction. Seventeenth-century preachers sometimes made the socially useful point that poverty might be the result of idleness but they usually argued that it was God's providence which determined who should be rich and who poor. However, as the temporal confidence of the middle sort grew in tandem with their wealth, one finds a subtle change in the teaching of the clergymen who stood above them in their pulpits. When Joseph Butler preached before the Lord Mayor in Easter-week of 1740, it was no longer providence which determined the distribution of wealth. 'The hand of the diligent maketh rich and, other circumstances being equal, in proportion to its diligence.'[24] The implication was obvious. The poor were poor because they were idle and deserved to be poor.

Enough has been said to demonstrate that contemporaries were well aware of the growth in numbers, wealth and self-confidence of the middling sort of people. Social conservatives disapproved, but found it difficult to ignore the new reality. Other writers, perhaps the majority, welcomed these new and thrusting people who were making England the richest country in Europe, and modified their ideas to accommodate them. The middle classes, so often rising in previous centuries, had finally arrived. In the second and third parts of this book, a profile of this dynamic group in English society will be drawn. Their social and geographical origins, their education and apprenticeship, will be examined and then their business methods and the factors which tended to make for success in business will be discussed. The ability to make money was an essential feature of such people, but the aim will be to look at them as complete human beings, rather than just as cyphers with a certain economic function, by examining their choice of wife and their family life, their role in civic life and their patterns of consumption. The whole range of middling people will be examined, from small shopkeepers and small manufacturers who were close to artisans in status to very rich merchants and bankers whose wealth enabled them to dominate the commercial and, to a lesser extent, the political world of the metropolis.

An individual's wealth or assets and, less often, his income will be referred to in order to provide a shorthand indication of his position in the long hierarchy of the London middle classes. Such figures have little intuitive meaning for those not familiar with the period and a conversion to figures understandable today is virtually impossible, so great have been changes in relative values. Some idea of where contemporaries saw the key dividing line in the wealth hierarchy is indicated by the fact that the framers of taxation selected individuals with personal wealth from £300 to £600 upwards as persons who might reasonably be charged surtaxes.[25] Personal wealth of a few hundred pounds and an annual income of about £50 thus provide a lower bound for the middle station, though some people with rather less appear in the book.

A fortune of a few hundred pounds or an income of £50 a year does not sound very much in these inflationary days but it was a reasonable competence in Augustan London, enough to live a comfortable lower-middle-class life. An income of £50 was some three, four or even five times the annual income of a labourer and would allow a family to eat well, employ a servant and live comfortably, while an accumulation of a few hundred pounds would enable the same family to own the long lease of a house, to furnish it in some style and still have plenty left for working capital or investment. Anyone with a personal fortune between £1000 and £2000 was already very well off by contemporary standards. Such people represented the average of the London middle classes and they lived very well indeed. Their fortunes would exceed those of nearly all provincial townsfolk and their life-style would be equivalent to that of a very prosperous farmer. When one comes to the large numbers of middle-class Londoners with fortunes over £10,000, one is in the ranks of the wealthy rather than the merely prosperous. These were men who could purchase virtually anything which their age could offer and whose wealth enabled them to live better than the majority of country gentlemen. But even £10,000 was only a moderate fortune for a London merchant, financier or big wholesaler. Many such men had fortunes of scores of thousands of pounds and a few passed the magical hundred thousand mark and so became a 'plum', the contemporary equivalent of a 'millionaire'. One or two plums will be met in this book and several very wealthy men with five-figure fortunes, but most middling people were men with fortunes between £500 and £5000, men who enjoyed a very pleasant, well-cushioned comfort, men whose lives offered a quite incredible contrast to those of the poor.

The sources used include private business papers, diaries and autobiographies, wills and inventories, fire insurance policies, the records of the London livery companies, government papers and the records arising out of litigation, as well as the contemporary comment which has been used in this introductory chapter. Such sources are used for description and for illustration and, to a certain extent, they form the basis for some of the large number of generalizations which a book of this sort inevitably contains. However, in order to provide a rather more solid framework, a sample of the middling sort of people has been used for more detailed investigation and analysis. Most of the information about these people comes from post-mortem inventories drawn up for the London Court of Orphans, an institution whose function was to supervise the division of deceased citizens' estates between their children. The information from the inventories has been supplemented by using other sources about the same people, particularly genealogical and apprenticeship records. The resulting sample consists of 375 London citizens who died between 1665 and 1720 and who between them cover almost the whole spectrum of London middle-class activities.[26]

These magnificent inventories provide a superbly panoramic view of the lives of the middling people of London. Complete and detailed lists of the furniture and other contents of houses, room by room, enable one to see just what domestic comfort meant to this class, while the trade part of the inventory lists the stock which the businessman kept in his shop or warehouse and so enables one to understand what the business of the haberdasher, the jeweller, the undertaker or the apothecary involved. In one inventory, the researcher may be struck by the richness and the wide range of the domestic possessions which had been amassed by the deceased citizen. He will note the silk bed-curtains, the cane chairs, the silver plate, the pewter and copperware in the kitchen, the coal and beer in the cellar. Where did all these things come from? As often as not, the answer comes in the next box of inventories. Here is the inventory of the merchant who imported the silk cloth or, if it was made in London, the master-weaver who organized its manufacture. Here is the inventory of the upholsterer who supplied the curtains and the chairs, the pewterer, the silversmith and the coppersmith who made the plate and the kitchenware, the coal-merchant who delivered the coal and the brewer who sold the deceased man his barrels of beer. For London was a place where what was accumulated or consumed in the house was very often supplied or made by other Londoners. This will become only too clear in the next chapter, where the scene is set for the detailed study of the middling sort of people in the second and third parts of the book by examining the multi-various nature of the London economy.

2 The Metropolitan Economy

The main characteristics of the middling sort of people have been defined as accumulation, self-improvement and the employment of labour and capital. In this chapter, the metropolitan economy is surveyed in order to see the ways in which such people chose to exercise their talents and their capital. This is a big subject, for London was already a real city even in modern terms and not just a large town. The population in 1700 was about half a million,[1] making it the fourth largest city in the world, exceeded only by Constantinople, Peking and Edo (the future Tokyo). This great city dominated England and the English economy during our period as it had never done before and was never to do again. Just to say that about one in every nine Englishmen lived in London is not enough, since one in six or seven were to live in Greater London in the late nineteenth century, when London was relatively less important in the economy. The real point is that there was nowhere else in England which was more than a moderately large town, even by contemporary standards.[2]

London was the seat of government, the main residence of the court, the only banking centre, virtually the only publishing centre and the home of the majority of professional people. The metropolis controlled three-quarters of England's foreign trade, owned nearly half her merchant fleet, dominated inland trade and had much the largest concentration of industrial workers in the country. Needless to say, such a concentration of professional, commercial and industrial activity led to a concentration of wealth. Man for man, Londoners were richer than their counterparts in the provinces. The merchants, wholesalers and financiers in the city were many times wealthier than those who strove to emulate them in provincial towns. The shopkeepers operated on a completely different scale from their often

part-time contemporaries elsewhere. Even the workers were
better off, being paid wages some 50 per cent higher than those
current in the provinces. Only one group, the great landowners,
could match and indeed exceed the wealth of the wealthiest
Londoners, and they were increasingly inclined to reside for a
large part of the year in London's West End and to spend there
much of their income, a pattern of behaviour which was itself a
major factor in making Londoners rich. Such a concentration
of people, economic functions and wealth in one city was unique
in Europe and was seen as a major factor in explaining
England's precocious development.[3]

What was the function of London in the national economy?
The metaphor used by Defoe was to describe the city as a heart
which circulated England's blood.[4] This heart drew in food-
stuffs, raw materials and manufactured goods from provincial
England and the wider world, which were then either distributed and consumed within London itself or pumped out again.
Some goods were consumed in London or redistributed with
little or no change, some were subject to embellishment and
some were totally transformed by manufacture in the metropolis. The first section of this chapter concentrates on these
manufacturing and finishing trades which found their home in
London; then commerce, catering and services are considered
in the rest of the chapter. The distribution of material between
the sections is somewhat arbitrary, since there was considerable
overlap between these functions, and the arrangement has been
made mainly for ease of exposition.

i Manufacturing

To start, then, London will be considered as a manufacturing
city, a facet of the metropolitan economy often overlooked by
historians, despite the fact that London was the greatest
manufacturing city in Europe and was at its all-time peak as an
industrial centre relative to the rest of the country. The range
of manufactures in general use grew rapidly in the seventeenth
century, and more and more were made in England as the
country overcame its former technical inferiority. The wide
range of skills among the male labour force, the existence of a

large low-wage labour force of women and children, the presence of much the largest and richest market, and easy access to raw materials combined to make London an obvious location for such new industries. At the same time, London's old industries expanded in response to the growth in numbers and prosperity of the population. London was later to lose many of her industries to the lower wages, food prices, rents and fuel costs of the provinces. However, this dispersal of industries required the development of provincial skills and capital, and a general improvement in inland transport and information networks. These things were happening, but they were happening slowly and the countervailing attractions of London skills and the London market were sufficient to limit the exodus of industries before 1730.

London's industries either made completely or at least added some value to the great majority of artefacts that were used in the capital city, with the result that manufacturing, in the broadest sense, employed a vast number of men, women and children. A recent study by Dr Beier, based on occupations recorded in a sample of burial registers, has suggested that as many as 60 per cent of the occupied labour force was engaged in 'production'. This seems too high, possibly as a result of a bias in the parishes chosen, but the author's proposition that London was a far greater manufacturing centre than is generally realized seems quite correct.[5] No data exist to provide an exact breakdown of the occupational structure but, from a general survey of the available literature, I would suggest that something like 40 per cent of the labour force were engaged in manufacturing, higher than in either commerce or services, the two types of occupation which are normally stressed by writers discussing the metropolitan economy.[6]

Much the biggest industry or group of industries was the manufacture or finishing of textiles and their conversion into clothes or furnishing materials, a group of industries which alone may have employed some 20 per cent of the London labour force, including a high proportion of women.[7] Pride of place must be given to the silk industry, which grew rapidly during our period and expanded from the north-east part of the City to Spitalfields, Bethnal Green and Southwark.[8] The most expensive silks were imported, mainly from France and Italy, but London produced a wide range of cheaper silks which were well within the reach of the middle class and even lower in the social hierarchy, while those who could not afford dress-lengths could buy silk handkerchiefs, scarves and ribbons and so bring a little glamour into their lives. All this demand gave rise to four main types of work – silk-throwing, which gave employment to several thousand women and children in the East End who prepared the imported raw silk by twisting and winding it on to reels;[9] narrow silk-weaving, which produced such articles as ribbon and braid; broad silk-weaving, which produced fabrics; and the manufacture of gold and silver thread by twisting silk thread with flatted gold or silver wire, an industry concentrated in the parish of St Giles Cripplegate and a good example of the very skilled employment which might be generated by the vagaries of fashion in such a centre of luxury as London.[10]

Silk thread also provided the raw material for lacemakers and, particularly, silk stocking knitters, some of whom worked by hand but most of whom used the knitting-frame, a very complex machine of which there were some 500 in London at the beginning of our period and 2500 at the end.[11] Finally, one should note that, although silk was much the largest branch of London's textile manufacturing industry, there were also spinners and weavers producing pure woollens and worsteds, mixed fabrics of silk and wool, such as stuffs and camlets, and fabrics made of cotton and linen or pure cotton using imported Indian yarn.[12] How many people were engaged in all these trades is impossible to say but even the most modest modern estimate puts the number of looms in the Spitalfields silk industry as over 10,000 in the early eighteenth century, while earlier estimates put the figure much higher.[13] Each loom employed well over one person, sometimes three or more, and to these numbers should be added perhaps 5000 for the knitting industry at its peak, many thousands of silk throwsters, not to mention gold and silver threadmakers, lacemakers and a host of lesser trades such as fringe and tassel makers. It seems likely that the total numbers engaged in silk manufacture and allied trades would have been somewhere between 40,000 and 50,000 in the early eighteenth century, nearly a tenth of the population of the metropolis and a much higher proportion of its work-force. If this figure is approximately accurate, it puts East London into the class of such famous textile centres on the continent as Lyons, Leyden or Florence.

There were also many thousands of workers who earned their living from textiles without making them. Although most woollen cloth was produced in the provinces, much of the finishing trades, such as shearing, pressing, calendering, packing and dyeing, were concentrated in London, the city which accounted for some two-thirds of all cloth exported overseas,[14] as well as being the biggest centre for the domestic consumption of woollens and the base of most of the wholesale woollen drapers who redistributed the cloth throughout the country. London was also a major centre for the preparation and distribution of textile raw materials, such as wool, which was bought from the graziers and country dealers and then cleaned, sorted, graded, mixed and often combed and spun in London before being sent back to the cloth-producing areas.[15] London's function as an entrepôt also created work in the finishing trades relating to the other two textiles in general use, cotton and linen, the most important of which was the calico-printing industry, which started in the 1670s and was given a great boost in 1701 by the ban on the retained import of the printed calicoes from India which had first inspired it.[16]

The conversion of all these textiles into clothing and furnishing materials must have provided almost as much employment as the textile industries themselves, for tailors and breeches-makers, milliners, mantua-makers and seamstresses, a veritable multitude of poor men and poorer women slaving away with scissors and shears and needle and thread.[17] Many of these were involved in a seasonal trade, creating fashionable clothes for the aristocracy and gentry who lived in the West End or visited it to renew their wardrobes, or for the men and women of the middle station who aspired to imitate the dress of their betters. But as many again, perhaps even more, were engaged in the ready-made trade, producing shirts and smocks, hoods and caps, cravats and bands, suits for men and boys, and mantuas, petticoats and gowns for women and girls. Historians have been slow to realize the size or even the existence of this ready-made industry, but the stock-lists of haberdashers, milliners and mercers and especially of those specialists in ready-made outerwear, sometimes called salesmen and sometimes shopkeeping tailors, leave one in no doubt of the size of this industry.[18] The sweat-shop is not an invention of the nineteenth century.

Gregory King estimated that about a quarter of the national income was spent on clothes, so one should not be surprised that textiles and clothing manufacture was much the biggest industry in London.[19] However, it was far from being the only one and some of London's other major industries will now be briefly considered before looking at the way in which they were organized and the opportunities that they provided for the men and women of the middle station. There are no data which could be used to calculate the size of any of these industries but the second biggest, after textiles and clothing, was probably building, an industry with many ramifications, which offered a wide variety of employment to skilled men such as masons, bricklayers, tilers and carpenters and their journeymen and apprentices and also to an increasing number of unskilled labourers who were employed on such tasks as clearing sites. Building was particularly buoyant in the first twenty-five years of our period, which saw the rebuilding of some 9000 houses after the Great Fire of 1666 and, almost simultaneously, the erection of streets and squares on previously unbuilt land in both the East and West Ends as well as much construction on the south bank of the river.[20]

The next two largest industries were almost certainly metal-working and leather manufacture, probably employing some 10,000 workers each.[21] Both were complex industries with a wide variety of employment. Hides were tanned mainly in Southwark and were then sold to the curriers who prepared the material for the saddlers and shoemakers, the latter often buying from middlemen who cut up the hides into soles and uppers. Lighter skins were prepared by the leather-dressers for such final manufacturers as the makers of buff-coats and oil-skin breeches, the trunkmakers and bookbinders and, especially, the glovers. All these trades were carried out in London, though tanning was increasingly being done in the country, and both gloving and ready-made boot and shoe manufacture were also beginning to flee the metropolis to seek out cheaper rural labour.[22]

Metalworking was an even more complex industry, producing finished goods in gold, silver, pewter, copper, brass, tinplate, lead, iron, steel and combinations of these metals, with London dominating national production in all these finished metal industries, except for goods made of iron.[23] Metalwork, like many other London industries, became an increasingly specialized activity, so that founders became separate from forgers and forge work was split into its component parts, 'the fire-man who forges the work, the vice-man who files and finishes it; the hammer-man who strikes with the great hammer'. Craftsmen also increasingly specialized in making just one product or a very narrow range of products, so that by 1747, when Campbell wrote his valuable guide to the London crafts, *The London Tradesman*, one has candlestick-makers or tweezers-case makers rather than non-specific braziers or goldsmiths, the latter terms being more often used to describe those who sold brass or gold goods rather than those who made them.

Specialization and division of labour went furthest where the final object could be made in parts, such as in locks and handguns and in the manufacture of clocks and watches, a very rapidly growing branch of metalworking, which was concentrated in Clerkenwell. 'At the first appearance of watches', wrote Campbell, 'they were begun and ended by one man, who was called a watchmaker; but of late years the watch-maker, properly so called, scarcely makes any thing belonging to a watch; he only employs the different tradesmen among whom the art is divided, and puts the several parts of the movement together.'[24] Such developments made it possible for masters to seek out cheaper skilled labour in the provinces, so that by the late seventeenth century many London watch parts were made in south-west Lancashire and parts of London hand-guns in Birmingham, the London gunmaker merely assembling the weapon and stamping his name on it.[25]

Apart from those already mentioned, there were at least five more London industries which certainly employed several thousand people each, though as usual exact numbers are impossible to obtain. Woodworking included box-making, turnery-ware and especially furniture and cabinet-making, which had a growing export component and was concentrated in the area north of the Strand.[26] Slightly further north, around Long

Acre, was the home of coachmaking, the contemporary equivalent of the automobile industry and, like its modern counterpart,
an employer of a wide variety of tradesmen who probably spent
more of their time in maintaining and repairing the vehicles
than in making them.[27] Over the river in Southwark, Lambeth
and Wandsworth was the main centre of hat-making, an
industry which, like silk-weaving, was a major beneficiary of
the skills of the Huguenots who flocked into England in the
1680s, ruining the French industry and leaving the English
hatters without serious rivals.[28] The fourth of our five industries,
baking, probably employed some 5000 workers scattered in
small units throughout the metropolis,[29] while the last, shipbuilding and allied trades, was necessarily found along both
banks of the river.

'The whole river, in a word, from London-Bridge to Black
Wall, is one great arsenal,' wrote Defoe, who estimated that
there were thirty-three shipbuilding yards below London
Bridge.[30] Some of these were very big employers, such as the
two royal dockyards at Woolwich and Deptford, and Blackwall
Yard where most of the East-Indiamen were built. Other yards
were quite small, though there were at least twelve private
yards big enough to build the lesser men-of-war in times of
emergency.[31] Londoners owned 43 per cent of all English
shipping tonnage in 1702 but a substantial and increasing
proportion of this was built at cheaper yards on the east coast,
whilst much of the coastal shipping which plied to London was
also built elsewhere.[32] Nevertheless, the industries of the river
were major employers, much of the work being provided by
fitting-out and repairs rather than in the initial building of the
ships. Such work employed not just shipwrights but also a host
of other trades such as mastmakers, coopers, ironmongers,
compass-makers, sailmakers, ropemakers and anchorsmiths,
the last three being important industries in their own right,
ropemaking in particular being a highly capitalized industry.[33]

Brewing and distilling were two other industries which can
have been only slightly smaller employers than the five mentioned above. By 1700, brewing was dominated by the 200 or
so 'common brewers', who produced for a wide metropolitan
market and also for export and the shipping industry, economies
of scale having enabled these big brewers to undercut the

victualling or publican brewers who brewed on a small scale for their own retail outlets.[34] The big brewers were to be challenged in their turn, for our period, amongst other things, was the 'Gin Age', a period when spirit-drinking became a national and particularly a London vice. Beer production actually declined slightly, while spirits took off, domestic production rising from half a million gallons in the 1680s to a peak of over eight million gallons in the 1740s, a period when the national population hardly grew at all.[35] Such a thirst meant plenty of work for the distillers, both the fairly small number of wealthy malt distillers, nearly all Londoners, who produced the raw spirit, and the much larger number of compound distillers who re-distilled, flavoured and watered it. Some of the latter were big operators, but most were small men or women who rectified malt spirits on their own premises and sold the resulting lethal concoction to that motley collection of customers who claimed to be able to get drunk for a penny and dead drunk for twopence.[36]

The growth of gin consumption was good news for the glass manufacturers, one of several smaller London industries employing about 1000 to 1500 people each. There were twenty-four glass-houses in London in 1695, mainly on the south bank of the river and in Whitechapel. These were big operations by contemporary standards, employing 50 to 100 men each, and they produced bottles, window glass, drinking glasses and mirror glass, all products which had been luxuries in the sixteenth century but were commonplace in our period.[37] Glass was also an input into other important London industries, such as looking-glass manufacture and the production of spectacles and scientific instruments. Other industries of roughly the same order of size as glass included soapmaking, candle manufacture, sugar and tobacco refining and printing and publishing, all industries which were growing rapidly and in most of which London dominated national production.[38] Most of these industries employed quite sophisticated techniques and were also heavily capitalized, especially glassmaking, soapmaking and sugar refining.[39]

Such were the major industries of London, though there were scores, perhaps hundreds, of lesser ones, ranging from sophisticated industries like pottery,[40] 'engine-making' and the manufacture of musical instruments, through important food-processing industries such as bacon-curing and the manufacture of ships' biscuit to relatively trivial but cumulatively important activities such as fanmaking, brushmaking, sievemaking and basketmaking. One must now consider, in very general terms, how all these industries were organized in order to see what opportunities they were likely to offer to the people of the middle station.

Such organization must obviously have varied considerably and a large shipyard producing men-of-war for the navy would have been a very different place from the premises of a small boxmaker. Nevertheless, the generalization may be made that the typical unit of production in the great majority of London industries was the individual master artisan working in his own workshop with his apprentices and journeymen, this small labour force often living above the shop with the master and his family. This is the picture which one gets from inventory after inventory of such master craftsmen as weavers, tailors, pewterers, goldsmiths, joiners and the like.

Such a picture helps to maintain a superficial continuity with a past in which a progression from apprentice to journeyman to small master had not been an unrealistic expectation for the majority of young craftsmen.[41] However, although this continued to happen, a number of factors were combining to undermine the independence of many small masters and to make it increasingly difficult for journeymen to become masters, with the result that the numbers of permanent journeymen with no prospects of advancement were increasing rapidly in our period. The most important factor was simply that nearly every branch of London industry required a greater capital to run it as time went on. This requirement reflected the widening, deepening and greater sophistication of the market as incomes rose, the variety of products available increased and it became increasingly common to buy goods from a retail shop rather than from the man who had made them. It also reflected the growing ubiquity of retail credit, which meant that manufacturers might need to wait a very long time before they received payment for their goods, while being liable for payment to their journeymen every Saturday and for their raw materials within a comparatively short time, such as three months.[42] This obviously greatly increased the need for working capital, as did the growing necessity to have a well-stocked shop in order to attract customers.

Such developments naturally made it harder for most journeymen to consider opening their own shops; they also had the effect of undermining the independence of many small masters, who tended more and more to sell to big masters or to specialist shopkeepers and wholesalers, at trade prices but for quick and fairly sure payment, rather than to the public. The specialization and increasing division of labour, which were observed in the metal industries and were common in many other industries, only served to reinforce this trend.

The result was that, in many industries, a hierarchy developed, which has been well described by the historians of the pewter industry, who distinguished four main groups. At the top were merchant pewterers supplying wholesale customers in England and overseas, and producing only a fraction of what they sold. Then there were more modest retailers, who produced for their own customers and for the wholesalers. These might buy in products from other pewterers to make up a respectable retail stock. At a lower level were the small masters, who derived most of their income from manufacturing rather than retailing and sold their output to retailers and wholesalers. Finally, there were the journeymen-pewterers, who might work for any of the other three groups.[43]

A very similar hierarchy can be observed in most of the other branches of the metal industry, the big jewellers or ironmongers replacing the master-pewterer at the highest level.[44] It can also be found in woodworking, where a man like John Rayner, described as 'a merchant in turnery ware', sold such things as bowls, trenchers, ninepins, bed-staves and rolling-pins produced by a host of smaller masters. In the furniture trades, the key men were the upholsterers, who kept a complete range of furniture displayed in appropriate rooms in their houses for customers to view, and the big cabinet-makers such as Edward Treherne of St Martin's in the Fields, a looking-glass manufacturer by trade who also kept stocks of inlaid and carved cabinets, chests of drawers and other furniture which would have employed many small masters in independent workshops who were never themselves visited by prospective customers.[45] The latter might run their own small businesses but they could easily degenerate into mere wage-earners or piece-workers as economic power tended to move away from the maker to the seller.[46]

Even in industries where the product was not made in a workshop, such as building, a hierarchical structure was likely to develop. In the past, most building had been done by craftsmen engaged directly by the owners of sites and paid individually. However, by our period, such direct labour was being superceded by the contract system in which a master-builder was engaged and paid a lump sum for the job, an obvious advantage for the man of capital, while much building was also undertaken as a speculative venture by the builder himself. As a result, one finds at the top of the building hierarchy a few very big entrepreneurs, of whom Nicolas Barbon, a speculative builder on a vast scale, was the most famous. More typical were the wealthier master craftsmen, who might be engaged on a fair number of building contracts simultaneously, sometimes to order and sometimes as a speculator. Some of the work was done with their own labour force, but most was subcontracted to small masters employing a few journeymen and apprentices, who made up the majority of the employers. Easy credit terms from suppliers and a well-organized mortgage business meant that such small men faced a constant temptation to speculate in their turn and so move up the building hierarchy. Some did so successfully but it was a notoriously risky business, then as now.[47]

Building saw few, if any, technical innovations in our period, but innovation, especially the increasing use of machines and other labour-saving devices, was another factor tending to play into the hands of those masters with greater capital. Three good examples are the knitting, ribbon-weaving and silk-throwing industries, in all of which a labour-saving machine was to triumph in the course of the seventeenth century.[48] None of these machines was very expensive, but they were normally too much for poor men, who had to work either in their own homes on machines hired at exorbitant rates or on machines grouped together in workshops owned by the big masters. Some of these masters were very large operators, employing as many as 500 workers, despite attempts to limit the extent of manufacture by any one master.[49] Naturally, these big masters, with their considerable turnover and sometimes with some economies of scale, for example, in the purchase of raw materials, were in a position to undercut the independent small masters and so reinforce the trend towards the concentration of the ownership of the machines into fewer hands.

The development of workshops in which large numbers of journeymen worked together did not necessarily require the invention of machines or other innovations, since these 'proto-factories' had their own economic logic. They reduced the wastage and embezzlement which was a common feature of work put out to journeymen or small masters in their own homes; they enabled masters to maintain a closer supervision of work and also to reap the benefits of any economies of scale or division of labour which might be possible in a particular industry. Large workshops were common in most of the ready-made clothing trades, amongst 'shopkeeping' tailors and shoe-makers, for instance, and also amongst the big hatters of Southwark. Such men, who controlled the supply of raw materials such as beaver fur, were amongst the richest manufac-turers in London. They owned large complexes of buildings, comprising dwelling-house, workshops and warehouses where they might employ scores of journeymen directly, as well as subcontracting work to smaller masters with fortunes of a few hundred pounds at most.[50]

What one is seeing, then, is an increase in the scale of the operation of the wealthier masters, sometimes in the form of bigger workshops, sometimes through an extension of a 'put-ting-out' system and sometimes simply through the use of their economic power in the market, which enabled them to buy raw materials more cheaply and on better credit terms and to sell goods cheaper to the final consumer, a factor which in itself was likely to increase their turnover and the size of their business. All this did not mean that the small master could no longer become a big one. Many skilful, enterprising or lucky men continued to do just that and so move up the hierarchy of their particular industry, but such improvements in status became increasingly difficult over time, as the world became one in which the big masters, shopkeepers and wholesalers tended to hold most of the cards.

So far, most of the industries considered produced relatively small and cheap articles using simple hand tools or machines which could easily fit into the humble living-space of a journeyman or small master. However, many London industries were not like that. Industries such as building, coachmaking and shipbuilding produced large and expensive articles which required the co-ordination of many different craftsmen over a fairly long period of time. Such work was mainly bespoke and some customers paid in instalments, but it is clear that one could not envisage making houses costing several hundred pounds or ships sometimes costing thousands without large reserves of working capital or very good credit. Fixed capital costs were also quite high, since, although the tools used by the individual craftsman might be cheap, such industries normally required a lot of expensive space – the yards and lofts of the coachbuilder or the yards, warehouses, sawhouses and wet and dry docks of the big shipbuilder.[51]

It is a cliché of economic history that working capital was always the main requirement of the manufacturer in this so-called 'pre-industrial' age. However, space was always a major fixed cost in high-rent London and some industries used considerably more fixed capital in the form of equipment and machinery than others – glassmaking, ropemaking, soapmaking, printing, dyeing and other branches of the cloth-finishing trades such as packing and pressing, sugar-refining, brewing, malt-distilling, to name but a few in which equipment worth at least a few hundred pounds was normally required.[52] The last three industries also had important economies of scale which encouraged a growth in unit size. The big brewers, for instance, used very large utensils, such as vats and coppers, whose price did not rise in proportion to their size, and the same was true of distilling and sugar-refining. Since it was liquid, beer could be moved about the brewery by pumps rather than by labourers, so that labour costs also did not rise in proportion to the quantity produced.[53]

The industries listed above also needed large stocks of raw materials, a fact which increased their needs for working capital but might be a positive advantage for the bigger operator. Wealthy brewers, for instance, could buy their stocks of coal in the summer months when coal was cheap and many diversified backwards into malting or contracted to buy their barley while it was still in the field at prices well below the market rate. Other manufacturers, such as soapmakers, dyers, ropemakers and sugar-refiners, were major consumers of imported raw materials and could reduce their costs by moving into foreign trade themselves and so cutting out the merchant's middleman profit.

It should be obvious from the above that London's industries offered a very wide variety of opportunities to the potential middle-class entrepreneur and that the size of businesses and their rewards varied accordingly. At one end of a long spectrum were very small men, artisans with no middle-class pretensions and no real hope of improving themselves, such as the small bakers, who were often little more than the employees of their flour suppliers, or the small joiners who made chairs and tables for the upholsterers. At the other end were some very big businesses whose owners had fortunes comparable to those of the merchants and wholesalers who dominated the commercial world of the metropolis.

Some idea of this variety is given in Table 2.1 overleaf, which sets out the fortunes at death of the 97 manufacturers in our sample, just over a quarter of the whole sample. This certainly illustrates the variety of experience which might be expected from what has been said previously. Builders, for instance, can be found in every one of the six wealth groups and distillers in all but one. It also suggests that the average fortune of the manufacturer was rather less than that of the more purely commercial man, the median fortune of manufacturers being less than two-thirds of that of the whole sample. This is clearly because of the large numbers who fall into the lowest wealth group with fortunes less than £500. All these men were masters and it is clear from their possessions that many of them had genteel ambitions. Nevertheless, they functioned in the economy as independent artisans, one step above the journeymen but at the lowest level of the manufacturing hierarchy discussed above. If some of them had lived a little longer, they might have improved their fortunes sufficiently to move up one or even two wealth groups but such men were never likely to get really rich in the London of our period.

To get rich you had to start rich or at least comfortably well off, as will be discovered later in the book, and there is no doubt

TABLE 2.1: Fortunes of London Manufacturers

Fortune at Death	Occupations
£10,000 & over	Builder/mason; cloth-finisher; distiller; bodice-maker
£5000–£9999	Soapmaker; publisher; builder/carpenter; candlemaker; distiller; packer
£2000–£4999	Distiller; dyer; builder/mason; tobacco-refiner; sugar-refiner; cloth-finisher; soapmaker; metalworker; metal-refiner; cooper; publisher; brewer; printer; distiller; trunk-maker; distiller; brewer; tobacco-refiner; dyer; distiller; dyer
£1000–£1999	Soapmaker; wire-drawer; silk-weaver; soapmaker; looking-glass maker; combmaker; gunmaker; brewer; carpenter/builder; pewterer; soapmaker; horner; brazier; mason/builder; silk-weaver; coachmaker; printer
£500–£999	Brazier; loriner; plumber; distiller; publisher; cloth-finisher; silversmith; clockmaker; carpenter/builder; currier; glazier; tortoise-shell worker; dyer; brewer; coachmaker
Less than £500	Packer; working goldsmith; silk-weaver; dyer; hatband-maker; map-printer; distiller; builder/mason; tailor; distiller; carpenter/builder; pewterer; wire-drawer; pewterer; hatter; founder; publisher; joiner; cutler; joiner; candlemaker; cloth-presser; brazier; hatter; distiller; candlemaker; bricklayer; brass-founder; brazier; distiller; cooper; tiler; turner; cooper

Median fortune of manufacturers: £1003
Median fortune of whole sample: £1717

Source: Sample (for details, see Appendix A, p. 394). The occupations within each wealth group have been listed in order of wealth of the deceased man. The last man on the list, a cooper, was insolvent. While this table is fairly representative of London manufacturing, the chance inclusion of a particular man in the sample does not mean that his fortune is necessarily typical of his trade (the numbers in each trade are too small to make that asumption). Some trades are also very poorly represented in the sample. There are no shipbuilders or allied river trades, no glassmakers, no silk-throwers and very few weavers considering the size of the silk industry, and very few leather workers except the leather-sellers whom I have included as wholesalers in Table 2.2 (p. 36)

that all the men in the top three wealth groups would have started their businesses with a capital of several hundred pounds and often with much more. Such a large starting capital was essential in some industries requiring large amounts of fixed equipment, but it could be employed in virtually any industry, as was seen in the discussion of the London manufacturing world and as is illustrated by the wide variety of occupations included in the top three wealth groups.

In no group is this variety more apparent than in the top group, which comprises four men who are representatives of scores of other London manufacturers who were worth more than £10,000, a very comfortable fortune for the age. Joshua Marshall, who died worth just under £14,000 and was marginally the richest of the four, was one of the great master builders of Restoration London, who succeeded his father as master-mason to Charles II in 1675. He worked for the King at Windsor Castle and for Sir Christopher Wren on St Paul's Cathedral, rebuilt six other London churches after the Fire, built the Monument and was an important speculative builder in his own right as well as being a dealer in stone and monumental masonry. Joel Andrews, who died in 1692, was a cloth-finisher whose inventory includes such items of the trade as shears and packing presses. However, this manufacturing side of his business had probably produced only a comparatively small part of his fortune and Andrews' main activities were as a middleman in the cloth trade, buying from the country clothiers, selling to the exporting merchants and sometimes exporting himself, what contemporaries normally called a Blackwell Hall Factor after the market where woollen cloth was supposed to be bought and sold in London.[54]

Robert Maddox, who also died in the 1690s, was a big malt distiller, producer of the raw spirits which fuelled the early years of the Gin Age. He had a distillery and vaults in Thames Street, warehouses in York and Exeter, and his inventory lists 835 separate debtors – merchants, dramshops and other drink outlets – from 205 places all over the country.[55] The last wealthy manufacturer, William Ladds, reflects a different type of fashion, being a bodice-maker, hardly the first product that one thinks of when considering big business. But Ladds was a giant in the trade, whose business extended as far as New England. The scale of his operations is indicated by the eleven tons of whalebone which he had in stock when he died, while his unpaid debts to the bone-cutters who boiled and split the whale fins remind one of yet another unknown London industry.[56]

People like Ladds, Maddox and Andrews can be defined as
manufacturers, as they are here, but they were of course just as
much merchants and wholesalers, the two groups of the London
middle class which together with shopkeepers and financiers
are considered in the next section.

ii Commerce

Most people who discuss the middle class of early modern
London frame this discussion in terms of merchants, no other
type of middle-class person coming readily to their minds. This
narrow misconception should be dispelled in the course of this
chapter but, for all that, merchants, defined as people trading
overseas, were rather important and occupied a very special
place in the upper ranks of the London middle class.

Merchants were singled out by contemporaries as a race
apart from other members of the commercial world, their
occupation being seen to have a certain nobility which distinguished it from the dross of shopkeeping and manufacturing.
Even the snobbish Edward Chamberlayne acknowledged 'their
great benefit to the publick, and ... their great endowments
and generous living', 'generous' of course meaning that they
lived like the gentlemen that many claimed to be.[57] Merchants
naturally encouraged this image, as did contemporary writers
on trade, who were prepared to list an unbelievable range of
qualities thought necessary for a 'perfect merchant'. 'He ought
to be a good penman, a good arithmetician, and a good
accountant', a master of several foreign languages, a good
geographer, a skilful navigator and a superb judge of his fellow
men, as well as knowing absolutely everything about the
produce, habits, laws and trading customs 'of all forraign
countries'. Whether many merchants were quite such poly-
maths is doubtful, but the image stuck. 'A merchant in his
counting-house at once converses with all parts of the known
world,' wrote Defoe. 'This, and travel, makes a true-bred
merchant the most intelligent man in the world.'[58]

There were probably some 600 to 1000 full-time merchants
in London in the later seventeenth century and perhaps as
many people again were engaged in foreign trade on a part-
time basis, investing in the occasional 'adventure' abroad or

trading overseas as an extension of their main home-based occupation.[59] Between them, the merchants proper owned much the biggest accumulation of wealth in London and individual merchants predominated amongst the city's richest men. However, there was a hierarchy in overseas trade as in most of the industries discussed in the last section and there was a huge difference in wealth between the richest merchants and the average. At the top, there were some ten or twenty veritable merchant princes, men who dominated the overseas trading world of their day and engaged in a variety of other economic activities, particularly finance, as well as very often playing a part in the political world. Their fortunes often overtopped the magic six-figure mark and there is one in our sample, Peter Vansittart, an immigrant from Danzig, who was worth over £120,000.[60] The only other men who could hope to leave such a fortune, apart from great landowners, would be top financiers and lawyers, a few doctors and the more unscrupulous public servants.

However, men like Vansittart were quite exceptional and it would be wrong to generalize about merchants on the basis of their richest representatives. Only one other merchant out of the forty-two in our sample had a fortune over £50,000 and a further seven left over £20,000. The median fortune was only £9050 and just over half the merchants had fortunes between £5000 and £15,000, which can be taken as a typical accumulation. This certainly meant that they were well off, but it does show that the typical merchant was not quite the plutocrat he is sometimes taken for.[61] The fortunes of the richer manufacturers came into the same range, as has been seen. So did those of wealthy wholesalers, as Table 2.2 overleaf demonstrates. Nevertheless, a career as a merchant was an attractive one, not least because you did not necessarily have to start with a very large capital. A typical career pattern involved several years abroad as a factor or commission agent for established London merchants, before returning home to trade from London, and the commissions thus earned formed a valuable addition to what capital had been raised from parents and relations.[62] Success in foreign trade however required that the young aspirant received the right training and made the right contacts and parents paid

TABLE 2.2: Fortunes of London Merchants, Wholesalers and Shopkeepers

Fortune at Death	*Occupations*
£10,000 & over	Merchant; merchant; banker; merchant; merchant; merchant; merchant; merchant; merchant; merchant; haberdasher; merchant; tobacconist; oilman; merchant; haberdasher; merchant; merchant; draper; draper; merchant; merchant; haberdasher; draper; merchant
£5000–£9999	Merchant; merchant; merchant; merchant; merchant; draper; drysalter; haberdasher; merchant; merchant; wine-cooper; merchant; merchant; wool-stapler; merchant; cheesemonger; jeweller; bookseller; merchant; merchant; leather-seller; leather-seller; merchant; merchant; druggist; merchant
£2000–£4999	Oilman; salter; merchant; merchant; haberdasher; merchant; mercer; haberdasher; silkman; leather-seller; tobacconist; draper; draper; haberdasher; tobacconist; merchant; grocer; coal merchant; silkman; cheesemonger; merchant; jeweller; draper; ironmonger; cheesemonger; draper; draper; coal-merchant; bookseller; salesman; grocer; merchant; mercer; upholsterer; grocer; paper-seller; mercer; tobacconist; tobacconist; merchant; upholsterer; merchant; laceman; silkman; draper; mercer; haberdasher; pawnbroker; jeweller; merchant; ironmonger; hop-merchant; haberdasher; hosier; mercer; grocer; furrier
£1000–£1999	Timber-merchant; salter; mercer; merchant; draper; draper; ironmonger; mercer; salter; haberdasher; leather-seller; haberdasher; grocer; bookseller; butcher; mercer; milliner; upholsterer; yarn-dealer; cheesemonger; salter; druggist; upholsterer; haberdasher; haberdasher; jeweller; salter; leather-seller; haberdasher; pawnbroker; corn-chandler
£500–£999	Hardware; tobacconist; salesman; grocer; milliner; salter; merchant; stationer; bookseller; haberdasher; cheesemonger; mealman; poulterer; grocer; timber-merchant; draper; grocer; milliner; grocer; draper; mercer; upholsterer; grocer
Less than £500	Milliner; leather-seller; confectioner; hardware; jeweller; milliner; haberdasher; haberdasher; salter; cheesemonger; stationer; ironmonger; haberdasher; salesman; ironmonger; chandler; jeweller; jeweller; coalman; milliner; milliner; poulterer; poulterer; haberdasher; grocer; ironmonger; chandler*; milliner*; grocer*; seedsman*; glass-seller*; haberdasher*; laceman*; draper*

* These last eight men were insolvent, i.e. their liabilities were greater than their assets.

Source: As for Table 2.1 (p. 32)

heavily for their sons' apprenticeships to ensure that this would happen.

English foreign trade was organized in three main ways in our period. First, there were the joint-stock companies, of which the East India Company and the Royal African Company were the most important. These companies traded with a capital supplied by their equity-holders, supplemented by money borrowed on bond, and their charters gave them a monopoly of the trade with the Indian Ocean and West Africa respectively. The companies were run by a salaried staff at home and abroad, and were supervised by 'committees' or directors who were themselves usually merchants with many other interests.[63] Then there were the regulated companies, the most important being the Levant Company in the eastern Mediterranean, the Eastland Company in the Baltic and the Merchant Adventurers or Hamburg Company. These companies also had a monopoly of their particular area of trade, but did not operate a joint-stock. Merchants acquired the freedom of the companies on payment of a fee and supported the companies' running costs by a levy on their trade, but traded for their own and not for the companies' profit. The companies, in turn, enforced the monopoly, lobbied parliament if necessary, made rules for the conduct of trade and kept consuls and agents abroad to smooth the passage of the traders and to negotiate with the local rulers.[64] Both joint-stock and regulated companies were under virtually continuous attack as monopolies, and only the East India Company and the Levant Company of those mentioned survived throughout our period and even they had to face considerable challenge from 'interlopers' who traded illegally in their areas of monopoly.

English trade was thus becoming increasingly open to all-comers in the areas of former monopoly, as it was in most other parts of the world. Here, individual merchants or partnerships were free to trade as they wished, provided they observed the laws of England and of the countries to which they traded. One result of this freedom was that many more small men traded to such places as Spain, Portugal, France or Holland and to the English colonies in America, particularly in the earlier part of our period. However, there were economies to scale in overseas trade, as there were in many industries, and what evidence we have suggests that, by the early eighteenth century, nearly every branch of English trade was being engrossed into fewer and fewer hands.[65] In the world of the merchants, as in that of the manufacturers, the small man was being squeezed out.

Most merchants at least started as specialists, confining themselves, for instance, to the wine trade and often a particular branch of the wine trade, or to the trade with the Baltic or the Levant, these 'Turkey traders' being almost a synonym for great wealth in the later seventeenth century. Such specialization made good sense, enabling the young man to know everything he needed to know about specialist products, the problems, laws and customs of trading with particular areas, the qualities of his competitors and foreign trading partners, and in general to get the best advantage of his training, which would have often involved the learning of one or more foreign languages.

However, it is clear from inventories that an initial specialization very often overflowed into considerable diversification. The basic form of the Levant trade, for instance, was an exchange of English broadcloth for Turkish and Syrian raw silk and many traders confined themselves to that, with the addition perhaps of some other English exports, such as lead, and a few other Levantine imports, such as cotton and dyestuffs. However, many Levant merchants traded also with Italy, North Africa and especially with Spain, an attractive business which provided cash in the form of pieces of eight, which in turn eased the problems of paying for their main return cargoes of raw silk. Some Levant merchants diversified much further. Some combined Mediterranean trade with re-export to Hamburg or the Baltic; some developed a West Indian business on the side. Some, like Sir Jonathan Dawes, who died in 1672 worth over £38,000, might still have a basic Levant trade at the heart of his business, but actually traded just about everywhere in the known world.[66]

The same patterns can be seen in every other trading area. The Baltic posed a problem for the merchant, since it was unable to absorb very large quantities of English exports, and many traders specialized almost entirely in imports from one particular area, such as John Ferney whose business was devoted to the import of iron and pitch from Sweden. But the very nature of such an unbalanced trade encouraged diversification. Some merchants engaged in a clandestine trade with the Spanish colonies to provide them with a flow of cash to pay for their Baltic imports. Others financed their Baltic trade through re-export of Asian, Mediterranean or American goods, as did Peter Vansittart, who traded in all three.[67]

The main business of traders to America and the West Indies, the fastest growing section of English overseas trade,[68] was the import of sugar and tobacco in exchange for what was called a 'sortable cargo', a mixed cargo of textiles, clothing, metal goods and furniture, wines, spirits and beer, re-exports of Asian goods and anything else 'that may furnish the tradesman there with parcels fit to fill their shops and invite their customers'.[69] However, these sugar and tobacco merchants diversified like everybody else, often into the slave trade from Africa, a logical direction in which to move since the planters who supplied them with their exports were always complaining that the Royal African Company, the official monopolists, did not deliver sufficient slaves. They also engaged in re-export of their wares to Europe, since England was unable to absorb all of the increasingly large imports, a process which could lead to the sugar or tobacco merchant becoming a Baltic merchant as well.[70]

These merchants also acted as agents or factors for the planters, selling their goods on commission and providing many other services. They lent money to the planters by allowing them to draw on them for cash, they searched out delicacies unobtainable in the colonies, looked after the planters' children, lobbied parliament and provided information for the Board of Trade which might further their own interests and those of the plantations. Such services played a vital role in linking together the far-flung parts of the English trading empire and were by no means confined to the American trade. 'Most merchants are factors for one another in this shape and reckon it the most certain, though not the most profitable part of their business.' The factorage business and hence the general efficiency of the London market was helped by the large numbers of foreign merchants who settled in London in the late seventeenth century. This influx of Huguenots, Jews, Dutchmen, Germans and merchants like Vansittart from the Baltic was to give the mercantile community that cosmopolitan quality that it has had ever since. Their presence in London also signalled the fact that England had now finally arrived as a trading nation.[71]

Shipowning was another important activity in which merchants engaged. Most ships were owned by syndicates, the commonest share held by an individual being one-sixteenth or one-thirty-second for the really large ships. Shares could be sold or mortgaged and so provided a useful liquid asset, and merchants were much the commonest owners of shares, followed by mariners and people engaged in shipbuilding or the supply of equipment, who often accepted shares in lieu of payment. Few people could be described as shipowners pure and simple, for it was rare to invest a high proportion of one's fortune in such an expensive and risky asset, liable to become a total loss in a storm or to capture by privateers in wartime.[72]

Ships could of course be insured and marine insurance was another activity in which merchants played a prominent role, most underwriters being merchants. Other pursuits included finance and the management of the trading companies, while some merchants had domestic interests in wholesaling, manufacturing or property on top of their overseas business. A few even had retail interests, though most contemporaries thought it beneath the dignity of a merchant to keep shop.[73] Most merchants, then, were busy as well as prosperous men. They were also employers of large numbers of subordinates: warehousemen to manage their extensive storage space, factors overseas and apprentices, clerks and book-keepers in their counting-houses, the equivalent of the modern office.[74]

The hub of the London mercantile world was the Royal Exchange, where merchants trading to different regions each had their separate walks, 'the place where the merchants assemble every day to transact business'.[75] Here was the place to seal a bargain, to charter a ship, to fix up an insurance. Here was the place for gossip, news and advice about the myriad byways of the English trading world. The Exchange was also the place where merchants were likely to meet wholesalers, a vitally important middle-class group who have been very little studied by historians.[76] Some London wholesalers doubled as overseas merchants, retailers or manufacturers, but their main function in the English economy was to make London work as an

entrepôt, acting as middlemen between merchants and manufacturers, between merchants and shopkeepers and, above all,
between the great market of London and the provinical traders,
who so depended on the metropolis both as a market for their
goods and as the source of supply for those other goods which
were not available in their vicinity. The wholesalers, in short,
acted as the pump which, in Defoe's metaphor, circulated
England's blood to and from the heart that was the metropolis.[77]

Most wholesalers specialized as middlemen in the market for
a particular product.[78] One group of these specialists has
already been mentioned, the Blackwell Hall Factors who acted
as intermediaries in the cloth trade, selling cloth made in the
provinces on commission to exporting merchants and to the
London woollen-drapers, another important wholesaling
group.[79] They also supplied the clothiers with raw materials,
such as oil and wool, and were often rich enough to give credit
to clothier and cloth exporter or draper alike, thus providing an
invaluable service to England's largest industry. Such a business obviously favoured the man with a big capital, as indeed
was true of every wholesale trade, and as a result the number
of factors shrank from about fifty in the late seventeenth century
to just a few very wealthy men half a century later. The
Gentlemen's Magazine summed up the position in 1739: 'The
Blackwell-Hall factor, originally but the servant of the maker,
is now become his master, and not only his, but the wool-
merchant's and draper's too.'[80]

Few importing merchants dealt directly with the final users
or consumers of their wares, preferring to sell in bulk to a
wholesaler and so turn over their trading capital more rapidly.
There were, as a result, specialist wholesalers in every major
import trade. One group were the silkmen, who combined
dealing in imported raw silk with silk-throwing, selling the final
yarn to weavers in London and the provinces.[81] Leather-sellers
performed a similar function, dealing in hides and skins, which
they often had dressed before selling them to glovers and other
manufacturers.[82] Then there were the linen-drapers, who
bought cotton textiles at the quarterly sales of the East India
Company and linen from merchants who specialized in its
import, sometimes organizing the finishing of the cloth before
selling to retailers in London and provincial towns and also to

salesmen called 'Manchester men' who travelled all over the country.[83] In the imported food trades, there were the wholesale grocers, who, together with the refiners, were the main purchasers of the sugar retained on the home market, and the wholesale tobacconists, who acted as intermediaries between the importers and the retail tobacco shops, men like Sir Richard and Francis Levett, who had a working capital of between £30,000 and £40,000 in 1705 and traded on a bigger scale than any of the merchants from whom they bought tobacco.[84]

The supply of food to London provided opportunities for many other specialist middlemen, who made a mockery of a large body of ancient statute law which said that farmers were supposed to sell direct to housewives or bakers in the market.[85] A few wealthy farmers did bring their grain to market or at least sold it in London through commission agents, but most grain consumed in the metropolis was sold by wholesalers, who 'buy the corn even in the barn before it is thresh'd, nay sometimes they buy it in the field standing, not only before it is reap'd but before it is ripe'.[86] Many groups competed for the profits to be made out of London's huge imports of grain, flour and malt – corn-factors, who bought as described above or sold on commission for farmers and country wholesalers; jobbers, who were speculators pure and simple; mealmen and rich bakers, who competed for the flour market; and millers and maltsters, who bought and sold grain as well as processing it. Carriers also developed functions as wholesalers in addition to their basic role – the bargemasters of the Thames and Lea valleys, the Kentish hoymen, and the carters and waggoners, of whom a writer complained in 1718, 'They having, by their quick and frequent passing and repassing between Town and Country, a better opportunity of knowing how the markets are likely to rise and fall; and by these means they draw off a considerable, though a very unjust gain out of all provisions of this kind.'[87]

Londoners did not live on bread alone; indeed, according to John Houghton, they were consuming 88,400 beeves and 600,000 sheep a year in the 1690s, or about one beef animal for every family and just over a sheep a head. They also consumed large numbers of pigs, some of which were bred on the spot and fed on the city's waste or on the mash left over in the breweries.

Naturally enough, there were wholesalers in these meat trades as well, in this case the 'carcase butchers', who bought the live animals from drovers and graziers and were often major graziers themselves, using their own pasture land to fatten the beasts which they had bought 'at the town's end'.[88] The other major wholesalers in the food trades were the cheesemongers, who dealt in both cheese and butter. These men kept factors in the dairying regions to buy at fairs or direct from the farmers, and they owned most of the vessels which shipped cheese and butter coastwise to London. Some of them ran very big businesses, such as Abraham Daking, who, in 1733, sold about one-fifth of all the butter traded on the London market in addition to a very large cheese business.[89]

The biggest, or at least the bulkiest, of all London's import trades was that in coal, which was averaging nearly a ton per head of London's population in our period.[90] Nearly all of this was shipped from Northumberland, Durham and the east coast of Scotland, passing through the hands of several middlemen on its journey from the pits to the Thames, by which time it was usually the property of the owners of the colliers, the ship-masters acting as travelling merchants. It was then sold to the London wholesale coal merchants, who broke the cargoes down into smaller lots to sell either direct to manufacturers or the wealthier private users or to the retailers or small-coal-men who hawked the fuel to the final consumers.[91]

London may have got its food and fuel from the provinces, but it sent plenty back in return, the metropolis supplying provincial industry with much of its raw materials and provincial shops and travelling chapmen with their stock in trade. Such goods might be purchased direct from the warehouses of the London wholesalers, from servants travelling on behalf of London firms, from factors established in provincial towns or at the country fairs which still flourished in our period. The historian of Nottingham described how, in the late seventeenth century, the local shopkeepers 'depended upon the great annual Martin-mass Fair at Lenton, a village about a mile distant from Nottingham, where they used to buy their mercers, drapers, grocers, and all sorts of goods they wanted, brought thither by the Londoners'.[92]

The greatest fair of all was that held in September at

Stourbridge, outside Cambridge. Defoe, who describes it in his *Tour*, was especially impressed with the 'wholesalemen, from London, and all parts of England, who transact their business wholly in their pocket-books, and meeting their chapmen from all parts, make up their accounts, receive money chiefly in bills, and take orders. These they say exceed by far the sales of goods actually brought to the fair, and deliver'd in kind; it being frequent for the London wholesale men to carry back orders from their dealers for ten thousand worth of goods a man, and some much more.' The debt-collecting aspect of the fairs was particularly important and is reflected in inventories, such as in that of the wholesale tobacconist, Francis Levett, where debts collected at Lenton, Gainsborough, Boston, Beverley and Houlden Fairs are listed.[93]

'You cannot go to a shopkeeper of any note in the remotest town in England, but he holds some correspondence at London,' wrote Defoe, 'or else he must be a mean tradesman, that buys his goods of some of his better furnish'd neighbours, and they buy at London. . . . As all these country tradesmen buy at London, so they are all in debt at London more or less.' The truth of Defoe's observation is only too apparent when we look at the names and addresses of the creditors of provincial bankrupts. In the years 1711–15, for instance, 154 provincial bankrupts from 41 English and Welsh counties were sued by Londoners. Nearly four-fifths of the debtors were retailers of textiles, food, drink or tobacco and three-quarters of the creditors were wholesale distributors of these same products, linen-drapers, mercers and haberdashers being the commonest of the London creditors.[94]

These London wholesalers were the creditors not just of provincial but also of London shopkeepers, the next group of metropolitan traders who will be considered. Shopkeepers, indeed all retailers, were seen as rather lowly creatures in the social hierarchy, above the 'lusty mechanicks or handy-craftsmen' but below the 'whole-sale-men' and in a completely different social world from the 'merchants of forrein traffick'. This did not seem to worry the young men of our period, for retailing was seen to be 'an easy life and thence many are induced to run into it', with the result that shopkeepers formed one of the larger groups in the middle station.[95] Many writers thought it too easy a life and complained that too many young men were being drawn into retailing by the generous credit offered by wholesalers. Shopkeepers certainly were vulnerable in a world that expected long retail credit and well-stocked shops but, for all that, most retailers made a respectable living. There are, for example, twenty-nine shopkeepers in our sample who could be described as haberdashers. Two died insolvent, another left only £20 and a further ten under £1000. All the rest left over £1000, three of whom were mainly wholesalers and left over £10,000. It may have been 'an easy life' but, for most who tried it, the life was not an unprofitable one.[96]

There had been shops in London since the middle ages, but it is really only in the late sixteenth and early seventeenth centuries that shops and shopping as we understand them came of age. This was mainly a function of the growth of the market and the separation of retailing from manufacture, which was discussed in the last section when considering such people as pewterers and ironmongers. Many people did still buy goods from the 'shop' at the front of industrial premises; many bought goods from wholesalers or from merchants. However, for most articles, except for food bought in the markets, it was the normal practice by the late seventeenth century to go to a well-stocked shop and there to bargain with a specialist retailer for their purchase.

The appearance of the shop was altering in line with its development as a specialized retail outlet. Some of the early shops were little more than stalls or sheds encroaching on to the pavements at the front of houses. Such ramshackle structures survived at the bottom end of the retail business, but the permanent shop occupying the ground floor of a house was becoming the norm. Some of these had very little depth and customers were served through the open window, over which a hinged shutter or awning offered protection from the weather. Others, probably the majority by the end of the seventeenth century, were fully enclosed shops with glazed windows through which the prospective customer could admire the choicer goods on offer before being stampeded by the shopkeeper or his apprentice standing at the door.

Mercers, drapers and high-class haberdashers had the smartest shops. Joseph Floyd, a mercer of Milk Street, had what was

quite a common arrangement, a front shop lined with wainscot-
ting and a back shop (often called a warehouse) separated by
an arch. The shop furniture included leather chairs for his
customers to sit on, looking-glasses in which they could admire
themselves, several presses and chests to hold his stock, shelves,
counters and twenty 'specklewood' ells and yards with which to
measure out the silks and stuffs which he sold.[97] A good idea of
the interior of such shops can be seen from the fine engravings
which sometimes illustrate the trade-cards of high-class retailers.[98] These enable one to see that London shops could be
attractive places in which to pass the time. They looked indeed
very like the high-class drapers' shops familiar to our grandpar-
ents, though the absence of gaslight or electricity made for
gloomy interiors, and the dangers of being fooled when buying
things by candlelight form a recurring theme in the literature of
the period. These mercers' and drapers' shops were, however,
decidedly up-market and most London shops were fairly chaotic
places, with floor, shelves and counters all overflowing with
packets and parcels containing a little of this and a little of that.
Many shops were subdivided, such as that of Sarah Kellett,
milliner, whose shop-goods were 'on one side of the shop only'
and Edith Clarke, hosier, who traded 'on the other side of the
said shop'.[99]

If a haberdasher is defined as 'a dealer in small articles
appertaining to dress, as thread, tape, ribbons etc.', in other
words as someone who is virtually synonymous with a milliner,
then haberdashers were much the commonest type of shop in
London, apart from food and drink outlets. Many of them
specialized in particular branches of the trade and so were
known as threadmen, ribbon-sellers and the like, but nobody
specialized so much that they did not overlap not only with
every other haberdasher but also with what were usually
thought of as completely different trades, such as mercers,
drapers, paper-sellers, jewellers or those sellers of fancy metal,
ivory and horn goods known as toymen. Thomas Pead, for
instance, specialized in thread, tape and ribbon, and sold most
other sorts of haberdashery, but he also sold paper, playing
cards, primers and hornbooks, all of which pertained to the
bookseller's trade.[100] Total concentration on any one type of
product was in fact fairly unusual. Mercers sold chess-boards

and looking-glasses, as well as silk fabrics; jewellers sold lace as well as jewellery. Some dealers traded in an amazing variety of goods. Thomas Oldham, a member of the Girdlers' Company, sold whips, canes, sticks, spurs, powder and drinking horns, knives, forks, scissors, combs, chess and backgammon men, leashes, hawking bags and other equipment for hawking and cock-fighting such as collars, swives and heel spurs . . . as well, surprisingly, as girdles. It was, perhaps, too varied a stock to bode well for, when he died in 1672 aged thirty, he was insolvent.[101]

Much of the Londoner's food was bought in the markets, the City proper being especially well served after the Fire, when new and better arranged central markets were built.[102] Much was also bought from the great army of mainly female hawkers who roamed the streets of the city and suburbs selling bread, meat, fish, fruit and vegetables, much of it carried in baskets on their heads. However, there were also large numbers of food shops – butchers, bakers, cheesemongers and, commonest of all, the chandlers, who dealt 'in all things necessary for the kitchen in small quantities' and thus were the main resort of the poor, who would buy here in pennyworths what their wealthier neighbours might buy from more specialist food retailers.[103]

Finally, there were the salters and grocers, the grocers concentrating almost entirely on imported goods and selling more or less what one would expect them to sell. Samuel Hayward had a typical stock in his City shop when he died in 1700. His main lines were sugar, molasses and raisins of various kinds, but he also sold figs, prunes, dates, rice and virtually the whole range of oriental spices.[104] He also sold tobacco, as did nearly all grocers and many other types of shop, though there were also specialist tobacconists, in many of which one could smoke the weed in the shop's pipes. Tea and coffee, which later became part of the normal stock of grocers, were usually handled by specialist dealers or sold from coffee-houses in these early days.

Grocers were quite distinct from salters, who dealt in 'wet goods' and also in a range of other things related to the chandler's and hardware trades. A typical salter's stock would include oil, salt, vinegar, soap, anchovies, capers, cucumbers

and olives.[105] Many also sold bacon and ham. John Pott of
Cornhill had a very smart business, stocking the very finest
Florentine and Genoese olive oil, caviar, mangoes, samphire,
pickled mushrooms and walnuts, as well as the normal range of
salter's wares. No wonder he included the Archbishop of
Canterbury and Brasenose College amongst his customers.
Other salters kept a line in such household necessities as
brooms, blacking, bedcord and string, thus gradually merging
into other trades such as hardware dealers and suppliers of the
specialized requirements of fishermen and gardeners.[106]

Nearly all these shopkeepers needed to borrow money to run
their businesses and this section concludes by looking at where
they were likely to get it from. Our period is sometimes
described as the Financial Revolution, what one might call the
first 'Big Bang', a description which normally refers to the
revolution in public finance which started in the 1690s and saw
the founding of the Bank of England and the creation of a long-
term national debt, developments which were to make it much
easier for the government to borrow money and so win wars.[107]
The same decade sees a rash of company promotion and the
development of a fledgling stock exchange, complete with
jobbers and brokers, whose ability to manipulate the market
made them a much-hated race. Meanwhile, ever since the
1630s, there had been an expansion in the provision of banking
services in the city.

Two main groups competed for this work. Probably the first
to develop were the scriveners, a very active group whose
original work had been the writing of bonds and other legal
documents, work which placed them in a good position to put
borrowers in touch with lenders and so earn a 'procuration' for
the introduction, such commissions earning the scrivener some
two to five per cent of the sum lent.[108] But scriveners did much
more than this, as can be seen from the papers of Paul Wicks.[109]
He wrote all sorts of bonds, mortgages and other legal documents to do with property, such as conveyances. He introduced
his customers to people who wanted to borrow money on bond
or mortgage, collected the interest and attended the law-courts
should litigation ensue. He bought and sold houses, drew up
leases and managed London property for clients, collecting
rents, seeing to repairs and dealing with recalcitrant tenants.

He acted as the man of business for people in the country, receiving their rents, collecting their pay if they held a government office, paying their bills and carrying out a wide variety of other commissions. The relative importance of such activities obviously varied from scrivener to scrivener. Some did little more than draw up legal writings for a fee. Some specialized in estate agent business. Some were virtually bankers.

In this last respect, the scriveners were competing with the goldsmith-bankers, a 'new fashioned' tribe who had been growing up since the Civil War.[110] The ordinary work of the goldsmith was to fashion articles out of gold or more often silver, make jewellery and deal in coins, jewels and precious metals. What was happening in the middle of the seventeenth century was that some of the wealthier goldsmiths were taking in deposits of cash and precious metals from their customers, initially because their premises offered good facilities for safe keeping, an activity which led them into the business of lending out this idle money, so that soon they became true deposit bankers. The receipts issued by the bankers for deposits operated as a sort of bank note and, at the same time, an infant cheque system grew up, a simple written order to the banker being sufficient for payment to a third party. Meanwhile, the banker lent out the money deposited with him in order to make his profit. In 1677, the first London directory listed forty-four goldsmiths who kept 'running cashes' or, in other words, allowed their customers the drawing and chequeing arrangements discussed above. By 1725, bankruptcy, death, retirement and consolidation had reduced the number of private banks in London to twenty-four, which was probably a more realistic number for the business available.[111]

Banks and banking tend to attract the attention of historians, because of their modern importance. However, they never dominated the financial world of our period as they were to do later. Most people who wanted to borrow money did so in fact from some sort of money-lender rather than a banker.[112] The commonest type was the pawnbroker, dealing mainly with the poor and advancing money on a variety of pawns, mostly of low value. Such businesses were very necessary in the London of our period, when few people had a regular income and when many of the working population might expect to be unemployed

for several months of the year. Loans were not simply used for
consumption purposes but also as a source of working capital
for small-scale handicraftsmen and for hawkers, 'such as persons who cry fish, fruit or other wares . . . to purchase the
several commodities they deal in'. Some idea of the return to
pawnbroking is given in a pamphlet of 1706, which claimed
that pawnbrokers 'commonly take six pence in the pound per
month for what they lend upon pawns, which is 30 per cent per
annum' and that they rarely lent more than a quarter or a third
of the value deposited. The rates on very low value pledges
were even higher, a witness in 1745 saying that 'for every pledge
of the value of 1s. he took a ½d. per calendar month' or 50 per
cent per annum, good business when the maximum legal rate
of interest was supposed to be five per cent.[113]

A rather more respectable business was that run by the
money-lender, who lent in larger amounts against paper securities, a common business for the men of the middle station.
Nathaniel Axtell, for instance, who died in 1672 worth over
£7000, was a member of the Vintners' Company but the only
wine in his household was for his own consumption. All his
assets, apart from domestic goods and cash, were in advances
made from his own capital. His liabilities totalled a mere £126,
of which £100 consisted of legacies owing to his children from
their grandmother.[114] Money-lending did not of course need to
be the citizen's only activity and we can find many examples of
businessmen who combined a very considerable degree of
money-lending (and other forms of investment) with their
everyday business. Men of any occupation at any time in their
life-cycle might decide to do this, since money-lending at five or
six per cent might well seem as good a prospect as selling cheese
or linen. There was, however, a tendency for men to lend out
more of their assets as they got older, many men in their fifties
and sixties being effectively retired, with all their assets in loans
or investments and no sign of any former trading or manufacturing activities in their inventories. It is also possible to discern
various groups who were particularly inclined to lend out a
large proportion of their assets, however old they were. Widows
were one such group, many of them having no practical business
skills and thus relying for their incomes on the interest which
they could earn by investing or lending out their former

husband's business assets, often using a scrivener as intermediary. The other main group were the professional people whose earnings were mainly in fees and perquisites and who had no need to plough back those earnings into a stock in trade.[115]

The men in commerce considered in this section probably represented the largest section of the middle class. Some idea of the relative wealth and the variety of occupations of the people in this group can be seen in Table 2.2 on p.36, which can be compared with Table 2.1 (p.32), where the wealth of the manufacturers was shown.[116] The table certainly makes clear the dominance of the merchants amongst the wealthy members of London's commercial class, no less than sixteen out of the twenty-five people who left over £10,000 being overseas traders.[117] However, what the table also shows and what I hope has been made clear in this section is that many wholesalers were in very much the same financial class as the average merchant, even if few were numbered in the really top ranks with fortunes over, say, £20,000. Historians have begun to realize that inland trade was rather important in early modern England; what they need to do now is to find out rather more about the inland traders who drove this commerce.

iii Catering and Entertainment

One major sector of the commercial world was omitted from the last section – the sale of drink. This was a very important part of the metropolitan economy, which may well have employed some 30,000 people.[118] The thirst of Londoners also provided many opportunities for the men and women of the middle station, though it is probable that the majority of drink outlets were too humble to earn their owners any more than an artisan income and often not even that. Indeed, many such places were run by former artisans or their wives, the ambition of workmen to retire and keep a pub being no less strong in the seventeenth century than it is today.

Few artisans could, however, have aspired to take over the city's inns, the largest and most venerable of London's catering establishments, of which there were between 150 and 200, most of them quite easily distinguished from other eating and drinking places by their extensive lodging and stabling facilities.

Many inns also had an important part to play in the country's transport services, being the termini of the carrier and coaching routes which radiated from the capital. This role gave them a particular regional flavour, depending on the routes which they served, and provided a link between the metropolis and the provinces from which coachmen and carriers could be relied on to provide the latest news.[119]

The layout of inns can be seen in contemporary maps, which show that most had a comparatively modest frontage with a gateway which allowed waggons to pass through into a series of yards set well back from the high rentals of the principal streets. These yards were surrounded by buildings containing the taproom or bar, lodging rooms for guests, often with the galleried access so familiar from old prints, coach-houses, stabling, farrier's, smith's and ironmonger's shops. Inns operated as markets as well as places of lodging and refreshment, and many kept warehousing space for goods in transit or as a permanent facility for those with no business premises in London. The Blossom in Laurence Lane and the Cross Keys in Wood Street had stockrooms for twenty-four separate provincial hosiers by the 1760s and many other provincial businessmen found it convenient to organize their businesses in this way.[120]

The social role played by inns in country towns was normally filled in London by the taverns, the most up-market drinking establishments, where Londoners went for good food and drink and lively company. Taverns sold wine almost exclusively and they were also the fashionable restaurants of the day, most of them offering a fixed-price 'ordinary' for their clientèle, a very convenient arrangement thought Samuel Pepys, 'because a man knows what he hath to pay'. The ordinary normally consisted of plain English fare, but our period also sees the beginning of that fondness for French cuisine which has been a feature of eating-out in London ever since. A passion for things French might simply involve the disguising of bad meat by a bad sauce, as Jonathan Swift discovered in 1710 when he had 'a neck of mutton dressed à la Maintenon, that the dog could not eat'. It could also involve outrageous prices, as Ned Ward warned his readers: 'Every fop with a small fortune, who attempts to counterfeit quality, and is fool enough to bestow twenty shillings worth of sauce upon ten penniworth of meat, resorts to one of these ordinaries.' But London, or at least the West End, was full of fops with small fortunes and the French ordinaries prospered.[121]

Most taverns had a big ground-floor room called the bar-room, buttery or simply the tavern. Here was the place for general eating and drinking, and some idea of contemporary drinking habits can be gleaned from such items as bar-boards or score-boards for marking up credit; gallon, quart and pint measuring pots for serving out wine; 'drinking towells', presumably for clearing up the mess; and chamber pots indoors and pissing cisterns in the yard. The most striking aspect of the rest of the tavern was the large number of private drinking-rooms, which might be used for business meetings, gambling or amorous assignations. Each room would have one or more tables, several chairs and nearly always its own fire, while the better quality rooms had carpets, window-curtains, hangings, pictures and other ornaments. Most taverns also had at least one very large and handsomely furnished private room which could be used for social, business or political meetings, such as the best room in the Crown in Threadneedle Street, which was used for suppers by Fellows of the Royal Society after their meetings.[122]

The main working quarters of a tavern, apart from the bar, were the kitchens and the cellars and vaults. The kitchens usually had an impressive range of equipment, with ten or more spits and over half a ton of pewter listed in their inventories. However, it was the wine in the cellars which dominated the capital investment made by tavern-keepers. The wine stocks of the twenty tavern-keepers in our sample averaged over £1000, this often being more than the net worth of the owner. Canary and, particularly, claret were the most popular wines in the early part of our period but, from 1678 onwards, government policy was to create an enforced change in English taste, as the import of French wines was either prohibited or subject to very high duties. In the long run, this policy worked in favour of the wines of Spain, Portugal and Madeira, though many tavern-keepers still kept French wines even during periods of prohibition and the English taste for claret was not easily to be eradicated.[123]

A challenge to claret and canary, and indeed to taverns as a whole, came from the coffee-house, which developed to serve essentially the same clientèle. This by-product of England's trade with the Levant first appeared in London in 1652 and was immediately successful. Ten years later, there were eighty-two coffee-houses in the City alone and many more in the rest of the metropolis, while Londoners wondered how they had ever been able to do without them. Coffee-houses were cheap – a penny gained admission for anyone respectably dressed – and they offered a simple, but valuable, range of amenities: coffee as a morning drink instead of 'ale, beer or wine, which by the dizziness they cause in the brain, make many unfit for business'; pipes and tobacco for the smoker; newspapers and gossip for the curious; and an address for those who did not want to stay at home all day. Indeed, as Macaulay noted, the coffee-house was the home of many Londoners: 'Those who wished to find a gentleman commonly asked, not whether he lived in Fleet Street or Chancery Lane, but whether he frequented the Grecian or the Rainbow.'[124]

The typical coffee-house was in fact a coffee-room, a single large room with one or two long tables round which the clients sat and talked or read the newspapers which were on display. Further useful information could be gleaned from the broadsheets and advertisements with which the walls were often adorned. Presiding over the entertainment would be the proprietor, or more often his handsome wife, while boys would distribute dishes of coffee, pipes and tobacco. Sometimes, the atmosphere would be one of sepulchral calm, quiet conversation and the occasional flash of wit. Sometimes, it was one of pandemonium. 'In we went, where a parcel of mudling muck-worms were as busie as so many rats in an old cheese-loft, some going, some coming, some scribbling, some talking, some drinking, some smoaking, others jangling and the whole room stinking of tobacco like a Dutch scoot or a boatswains cabbin.'[125]

Something of the same atmosphere could often be found in the alehouse, the forerunner of the modern pub. In the alehouse kept in Little Moorfields by Thomas Crooke, for instance, you could drink his home-brewed beer in the parlour or the 'great room', but you would also be able to enjoy most of the extraneous facilities offered by a coffee-house, as can be seen from his unpaid debts for tobacco, pipes, newspapers and candles. Crooke would have been unusual in brewing his own beer, most of which was supplied by the common brewers. However, with nearly 6000 alehouses in the metropolis by the 1730s, there was room for a little individuality and alehouses came in all sorts, as is indicated by the varied nomenclature which was used by contemporaries. A dive, boozing ken or tippling house does not sound as though it is in quite the same class as even an alehouse, let alone a public house, an expression which was just coming in.[126]

Most customers of alehouses belonged to the 'mechanick part of mankind', who found there many other services apart from a plentiful supply of drink. Many alehouses offered lodging on a permanent or temporary basis. Others served as a focus for workers in a particular trade, providing a club-room for communal entertainment and operating as a 'house of call' in which information about possible employment could be obtained. Other publicans enhanced their income by serving as the poor man's banker, lending money on the security of pawns or serving beer on tick until the Saturday pay-day. Most alehouses also served food, the usual fare being bread and cheese. However, some establishments combined the functions of an alehouse and a cook-shop, an important part of the London eating scene, which had once been the monopoly of the Company of Cooks but which, by our period, had been invaded by all-comers.[127]

At one level, the cook-shop offered meals similar to those served at the tavern ordinary. Misson gives a good description of a high-class establishment: 'Generally four spits, one over another carry round each five or six pieces of butchers (never anything else; if you would have a fowl or a pidgeon you must bespeak it) meat, beef, mutton, veal, pork and lamb. You have what quantity you please cut off, fat, lean, much or little done, with this a little salt and mustard upon the side of a plate, and a bottle of beer and a roll, and there is your whole feast.' At a much lower level, the cook-shop provided cheap, hot meals for the poor. Roderick Random visited one situated in a cellar where he was 'almost suffocated with the steams of boil'd beef, and surrounded by a company consisting chiefly of hackney-coachmen, chairmen, draymen, and a few footmen out of place, or on board wages, who sat eating shin of beef, tripe, cow-heel or sausages at separate boards, covered with cloths which turned my stomach'. He may not have been delighted with the company, but both food and price were delicious, 2½d. for shin of beef, small beer and bread.[128]

The last and lowest form of drinking establishment was the brandy or dram shop, the numbers of which began to expand rapidly as small shopkeepers and poor housekeepers realized that an investment in a few gallons of spirits and some glasses could add some easily earned pennies or shillings to their weekly income. In 1739, at the height of the gin craze, William Maitland claimed that there were 8659 brandy-shops in the metropolis. He showed, as one might expect, that the density of brandy-shops was greatest in poor areas, there being one for every eight houses in the East End and Southwark and only one in thirty-nine in the City, where the density of taverns and coffee-houses was correspondingly higher.[129] The dram-shops do not seem to have provided any of those elementary comforts which could be found in even the poorest class of alehouse. They existed in the dreariest of surroundings, in damp cellars or back rooms, in sheds and holes in the wall. Here, there were no tables and benches, just a shop counter from which the spirits might be dispensed and a pile of straw for those who could drink no more.

There seems little doubt that drinking, often to excess, was the main entertainment of contemporary Londoners. There were, however, many other things that they could do to amuse themselves. The drink outlets themselves often offered music and dancing, some being specifically described as 'music houses', while many pandered to the Londoner's love of the curious and bizarre. A mermaid or a dancing bear soon drew in thirsty customers while, in the mid-1680s, the great coaching inn of the Belle Sauvage on Ludgate Hill was making £15 a day from a rhinoceros, a marvel indeed, for which the management charged 1s. for a look and 2s. for a ride.[130]

Taverns and alehouses also provided facilities for games such as cards, dominoes and backgammon, while some had billiard-rooms and bowling alleys. Gambling was in fact second only to drinking as a London amusement and it took place in every possible sort of venue, from the Court to taverns and the street, Daniel Defoe proposing in 1725 that 'gaming at orange and gingerbread-barrows should be abolish'd'. There were also specialist gaming-houses, whose owners were thought to have huge fortunes, one former drawer from a tavern being said to be worth £60,000 after a few years as the proprietor of a faro table in Covent Garden. The houses were well organized, each having 'a commissioner, always a proprietor, who looks in of a night, a director who superintends the room, an operator who deals the cards . . . two crowpees who watch the cards and gather the money for the bank, two puffs who have money given them to decoy others to play, a squib, a puff of a lower rank', as well as a waiter, an usher, a porter and an orderly man 'who walks up and down the outside of the door to give notice . . . of constables'.[131]

Further amusement was provided by the various forms of animal baiting sports which were so rife in the city, such as the rat-pits where punters betted on how many rats a dog could kill in a given time, the cock-pits and the bull and bear baiting establishments. Cock-fighting was a very popular sport which drew its audience from the whole gamut of London's social hierarchy, as Samuel Pepys noted when he visited the Shoe Lane cock-pit in December 1663: 'But Lord! to see the strange variety of people, from Parliament men . . . to the poorest 'prentices, bakers, brewers, butchers, draymen, and what not; and all these fellows one with another cursing and betting.'[132] Pepys also went to the Bankside Bear Gardens in August 1666 'and saw some good sport . . . but it is a very rude and nasty pleasure', sentiments which were echoed rather more strongly a few years later by Evelyn, who left the bear-baiting early, 'most heartily weary of the rude and dirty pastime'. Such sentiments were not common, however, and if appetites did become jaded by the antics of the bulls and bears, the proprietors had the answer, introducing an African tiger which was baited by six bull and bear dogs or a leopard to be baited to death in the bear-garden at Soho Square, the audience paying 2s.6d., 5s. or 10s.6d. for a ringside seat. With admission charges exactly the same as at the opera, it would seem that it was not just rude and nasty people who paid to watch these spectacles.[133]

The bear-baiting arenas were also increasingly used for prize fights where men would fight for large purses with a variety of weapons. As prize fighting became more popular, purpose-built

amphitheatres were erected to stage the sport, of which the best
known was Figg's Amphitheatre near Cavendish Square. 'Here,
commonly once or twice a week, is a challenge between two
champions, who, like the Roman gladiators, fight at back-sword
and other weapons, and very cruelly wound one another. There
is also wrestling and playing at cudgels; and what is still more
to be admired, women often, like intrepid amazons, appear
upon the stage, and with equal skill and courage fight with the
same weapons men use. This commonly draws much
company.'[134]

Rather less savage entertainment could be had by listening
to music. Concerts where one paid to hear good music made
their first tentative start in the 1670s and, by the reign of Queen
Anne, several places were putting on performances on a weekly
or more frequent basis, the most famous being Thomas Hick-
ford's Great Room off the Haymarket, which opened in 1691,
and the concert room in York Buildings, which had been
opened by musicians 'determined to take the business in their
own hands'. Roger North said that 'all the quality and beau
mond' went to York Buildings and the proprietors made sure
that it stayed that way by charging 5s. or as much as a guinea
on special occasions. The concert room held 200 comfortably,
so that the musicians could expect a reasonable return for their
labours.[135]

If you wanted to do more than just listen to music you could
go dancing, which was another very popular form of entertainment in Augustan London. The dancing masters were familiar
figures, moving from house to house to teach the children (and
often the adults as well), despised for their supposed effeminacy
but in constant demand for the social graces which they were
able to impart. Many enhanced their incomes by running public
dances at their own schools or at such places as the City Livery
Halls, which were let out on a regular basis for this purpose.
There were also much more public hops at the spas which
flourished on the outskirts of London. Lambeth Wells, for
instance, opened on Easter Monday and 'had public days on
Mondays, Thursdays and Saturdays, with musick from seven
in the morning till sunset; on other days till two. Admission
3d.' Sadler's Wells and its close neighbour and rival Islington
Spa or the New Tunbridge Wells were other favourites for

music and dancing. Ned Ward describes a day out at Islington in 1699 in his salacious poem, *A Walk to Islington*, and provides one with a vivid picture of the crowds of citizens and their wives, apprentices, law students and domestic servants who mingled with members of the lower and criminal classes who flocked to such places for amusement and profit.[136]

Music and dancing were also increasingly important aspects of the entertainment offered by the London theatres, both before, after and during plays, and in the opera, which became more or less permanently established in London in the early eighteenth century. London had only two theatres in the first half of our period and only one between 1682 and 1695, but there was some expansion in the reign of Queen Anne and in the 1720s, so that there were six theatres by the time that Covent Garden opened in 1732, not to mention a considerable amount of fringe theatre in taverns and other venues.[137] All this became increasingly popular with the men and women of the middle station as time went on, few middling people going to the theatre in the early part of our period, hardly surprisingly since so many of the plays performed on the Restoration stage were designed to mock the pretensions of the cits and to insult the honour and taste of their wives.

The theatre, like other forms of entertainment, offered scope for the entrepreneur, most theatre buildings being built and owned by investors who received an income of so much per acting day from the theatrical companies. These companies were often organized on an equity basis, with a small number of sharing actors and a much larger number of actors, dancers, musicians and non-acting personnel on salaries. Rewards were on the whole good. In the 1690s, for instance, the leading actor Thomas Betterton, who had withdrawn from a sharing agreement, was being paid £5 a week and an annual present of 50 guineas, and other actors and actresses got wages from £4 down to £1, while an apprentice actor like the young Colley Cibber got 10s., incomes which suggest that the leading actors and actresses were members of the middle station in material terms, even if by inclination they aspired to the West End and in actuality they belonged to their traditional demi-monde.[138]

London, then, was well provided with entertainment, as befitted a great city, which has been described by one historian

as 'a centre of conspicuous consumption'.[139] The most conspicuous consumers were the aristocracy and gentlemen of the West
End and their hangers-on, who seemed to have little other
purpose in life, but the poor had a great thirst as well, all grist
to the mill of the men and women of the middle station, who
might well find that running a tavern, a bear-pit or a gaming-
house could be just as profitable as any other type of business
in the metropolis.

iv Professions and Arts

The learned professions, which will now be considered, provided employment for at least a quarter and perhaps a third of
the London middle class.[140] The professions had grown particularly rapidly in the half century before the Civil War and this
growth was a major feature in the development of the metropolis, providing yet another focus for provincial men and women,
who looked automatically to London for specialized professional
services or thought of it as the place where a boy who shone at
school might go to make his living in an occupation which bore
none of the stigma of trade. The rewards varied enormously.
Nearly all teachers and most clergymen were very poorly paid.
However, doctors and lawyers, especially the latter, tended to
get richer and richer. 'It is safe to say', writes Professor Holmes,
'that in no other profession in late seventeenth and early
eighteenth-century England did so many men make so much
money, or make it so quickly, as in the law.'[141]

The law provided three main types of occupation, of which
the bar was the most eminent and potentially the most profitable. Incomes earned at the bar were growing over time, as the
fees charged for advocacy or for giving counsel in chambers
grew from a typical 10s. or £1 in the early seventeeth century to
£3, £5, £10 or more by the end of the century. Such fees
provided top-flight barristers with annual incomes of some
£3000 or £4000, far higher than those earned by any commercial
people except the very richest merchants, financiers and wholesalers. Success at the bar was, however, as today, an enormous
gamble, since 'lawyers get very little until they be very eminent,
and such as shall prove so must spend much before they be
so'.[142] Not many barristers did become eminent and the stake

necessary to venture on this gamble was a high one. A call to
the bar required only that one be enrolled as a student for seven
years and eat dinners in the hall of one's Inn for twelve terms.
However, simply living in the correct manner could cost £200 a
year and this high cost of maintenance, together with tuition
and other expenses, could involve the young man's parents in
an expenditure of £1000 to £1500 with no guarantee that he
would ever earn a decent living.

Barristers already confined themselves mainly to advocacy
and pleading in the courts and counselling in their chambers,
and few any longer prepared their own briefs or carried out any
of the other preparation necessary to process a case through the
courts. This 'mechanick' work was done by attorneys and,
increasingly, by solicitors. The latter were a new breed who had
to get business where they could, doing work which attorneys
could not be bothered to do and actively seeking out new
clients, as their name implies. Until 1729, anyone involved in
legal business could call themselves a solicitor; 'every idle fellow
whose prodigality and ill husbandry hath forced him out of his
trade or employment, takes upon him to be a solicitor', as *The
Compleat Solicitor* complained in 1683. Such untrained solicitors
or 'pettyfoggers' were the jackals of the profession, disreputable
men who were 'now indeed swarming and evidently causing
suits and disturbance by eating out the estate of people,
provoking them to go to law'. They were also, of course, eating
into the business of respectable attorneys and solicitors who
had gained their training through clerkships, 'at great labour,
expence and study'.[143] However, a five-year clerkship was cheap
relative to the cost of reading for the bar and the parents of
attorneys and solicitors rarely had to find more than £100 for
their education, a good investment since, despite the swarms of
pettyfoggers, the business available was expanding even faster
than the lawyers.

Such business included court work and litigation, but both
branches of the 'mechanick' side of the law also engaged in
much non-litigious work – drawing up deeds, wills and marriage
contracts, managing property or acting as intermediary between
borrower and lender. Earnings ranged from the pickings of law
business scratched up by an unsuccessful pettyfogger – a couple
of letters written in a coffee-house, a will or two and a rather

desperate action for debt – to the very handsome incomes of the top-rate London attorneys, whose prospects were as good as those of most barristers.

The last branch of the legal profession consisted of the bureaucracy who staffed the law courts in London and West-minster, an extraordinary profusion of clerks of various kinds and of officers with splendidly archaic names such as protono-taries and cursitors, filazers and exigenters.[144] Their incomes came mostly from fees extracted for real or imaginary duties carried out at every stage of the legal process. The Doorkeeper of the Court of Chancery, for example, was due 10s. for every cause heard, out of which he paid 2s. to the Usher of the Rolls, 2s.6d. to the Cryer, 1s. each to the Lord Chancellor's Tipt-Staff and the Register's Bagbearer, 6d. each to the Master of the Rolls' Tipt-Staff and the Court Keeper, retaining just 2s.6d. for himself. [145]

Both the numbers and the incomes of these legal bureaucrats seem to have been growing rapidly. The Six Clerks in Chancery, for instance, had become somewhat overwhelmed by the Sixty Clerks who served under them and who, by 1707, had become 'Ninety who, with their under clerks, dispatch the business of that office. Some of these Ninety do severally get four, five, or six hundred pounds per annum, or more.' Such incomes expanded with 'the alteration which Time has introduced into the practice of the Court . . . by the multiplying of petititions, bills, answers, pleadings, examinations, decrees, and other forms and copies of them, and extending them frequently to an unnecessary length'.[146] No wonder so many people complained of the convolutions and procrastinations of the law; no wonder so many died before getting a decision.

When one looks at the Church, one finds a very different scene from that of the lawyers, a scene of declining business, criticism and generally low incomes.[147] Religion still played a prominent role in politics, but contemporary evidence suggests that the religious passions of the first half of the seventeenth century died down after 1660 and even more after 1688, and that our period saw a growth in indifference and scepticism, which was reflected in a decline in attendance at church and in the moral standards of the people. This owed at least something to the quality of the clergy, according to contemporaries. Bishop

Burnet condemned the English clergy for the mercenary attitude of those who 'come into the priesthood for a piece of
bread', for their lack of pastoral care and for their general
dullness. Edward Chamberlayne wrote that the English clergy
were 'less respected generally than any in Europe' and the
theme of the 'contempt of the clergy' is one that runs right
through our period. Such contempt was generally said to arise
from the ignorance and poverty of the clergy.[148]

This brings one to the paradox of the clergy, which involved
a basic blindness to the laws of supply and demand. There were
quite simply too many ambitious young men seeking too few
livings, while those that there were tended to be poorly paid
and hardly commensurate with the dignity of a clergyman.[149]
This was strange behaviour for men who came 'into the
priesthood for a piece of bread', for the bread was dearly
bought, all clergymen being graduates who had spent several
years at university where expenses were on average about £60
a year. Such an outlay was high compared with that necessary
to enter most trades and professions, as Addison pointed out in
the *Spectator*: 'How many men are country curates that might
have made themselves aldermen of London by a right improvement of a smaller sum of money than what is usually laid out
upon a learned education.'[150]

There was, however, a vitality in the London church which
was far removed from the doom and gloom of most contemporary comment on clerical matters. The City and suburbs bristled
with Anglican churches and chapels[151] and the London parochial clergy seem to have worked hard for their living, filling a
timetable of services in the churches and parochial care outside
which would have driven most country clergymen to despair.
'Few of the hundred churches contained in this city', wrote
Hatton in 1708, 'but where there is divine service once, twice
or more in a day, and these at different hours, some in the
hours of business, which seem to be intended for masters and
those that have estates; and others in the evening when shops
are shut, or very early in the morning, most proper for servants
of all sorts and labouring persons.'[152] London clergy were also
exempted from that contempt which was the lot of their
colleagues elsewhere. A writer of 1739 'owned that the clergy in
and about Town had no reason to complain of contempt, they

had their full portion of esteem and respect', while Burnet praised the men of trade and business who were their congregations, 'the best body in the nation, generous, sober, and charitable . . . more knowledge, more zeal, and more charity, with a great deal more of devotion'.[153]

London could attract a learned clergy, pious and for the most part zealous in their pastoral care, because livings were well above the poverty-stricken norm of the rest of the country. The median living of the rectors and vicars of the 111 churches of 1732 was £150 per annum, with only nine below what was considered the minimum decent living of £80 and no fewer than twenty-five worth more than £300 a year.[154] Curates' pay was higher in London too, despite the complaints of Thomas Stackhouse, who reckoned that a London curate got paid less than 'an ordinary bricklayer or carpenter' or even a footman, grounds for contempt indeed in a materialist age. Some curates certainly were very badly paid, but the typical salary seems to have been about £60 per annum, which should be compared with £30 to £40 in the country as a whole.[155] A salary of £60 would provide a respectable lower-middle-class type of existence, but not all London clergymen lived so well. The metropolis, together with the two universities, was the clerical labour exchange. Here, if a young man could catch the right eye or tug the right lawn sleeve, was the place to find a curacy that would lead to something better, or a domestic chaplaincy in the household of a nobleman with the presentation to a good living. Many a poor clergyman found such places, but many did not. In 1684, the rector of St Martin's in the Fields told John Evelyn that there were 'thirty or forty young men in Holy Orders in his parish' looking for work, and his parish could hardly have been the only one housing such swarms of unemployed clergymen.[156]

London, then, was the home of all sorts of Anglican clergymen, very wealthy bishops who rarely left the metropolis for their dioceses, well beneficed and learned parish clergy, chaplains to prisons and chaplains to monarchs, and hordes of penniless young and not so young men seeking to place their foot on the first rung of the ladder of clerical preferment. London was also the home of many dissenting ministers, for it was amongst 'the men of trade and business' that nonconformity as well as the established church could hope for the biggest and most pious congregations.[157] Dissenters could be found in the very wealthiest mercantile and financial circles but their main numerical strength came from a rather lower stratum, from tradesmen, small shopkeepers and artisans. Such people supported a learned ministry to serve the sixty-one Presbyterian and Independent congregations and rather less well-educated pastors for the nineteen Baptist congregations, while the twenty-three Quaker meetings did not of course have a paid ministry, a fact which enabled them to support a generous system of relief for poorer Friends. Most nonconformist stipends were similar to those of the poorer Anglican clergy, though there were some twenty ministers with prosperous City or West End congregations who could live a modestly genteel life on incomes around £100 a year or more.[158]

London was famous for its schools as well as for its churches and chapels, and the quality of education available was yet another magnet drawing people into the metropolis. School for those who went to one started at about the age of six or seven and the high level of literacy in the capital in all classes and both sexes suggests that elementary education was widely available and reasonably competent.[159] Schoolteaching at this level was not necessarily a sole occupation and one can find among the teachers in petty or 'English' schools such people as curates and parish clerks, artisans such as shoemakers and tailors, a few shopkeepers and several housewives. Fees were cheap, a few pence a week being a normal rate, while many parish schools offered free education for the poor. This facility was expanded considerably by the Charity School movement, which started in 1699. This was supported mainly by middle-class money and aimed to create a dutiful and subordinate working class, with just enough education to turn the children of the poor from pagan savages into obedient and Christian apprentices or servants. It was an immediate success, producing 54 new schools in London and Westminster in its first five years and 132 schools, teaching over 5000 pupils at a cost of about £3 per head per year, by 1729.[160]

Primary education was all the education that the majority of London's children got, if they got that much. It was by no means the end of education for all young Londoners, however, and there was a very wide range of secondary schools, which were attended by nearly all the sons and daughters of middling people and also by many children of lower status, some of whom were able to continue their free education up to this level. The traditional form of secondary education was the grammar school, whose function was to teach boys the rudiments of Latin and sometimes Greek, this being for some a preparation for entry to university but for most an end in itself, a classical education being considered to be the best possible preparation for a young man to serve his God, his country and his family. Students typically stayed at grammar school until they were between fourteen and sixteen before going on to an apprenticeship or clerkship or up to the universities. Such schools had mixed fortunes in our period. Some earlier foundations collapsed or ceased to teach grammar, inflation having made the schoolmaster's salary too derisory to attract anyone above the elementary or 'English school' standard. On the other hand, new grammar schools were still being endowed, the future Archbishop Tenison, for instance, founding a grammar school for thirty non-paying scholars in St Martin's in the Fields in 1685.[161]

Many people and especially middle-class people were, however, losing faith in the educational value of the classics, for reasons summed up by Francis Brokesby in 1701: 'Many things in learning the grammar are imposed that are toilsome and needless, several things that may be useful are not taught in due season; . . . further, that the learning which is acquired at grammar schools is of little or no use to such as are set to ordinary trades, and consequently that time might have been better spent in attaining some useful knowledge, nay much more profitably in learning to write a good hand, arithmetic, and other things of this nature.'[162] Some grammar schools had appreciated the truth of such views for a long time. Dame Alice Owen, for instance, who founded her school in Islington in 1613, was well aware of the commercial opportunities in London and the school's curriculum reflected this. Few children stayed beyond the age of fourteen and writing, arithmetic and accounting were as important as the teaching of Latin. Half a century later, Christ's Hospital, much the biggest school in

London with nearly 1000 pupils, introduced similar innovations with its writing school, which gave scholars the 'opportunity of instructing themselves in writing and arithmetic, the more immediate and necessary qualifications for their preferment in the world'. The writing school was joined in 1673 by the Royal Mathematical School, in which forty scholars were taught mathematics and navigation with the object of apprenticing them into the Royal Navy or the merchant service at the age of sixteen, an innovation which after a shaky start was a great success.[163]

The spread of specialist writing schools and, to a lesser extent, mathematical schools was one of the most striking changes in the London education scene in our period, the usual practice being for boys to go to these establishments for a year or two in their early teens. Many writing and mathematical masters also put in a day or two at grammar and other general schools, as well as teaching pupils in their homes, a practice followed by other specialist teachers, such as Italian, French, dancing, singing and fencing masters. Writing masters almost invariably taught arithmetic and accounting and sometimes applied mathematics, as well as teaching their pupils an easy to read round hand which is much welcomed by historians.[164]

Our period also sees the development of more general schools or academies teaching non-classical and often vocational subjects. Such schools took many forms to suit different sorts of pupil. Some catered for the children of the aristocracy and gentry, such as that established by M. Henri de Foubert in 1680, 'who for his religion was driven out of France, [and] has set up an Academy near the Haymarket for riding, fencing, dancing, handling arms, and mathematics'. Little Tower Street Academy, which was set up in 1715, appealed to a lower class of pupil: 'The proper age for education here is from about 13 or 14 upwards; and the young gentlemen are not only such as are immediately designed for trades, merchandise, the sea, clerkships in offices and to attorneys, or any other employment in business at home or abroad, but those in general who are not designed for the Universities.'[165] One should finally note the dissenting academies, which began to appear soon after 1662, when the Act of Uniformity barred dissenters from going to university. Most of the early academies were small institutions which taught the traditional classical syllabus right up to university level and so prepared young men for the nonconformist ministry, but there were others, of which Newington Green Academy was the most famous, which were forerunners in the development of a more modern education.[166]

The growth of vocational education was the most important change during our period, but there was also a considerable expansion in the numbers of boarding schools in and about the metropolis. Some schools, such as Westminster and St Paul's, drew in boarders from all over the country because of their reputation and social cachet, but there were also many lesser boarding schools which grew up in a ring around the city, mainly to serve the children of the middle class. Such schools offered education of all types. Some were private classical schools offering the grammar school curriculum in a more intimate, tutorial type of environment, often with great success; others offered the range of modern subjects discussed above. Many specialized in teaching girls, such as the nine schools advertised by Houghton in 1694, all of which were run by women and sound similar to the sort of school which Becky Sharp attended in *Vanity Fair*.[167]

Providing all this education was a major occupation in London but, for the most part, a very poorly paid one, there being an even greater number of people qualified to teach than to preach the gospel, with inevitable results on their market value. At the top of the profession were the masters of the great schools, most of whom had fairly modest salaries but could swell their incomes by taking on extra pupils for a fee, by customary gifts and by the profit from taking in boarders. The income of Dr Busby, the famous Headmaster of Westminster, was said to be £1000 a year at its peak and that of his Second Master £800. Several educational entrepreneurs did well too. John Ayres of the Hand and Pen near St Paul's School was bringing in £800 a year in the late seventeenth century, which was thought to be 'a fine income for a writing master', while the Newcome family made a fortune out of Hackney Academy, which was the most fashionable of London's eighteenth-century schools.[168]

Such high incomes and success stories were, however, very much the exception. Good pay for a schoolteacher was £50 a year and those who got more were lucky. Most got considerably less. The salary of the master of Owens' School went up from £20 to £26 per annum in the course of the seventeenth century and a salary of £20 or £30 seems to have been quite normal for masters in the smaller grammar schools, despite their graduate status; this was no more than was being paid to charity school masters, who needed to have very little formal education, just a 'good character and religious knowledge', and were averaging £30 per annum in the early eighteenth century.[169] The low salaries of schoolteachers were often cushioned by free houses, free coal and other perks. They remained, however, low salaries and placed most teachers firmly in the lowest and most shabbily genteel rank of the rapidly expanding educated lower middle class, a stratum of society which included book-keepers, clerks, customs officials and similar types of occupation, a world of prototype Pooters striving valiantly to retain some dignity on incomes well below what could be earned by many skilled artisans.

The world of the Pooters was occasionally visited but rarely shared by those who practised medicine, the professional group who most raised their incomes and status in our period. It was a time when, paradoxically, all branches of medicine were mercilessly mocked in print while more and more people flocked to medical men in a desperate search for cure and comfort against the manifold pains and diseases of the age. Advances in medicine were few, but this did not stop more and more money being expended on the medicine that existed, much of it with a very long, two thousand years' old, record of ineffectiveness.

There were three main branches of the medical profession: physicians, who diagnosed and prescribed; surgeons, who did the necessary manual work; and apothecaries, who made up medicines to the physician's prescription. The physicians had been organised since 1518 in the London College of Physicians, whose charter laid down that no one should practise medicine within seven miles of London unless they were Fellows of the College or held the College's licence, a privilege only granted after examination by Fellows and the payment of a high fee. These physicians were very learned men who had spent many years studying the works of Galen and Hippocrates and their commentators. They had no hospital bedside training and the

university requirements in anatomy could be obtained in just
three days of a seven-year course, anatomy being taught at
Oxford in the spring, when four lectures were given on the
dissected body of a criminal executed at the Lenten Assizes.[170]
Such learning enabled them to diagnose and prescribe with
confidence, quite often without even seeing the patient.

The great physicians of Queen Anne's day were said to sit in
coffee-houses and there await the arrival of their apothecaries,
who would describe the symptoms of a series of patients, receive
a handful of 'bills' or prescriptions and then go off to make
them up and administer the medicines. Since the standing fee
of the physician was half a guinea or a guinea and coffee cheap
and good conversation free, this was a pleasant enough way of
making a living.[171] Fortunately for the fashionable London sick,
there was in fact rather more to the practice of medicine than is
suggested by this caricature. Physicians did visit patients from
time to time and there were improvements in practice which
were to make such visits more beneficial. Much can be attributed to the work and influence of Thomas Sydenham
(1624–89), who affected to despise medical learning and
stressed the virtues of common sense and observation. 'You
must go to the bedside,' he told the young Hans Sloane. 'It is
there alone you can learn disease.' Sydenham believed in fresh
air in the sickroom and the curative powers of nature, attitudes
which were shared by his successor at the peak of the London
medical world, Dr John Radcliffe (1652–1714), whose success
was not due to medical learning, according to his biographer,
'but to shrewd diagnoses, a strong personality and practical
common sense'. Since Radcliffe cured many of his patients and
got extremely rich in the process, his example and that of
Sydenham were very valuable in improving the quality of the
London physicians and so the medical chances of the wealthier
London sick.[172]

Physicians might prescribe bleeding or a course of medicine,
usually both, but it would have been beneath their dignity to
administer such cures themselves. This was the role of the
surgeons and apothecaries, both of whom raised their status
considerably in our period. The seventeenth century saw a
considerble improvement in the skills and knowledge of surgeons, much of it gained on the battlefield or at sea. Surgeons

also seem to have learned far more than did physicians from their observations of patients and from their work in the hospitals where the poor were treated free. Most remained unlearned, with no university degree, but they benefited rather than lost from their training being based on a practical apprenticeship rather than on the study of books alone, while their company ensured that their formal education was not neglected. Surgeons had once been rather despised figures, degraded by their association with the barbers, who continued to cup people and draw their teeth in addition to shaving them and making their wigs. By the end of our period, however, the better London surgeons had become well-respected men, much admired for their skill and much envied for their wealth.[173]

The rise in status and fortune of the surgeons provided little challenge to the physicians, despite the fact that several surgeons were practising medicine by the early eighteenth century. The rise of the more numerous apothecaries posed very different problems and led to much hostility from physicians fearful of a successful invasion of their monopoly of practising medicine. This hostility led to a long and tedious pamphlet warfare and, ultimately, to a famous test case, College of Physicians v. Rose, in 1703. This involved the right of apothecaries to give medical advice and was won by them on appeal to the House of Lords. It now became legal for apothecaries to practise medicine, so long as they did not charge for their advice, thus regularizing a situation which had existed for half a century before 1703.

It seems probable that a large number of London's 400 or so apothecaries did in fact act as doctors, as well as preparing and selling drugs, and there seems no reason to assume that their patients were any worse off than those who consulted physicians. Apothecaries were quite capable of absorbing contemporary medical knowledge, as was convincingly argued by the anonymous author of *Tentamen Medicinale*, one of the best defences of the apothecaries which came out in the pamphlet war. He pointed out the superiority of the apothecary's training to that of physicians. While the student of physick was poring over ancient books, the apothecary was undergoing an eight-year apprenticeship in which he thoroughly acquainted himself with all the drugs and herbs used in medicine and, by accompanying his master to the patient's bedside, he was able to learn the practical side of medicine as well. Here he would be able to 'improve him in the knowledge of the vertues of medicines, and by hearing of the alterations and effects they had upon the patient, learn something of the nature of diseases too, and how and what will cure them; or at least so much as would excite his curiosity to inform himself further by reading the best authors upon such subjects, which he may easily do, if he has but learnt before he came to apprentice the Latin and Greek tongues, especially the former'.[174]

The business of the apothecary was an extremely profitable one, in which huge bills could be sent in for drugs and herbs of very little intrinsic value. It was also a business requiring little capital since apprenticeship premiums were not particularly high and entry costs were modest compared with those of most shopkeepers. Hamnett Rigby, for instance, had just £16 invested in equipment and £17 in drugs and medicines when he died in 1671 aged thirty. If he had lived a little longer, the accumulation of high profits would probably have made him reasonably well off, if not downright rich. Both the median and average fortunes of the fourteen apothecaries in our sample were just over £2000, while the two richest were both worth over £5000. The giants in the business were very well off indeed. In 1708, it was said that 'there are eight or ten apothecaries gain their fifteen hundred or two thousands pounds a year', while Dandridge, Dr Radcliffe's main apothecary, rode on his master's back to accumulate £50,000 by his death.[175] Surgeons probably had similar incomes and fortunes, but neither of these two lower branches of the medical profession could compete in wealth with the great physicians. Dr Radcliffe was said to be making 20 guineas a day in 1684, his first year of practice in London, and had accumulated over £30,000 by 1692 and £140,000 by his death in 1714, such a rate of accumulation putting him amongst the very top lawyers and merchants. Radcliffe was, of course, quite exceptionally successful, and a bachelor to boot, but even a fraction of such earnings could make a very comfortable living for a lesser physician, many of whom counted their fortunes in the tens of thousands.[176]

Several smaller professional groups were also expanding in our period, such as architects and surveyors, while other occupations were adopting a more professional approach, such as accountants and other 'men of business' like the scriveners, whom we have already met, and the stewards who managed the estates of noblemen and gentlemen. This developing professionalism could also be found in the civil service, the period seeing the emergence of a new type of efficient and fairly honest administrator.[177]

By the early eighteenth century, security of tenure, internal promotion, reasonable salaries and a rudimentary pension scheme made public service attractive for young men of the middle and upper classes, who, with promotion, might expect to earn £100 a year or more, an income equal to that of a middling shopkeeper with none of the stigma or risk of trade. The numbers involved were still minuscule by the standards of today, perhaps 5000 in all types of civilian government employment in London, and many of these jobs were fairly menial. Nearly half were in the two booming branches of the revenue service, the customs and excise, a great army of land-waiters and tide-waiters, gaugers and searchers earning around £50 a year and swelling the ranks of that burgeoning educated lower middle class who have already been noted.[178]

The main tasks of government were to raise money and spend it on the armed forces and these last, particularly the army, provided the other main type of government employment in and about London. The army, which like the civil service was becoming more professional, was minute by continental standards but numbers grew with every war and rarely declined afterwards to the previous level. The officer corps grew even faster than the army as a whole, especially after 1713 when half-pay for disbanded officers became a regular institution, and a military presence was very visible in the more raffish section of West End society. This larger army provided a useful niche for the younger sons of gentlemen, a trend which was eventually to reduce the numbers entering trade and thus encourage a snobbish disdain for business as the eighteenth century went on.[179]

Another rather raffish section of London society was made up of writers and painters, who, together with musicians and actors, formed a demi-monde halfway between the gentlemen of the West End and those commercial and professional people with whom this chapter has been chiefly concerned. Our period is one in which many musicians, painters and writers came out from under the umbrella of court and aristocratic patronage as a result of a developing commercial demand for their services, often provided by a middle class eager to display such evidence of their taste and culture. The combination of patronage and the market provided actors and musicians with a reasonable income, as has been seen, and the period was also a prosperous one for painters, the supply of competent artists not being sufficient to swamp the rapidly increasing demand for their services.

The inventories of royal and aristocratic palaces and houses show a very considerable increase in the number of pictures which were on their walls from the Restoration onwards. Much of this was supplied from abroad, where there was a brisk market in 'old masters' and an even brisker supply of paintings by the yard to fill aristocratic picture galleries.[180] But much was also painted in England, either in the artist's studio or directly on to the overmantel or overdoor which was required to be filled, such domestic commissions being a welcome addition to the wall painter's traditional market in churches and other public buildings. By 1700, the aristocratic taste for paintings had filtered down to those of the middle station, many of whom owned scores of pictures and some of whom rivalled their betters in the commissioning of decorative art in their homes, such as the East India merchant who in 1696 got Robert Robinson to paint his panelled room in Botolph Lane with a delightful composition of pagodas, pavilions, palm trees, princesses and other oriental exotica.[181] The rewards for competent artists were substantial. At the top were the two immensely successful portrait painters, Sir Peter Lely and Sir Godfrey Kneller, who both died very rich indeed, but lesser men could do well too. Few people today have heard of Thomas Stevenson, who is described in a very off-hand way in dictionaries of artists. Yet Stevenson, who was only thirty-one when he died in 1679, was owed money by several members of the aristocracy and left over £1000, a fortune which suggests that his was not the garret existence of the stereotypical artist.[182]

Writers did not do so well and, despite a considerable widening of outlets, most were poor and despised for the mercenary activity to which poverty drove them. Many a man who aspired to be a Dryden or a Pope ended up in Grub Street as a drudge of the booksellers producing cheap ephemera, a sad fate for men who were largely drawn from the educated but impoverished upper classes and had spent their youth admiring and imitating the work of the best classical authors of Greece and Rome.[183]

Some of these men were fortunate enough to find a patron amongst the cultured and politically influential members of West End society who could reward them with a cash gift for an admired piece of work, pay them a retainer or find them some other source of income. Other writers did reasonably well from the theatre. The dramatist normally kept the receipts taken on the third night, if his play lasted that long, a reward which averaged about £50 in the 1680s and was to become higher in the early eighteenth century.[184] Most writers, however, got their living from the owners of newspapers and from booksellers. Here, the market was very much against the author, who had little option but to take the best offer made for his manuscript or starve. Some publishers had reputations as generous men, but most used their market position to pay what seems to us to be derisory amounts, such as the £5 which Samuel Simmons paid Milton for *Paradise Lost*. Milton did at least receive £5 more for both the second and third editions, £15 in all, but most authors got just a single fee and received no royalties. Other writers worked directly for the newspapers or the booksellers at so much a page or a line, needless to say at very low rates. These were the true Grub Street hacks, slaving away in garrets translating French trash into English trash or doing a scissors and paste job on the work of their predecessors.[185]

Some writers did better than this and some did very well indeed, such as Dryden and Pope.[186] However, no author could be called really rich by the standards of the day, while the vast majority of London's hundreds of professional writers lived extremely poorly and might well have envied the £20 or £30 earned by a charity school teacher. The truth was that there were just too many pens for the work available, leaving the writers with even less bargaining power than other impoverished members of the educated classes, such as clergymen and teachers.

v Other Services

It might be thought that by now the possibilities of middle-class employment in London have been exhausted. However, a big city is a very complex organism and there are many legitimate types of business which have not yet been discussed, not to mention those illegitimate occupations which flourished in the city of Macheath, Moll Flanders and Jonathan Wild. For example, no mention has yet been made of two of the largest sources of employment in the metropolis: domestic service and carriage by land and water, each of which probably employed between 30,000 and 40,000 people.[187] Domestic service was of course hardly a middle-class occupation, though many servants married into the lower strata of the middle class and many upper servants, such as butlers and housekeepers, certainly had genteel pretensions.[188] Most people employed in carriage also belonged to the 'mechanick part of mankind', but this sector of the economy provided many opportunities to middling people as well.

The most important group were probably the master mariners, who stood at the peak of a hierarchical pay structure in the merchant service, which provided an incentive for ambitious youths who hoped to make their fortune at sea. Ships' captains drew their income from many sources. Their wages for commanding a ship might be £6 a month or more all found, sufficient in itself to place them in the ranks of the middle station. Many captains also had a share in the ships that they commanded and so would enjoy a corresponding share of any profits made from freight. They also often acted as supercargoes or travelling commission agents for the merchants who freighted their ships, as well as shipping goods on their own account. This combination of wages, commissions and profits could make a master mariner a wealthy man, ready to retire from the sea, buy a house in Deptford, Greenwich or Wapping and maybe become a merchant himself.[189]

The opportunities for the middle class in river carriage and in carriage within the city were more limited, most watermen, carters and coachmen being self-employed men with comparatively modest fortunes. However, that principle of accumulation which has been stressed so often in this chapter operated in this field as well. Most watermen owned their own boats but a growing number, especially those who worked on the more expensive lighters, were employees of men of the middle station with several vessels. One surviving register shows that, by the end of the eighteenth century, 9 men, each with over 20 lighters, owned 300 out of the 756 lighters which it lists. One finds the same principle operating in land carriage, as large-scale operators accumulated the hackney-coaches which plied for hire within the city and the stage-coaches which were serving 216 provincial towns by 1715. The stage-coaches were often owned by the keepers of the inns which were their termini and who had obvious economic advantages over the individual coachmen who had often inaugurated the services.

Even the humble carts which carried goods within the city did not evade the attention of the accumulator. The number of carts was limited to 420, not counting those belonging to brewers and coal-merchants, and a system of licensing was introduced; these licences, which were known as 'carrooms', rose in value from £50 to £150 in the course of our period. Such valuable property was unlikely not to be observed by members of the middle class and so one finds a man like John Barber, who owned twenty-four carrooms at his death in 1734, a haulage contractor rather than a mere carter.[190]

Such carts were normally leased out to poorer working carters, but some entrepreneurs used them for their own profitable businesses. Thomas Rowe, for instance, claimed in 1681 that he had invested £2000 in carts and other equipment needed for the scavenging business of the parish of St Giles in the Fields. He had taken out to the country nearly 2000 loads of dirt and ashes in three months, a task which gave him a double income, from the rates for removing the rubbish and from the farmers and market-gardeners who spread it on their land. Such a contract made good sense to the local authorities, who could hope that the profit motive would lead to a more efficient disposal of the parish rubbish, a task normally done by labourers called rakers under the supposed supervision of unpaid parish officials known as scavengers.[191]

The substitution of the profit motive for a former system of individual or public responsibility was in fact a common way of improving amenities and local services. Water supply, for instance, which until the sixteenth century had been the responsibility of the City Corporation, was in our period nearly all carried out by private companies, who brought water into houses in return for a rental of about £1 a year. The two largest companies, the New River Company and the London Bridge Water Works, were very big operations, with a capital value of £170,000 and £150,000 respectively in 1708.[192]

Street-lighting is another example of the same trend. The old system required householders to display lanterns with candles lit from dusk to nine o'clock on moonless nights during the winter; as one can imagine, it was a fairly ineffective system which kept most Londoners at home after dark. However, the 1680s saw the development of street-lighting companies, which contracted with individual householders to take over their lantern responsibilities for an annual payment. The companies used oil-burning lamps incorporating mirrors and bull's-eye lenses to intensify the light, an improvement which was sufficient to encourage a much greater public use of the evenings, as theatres opened and closed later and more people went on to taverns and coffee-houses afterwards. The new system was gradually extended and improved, so that by 1736 the City was lit from sunset to sunrise throughout the year, making it the best lit urban area in the world.[193]

Improvement inspired by the profit motive can also be seen in the development of fire insurance in the late seventeenth century. The impetus in this field came as might be expected from the dreadful example of the Great Fire and from the rebuilding regulations which were intended to reduce the risk of fire in the future, such as requirements to build in brick and tile. Such regulations were effective and, although there were to be some serious fires, there was never again to be devastation remotely on the scale of 1666. This reduction in risk made fire insurance a realistic commercial proposition, the first successful office opening in 1681, and over 20,000 houses in London were insured by the early eighteenth century. At first only buildings were insured but, from 1708, policies could be taken out to protect goods and merchandise as well.[194] The development of fire insurance greatly reduced one of the major risks of early modern commercial life and so not only enabled the citizens to sleep more soundly but also encouraged them to keep larger stocks, thus reinforcing the general trend towards a bigger scale of business.

A very wide variety of businesses has been looked at in this extended ramble round the metropolitan economy and it may be appropriate to close this survey with a brief consideration of the death business, a phrase which is not as facetious as it might seem, since death, like so many other things, was becoming increasingly commercialized. Mortality rates were some three times higher than they are today, with some fifty to eighty deaths per day, so the business was a big one, providing benefits for a wide range of people whose income started when that of the physicians and apothecaries finished, such as the searchers who ascertained the cause of death, the gravediggers and professional bearers and the makers of mourning cloth, mourning rings and tombstones.

Funerals were another institution which illustrated the increasing penetration of the profit motive into the fabric of society, the main innovation here being the rise of the professional undertaker from the 1680s. These specialists not only took over the organization of funerals but also specified the form that they should take and the paraphernalia that were necessary if one was not to lose face before the neighbours. Such a development naturally increased the overall costs of funerals as people bought goods and services which they would not have thought of by themselves. Richard Phipps was one of these early London undertakers. In his shop, he had 157 coffins in stock, 71 of them being described as small, a necessary distribution in these days of high infant and child mortality. Upstairs in his house, Phipps had a large stock of coffin nails and handles, black hatbands, cloaks and gloves, yards of black cloth for mourning, coffin pillows, shrouds and other upholstery. He also had flambeaux and black links, necessary to provide illumination for night-time funerals, which had become increasingly fashionable among those of the middle station, in imitation of aristocratic practice. With such an extensive stock to draw on, there is a certain irony in the fact that Phipps' executors had to pay out £70 18s. on the undertaker's funeral.[195]

This chapter has moved a long way from the discussion of London as a manufacturing city to this last brief description of the business of the undertaker, but this panoramic survey of the metropolitan economy has aimed to show the range of occupations open to middle-class people in London. It has also been intended to show, or at least hint at, the way in which a great early modern city actually worked, how the various bits and pieces of the economy fitted together, how God's providence, the 'invisible hand' and the market were able to put supply in touch with demand. This economy was far from static, some sectors growing and some declining as time went on, with a general picture of slow but significant growth. The methods and scale of business were not static either and it should be clear that this was a city in which 'capitalism' was becoming more important, big business was becoming more prominent and all business was growing in scale, while the profit motive was finding its way into many new aspects of individual and neighbourhood life. At the same time, the professions were becoming more professional and growing in scope and status, and even art was becoming more commercial. It was indeed a good city in which to be middle-class.

In the second part of the book, some aspects of business life will be looked at in more detail, starting with a consideration of the social and geographical origins of these middle-class businessmen, their training and the life that they experienced as apprentices. First, however, it may be useful to give some idea of the numbers who might be included in the middle class, though this is largely a matter of guesswork since no data exist which could give the true figure. To start with Paris, the only city in Europe of comparable size and structure and one where the definition of 'bourgeois' was rather more precise, Pierre Léon has suggested that, in 1749, some 30 per cent of Parisians were 'bourgeois', 3 or 4 per cent were 'privileged' and the remaining two-thirds belonged to 'le peuple'. For London, one has the intelligent guesswork of George Rudé and the detailed analysis by Leonard Schwarz of the returns of the collectors of assessed taxes in 1798, both approaches coming up with similar figures to those of Léon, with some 3 to 5 per cent in the upper class, some 20 to 30 per cent in the middle class depending on definition, the remainder being wage-earners or self-employed artisans.

Let us assume then, for the purposes of this book, that about a fifth or a quarter of all households belonged to that middle station which is the main subject here, proportions which would suggest that there were some 20,000 to 25,000 households in this group in the early eighteenth century. Above them were some 3000 to 5000 families of the West End gentry and what one may call the upper middle class. The remaining two-thirds or three-quarters of the metropolitan population belonged to the various sectors of the 'mechanick part of mankind'.[196]

Two

Business Life

3 Apprenticeship

Much of the rest of this book will discuss how people got rich and spent and enjoyed their riches in Augustan London, but first the humbler beginnings of the careers of London businessmen will be considered. These started for the great majority with seven or eight years' apprenticeship, a period of 'genteel servitude' according to a contemporary writer.

This was an attractive institution for the masters since apprentices paid substantial premiums to enter into their servitude, while the free labour might make a net addition to the master's income even in the apprentice's first year and would almost certainly do so by the third or fourth year.[1] The advantages to the apprentices were less obvious, especially for that majority who had no hope of ever becoming a master.[2] Most trades certainly did not require seven years' training – many could be mastered in a few months according to critics – and the restrictions on the freedom of apprentices were irksome.[3] On the other hand, apprenticeship was the commonest way to become a full member of a Livery Company and acquire the freedom of the City, a status which gave social prestige in itself and also provided rights of franchise, rights to office, rights to charitable maintenance in old age and, more significantly for business, various beneficial trading rights, the most important being the right to trade or open shop within the City.

The formal advantages of apprenticeship were to diminish over time as membership of Livery Companies became increasingly open to purchase and as the expansion of the metropolis led to more and more business being done outside the City. Such considerations caused apprenticeship to decline both absolutely and relatively in the eighteenth century,[4] but this was a slow process and for the men considered in this book, most of whom were born between the 1630s and the 1670s,

seven years' 'genteel servitude' remained the commonest introduction to the world of business.

i The Origins of London Apprentices

London was a city which relied for its continued growth on an
annual stream of immigrants from the provinces and from
overseas, and large numbers of these came to the metropolis in
their teens to enter on formal indentures of apprenticeship.[5]
Such young men, and a few women, came from all over the
country but there was a tendency over time for an increasing
proportion to be drawn from south-eastern England as opportunities opened up elsewhere for young people to learn a trade
or start up a business.[6] Nearly two-thirds of our sample, for
instance, came either from London itself or from the eastern
and south-eastern counties. Despite this, there are representatives from almost every county and from Scotland, Wales and
overseas. Opportunities in the provinces might be growing, but
London remained the place where the really ambitious youth
was likely to seek his fortune and for many trades it was
virtually the only place where a satisfactory training could be
obtained.

Historians have noted a marked rise over time in the social
and economic status of the fathers of young men who took up
London apprenticeships. In the sixteenth century, it was possible to find many fairly poor people, such as husbandmen, as
the fathers of London apprentices. This became increasingly
unusual and, by our period, most apprentices, or at least those
likely to end up as independent businessmen, were the sons of
yeomen or gentlemen if they were countrymen, while increasing
numbers were the sons of urban professional or commercial
people or of such 'middling' members of rural society as
innkeepers, clothiers, millers and the like.

The most obvious reason for this change in social origins was
the increasing cost of a London training. However, the development also reflects the changing attitude towards trade, which
was considered in Chapter 1.[7] This can be illustrated by the
large number of apprentices whose fathers were described as
gentleman, esquire or even knight in their indentures. Nearly a
quarter of our sample were the sons of gentlemen and they were

trained for a wide variety of occupations. Ten became drapers or silkmen, eight merchants, six money-lenders or bankers, three tobacconists or tobacco factors, two each became apothecaries, grocers, haberdashers and cheesemongers, and one each was trained as an ironmonger, jeweller, leather-seller, tavern-keeper, silversmith, bookseller, salter, druggist and looking-glass manufacturer. The sons of gentlemen thus permeated the London business world fairly thoroughly, though they tended to be concentrated in such potentially profitable occupations as overseas trade, linen-draping and finance.

Just what it meant when a man described his father as a gentleman in a document is difficult to say, since the temptation to upgrade one's status when beginning a career in a strange town must have been considerable. Lawrence Stone has suggested that most of these fathers were really 'pseudo-gentlemen', that is, moderately respectable urban tradesmen, a hypothesis which leads him into some delightfully unacademic snobbery. 'They were men of limited means, were actively engaged in retail buying and selling, and probably did not own a single acre of agricultural land, certainly not a country house. They had no knowledge of Latin. They did not dream of swaggering around with a sword at their side, and they would have been completely at a loss if anyone had challenged them to a duel. By any sociological definition, they did not count as gentlemen, yet gentlemen is what they called themselves on public documents.'[8]

Stone's hypothesis is certainly refuted by those men in our sample who were described as sons of gentry. Only eight had fathers with the urban address which seems necessary of his pseudo-gentry, three in London and its suburbs and one each in Canterbury, Gloucester, Bath, Colchester and Norwich. The remaining thirty-nine had rural addresses, which were scattered much more widely across the country than was the overall distribution of apprentices' origins. Some may well have been sons of 'parish' gentry, rather than the more distinguished 'county' gentry, as Stone also suggests. However, the fact that twelve fathers were described as Esquire suggests that the gentleman label is not quite as trivial as Stone would have us believe. And indeed if none of these fathers were really gentlemen at all, it seems unlikely that there would have been so much contemporary comment on the subject as there was.

The seventeenth century was in fact rather a difficult time for the sons of gentlemen, especially the younger sons. It was then that the practice of primogeniture took a firmer grip in landed society, with the result that few younger sons could look forward to inheriting a landed estate to support them in the idleness to which their elder brothers were destined. There were also more younger sons than usual as a result of increasing total numbers of gentry and improving mortality chances for their children. What was to be done with them all? The obvious solution was either to educate them for the professions or apprentice them to trade.

The preferred solution in a status conscious society was probably to train them for the professions, though the opportunities for those born in the middle decades of the seventeenth century were fairly limited and some professions which would later absorb large numbers of younger sons, especially the army, had hardly been developed at all. Success in the learned professions also required academic abilities, which only a minority of gentlemen's sons were likely to have, a fact of life quite obvious to most parents. The Sussex gentleman, John French, declared in his early seventeenth-century will that if his younger sons were 'not capable of being scholars', they were to be sent to London to be apprenticed, and such an attitude was a common one. George Boddington showed no great signs of learning at grammar school and so was sent by his father to writing school and then put to learning business. Dudley North, destined to be a wealthy Levant merchant, one of the very few who ever learned Turkish and one of the most respected of early English writers on economics, was 'an indifferent scholar' and his 'backwardness at school and a sorry account that the master gave of his scholarship' led him into a merchant's apprenticeship, though his 'strange bent to traffic' which was demonstrated by successful trading with his schoolfellows was an important indication of his vocation.[9]

Dudley North and his elder brother, the lawyer Lord Keeper Guilford, both claimed that they would never have pursued their careers if they had been assured of even quite a small private income: 'I have heard him say more than once that, if he had been sure of a hundred pounds a year to live on, he had never been a lawyer.' But their family 'was not in a posture to sustain any of the brothers by estates to be carved out of the main sustentation of the honour', and such was the position of many another estate. Gentry estates were particularly hard hit after 1650 as a result of the accumulation of debts in the Civil War and its aftermath, high taxation and low agricultural prices, but the carelessness or irresponsible behaviour of gentlemen themselves was often the cause of their sons having to seek a career in trade. George Boddington's grandfather, for instance, 'waisted a good estate by gayming and was thereby constrayned to sell all he had to pay his debts'. All three of his sons were put out to apprenticeships in London.[10]

This is not to suggest that only the stupid or the sons of the unlucky sought a career in trade. Such careers were increasingly attractive for their own sake, as the status of trade improved and the potential rewards escalated. There is also no reason to assume that the intellectual quality of London businessmen was below the norm of their day. They might not have been particularly good at Latin, but they seem to have had the ability to learn modern languages and to raise the general level of mathematical competence, while their correspondence suggests that they were quite capable of communicating adequately in their own tongue. This was a highly literate class who had spent several years at grammar school or at the new vocational schools which were discussed in Chapter 2. Such an education was often completed by a year or so at writing school in London before they entered into their apprenticeship, typically at the age of sixteen, though the starting ages of our sample ranged from a technically illegal thirteen to twenty.[11] However, before they could start their apprenticeship, they had to decide what occupation they wished to follow, find a suitable master and settle terms, all difficult decisions to make.

ii Finding a Master

One of the most responsible and difficult duties of parents was to see 'their children well dispos'd of, well settled in the world'. This involved the provision of a sound moral upbringing, an education suitable to their talents and expectations in life, and a considerable outlay in money to see them apprenticed and started in the world. Parents were also expected to help children choose the particular career that they were to follow, ideally helping them discern their vocation and in any case using their worldly wisdom to distract them from unsuitable, unworthy or unprofitable occupations. This was a very difficult task, where parental ambition or fondness could easily lead to serious mistakes. 'Pride, avarice, or whim are the chief counsellors of most fathers when they are deliberating the most serious concern in life, the settlement of their children in the world,' wrote Campbell.[12]

Campbell was sufficiently worried by the problem to produce in 1747 the first really useful guidebook to the London trades, written specifically to help parents make their choice. He outlined the innate skills and talents necessary for each trade, occupation or profession, together with the probable costs of acquiring the competence to practise them and their likely monetary rewards. Before the appearance of this book, it must have been extremely difficult for parents and their adolescent sons, particularly that majority who lived in the country, to have had much idea of what might be a suitable occupation to follow in London and even more difficult to know which master to choose for the period of apprenticeship. Books written on apprenticeship before Campbell considered the subject in such a general manner as to be virtually useless in terms of practical guidance. It was in fact the morals of the master rather than his competence as a businessman or teacher which were most often emphasized.[13] Moral qualities were clearly important in the man who was to be master of one's son for seven years, but they needed to be coupled with practical qualities if a young man was to get on in the world. How then did apprentices find masters in Augustan London?

Family relationship was one obvious link between master and apprentice. Thomas Purcell, for instance, was the son of a gentleman from Shropshire, who was apprenticed to a silkman in 1618. His own apprentices included virtually all the male members of the next generation of his family, the son of his elder brother, two sons of his younger sister and two of his own sons. The cloth merchant, John Randall, followed a similar pattern, five of the apprentices whom he took between 1648 and 1669 being called either Randall or Claxton, his wife's maiden name. Other obvious links included geographical propinquity and trading partners. Thomas Williams, the son of a yeoman of Walford in Herefordshire, was apprenticed to a stationer in 1635 and nineteen years later he took as his own apprentice, John Harris, the son of another yeoman from Walford. Luke Meredith, a London bookseller, took as an apprentice in 1692 William Wilmot, the son of an Oxford bookseller who was one of his major customers.[14] Such examples could easily be multiplied, but the importance of such relationships should not be exaggerated. Very few men in our sample were in fact apprenticed to masters of the same surname or of that of their mother's family and most apprentices seem to have found masters with whom neither they nor their parents had any prior relationship of any sort.

A master might be found by a professional intermediary, such as a scrivener. In 1676, for instance, Mary Sturges, the widow of a Leicester mercer, 'authorized Mr Hunt, a scrivener in London, to finde some fitt able and discreet person to place her son apprentice to' and this turned out to be Leonard Compeere, citizen and leatherseller, who followed the trade of milliner in the Royal Exchange. This was probably a common role for a scrivener to perform, used as they were to carrying out other services for provincial customers. Advertisement was another source of introductions. John Houghton, a pioneer of newspaper advertising, included several notices of apprentices seeking masters and vice versa in his *Collections*. 'By reason of my great correspondency', he wrote in February 1693, 'I may help masters to apprentices and apprentices to masters. And now is wanting three boys, one with £70, one with £30, and a scholar with £60.' Similar advertisements can be found in early eighteenth-century newspapers but they would have satisfied only a fraction of the market and most introductions were made on a much more personal basis.[15]

Most apprentices seem in fact to have found their masters through the mediation of 'friends', a word which had a rather different connotation in our period than it does today. A man's friends played a very important part in his life, similar to that played by the kin group in many societies. They tended to be older people, usually male, of the sort that even today one might have to invite to a wedding party whether you liked them or not. They might include relatives such as uncles, possibly god-parents, business or social associates of one's father and similar people who could be expected to be wise in the ways of the world and often comparatively well off. They were people who needed to be cultivated with care and treated with respect, for a man's friends were his best source of prudential advice and financial assistance and were likely to be his advocates and the upholders of his good character in times of trouble.

Because of the continuous migration into London and the growth of inland trade, most provincial families had at least one 'friend' in the metropolis. Most had several and it was these friends who would seek out a suitable master for their sons and would then keep an eye on them and, if necessary, mediate if they ran into difficulties. The friends of John Parker, the son of a Lancashire man, for instance, were John Ashurst and Edward Rigby, both members of the Merchant-Taylors' Company and countrymen of his father, and Anthony Parker, a lawyer of Gray's Inn, presumably a relative. When John Parker's master turned him out of his house, he went to see Ashurst, and Ashurst and Rigby then went to the master's house to mediate. The friends of William Bullivant, who was apprenticed to a worsted-seller in the early 1650s, were his two uncles, Samuel Holland, a merchant-tailor who arranged the apprenticeship in the first place and often visited the shop to check on the boy and ask 'whether he was being faithless and untrusty', and John Holland of the Charterhouse, aged sixty-five, who also 'oftentimes came to visit him'.[16]

Whoever fixed up the apprenticeship had a lot of work to do. They first had to decide what occupation the boy should follow or interpret the rather vague instructions of parents or widows on this point, decisions which were affected by the amount of money available for the boy's training as much as by any apparent talents that he might have. They then had to find a master following this occupation who wanted an apprentice, who had the reputation of being kind, moral and competent at his job, and whose business was large enough and varied enough to enable an apprentice to get a broad education in the trade. Finding such things out required visits to the prospective master's house to make a judgment on his domestic relationships – a squalid household or a dominant wife, for instance, being seen as a bad sign – and a round of the taverns and coffee-houses in the vicinity to discover the master's 'reputa-tion', the opinion of neighbours as to his character and business competence being seen as crucial.

Once a decision had been made on a master, it was necessary to hammer out the details of the contract, a process which could take several months. The actual form of the apprenticeship indentures, covering the reciprocal rights and duties of the two parties, was fairly standard. The master agreed to teach and instruct the apprentice 'by the best means that he can' and to find 'his meat, drink, apparel, lodging and all other necessaries' (such as the cost of medical attention), according to the Custom of the City of London. The apprentice promised rather more:

> The said apprentice his said master faithfully shall serve, his secrets keep, his lawfull commandments every where gladly do. He shall do no dammage to his said master . . . He shall not waste the goods of his said master, nor lend them unlawfully to any. He shall not commit fornication, nor contract matrimony within the said term. He shall not play at cards, dice, tables, or any other unlawfull games, whereby his master may have any loss. With his own goods or others . . . without licence of his said master, he shall neither buy nor sell. He shall not haunt taverns or play-houses, nor absent himself from his said master's service day nor night unlawfully: but in all things as a faithfull apprentice, he shall behave himself towards his said master.[17]

This was standard stuff. Where the negotiation lay was in the details, such as the number of years' service, which was usually seven, but eight for apothecaries and quite often for younger apprentices or in respect of a lower premium.[18] Another bar-gaining point was who provided the apprentice's initial ward-robe, how extensive this should be and who was to keep this wardrobe repaired and replaced – no small matter since the clothes suitable for a merchant's apprentice might well cost his parents or friends £40 and the very cheapest outfits for those apprenticed to low-grade trades were likely to cost between £5 and £10.[19] Then, there was the question of security. 'Generally tradesmen who have any considerable trust to put into the hands of an apprentice, take security of them for their honesty by their friends.' Signing bonds for the good behaviour or 'truth' of apprentices must have been a worrying moment, since they had access to large sums of money and some were far from honest. The penalties of such bonds were sometimes very large, £1000 for apprentices in the Levant trade before they went abroad, £500 for the apprentice to a goldsmith-banker, £100 for a scrivener's apprentice, £150 posted by Eleanor Palmer to persuade a linen-draper to take back her scapegrace son after he had stolen some goods and a promise to take him away if he offended again.[20]

Finally, there was the settlement of the premium. This down payment to the master seems to have been an innovation of the seventeenth century and indicates the value that a London apprenticeship was deemed to have. There seems little doubt that the premiums demanded were increasing but, even at the beginning of our period, they were high enough to explain why so few poor men were the fathers of apprentices. The premiums for merchants' apprentices which we have found between 1650 and 1680 ranged from £100 to £860 asked for a Levant merchant's apprentice. Most were between £200 and £500. A witness in a court case of 1653 said that the typical premium for a woollen-draper was £100 to £120 and similar sums were paid by mercers' and drapers' apprentices in the 1670s. In the same decade a boy apprenticed to a milliner was asked to pay £30 and to a yarn-seller £40, figures which reflect the range of premiums paid in the haberdasher type of business. The premiums paid by artisans were rather lower, though still high enough to deter the fathers of the poor: £10–£35 for coopers, £20–£50 for working goldsmiths, £10–£35 for cutlers, figures which reflect six months' or a year's pay for journeymen in these trades.[21]

These were big sums for parents to pay, though they were only the beginning of the financial outlay necessary to set a young man up in business. There were, however, many sources from which a boy's premium might come and so alleviate the pressure on parents. Friends and relations might well contribute to this vital payment to ensure a boy's future, while legacies (especially by uncles) were often specifically designed to pay a premium. The provision of a fund whose interest was used to pay the premiums of deserving poor apprentices was also a common form of charitable bequest. Then there was the possibility of deferred payment. The father of an apprentice to the cook's trade was given eighteen months to pay his premium in 1678, while a glover agreed to pay the balance of his son's premium to Robert Foyce, a surgeon, in 'as many gloves as should be expended at the christening of the said Robert Foyce's next child', an interesting gamble in an age of high infant mortality.[22]

Contracts often specified that there should be a period of a few months' trial or 'liking' before the formal binding. John Dunton, for instance, was 'not fasten'd for good and all at this time, but my master and my self were left to make the experiment how we cou'd approve each other'. Dunton in fact ran away after a few days, like many another homesick lad, but his father persuaded him to go back and 'after a month's liking was bound'.[23] All that remained now was the formal enrolment of the new apprentice, first before the Master and Wardens of the master's Livery Company and later before the City Chamberlain, 'who is Guardian of all apprentices and has a right to see justice done between them and their masters'. Enrolment before the Chamberlain was supposed to be done within a year of binding and was the final stage in the process by which master and apprentice committed themselves to seven years in each other's company. Failure to enrol was grounds to break the contract and, judging by the number of cases where such grounds were presented before the Lord Mayor's court, it seems that it was common practice deliberately to neglect this formality in order to give the parties an easy way out of what was otherwise a difficult contract to break.[24]

iii The Learning Process

What did the apprentice do and how well was he instructed in his master's trade? The answers to such questions naturally varied enormously and depended on the type of occupation, the diligence of the apprentice and the character and expectations of the master. Some masters did their duty very conscientiously; but many neglected to instruct their apprentices almost completely, some from idleness or because they were rarely resident in London, many from a fear that too much instruction would create a dangerous competitor in the future and many because they saw their apprentices as unpaid menial servants and nothing else.

Complaints that apprentices were set to menial tasks and denied instruction were a common theme. Sir John Fryer, a future Lord Mayor who was apprenticed to a pewterer, was set to 'doing the servile part of ye trade, such as turning ye wheel, oileing and cleaning ye ware when finished, carrying of baskets of goods to ye inns and other such like things not commonly done by other apprentices'. Such work should have been done by journeymen and porters and not by a young apprentice, whose 'dear mother had not inured me to any hard labour'. Many similar complaints can be found in the records of the Mayor's Court: a soapmaker's apprentice who was 'put to doe such servile and drudging work as was fitter and most usually done by labourers', the apprentice to the master of an East Indiaman who had to do 'the slavish and most drudging parts of the ship's work', was ranked as a seaman, not a midshipman 'in his dyett and labour' and was not instructed in navigation 'in such manner as is usuall and necessary for mariners' apprentices'.[25]

One does not have to believe such complaints, since they were normally denied by witnesses for the masters, but the fact that they were denied helps to define what was expected of apprentices. The language is revealing too, the repeated use of words such as 'servile', 'slavish' and 'drudging' suggesting that public opinion thought that apprentices who had paid large premiums should be taught the business side of a trade and the skills associated with it, but should not be employed as menial servants. The connection between size of premium and type of work is made explicit by Benjamin Clements, a wire-drawer, who claimed that he accepted Thomas Brown as his apprentice with a premium of only £7 10s., instead of the usual £20 or £30, specifically because he was 'not to be trained as a wire-drawer for the first two or three years but only to run errands, he being then young and small of his age'. Witnesses in a case relating to the Norwegian timber trade stated that there were two levels of premium, one much higher than the other for those apprentices who were to be sent abroad to learn the trade at their master's expense.[26] It seems, then, that one might expect to get the instruction one had paid for.

Drudgery and hard labour actually connected with a trade might well be seen as a necessary part of training; drudgery in the service of the household clearly was not, though many people thought that such work should be done by apprentices. Daniel Defoe, writing in the 1720s, bemoaned the fact that apprentices no longer cleaned their master's shoes and waited at table, tasks which he claimed they had done as a matter of course in the past.[27] However, Defoe had a habit of idealizing the past and there is no doubt that apprentices objected to doing domestic tasks even before he was born. Once again, the fact that masters took the trouble to produce witnesses to deny allegations on this score suggests that contemporaries agreed that there should be a distinction between work done by domestics and apprentices.

For all that, much domestic work was done by apprentices. Francis Kirkman, apprenticed to a scrivener in the 1640s, learned to draw up documents but also did other petty services – cleaning shoes, carrying ashes, sweeping, cleaning the sink, drawing beer, fetching coals. 'When I have bin seriously a drawing writings in the shop, and studying and contriving how to order my covenants the best way, a greasy kitchin-wench would come and disturb me with her errants.' Such complaints were commonplace. In the 1670s we find a merchant's apprentice with a £200 premium 'employed in cleaning shooes, sweeping of cellars and chambers and making of beds'. He asked whether it was 'usuall or common for merchants' apprentices . . . who give considerable sums of money to their masters to do such inferior and drudging business', clearly expecting the negative answers which his witnesses supplied.[28]

Evidence on the master's behalf in this case gives some idea of what was actually expected. One discovers that he was 'kind and loving to former apprentices and used them well in his service and sufficiently instructed them and endeavoured their advancement and preferment in the world and sent them beyond seas with considerable cargoes and also has sent and consigned goods to them both before and after their being his servants'. Such instruction included learning how to enter goods at the Customs House, how to keep accounts and how to buy

cloth at Blackwell Hall, while the apprentice would simultaneously be trying to build up a good reputation with other
masters who would be his future customers and correspondents.
The merchant's apprentice had to work hard to be competent
at his business before being sent abroad in his third or fourth
year, there to build up his trading capital through commissions
as a factor, before returning to London many years later to set
up on his own and take on apprentices in his turn.[29]

Much less had to be learned in shopkeeping trades, Campbell
claiming that the 'mystery' of most retail businesses could be
learned in a month or two. 'Their skill consists in the knowledge
of the prices, properties, the markets for such goods, and the
extent of the demand for the various articles they trade in:
buying at one price, selling at another, weighing and measuring,
is the whole mystery of the retailers in general: the greater
number of articles they sell, the greater memory and acuteness
is required, but a moderate share of wit serves their turn in
general.' Shopkeepers' apprentices therefore found themselves
behind the counter fairly quickly. William Browne had only
been in the service of a draper for six months when he was
acting as his cash-keeper, a fact which we learn when his master
accused him of embezzlement. Benjamin Giles served in Jacob
Rogers' mercer's shop from an early date in his term and one of
Rogers' customers deposed that he 'could sell any goods in the
defendant's shop in his absence as well as the defendant
himself', though reflection led him to change his deposition to
the more politic 'almost as well'. He was after all the master's
witness. Wholesalers' apprentices also served in the shop but
might well be sent into the country on their own to sell their
master's goods, as a distiller's apprentice was in 1679. The
other main job was the perennial one of collecting debts, both
in the town and the countryside, tasks which are normally
heard about because they gave rise either to the fairly trivial
complaint that the apprentices, once freed of the shop, spent
hours loitering, visiting taverns or staring into the Thames or,
more seriously, took the opportunity to put some of the money
collected into their own pockets.[30]

It might be comparatively easy to learn to be a shopkeeper
or a wholesaler, though one feels that Campbell minimizes the
problems of learning to trade successfully, but it was far from

simple to acquire the necessary skills to do well in many other occupations. Most skilled artisans really did need several years to enable them to equal their masters in a period when London was famed for the extremely high quality of many of its manufactures. Lawyers' clerks, who normally served five years, could expect their fair share of drudgery but would also have to study seriously if they hoped to set up independently, and the same was true of scriveners, who usually served seven or eight years. Even more knowledge had to be crammed in by the apprentices of apothecaries and surgeons, who were amongst the few young Londoners whose competence was tested by examination at the end of their term, though some skilled trades such as goldsmiths and pewterers still required apprentices to produce a masterpiece before being made free of their companies.[31] Simon Mason was apprenticed in 1715 to Mr Ralph Cornelius, an apothecary 'who was a very good master to me'. 'I first endeavour'd to obtain a knowledge of simples and their virtues, next the art of composition and making medicines, and to acquire a compleat knowledge of quantity and quality. And as I advanc'd farther in my apprenticeship I attended the sick and made the most strict enquiry into the nature of distempers.' He also read widely and attended St Thomas's Hospital as often as possible. Before the end of his term, he was visiting patients on his own and 'directing most of the medicines our patients took'.

Cornelius was well pleased with Mason's progress and, as a reward, gave him 'a priviledge he never did to any apprentice before', allowing him to treat 'young gentlemen in the venereal way', getting the medicines at cost and keeping the fees, which earned him nearly £50 a year 'which kept me handsomely in clothes and pocket money'. Trading or practising independently of the master, with or without his permission, seems to have been quite common. Merchants' apprentices, for instance, normally took some of their own capital when they were sent abroad, £1000 being typical for a young factor in the Levant trade, and anyone with an easily saleable skill, such as a surgeon or a scrivener, was likely to be trying to make something on the side towards the end of their term. Many shopkeepers' apprentices interpreted such possibilities in a rather liberal manner, such as the bookseller's apprentice John

Martin, who not only sold the books he stole but spoiled the market by selling them cheap, 'one booke that he hath sold for a groat that the defendant did usually sell for half a crowne'.[32]

Other apprentices used their growing skills to bargain with their masters to pay them wages, though taking wages technically disbarred them from acquiring the freedom of the City and so setting up shop on their own. However, by the early eighteenth century, the payment of wages towards the end of an apprentice's term was quite common, the threat of desertion on the grounds of the master's cruelty or some other pretext being a common bargaining point. And indeed, by this stage, most apprentices would be worth wages since their skills were likely to be equal to those of journeymen long before the end of their terms. This was usually the test of competence in court cases, such as that relating to Luke Butler, apprentice to a wine-cooper, who was said to be able to do the work 'the same as a journeyman and could deserve a good wage at it', a point which simply emphasizes the fact that in most trades seven years' apprenticeship was merely a racket which provided masters with cheap labour.[33]

iv The Life of the Apprentice

Service in another person's household may seem to us one of the strangest institutions of earlier times, but there was of course nothing strange about it to contemporaries, and service as a farm servant, a domestic or an apprentice was the normal experience of the majority of young people.[34] There were, however, two features of service as an apprentice in London which clearly distinguished it from the normal run of such occupations. In the first place, one's parents or friends paid handsomely for the privilege; in the second, most apprentices of the sort discussed in this book were at least of the same social standing as their masters and many came from families of distinctly higher status. Both these factors caused frictions in the household, quite often leading to a breakdown in the relationship between master and apprentice, though one should not exaggerate this. Many masters treated their apprentices as real members of the family, another son, and were carefully chosen because they promised to do so. However, many were unable or unwilling to develop such a relationship, the apprentices themselves not always being very helpful in this respect. Young men from good families are not always very tactful or respectful, and a master might well object to being called 'puppy and puppy dog and other ill names' by a youth who must have seemed no more than a puppy to him.[35]

It must have been a fairly traumatic experience for the young apprentice when, at the age of sixteen or so, he arrived with his box of clothes to start his term. For most young men, it was probably the first time they had been away from home and the first that they had seen of the basically hostile environment of the big city. Working conditions varied, but the hours were long, typically from seven in the morning to nine at night with a break of two hours for dinner at mid-day, and it is hardly surprising that young people from leisured homes where they had not been 'inured to labour' should complain of drudgery. Living conditions varied from master to master and depending on the 'degree and quality' of the apprentice, but there was a pecking order which required that the youngest apprentice 'was to be commanded by everyone', a general dogsbody who might well find himself sleeping on a truckle bed beneath the counter in the classic tradition. Food might well be poor and shared with the menial servants rather than above stairs with the master and mistress. Such discomforts might be compounded by harshness and cruelty. One should not take the complaints of apprentices at face value, but beatings and blows from angry, drunken or sadistic masters do seem to have played a fairly regular part in their lives. One can find apprentices who were locked into their room or out of the house, thrown down the cellar stairs, beaten with canes, pistols, spurs or horse-whips, some of these punishments leading to serious injury.[36]

Life could be hard for the apprentice, too hard for many homesick and miserable young people, who took the first opportunity to run away, many never to come back. There were, however, good reasons for masters to treat their apprentices harshly in many instances. An apprentice who bullied the master's children, insulted his wife or caused domestic discord by abusing his servants was hardly likely to be treated kindly, nor was one who lost his master money by his surly demeanour in the shop or by such carelessness as burning cloth in a hot press. Embezzlement and theft were also rife, not surprisingly given the enormous temptations placed in the way of young apprentices by the careless business methods of many masters, such as the linen-draper who instructed his apprentices to leave the takings 'in bags between the piles of cloth behind the counter' and only counted them and placed them in custody on Saturday night. Some apprentices were simply bad, thieves who broke open tills or their fellow-servants' boxes, louts who came in drunk and woke the household in the middle of the night or went to bed with their clothes and dirty shoes on and so damaged the bedding. Some apprentices were actually dangerous, such as William Palmer, who not only kept low company and was extravagant and idle but was also subject to mad fits, on one occasion attacking his fellow apprentices with a knife and who ended up trying to hang himself in the cellar.[37]

The miserable junior apprentice did not remain so for ever. After a year or two's unpleasantness, there was likely to be a new junior to bully and an improvement in status, a move from the truckle bed under the counter to a room in the house, perhaps a move from the kitchin to the master's table. Custom also allowed senior apprentices greater latitude in dress, even such privileges as wearing their hats in the shop and the house. By this time, apprentices knew their way about London and how to enjoy themselves, even if some keen young men might spend their nights and play-days learning shorthand. Parents who could afford large premiums could afford pocket-money and some apprentices had plenty to spend. They spent it as one might expect, on drink, gambling, the theatre and the dancing school, on late-night feasts of oysters and lobsters in their rooms, and perhaps most extravagantly of all on women, a mistress or a miss being a sure sign that the high-living apprentice had arrived. In short, apprentices systematically ignored every one of the moral clauses in their indentures.[38]

Some young apprentices behaved just as badly as the rakes in Restoration comedies, who could have provided a model if one had been needed. An example is John Todd, the son of a gentleman who was apprenticed to Nicholas Wild, a merchant. According to Wild's younger brother Ralph, who lived in the same house, Todd's behaviour was simply outrageous. He frequently came home drunk very late at night and put the house into disorder. He would forget to carry letters to the Post Office, sometimes keeping them a week before delivering them. He kept a wench in Covent Garden, where he had taken a chamber for her, and was said to have spent £40 or £50 on her clothes and other expenses. Worst of all, he once pawned the poor girl for 22 shillings when he was losing at hazard and she was forced to leave her petticoat behind as a pledge before being allowed to go home.[39]

Other high-living apprentices were more discreet; sober and reasonably well-behaved in the master's house, wild and far from sober once out of the neighbourhood. Many kept the paraphernalia of high living far away from their master's house, a sword 'at the other end of the town', a mistress in Whitechapel or Covent Garden, and some fighting cocks in Old Street, like Titus Manley who kept six at a time and paid someone to look after them, often winning or losing £5 in a day from gambling on the birds. One often learns such things from the very people who benefited from their licentiousness, keepers of taverns giving evidence of their drunkenness, neighbours of their mistresses attesting to their lewd reputation. Even a servant treated to a night out might provide evidence of an apprentice's extravagance, such as Mary Bethell, who told the Mayor's Court that her master's apprentice had taken her to the playhouse and then out to supper, where he had plied her with oysters and wine, confirming that 'the same was a considerable charge and expense to him'. The same apprentice's addiction to cock-fighting was revealed by Anne Swinstead, another fellow-servant, who when asked how she knew that he went to cock-pits replied rather disingenuously that she had seen him 'pull out of his pockets cocks, spurs and implements belonging to such business'.[40]

Many apprentices were accused of offences, and many confessed to them, which could have led them to the gallows under England's harsh penal code. Some were indeed hanged, the wayward apprentice being one of the stereotypes found in biographies of criminals. However, prosecution was expensive and the outcome doubtful, and a hanged apprentice was of no value to a master, so only a few apprentices were prosecuted before the criminal courts. It was much more effective to extract 'an ingenious confession on paper' by entreaty or violence or the threat of violence or prosecution. Such confessions could then be used to recover losses from the apprentice's parents or friends and held in reserve as a guarantee of the apprentice's future good behaviour. Threat of exposure to loving parents was another effective way of bringing an erring apprentice to heel, a maid, Joyce Knight, deposing in one case that 'if his father knew of something he had done, it would breake his heart'.[41]

The other main way to deal with troublesome apprentices was to complain to the City Chamberlain, who might simply give the lad a serious avuncular talk or, more likely, order him to be whipped or imprisoned for a few days in Bridewell, or both. The Chamberlain also acted as mediator in disputes between master and apprentice, hearing evidence from both parties and their witnesses and friends, and arbitrating himself or appointing arbitrators, a role also performed by the Wardens of the master's Company. The Chamberlain often went to great lengths to try to persuade a master to take back an erring apprentice or to convince the runaway that his best interests lay in returning to his master's service. Such intervention was often successful, but by no means always, most of the evidence used in this chapter coming from cases heard before the Mayor's Court, a fact which normally meant that all arbitration and intervention by Chamberlain, Company, parents and friends had failed.[42]

The apprentice has so far been considered as an individual, but 'the apprentices' or more often 'prentices' appear frequently as a generic term in contemporary literature, sometimes meaning what it says but quite often being a synonym for youth in general. Apprentices formed a large group in London society, modern estimates of their numbers in the second half of the seventeenth century ranging from 11,000, which is certainly much too low, to 40,000, which is far too high. In some areas, particularly in the City, they might form as much as 10 per cent of the population of a parish and, since they were nearly all young and male, could make their presence felt in a number of ways from simple youthful high spirits, such as playing football in the streets, to drunken disorder, riot and even the occasional intervention in politics.[43]

However, it is wrong to think of the apprentices as a

homogeneous group since, despite a superficially similar status and experience, they differed one from the other as much as adolescents as they were to do later when they had completed their terms. Older apprentices differed from younger apprentices, merchants' apprentices from butchers' apprentices, sons of gentlemen from sons of husbandmen, and these differences were much more important to the young men than the fact that they were all apprentices. London society was hierarchical at all levels, a fact only too obvious towards the end of the period of service when the majority of apprentices had nothing more to look forward to than a lifetime as a journeyman or clerk, while that minority who are discussed in the rest of the book would be thinking of setting themselves up in business and, before long, taking on apprentices in their turn.

4 Business

Business is not discussed in detail here since different types of business had their own particular characteristics, some of which have already been discussed in Chapter 2. Nonetheless, all businesses had some elements in common and it is this common ground that is considered in this chapter. How people started a business is examined first, then the central problem of cash flow, a problem which governed most of the tactical and strategic decisions of the businessman, and, finally, some idea is given of the rates of profit and accumulation in the London business world.

i Starting a Business

The most obvious initial problem for a man starting a business was to raise the necessary capital. There had been a time when this could be done by spending a few years as a journeyman or factor and saving wages or commission income.[1] However, by the late seventeenth century, it was unrealistic to expect to save enough from wages alone to set up in business, except in the lowest levels of shopkeeping and catering and in artisan trades. Few journeymen or book-keepers got more than £20 a year on top of their board and even several years of such wages would not go very far towards the cost of establishing a shopkeeping or mercantile business, as can be seen in Table 4.1 opposite.[2]

Two mid-eighteenth-century books provide information on start-up costs for London businesses and a selection from this material is presented in Table 4.1.[3] The table shows that, except for some artisan trades, at least £100 was needed to start almost any sort of business. Most shopkeeping businesses required at least £500, while such genteel trades as draper or mercer needed at least £1000 and a man wanting to deal in a big way would

TABLE 4.1: Start-up Costs for London Businesses (in £s)

Type of Business	Campbell (1747)	Collyer (1761)
Apothecary	50–200	100
Bookseller	500–5000	100–200 (small retail shop)
Box-maker	20–100	100
Brewer	2000–10,000	2000–10,000
Carman	60–100	100
Cheesemonger	100–500	100 (retail) up to 1000 (wholesale)
Coachmaker	500–3000	500–2000
Distiller	500–5000	500 (compound) 3000–4000 (malt)
Dyer	100–500	100–500
Glover	50–500	100–1000
Goldsmith	500–3000	500–3000
Grocer	500–2000	500 (at least)
Haberdasher	100–2000	500–1000 (in a genteel way)
Hosier	500–5000	500 (at least retail) up to 5000 (wholesale)
Ironmonger	500–2000	500 (in the common way)
Linen-draper	1000–5000	1000 (genteel retail shop)
Mason	100–500	100–500
Mercer	1000–10,000	2000–3000 (at least)
Merchant	Unlimited	3000–4000 (at least to engage in foreign trade to any great advantage)
Packer	300–500	400–500
Pawnbroker	500–2000	1000
Pewterer	300–1000	500
Poulterer	20–200	20
Printer	500–1000	700–800 (genteel way)
Salesman	100–1000	300–1000
Silkman	Unlimited	1000–4000
Soap-boiler	2000–5000	2000–5000
Stationer	100–2000	50 (retail) 1000 (wholesale)
Sugar-baker	1000–5000	1000–5000
Tailor	100–500	200–300 (middling)
Tallow-chandler	100–200	200 (middling way)
Tanner	100–1000	500 (at least)
Upholsterer	100–1000	100–1000
Vintner	100–500	500
Woollen-draper	1000–5000	1000–5000

Source: Campbell (1747) pp. 337ff; Collyer (1761) *passim*

have had to double or treble these sums. Even £100 was a substantial sum for a parent to find and these start-up costs confirm that most parents of potential London businessmen must have been in the middle station themselves.

These figures are of course drawn from a period rather later than ours. However, the intervening years were not ones of inflation and there seems little doubt that young businessmen needed similar sums in our period. This is illustrated in Table 4.2 opposite, where the assets of some of the sample who died young and so had not accumulated very much are compared with the mid-eighteenth-century start-up costs of their occupations. The fit is not perfect but it is good enough to indicate that comparable sums were already required to set up business in Augustan London.

Start-up costs were related both to apprenticeship premiums and to the fortune that a man could hope to accumulate in his lifetime, as is shown in Table 4.3. opposite. The table shows that in most cases those who ended up rich started off rich or at least pretty well off. It also indicates that in most trades accumulation was fairly modest since most of the median fortunes are only about twice the average start-up costs for that occupation. The two main exceptions were artisans and apothecaries. In most artisan trades it was possible to start in a small way, often saving one's initial capital from wages, and the lucky or talented man could expand from this basis into a substantial business, especially in the building trades. However, such opportunities paled beside those of the apothecary and it was this business that the sensible but relatively poor father should have chosen for his son. 'There is no branch of business in which a man requires less money to set him up than this very profitable trade,' wrote Campbell. 'Ten or twenty pounds, judiciously applied, will buy gallipots and counters, and as many drugs to fitt them as might poison the whole island. His profits are unconceivable; five hundred per cent is the least he receives.'[4] The profits may be exaggerated but there is no doubt that the substance of Campbell's observation was true.

It has so far been assumed that parents provided the young man's trading capital and this was certainly the commonest source of funds. There were, however, several others. Other members of the family often helped, either by an outright gift

TABLE 4.2: The Assets of Young Businessmen

Sample No.	Age	Occupation	Gross Assets (£s)	Net Assets (£s)	Start-up Costs (£s)
S.5	30	Joiner	301	280	100–500
S.18	27	Tavern-keeper	734	427	500+
S.46	28	Compound distiller	239	66	500
S.54	26	Carman	204	172	100
S.104	26	Distiller/tobacconist	1050	896	500–1000
S.113	27	Apothecary	161	130	50–200
S.121	28	Brass-founder	223	115	100
S.178	30	Compound distiller	420	402	500
S.207	28	Haberdasher of hats	6990	4003	100–2000
S.238	29	Tavern-keeper	2966	2503	500+
S.240	30	Poulterer	145	131	20–200
S.241	28	Bookseller	1487	831	500–5000
S.265	28	Apothecary	1513	1217	50–200
S.267	29	Inn-keeper	867	489	500
S.283	24	Cutler	236	223	50–300
S.373	30	Barber	484	231	50

Source: Assets from inventories; start-up costs from Campbell and Collyer.

TABLE 4.3: Start-up Costs and Fortune at Death

Occupation	Apprentice Premium (£s)	Start-up Costs (£s)	Median Fortune (£s)	No. of Cases
Merchants	100–500	3000–4000+	9050	42
Mercers etc.	50–400	1000–3000+	2250	29
Apothecaries	20–200	50–200	1146	16
Tavern-keepers	20–50	500	1025	20
Grocers	20–100	500–2000	922	19
Haberdashers etc	10–50	100–1000	903	33
Artisans	5–40	20–100	390	52

Mercers = Mercers, drapers, lacemen, silkmen
Haberdashers = Haberdashers, milliners, salesmen, threadmen
Grocers = Grocers, salters
Artisans = Metal and wood workers and building trades

Source: Fortune from inventories; premiums and start-up costs from Campbell and Collyer.

or a loan. An uncle or grandfather might leave £50 or £100 to help set a man up, while aunts, brothers, sisters and cousins could often be touched for a small loan to stretch the beginner's resources. Osbaston Hunlocke, for instance, an apothecary whose business assets were £70 when he died aged twenty-seven, owed £10 each to three people called Hunlocke, while the fledgling linen-draper James Hudson must have been pleased to hear from his brother in Cumberland that 'Sister Ann says she will forgive the first years interest but she wants the second' on the £13 that she had lent her faraway brother.[5]

An early marriage might be another solution to a young man's financial problems. About a third of the sample got married when they were twenty-four, twenty-five or twenty-six, almost immediately after completing their apprenticeships, and such timing must have greatly assisted their initial establishment in business.[6] Fortune in this respect normally favoured the already fortunate, since the size of the dowry usually matched the wealth or prospects of the bridegroom, but there were exceptions. John Tarry was a journeyman with no capital when he married Jane Warren, who brought him £900, in 1689. The successful wholesale spirits business which he set up in his wife's house had a turnover of £5000 a year by 1701. The scenario of the apprentice who married his master's daughter and took over his business was also one that happened in reality as well as fiction, while masters could be generous even if one did not marry their daughters. Some left their apprentices or such trusted servants as book-keepers a sizeable sum in their wills, while others loaned money to former servants at low rates of interest. William Ladds, for instance, a bodice-maker in Milk Street, bequeathed a loan of £1000 at 4 per cent 'for the better enabling my servant Jacob Webster to maintaine and carry on the trade by me driven and exercised'.[7]

Charity was another source of low cost loans and W. K. Jordan has shown that, up to 1660, nearly £44,000 had been willed by Londoners to provide loans at no interest or at nominal rates to young men starting in business and nearly as much again had been left to create revolving loan funds 'to be lent with great discrimination' at market rates. John Kendrick, for instance, left £900 to the Merchant Adventurers in 1624 to be lent in amounts of £300 to each of three 'honest, industrious and frugal young men' for three years without interest. In all, there must have been sufficient of these charities to loan money to several hundred young men a year, though the sums which had seemed sufficient to the charitable of Elizabethan London did not always go very far in our period.[8]

If all these sources of money were insufficient, then partnership was probably the best answer and indeed a partnership was virtually essential for those starting up in businesses with very high entry costs, such as mercers' and linen-drapers' shops and much of overseas and wholesale trade. Partnership was, however, potentially very dangerous in these days of unlimited liability when one's partner might 'incur debts for the partnership by bad judgment or simply by extravagance which could bring you both down'. Fear of the legal dangers seems to have made formal partnership fairly unusual, less than 10 per cent of the sample having such arrangements at their deaths, though considerably more entered into partnerships for a few years or for a particular trading venture. Defoe, who disapproved of partnership, thought that the best type of partner was a young beginner whom one knew personally and whose affairs were as yet unentangled by interests outside the business. Such young men could be watched over by an older and more experienced trader who might welcome the opportunity to withdraw from everyday management, and partnerships for a few years with an apprentice who had proved his competence were fairly common.[9]

The disposition as well as the raising of their initial capital posed problems for beginners, especially for those who needed permanent business premises. A merchant could invest every penny in trade goods and hope for the best; a shopkeeper had to decide how much to spend on shop-fittings, while still leaving sufficient money to acquire his stock and have something left over for living expenses and contingencies. The fashion for fancy shopfitting worried Defoe, who claimed that some tradesmen were laying out two-thirds of their fortune on their shops and so leaving their actual business badly under-capitalized. One suspects that he was exaggerating, but this was certainly a problem for a young starter who wanted both full shelves and a shop that was sufficiently attractive to entice customers into it. Another important decision for the starter was to determine how much to borrow or buy on credit in relation to his own capital. William Stout provides some information on this subject in his autobiography. His starting capital of £141 enabled him to fit up a shop and stock it with about £300 worth of goods, paying 'about halfe ready money, as was then usual to do of any young man beginning trade'. Nicolas Barbon confirmed this gearing convention in 1690. He stated that most retailers 'are usually trusted for more than double what they are worth'.[10]

These first six months were a desperate time for the beginner, a period of anxiety familiar to those who start a business on a bank loan today. He had probably borrowed some of his trading capital from relatives or, more alarmingly, from professional money-lenders. He then pledged himself to wholesalers for a sum equal to twice his capital, said a prayer and hoped that he could sell sufficient goods for cash or on short-term retail credit to pay the wholesalers' bills when they fell due. During this period, he would be competing with older men with much larger capital who would set the prices for the trade. Such men would almost certainly be able both to buy and sell on better terms than the young beginner, quite apart from having far greater experience in business. Life has never been particularly easy for the small businessman and many, then as now, failed to survive for very long, the dreams of a genteel existence in the middle station being rudely exchanged for the harsher realities of a journeyman's wages or, worse still, a debtors' prison. Nevertheless, most young men did survive and many prospered, and the problems that they faced in doing so form the subject of the next section.

ii Cash Flow

Nowadays, business is usually seen as separate from family and domestic life, but things were very different in our period, when household and business affairs were inextricably entangled. Some idea of the flow of payments in and out of the households of businessmen is shown in Fig. 4.1 on p. 113. Starting clockwise, there are first the positive and negative contributions to capital – portion, legacies, dowry and loans being offset by portions and dowries for children and outgoings for the service

FIGURE 4.1 Cash Flow of the Businessman

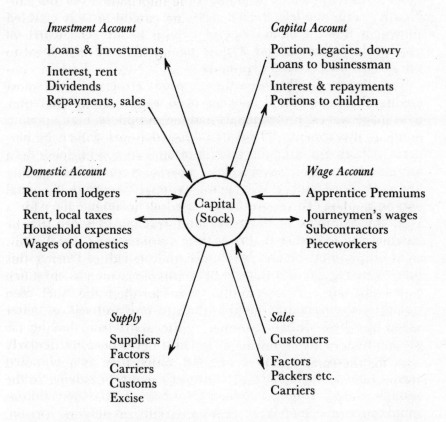

Investment Account

Loans & Investments

Interest, rent
Dividends
Repayments, sales

Capital Account

Portion, legacies, dowry
Loans to businessman

Interest & repayments
Portions to children

Domestic Account

Rent from lodgers

Rent, local taxes
Household expenses
Wages of domestics

Capital
(Stock)

Wage Account

Apprentice Premiums

Journeymen's wages
Subcontractors
Pieceworkers

Supply

Suppliers
Factors
Carriers
Customs
Excise

Sales

Customers

Factors
Packers etc.
Carriers

and repayment of loans. Below this is the wage element of the business, the influx of money from apprenticeship premiums being usually well overbalanced by wages to journeymen, porters and other casual labour and by payments to subcontractors and pieceworkers. At the bottom of the diagram can be seen the process by which stock in trade was fed into the business from suppliers and then progressively sold to customers, the incoming goods requiring payment to the suppliers, together very often with payments to carriers, commission agents and to the government for customs or excise, the outgoing goods naturally bringing in payment from customers but also often requiring payments to finishers, packers, factors and carriers. On the left of the diagram is shown the domestic side of life, mainly outgoings in the form of rent, local taxes,

household expenses and wages to domestic servants but sometimes counterbalanced to some extent by rent from lodgers.
Finally, in the top left, the businessman's investment account is
shown, a flow of money out of capital to advance loans or
acquire investments and a flow back reflecting repayments,
sales, rent, interest and dividends.

The distribution between these various groups of debits and
credits obviously varied between occupations – manufacturers
paid more wages, professionals had few suppliers, many people
made no investments. The distribution also varied over the life-
cycle – both investments and domestic outgoings tended to
increase with age. Nevertheless, nearly every inventory one
looks at illustrates this general pattern of incomings and
outgoings. The central problem of the businessman's life was to
keep this complex of payments and receipts in some sort of
balance and to ensure that over time more money came in than
went out, so that he and his family had enough to live on and
there were regular additions to his capital or, as it was normally
called, his stock. A simple approach to this problem is illustrated by a remark attributed to the lawyer Erasmus Earl when
asked how he kept his accounts. ' "Accounts, boy?" said he. "I
get as much as I can and I spend as little as I can; and there is
all the accounts I keep." '[11] In the absence of very effective
accounting methods, such an approach was probably common
enough, though it might be safer for a lawyer to adopt it than a
shopkeeper or a merchant. A lawyer relied mainly on fees for
his income and had few countervailing payments to make to
suppliers or other creditors, so the main problem would be to
remember who owed him money or, if he did not have a
particularly good memory, to keep a list of his debtors.

The problems of shopkeepers, manufacturers and merchants
were of quite a different order and most kept some sort of
accounts. Shopkeepers' accounts were generally in the form of
a day-book in which debit and credit transactions were recorded
on facing pages and from which amounts due to or from
outstanding debtors or creditors could be periodically extracted,
this exercise sometimes being assisted by posting material from
the day-book to a ledger. Many businesses, such as those of
coachmakers, jewellers and tailors, involved a series of bespoke
orders and these men would normally keep a job book or an

invoice book in which their expenditure and the amount due from the customer on each order could be recorded. Judging from surviving accounting records, only such high-flyers as merchants, big wholesalers and bankers kept a full set of books and even these were normally kept in single rather than double entry, though the latter was well known and was usually referred to as 'merchants' accounts'. Some surviving account books were beautifully and meticulously kept, but many are in a terrrible mess and hardly meet Defoe's requirement that 'next to being prepared for death, with respect to heaven and his soul, a tradesman should be always in a state of preparation for death, with respect to his books'.[12]

The problems of the businessman's cash flow were made much greater by the ubiquity of credit. There was of course a cash basis to the economy but credit, often for very long periods, permeated every aspect of economic life. Goods were sold, both wholesale and retail, on credit; wages, commissions, taxes and rent payments were normally in arrears; even portions, legacies and dowries were normally paid long after they were due. Terms of credit varied enormously, depending on the status, wealth and credit-worthiness of the debtor, the customs and conventions of different types of business and, perhaps particularly, on whether the creditor was sufficiently wide awake, efficient or grasping to claim the debt when it was due and to enforce that claim. The majority of people paid their debts in the long run and, if they did not, the legal system was weighted on the side of the creditor, but it might be a very long run.

Contemporaries always distinguished between retail credit and wholesale credit, the former being seen as undesirable and dangerous both for the customer and retailer. However, despite this, retail credit was a central feature of the London economy and one probably growing more important over time. This at least is suggested by the works of Defoe. On numerous occasions in his *Review* he attacked retail credit as an evil likely to bankrupt tradesmen and force their gentlemen customers into a desperate search for funds. 'Giving credit to the last consumer', he wrote in 1709, 'is the destruction of credit.' By the 1720s, however, he had completely changed his tune. 'Every trades-man both gives and takes credit, and the new mode of setting it up over their shop and warehouse doors in capital letters, NO

TRUST BY RETAIL, is a presumption in trade . . . and most of those trades who were the forewardest to set it up have been obliged to take it down again, or act contrary to it in their business.' In a pamphlet written a couple of years later, he hammers home the consequences for those who refuse to give retail credit. 'Thousands of buyers who laid out their money freely and who, tho' they might not always pay down upon the spot, yet paid tolerably well, went from shops and bought where they knew they could be trusted.'[13]

Indeed, 'trusting' was essential in a world where the majority of customers had no regular income, and the accumulation of numerous small debts of a few shillings or a few pounds can be found in almost any list of assets. The inventory of the apothecary Owen Crane, for instance, lists nearly 200 small debtors owing £150 between them.[14] What was necessary was not to let these small debts become large ones, to keep one's ear to the ground so that one knew when the customer was in funds, had himself been paid for piecework or had received some other overdue debt from his own customers. Then was the time to present a bill or to send an apprentice round to dun the customer for his money or at least something on account.

Such problems grew in magnitude when the customer was a gentleman or an aristocrat from the West End, as so many customers of London's luxury bespoke trades were. 'Never trust', wrote Tom Brown, '[and if you do] let it not be with men who are protected by their dignity or character.' Such advice was easier to write than carry out. A coachmaker or fashionable tailor had to trust or he would have virtually no business, but such trusting required good nerves and substantial assets or at least substantial credit from his own suppliers. Some idea of attitudes can be seen from a letter written by a gentleman in Penrith to his London tailor promising to pay him six months after delivery, 'which considering how you are generally paid in your way will be next to ready money'. When the famous cabinet-maker Thomas Chippendale ran into cash flow problems he called on Sir Edward Knatchbull to pay an outstanding bill but had no joy. 'As I receive my rents once a year,' wrote Sir Edward, 'so I pay my tradesmen's bills once a year which is not reckoned very bad pay as ye world goes.' There was no exaggeration in this; settling bills once a year, often at Christmas, was a common practice. Even a barber might have to wait a year for his pay, as can be seen from the diary of the accountant Stephen Monteage, who on 26 December 1738 paid £3 to William Stephens for 'a year's shaving due at Xmas'. Many retailers and artisans waited far more than a year for their money, and many of course waited for ever; one can feel sympathy for the nurseryman Thomas Greening, who found when he searched his books in 1740 that the only money due to him were two bills contracted in the mid-1730s by Lord Weymouth and the Duke of Marlborough 'which God knows when I shall receive'.[15]

It is difficult to discover the terms on which retail credit was granted. Many purchases on tick from shops or taverns were no doubt free of interest in the short run, the seller using tick as a means of increasing turnover, as a credit-card transaction does today. Most customers paid sooner or later and the seller would be better off than if he had refused them credit. However, once weeks of non-payment turned into months, negotiations would take place between seller and buyer involving the latter in a substantial interest payment, the refusal of further credit being a useful lever to obtain profitable terms for the credit already given. When selling goods and services to the wealthy and privileged, self-interest ensured that bills were well-padded from the start and that slow-paying dukes would eventually pay handsomely for their carriages and cloaks, first because the initial price was high and later because they would be charged interest as the months and years went by. This, of course, was the attraction of doing business with such people of 'dignity or character', as it was with the government, who also paid high prices in return for dilatory payment. Dilatory though they were, they paid in the end, as the merchant Michael Mitford wrote in 1704. 'The payment of the government is very certain, but the time when is also very uncertain.' Since the time when was usually years and sometimes decades after the event, such profitable business required a very long purse.[16]

A lower bound to the terms of retail credit can be given by looking at the terms on which wholesale credit was offered, since tradesmen were much better payers than governments or gentlemen and so presumably got better terms. Merchants trading overseas generally received the longest credit, from six months to a year or even longer being common, while whole-salers normally gave retailers three, four or six months to pay, with 'three days of customary grace'. Some idea of the cost of this credit can be obtained from the letters of merchants and wholesalers, which often quote the prices of the goods in which they dealt at 'ready money' and at various lengths of credit, such as 'at three months'. Such material is too scattered to give an average but it suggests that credit was nearly always offered at a cost higher than the maximum legal rate of interest and often at three or four times the maximum rate. Small men might find 'trust' even more expensive. In 1745, the pawnbroker Richard Grainger claimed that it paid a handicraftsman to borrow from him and buy his raw materials for cash, 'the difference of buying goods with ready money and upon trust, being more in proportion than the pawnbroker takes'. Such rates reflect the risk and inconvenience of giving credit but they also help us to understand why wholesalers tended both to start rich and die richer, despite a substantial proportion of bad debts.[17]

Borrowing and buying on credit naturally meant that most businessmen's inventories include a substantial proportion of liabilities and a breakdown of these is provided in Tables 4.4 and 4.5 on p. 119. These figures underestimate the real state of credit since inventories were often drawn up a long time after death so that executors had time to pay off some of the debts. However, even as a lower bound, the figures give a good idea of the web of debt in which the London business world was entangled. Table 4.4 shows that by the time the inventory was drawn up, the average man still had liabilities equal to nearly a quarter of his gross assets, while the lower quartile of the sample had liabilities equal to over half their assets.

In Table 4.5, the occupations of those with high or low proportions of liabilities are set out to see if any patterns emerge. Individuals from virtually every occupation appear on each side of the table but some tentative conclusions are suggested. Tavern-keepers and most small shopkeepers tended to have high levels of liabilities, reflecting their need to keep high levels of stock and the generally slow rate of turnover. On the other hand, the apothecary's business once again looks a good one to be in from this point of view, and most merchants,

---

TABLE 4.4: Liabilities as a Proportion of Assets

Liabilities/Gross Assets × 100	No. of Cases	
	No.	%
Less than 10%	93	24.8
10–24%	102	27.2
25–49%	89	23.7
50–74%	48	12.9
75–100%	29	7.7
Over 100% (insolvent)	14	3.7
	375	100.0

Median = 23%.

TABLE 4.5: Occupations of Low and High Scorers in Table 4.4

Occupations	Numbers	
	Less than 10%	50% & over
Apothecary, Surgeon	7	1
Building trades	6	2
Merchants	12	5
Rentier, moneylender	12	4
Manufacture	16	11
Draper, mercer	8	6
Leather trades	3	0
Food and fuel trades, apart from below	9	6
Grocer, salter, cheesemonger, tobacconist	3	14
Jeweller, toyman, bookseller etc.	1	10
Haberdasher, milliner	9	17
Taverns, inns	5	12
Ironmonger, brazier	2	3
	93	91
Average age at death	47.6	42.5

Source: Inventories of the sample. The average age at death of the whole sample was 45.1.

---

rentiers, moneylenders and, surprisingly, most of the building trades also seem to have been able to keep their liabilities down to a reasonable level. Finally, while men of all ages can be found on both sides of the table, the average age of those with high liabilities is five years younger those those with low liabilities, suggesting that the young were more inclined to over-extend themselves, from being in too much of a hurry or because their businesses were often financed by loans.[18]

The extent of liabilities may not seem all that much by the standards of today's mortgage-ridden citizens, but it was a worrying problem in a world of personal credit where the whole edifice was built on confidence in the ability of the debtor to pay and very few debts were supported by collateral. A casual remark in a coffee-house or a tavern might lead creditors to suspect that their debtor had no 'bottom' and to close in quickly for repayment. If this debtor belonged to one of the groups in the table with liabilities equal to 50, 75 or, worse still, 100 per cent of his gross assets, then such suspicion could lead very quickly to disaster.

Disaster could strike even the soundest of businesses for, as can be seen in Table 4.6 opposite, assets were far from liquid.[19] Cash ratios were low for all groups and few other assets could be turned quickly into money, except jewellery and plate. If the cause of the cash flow problem was 'deadness' of trade, then it was unlikely that stocks could be sold quickly or at a reasonable price. The same would be true of investments in the stocks of the trading companies or in ships, while most other investments – in property or government debt – were even more illiquid. This meant that, if a man was in trouble, he normally had little option but to press those debtors to whom he had advanced personal loans and trade credits. These together made up over half the gross assets of the average businessman and might involve literally hundreds of separate debtors. What a cash flow crisis involved was chasing these debtors, who would almost certainly be chasing their own debtors at the same time, since a crisis of confidence was likely to strike everyone together.

Table 4.6 also illustrates the differing structure of asset holding for a few common occupations or groups of occupations. In general, expenditure on domestic goods was inelastic in respect of wealth, taking up nearly 10 per cent of the artisans' assets and less than 2 per cent of the two wealthiest groups. The category 'stocks and fixed assets' is in nearly all cases dominated by stock in trade, most businesses having just a few such items as shelves, counters and presses as their total of fixed assets, not including buildings. Manufacturers naturally had

TABLE 4.6: Analysis of Assets
Percentage Distribution of Gross Assets

Group	DOMESTIC		BUSINESS		INVESTMENT					
	Domestic Goods	Jewellery & Plate	Stocks & Fixed Assets	Trade Credits	Personal Loans	Other Investments	Cash	Total	No. in Sample	Ave. Gross Assets
Whole sample	2.15	1.20	18.50	38.36	15.04	19.94	4.81	100	375	£ 5283
Merchants	1.36	0.95	23.04	35.72	8.91	26.22	3.80	100	42	17667
Textile wholesalers	1.95	1.06	21.26	53.76	12.12	5.33	4.52	100	34	7176
Rentiers/ moneylenders	2.33	1.70	0.08	4.00	24.34	64.08	3.47	100	21	6887
Manufacturers	3.00	1.52	18.49	46.81	13.40	12.89	3.89	100	29	3773
Tavern-keepers	2.97	2.68	38.29	14.80	21.82	14.75	4.69	100	21	2888
Apothecaries	4.73	2.68	6.83	34.08	27.16	19.14	5.38	100	16	2012
Textile retailers	4.70	1.72	25.90	43.22	12.69	7.29	4.48	100	32	1632
Artisans	9.42	4.14	19.76	37.14	10.19	16.78	2.57	100	38	620

Source: Inventories of sample. Textile wholesalers are defined as those worth net over £2000 selling textiles in any form and textile retailers those under £2000. Manufacturers include brewers, distillers, dyers, printers and soap, sugar and candle-makers. Artisans are defined as those in working trades worth net less than £1000. Investments consist of leasehold property, shares in ships, the stocks and shares of the trading companies and government debt. (See Chapter 5 for a fuller discussion of investment. For the method used to distinguish trade credits from personal loans, see note 19 of this chapter.)

the greatest fixed assets but no one in the sample had as much as £1000 in fixed capital. The two biggest were a distiller with £880 of equipment and a brewer with £538, which in both cases represented just over 15 per cent of their total assets, but most manufacturers had a far smaller proportion of their assets invested in fixed capital.[20] This is still a commercial society where stock in trade and not equipment is what matters. Much the highest proportional investment in stocks (almost entirely wine) was made by the tavern-keepers, which compares very strikingly with the very low investments in stocks made by apothecaries, while of course rentiers and money-lenders had virtually no stocks or fixed equipment at all. Tavern-keepers, on the other hand, were in more of a cash trade than most and so had to give relatively less trade credit than any other group except the money-lenders, while the textile wholesalers held over half of all their assets in the form of credit advanced to their customers. Manufacturers, too, were wholesalers in respect of the selling side of their businesses and they came second in the proportion of assets held as trade credits, nearly 47 per cent.

Investment will be looked at in more detail in the next chapter, but it can be noted here that merchants were relatively little involved in personal loans but were the most important group in other types of investment apart from those specialist investors, the rentiers and money-lenders. Apothecaries were the greatest investors of all groups who actually had a trading business, investing nearly half their assets outside that business, a reflection of the fact that they did not have to invest a lot of money in expensive stocks. If it had been possible to compare the asset structure of such professionals as doctors and lawyers with the others in the table, this would probably have fallen somewhere between the pattern of the apothecaries and that of the rentiers and money-lenders, that is, with high investments, low stocks and a relatively low level of trade credits in respect of their unpaid fees.

Most of the assets held by all these groups were safe enough and could be turned into cash in the long run, though that long run might be too long to satisfy impatient creditors. However, in nearly every case, there would be some assets which were not really assets at all. Inventories are inconsistent in recording bad debts and in any case it is not exactly clear what a 'desperate' or 'doubtful' debt meant in the conventions of the day. Sometimes such adjectives clearly mean what they say; sometimes, one suspects, they merely reflect laziness on the part of valuers or executors. However, if 'doubtful and desperate debts' are taken as an accurate description, they they represent just under a third of all debts due in those inventories which record them.[21] This may seem a huge proportion, but the number is swollen by the extreme reluctance of Augustan businessmen to write off bad debts. There are no data on the proportion of bad debts to turnover, but in 1734 Jacob Vanderlint suggested that one should expect bad debts to represent about 2 per cent per annum of trading capital.[22] If these were never written off, it would not be very long before they were a third of all debts due.

This approach to bad debts was a major cause of trouble for the London tradesman, whose treatment of them as assets allowed him to believe he was quite safe when he was in fact close to insolvency. Not that such self-deception was the only cause of problems in the juggling act between debit and credit which was performed by every London businessman. Many failed in this act and in the next section the tactics used to recover money from reluctant payers is looked at, followed by the problems of insolvency and bankruptcy in our period.

iii Debt Collection

The collection of debts, either in full or as near full as possible, was one of the major tasks of the businessman. Debt collectors, working on commission, provided some assistance but in most cases it was a task which the creditor himself carried out. The first stage was the same as today, a combination of wheedling appeals and threats in person or by letter, the language different but the content familiar to the modern creditor or debtor.[23] If letters and verbal demands had no effect, then it would be necessary to take sterner measures. One obvious procedure would be to secure the debt. This could be done by getting the debtor to bind himself to pay at some future date, the penalty of such bonds being the double of the debt. However, a bond was only secured by a signature and it might be better to find rather more solid collateral, such as a pawn of some of the debtor's goods, a mortgage on his property or an attachment or garnishee order on his own debtors. The latter were very common, the object being to divert to yourself money due to your debtor from a third party. 'This doth not hurt the person of him that owes the money, but only secures the debt, and is no very great disgrace to the debtor, nor any great charge, and is done with much privacy.'[24]

An alternative procedure was to sue for the debt, a process whose main object was to call the debtor's bluff but which might end up with putting him in prison for the rest of his life. Any creditor whose debtor owed him more than £2 could issue a writ to summons him to court or have him arrested and then either bailed or imprisoned until his appearance in court. Such writs normally worked like magic and a Commons enquiry of 1791 found that less than two-thirds of those issued with writs in the metropolis were actually arrested and less than a tenth went to prison, in most cases because the writ or at least the arrest was sufficient to get the debtor to pay, while many of the remaining tenth settled with their creditors before the hearing in court.[25]

The remaining fraction of non-payers were those who might have to suffer the full rigour of the laws against debtors. If the debt was proved in court, not always easy and one good reason to keep good books, the creditor had two options. He could proceed against the debtor's property by having the sheriff seize and sell his goods or he could proceed against the debtor's body by having him detained in prison until he repaid the debt or the creditor gave up and let him be released. The majority of creditors chose this latter course since it was rarely easy to settle a debt by seizing property. Neither creditor nor sheriff were allowed to break into the debtor's house, shop or warehouse, while what the law called 'choses in action' – bills, bonds, book-debts, stocks and shares, in other words most assets – were safe from the bailiffs' attention. On the other hand, imprisonment tended to concentrate the debtor's mind in a wonderful way, leading him to discover resources or friends which up to that time he had denied. However, in many cases the debtor simply could not pay and, as a result, there were normally several hundred London debtors languishing in prison at any one time, while many others fled to avoid 'the temporal hell of a gaol'.[26]

Debtors' prisons were periodically cleared of most of their poorer inmates by Acts of Insolvency which empowered magistrates to free prisoners who swore on oath that they had no estate above some small value such as £5 or £10 and whose creditors could not disprove the oath. There was also provision for debtors to live and even conduct business in strictly defined areas outside the prisons known as the Rules, some prisoners being quite wealthy men who chose to abuse the system rather than pay their debts. Nevertheless, debtors' prisons were unpleasant places and they aroused the humanitarian outcries one might expect, especially after a parliamentary committee of 1729 published a damning indictment of conditions in London's prisons. Attention was drawn to the old and unsuitable buildings, the overcrowding and, in particular, to the extortions of the venal wardens and other prison officers. The report sums up nicely the results of private enterprise in the prison service. 'The warden, who pays for the privilege of punishing others [£5000 in the Fleet], does consequently sell his forbearance at high rates, and repairs his own charge and loss at the wretched expence of the ease and quiet of the wretched objects in his custody.'[27]

These wretched objects did not prevent imprisonment for debt being generally supported by middling people, who saw it as essential if the system of credit was to be maintained, a system which was of course the basis of the whole expanding economy. No threat would be effective without the final sanction of prison and, as has been seen, the system did in fact work in the great majority of cases. Most debtors paid their debts and comparatively few went to prison. Defoe spelt out the logic in 1729. 'The retailer, being a woollen-draper, trusts his neighbour with a suit of clothes. How comes he to do it? perhaps the man has no extraordinary character; well but, says the retailer, he is a tradesman as well as I, and he must pay me, or he shall not be able to stand at his shop door or sit behind his counter, for I will arrest him and make him pay me; and upon this power of arresting the debtor and carrying him to prison, or whether he is carry'd to prison or no, the exposing him, disgracing him, and ruining his credit; I say, upon this is founded the freedom of the tradesman to trust him. If you destroy this power of coercion, you destroy the credit in trade; for if a man cannot be credited, he cannot buy; and if the tradesman cannot arrest him, he will not sell.'[28]

One flaw in this system was the fact that the process could only be begun if the debt was for a sum of £2 or more and of course many retail debts were for much less than this. This was no problem in the City where, since the reign of Henry VIII, there had been a 'Court of Conscience' to deal with small debts. This was not a common law court but one where commissioners consisting of two aldermen and twelve commoners made 'such orders between party and party as they shall find to stand with Equity and Good Conscience'. The court was the first to order debtors to pay by instalments – 'generally poverty is pleaded and the debtor is ordered to pay so much per week, 6d. or 12d. or what the Court thinks fit' – and it played an important part in City life. However, attempts to introduce similar courts elsewhere in the metropolis were unsuccessful until 1749-50 when Courts of Conscience for Southwark, Westminster and Tower Hamlets were set up, well-argued cases for the courts being repeatedly set aside by the opposition of the common lawyers and of gentlemen who objected to having 'to submit for small debts to a company of shopkeepers'.[29]

So far cases have been mentioned where the creditor was fairly certain, perhaps mistakenly, that his debtor could pay. What happened when the debtor's business was really unsound and there was no way that he could pay, at least in the short run? A variety of tactics was open to the creditor, but it was a well-worn maxim that 'the first offer is generally the best'; in other words a sensible creditor should accept what a debtor declared was the most he could pay and so avoid legal costs, delays and almost certainly a finally disappointing dividend. A common situation was for a merchant or trader, though fundamentally sound, to get his payments to creditors hopelessly unsynchronized with potential receipts from his debtors. If he kept reasonable books, he should be able to prove his basic soundness and ask his creditors for time, which, if they had any sense, they would give him. 'Whereas he finds himself not in a capacity to pay, he desires a Letter of Licence, and promiseth that in three, four, or five years (more or less, as you can agree) he will pay the debt, because he hath many debts out, and goods beyond the seas, and must have time to get them in.' Arrangements would be made for serial payments and the debtor bound for twice the debt.[30]

Where the business was not sound, it would still probably pay creditors to arrange a private composition. If the number of creditors was small and the debtor could establish his honesty if not his good business judgment, then a composition had the advantage of a speedy settlement and usually a higher dividend than if the debtor had been sued as a formal bankrupt. The simplest composition was where the creditors agreed to accept say 15s. in the pound of what they were owed and the debtor himself sold his property and called in his own debts in order to pay the agreed dividend within some pre-arranged time. In other cases, the creditors would appoint a trustee, possibly one of themselves, possibly someone more formal, such as a Master in Chancery, to whom the debtor would surrender his effects to be sold. Whatever the particular arrangement, such private compositions allowed the debtor to be discharged of the balance of his previous debts and, in Defoe's metaphor, to rise like a phoenix from the ashes of his former business, a free man who could get fresh credit, open his shop again and ideally recover his honour by paying the balance of his debts at some future date, even though he was not legally required to do so.[31]

Such arrangements were relatively friendly, speedy, cheap and generally in the best interests of both creditor and debtor. However, not all debtors were or were thought to be honest and not all creditors were friendly, while even the kindest of creditors might fear that he was somehow being cheated of an equitable dividend either by other creditors or by the debtor himself. In such situations and in the very common circumstances of the creditors being unable to agree to the terms of a private composition, there was no alternative but to sue out a commission of bankruptcy. In the first part of our period, this would have been done under the bankruptcy statutes of 1571 and 1624, which were very harsh to the bankrupt. Bankrupts were assumed to be fraudulent and creditors had to prove an 'act of bankruptcy', such as the debtor fleeing, keeping his house or allowing himself to be imprisoned for debt, before a commission could be issued. Commissioners were then appointed with wide-ranging powers – to seize and examine the bankrupt under oath, send him to prison if he refused to answer questions, to examine his wife and his debtors under oath and to do anything else necessary to determine the state of his affairs. 'They can break open houses, seize goods, sell them, extend lands, and in short, do any thing for the advantage of the creditors; and at last make a treasurer and cause a divident to be made to the creditors.'[32] For the dishonoured and now penniless bankrupt, this was not necessarily the end of the matter for he received no discharge and could be and often was later sued for the debts which had not been paid in the dividend. This was usually a purely malicious action by creditors, who could not hope to get any more money, but some creditors were malicious and bankrupts who were subsequently sent to debt-ors' prisons were the unhappiest of prisoners since, if the commissioners had done their work, they had no funds to sweeten the warders.

Statutes of 1705 and 1706 produced a major change in the bankruptcy laws. For the first time, a distinction was made between the fraudulent and the honest bankrupt, the man whose failure was 'his misfortune and not his fault'. A new stick and carrot situation was created where honesty was rewarded and fraud punished by death or, as one contemporary put it, 'all that run away shall be hang'd if they are caught, and all that surrender clear'd, if nothing is made out against the truth of their discovery'. Those bankrupts who surrendered them-selves within thirty days of notice and made a full and honest declaration of their affairs were given a certificate discharging them of the balance of their former debts. They were also entitled to be given five per cent of their net estate if the dividend paid was more than 8s. in the pound, to a maximum of £200. Such leniency was too much for many contemporaries and the law was modified in 1706 in two important ways. It was first declared that no one could become bankrupt unless he owed £100 to a single creditor, £150 to two creditors or £200 to three, thus barring small men from the benefits of the new act and, secondly, discharge certificates could only be issued if four-fifths of the creditors in number and value signed them, thus once again opening the door to the malicious who could 'keep his body, starve him, and never let him out of prison unless they and four fifths parts of them in number and value voluntarily please to agree to it'.[33]

Nevertheless, even the 1706 Act was a great improvement on the previous situation, so much so that in 1726 Defoe could write that 'men make so little of breaking that many times the family scarce removes for it; a commission of bankruptcy is so familiar a thing that the debtor oftentimes causes it to be taken out in his favour that he may the sooner be effectually deliver'd from all his creditors at once'. Most writers, however, still felt that formal bankruptcy was a slow and not very satisfactory method of dealing with the problem of insolvent debtors. As one put it in 1707, 'when the goods are sold, at 3 or 400 per cent loss, and the sittings, assignments etc. are payed, very little comes to the creditors'. This is probably exaggerated, but everyone agreed that very poor prices were paid at sales of bankrupt stock.[34]

The new legislation encouraged more people to sue out commissions of bankruptcy, so that in the last twenty years of our period there were usually between 150 and 200 bankrupts a year, of whom rather more than half were Londoners, while in the 1650s the numbers had rarely risen above 50. Roughly 100 Londoners a year were thus going bankrupt in the 1710s and 1720s, a number which should be compared with the population at risk, perhaps half of the 20,000 to 25,000 households which have been estimated to be in the middle station, since professionals were not subject to the bankruptcy laws and small traders would be unlikely to have debts large enough to satisfy the minimum requirements of the 1706 Act. This gives an annual rate of bankruptcy of somewhere between 1 and 2 per cent, but the rates varied enormously for different occupations. There were, for instance, somewhere between 400 and 500 each of apothecaries, cheesemongers and tavern-keepers in London in the early eighteenth century but the numbers of bankrupts in these three occupations during the five years 1711-15 were 3, 9 and 39 respectively, figures which suggest that the tavern-keepers with their huge wine stocks were amongst the most vulnerable of all businessmen, while the apothecary's business once again shows up as one of the safest.[35]

The overall bankruptcy rate of 1 or 2 per cent does not seem very high until one recalculates it on a career basis. Assuming that the average business career lasted twenty years and that those leaving the business world were matched by those entering it, then the career chances of bankruptcy rise to 10 or 15 per cent.[36] When one considers that private compositions remained significant, it shows just how important cash flow problems were in London business life. The commonest end to a business career was death, but bankruptcy must have run retirement very close in second place.

iv Business Strategies

'The chief end or business of trade is to make a profitable bargain,' wrote Nicolas Barbon in 1690, a sentiment with which no businessman then or now would argue.[37] However, the desire to make profits had to be tempered by the need to avoid insolvency and this section considers a few of the strategies employed in an attempt to garner profits without ending up in the bankruptcy court.

The simplest answer to the problem was to have no liabilities, since without them there could be no insolvency. Many Londoners, rich and relatively poor, old and young, adopted this strategy. They either invested all their capital or set up as money-lenders; they never bought trade goods, accepted no credit and lived on the 6 per cent or more that they could get as a rentier. If their capital was small, they would live fairly meanly but would have few fears since the worst that could happen would be one of their debtors turning out to be a bad one, which would make them poorer but not insolvent.[38]

Another simple and almost ideal approach, according to Defoe, was 'a few goods and a quick sale'. When small stocks were combined with certain, bespoke cash sales and purchases at three or four months' credit, then life might seem rosy, as it must have done for the jeweller Peter Webb in the mid-1730s. He made attractive and expensive jewellery for fashionable people, but his journal shows that he was in the unusual position of being paid nearly always in cash for his product, only two of his twenty-nine sales between September 1735 and September 1737 being on credit. Meanwhile, he acquired his working materials either from his customers themselves or on credit from other jewellers and goldsmiths. In this two-year period, he made over £250 a year with very little capital save his tools.[39]

Such a business could very easily come unstuck as a result of just one of his customers not paying the cash promised and maybe, since Webb's papers are in Chancery, that is what happened. It was, in any case, a fairly unusual business and most traders and manufacturers had very considerable liabilities. When payment of these became unsynchronized with incoming payments, there was generally little alternative but to borrow more to get out of trouble. William Stout, for instance, inspected his books after a year's trading and 'found that I had been too forward in trusting and too backward in calling, as is too frequent with young tradesmen'. He solved the problem by borrowing £50 on bond. This was all right if most people were not in the same situation and the bond market was fairly easy, but matters were not so simple in a general crisis. 'These breaking times will make all men more cautious,' wrote the merchant Thomas Boughey in March 1675.[40]

Caution has a price but, in our period, there was no easy mechanism for reflecting that price in a higher rate of interest. Most bonds were secured at or near the legal maximum rate of 6 per cent and the penalty for exceeding that was 'treble the value of the moneys, wares, merchandises, and other things lent'. This statutory limit to the rate of interest made the supply of funds in the 'last resort' much less liquid than it would otherwise have been and could lead to a sudden rush of interconnected bankruptcies, as T.S. Ashton pointed out many years ago. Nevertheless, there have always been ways round usury laws and our period was no different in this respect. The easiest way was simply to ignore them, as Mary Turner of Tottenham Court did in 1679 when she charged John Dawson 10 per cent on two bonds. When he complained that she was liable to be indicted for charging such extortionate interest, the lady replied that he should pay what he owed and indict her afterwards.[41]

Another way round the law was to disguise a loan as an undervalued annuity by calculating the years' purchase at an unrealistically low level. For example, the borrower might contract to pay the lender £100 a year for life in return for a payment of £300, or three years' purchase, the lender either letting the annuity run on until the annuitant actually did die or allowing him to repurchase the principal when he was in funds. Of course, if the annuitant did die within three years, the lender had no redress since he had no claim on the estate, though it was possible in the eighteenth century to insure the life for the value of the principal. A much simpler way of side-stepping the usury laws was to deduct some of the principal before handing over the money, this extra interest charge being known as a premium.[42]

Retrenchment was an alternative to borrowing oneself out of trouble, but it was a strategy that could rebound seriously on those who adopted it. Today, a man's credit would hardly be impaired if he stopped entertaining or sold the yacht, but matters were very different in the world of personal credit of Augustan London. One reason that Thomas Goodinge thought that 'many good men . . . do insensibly sink and decay in their estates [was] . . . living up to support a credit and shoar up a reputation (no mean mystery in this world)'. The irony of such a situation was not lost on Defoe. 'He must live as others do, or lose the credit of living and be run down as if he was broke. In a word, he must spend more than he can afford to spend, and so be undone, or not spend it, and so be undone.'[43]

The chronic problem of balancing liabilities and assets could be helped by re-scheduling one's asset structure or one's payments. A house and shop could be rented instead of purchasing the freehold or the lease, thus releasing capital but losing income. Trade credit at, say, 10 per cent could be converted into ready money by borrowing on bond at 6 per cent. Something could be done about payments to workmen, too, as Andy Federer has shown. Journeymen, at least those who lived out of doors, had to be paid on Saturday night or starve. Subcontractors might starve too, but they could be held at bay much more easily than a regular workforce, who had to be paid even when there was no trade, as the nurseryman Thomas Greening found in 1740. 'Trade is so bad', he wrote to his father, 'that I have not maid so much out of the nursery as will pay the workmen's labour.' Payment to a poor artisan or food retailer could be put off much longer than payment to a rich linen-draper, who would think nothing of the cost of going to court, while payment to some people could be put off almost indefinitely, such as the money due on bond to an aunt or legacies from a grandfather due to one's children.[44]

Price as well as cost could be adjusted, for, although some dealers faced situations of near-perfect competition, this was certainly not true of all traders. 'The price that the merchant sets upon his wares is by reckoning prime cost, charges and interest,' wrote Barbon, a simplistic cost-plus approach which may have been common but was certainly not universal. London was a much more aggressively competitive place than that, as Barbon, one of the sharpest businessmen of his day, certainly knew. Defoe complained bitterly about the price-cutting policy of the rich which undermined the cosy small shopkeepers for whom he wrote so many of his books. "Tis fatal to the poorer and little dealers about him; for they stand still, with their fingers in their mouths, as we call it, or walk about at their shop doors and have nothing to do, while they see all the trade run in the great channel of their neighbouring alderman's shop; who gives large credit at a ready-money price, or sells for ready money ten per cent cheaper than they can.'[45]

Price-cutting there certainly was – one good reason for the growth of the market – but the aggressive instincts of the price-cutter were shadowed by the defensive strategy of the monopolist. Where demand was inelastic and the number of suppliers small, there was likely sooner or later to be a ring. There is, for instance, a record of a ring amongst the manufacturers of copperas, a product sometimes called green vitriol which was used in dyeing, tanning and ink manufacture. The ring consisted of sixteen individuals or partnerships who controlled between them all twenty works supplying the metropolis. Their objective was to raise prices by reducing output but, then as now, it was not always easy to reach agreement. 'It is difficult to bring so many men to be of one mind be it ever so much for thare own good or profitt as we are assured this will when it is brought to a conclution,' sentiments familiar to those who have attempted to engage in restrictive trade practices. Such trade associations were not necessarily restrictive in the modern sense. Much of foreign trade was organized by regulated companies whose main functions, apart from keeping outsiders out, were collecting information, organizing shipping, negotiating with foreign governments and lobbying at home. Less formal organizations existed for other trades. Alison Olson has described the activities of the 'Virginia merchants', who were already well organized as an interest group by 1670, their mutuality assisted by the Virginia Walk on the Exchange and the Virginia Coffeehouse where they held their meetings to discuss lobbying parliament and other bodies on such subjects as taxation or convoying.[46]

Similar associations grew up for other overseas trades, but the interest group was not confined to merchants. Much of the work of the Livery Companies was of a similar nature, while this book has made much use of petitions sent to parliament by such groups as the 'Licensed Hackney Chairmen' or the 'Midling and Poorer Sort of Master Shoemakers'. Such activities required organization, meetings, agenda, minutes and so on, and were another aspect of the passion for clubs and societies which was a characteristic of the period. There is the agenda for a meeting of one such trade association, 'the dealers in tea', in the papers of Henry Gambier. The main business, not very surprisingly, was: '4. That the present execution of the laws of excise are a very great grievance.'[47]

One function of interest groups was to assist their members through the dissemination of information, but this was something that every businessman had to gather for himself if he was to survive for very long in the trading world. Published commercial information was growing in scope but was still thin on the ground and, in any case, what most tradesmen wanted was something exclusive to themselves. Every merchant and wholesaler therefore needed to establish a network of correspondents who could provide commercial and political intelligence, make sales and purchases, and assist in the vital business of remitting money over long distances.

Several letter-books have survived, which enable one to see such networks in operation. Between August 1686 and December 1688, for instance, the merchant Thomas Palmer shipped over £10,000 worth of cloth, tin and lead in twenty-eight consignments, mostly to Levantine ports. To support this operation, he sent 127 letters, over half of them to his factors and correspondents in Constantinople, Aleppo and Smyrna and in Cyprus, where he bought cotton as a return cargo. However, nearly a third of his letters went to the Italian cities of Venice, Genoa, Livorno and Messina, important centres of information on Mediterranean trade as a whole, but even more important as the residence of bill-brokers through whom payments could be arranged. A similar pattern can be seen in the letter-book of Michael Mitford, a Russian and Baltic merchant. He wrote to his agents in Moscow, Danzig and Konigsberg, to correspondents in many east and south coast English ports, but also to Amsterdam and Hamburg, where he acquired bills to settle his Baltic debts.[48]

It is difficult to find letter-books for wholesalers, but it is clear from the jumbled collections of letters that have survived that they too were eager correspondents. Some wholesalers traded throughout England, but most specialized in particular regions and their correspondence networks were often based on an extended kin network.[49] In such correspondence, one finds the same urgent need as in international commerce for information on prices and markets and on the credit-worthiness of customers, with just the occasional polite enquiry after a correspondent's health or a little bit of home news. One is struck, too, by the dominating influence of the seasons in trade and business generally. There was a season to sell gloves and a season to buy butter, goose quills or linen, while it was a waste of time trying to borrow from a grazier in February when he needed his money to stock his land. At the beginning of winter when he sold much of his cattle it might well be a different matter. [50]

Commercial correspondence also illustrates just how serious a problem remittance was in the days before a national banking and chequeing system. Quite a lot of business was still done by barter. Much of the Levant trade, for instance, consisted of the barter of broadcloth for raw silk, while, in the money-scarce world of the north of England, it was a question of finding the right purchasing medium with which to enter the market. 'I believe ye Spanish lamb wool may command felts sooner than fine hats will do.'[51] However, most business was done for money and arranging for payment could be a major task. Many wholesalers went down into the country to collect their debts in person from their customers and the seasonal fairs continued to play an important part in this activity. Nevertheless, an increasing proportion of business involved remittance through the medium of some sort of paper rather than through the shipment of bags of specie.

The international bill of exchange had been in use for centuries and played a vital role in the settlement of merchants' accounts, while inland bills were increasingly used from the middle of the seventeenth century. Merchant practice was always ahead of a power in law to enforce that practice, but our period sees some major legal changes which made the use of bills and promissory notes, the two main forms of deferred payment, very much easier and safer, so that merchants did not have to rely so much on the honour of their correspondents. A key date was 1666, when a judgment in the case of Woodward v. Rowe declared that 'the law merchant was part of the law of the land' and so allowed centuries of international custom relating to bills to become part of the English common law. By the end of the century, further legal judgments had determined the liability of the indorsers of bills and so made them truly negotiable, while an Act of 1704 confirmed the negotiability of promissory notes. Such changes, which enormously increased the effective money supply, were very much part of the legal spirit of the age, which in hundreds of large and small ways made the life of the businessman easier and property safer.[52]

The improved status of bills and notes in law did not solve all problems, since it was still necessary to arrange for someone to accept one's bills in London and vice versa, and a large proportion of all commercial correspondence is on this subject. As the trade of the provinces with London expanded, so did patterns of remittance emerge to ease the problem. Provincial merchants and manufacturers who sold in the London market played a key part in this, since they had money due to them in the metropolis and so could sell their 'bills on London' to their neighbours who needed to make payment there. Butchers and graziers were important in such remittance business, as were the country cloth manufacturers. The Huguenot David Compigne, for instance, a Wiltshire grocer and customer of Henry Gambier, a London tea and coffee dealer, was able to pay for some of his supplies by buying the bills of the West Country clothiers drawn on Blackwell Hall Factors in London. These could then be remitted to Gambier, who could present them for payment. Nevertheless, such networks could break down and alternative and less safe methods of payment had to be found. 'Les billes sont bien difisille a trouver,' Compigne wrote in June 1730. 'Je vous envoieray un billet de cent pieces [i.e. a Bank of England note for £100].'[53]

Such problems were not so great within London itself, where payment could be made at a periodic 'accounting' when the balance accumulated in book debts would be paid in cash. Nevertheless, payment and remittance were major problems for contemporary businessmen, just one more headache for people struggling with the problem of ensuring that they actually did make a profitable bargain in this difficult world of seasons, cash flows, 'breaking times' and other hazards. In the next section, an attempt is made to determine just how much profit people did make, not an easy question to answer but one that should be addressed in order to get some idea of how middling people accumulated and improved themselves.

v Profit and Accumulation

It is often thought that people made very high profits in the past, particularly in foreign trade and especially in its more notorious branches such as the slave trade. The evidence for this is often simply assertion either by a contemporary or by a modern historian or polemicist with an axe to grind. Real evidence of the rate of profit is difficult to obtain, partly because few business papers have survived and partly because contemporaries were not particularly interested in 'profit' in the economist's sense of the net annual rate of return on capital.

Most people were more interested in accumulation than in annual profits and some attempted to calculate this from time to time. Once a year, or at more uneven intervals, they would value all their assets, deduct their liabilities and arrive at a new figure for their 'stock', a process which amalgamated house-keeping and shopkeeping gains and losses, normally counted bad debts as assets and made no pretence at estimating a return on capital. Even those who kept really good accounts in double entry did not distinguish in their profit and loss accounts between business capital and total assets or between business and household expenses. 'There is scant evidence of any attempts at a precise calculation of profits and capital, or of any general endeavour to systematize and to refine the calculation of capital or profits,' writes an expert on the history of accounting.[54]

In such circumstances it is obviously difficult to calculate an average rate of profit. Commentators quite often referred to the average turnover of a business and sometimes related this to what the trader 'got' or 'got clear' from his business, an ambiguous concept which presumably meant the profit on turnover but which took no account of overheads or capital costs. A witness in 1696, for instance, thought that the owner of a public-house who 'took 40 or 50 shillings a day . . . could not gett less than £100 a year'. If his turnover on the basis of 300 days is taken as £675, then the return is about 15 per cent, though the exact meaning of 'gett' remains unclear. The business of pastry-cook seems to have been more profitable than the drink trade, even in 1697, a year when we are told that fruit, sugar and flour were very dear. Ayliffe White was said to take £200 a year or 12s. a day from his trade and his 'profitts' were estimated at 'above a fourth part of ye said summe in a year'. Another case concerned John Tarry, who sold strong waters, mainly wholesale. His business was said to be taking between £12 and £20 a day or about £5000 a year, from which witnesses estimated that Tarry 'does clearly gett ye sume of £300 a year', a rate of profit on turnover of only 6 per cent. This seems a low return for someone whom witnesses described as doing well, and what was meant by 'does clearly gett' was probably the amount that Tarry accumulated clear of all his household expenses in a year.[55]

Rates of profit on turnover can also be discovered in account books, many of which kept separate accounts for each trading venture, thus making calculation relatively easy. Such 'profits' were also generalized by contemporaries into statements that the normal profits in some particular trade were, say, 9 to 10 per cent on wool sales or 50 to 100 per cent in the China trade, to take two late-seventeenth-century examples.[56] These examples suggest a wide range, but profits on turnover in overseas trade normally seem to have been somewhere between 10 and 25 per cent, some individual transactions or risky trades providing much higher returns and many of course showing losses. In a business world increasingly characterized by free competition, it seems unlikely that much higher profits could have been kept secret for long from newcomers eager to enjoy them for themselves.

When profit on business overall is looked at, the accounting problems mentioned above are encountered. In an article published in 1969, Richard Grassby wrestled with these problems and came up with a set of data which is convincing and not very likely to be improved on. He collected profits and rates of accumulation from surviving account books and the published comments of contemporaries, and, although these naturally varied very widely, the end result of his enquiries was to suggest that profits were fairly modest. Thus, at one end of the scale, successful merchants were making annual profits of 20 to 30 per cent and sometimes more, while the unsuccessful might be earning from trade less than the 6 per cent which was the maximum legal rate of interest, a rate which Nicolas Barbon said was 'the rule by which the trader makes up the account of profit and loss; the merchant expects by dealing to get more than interest by his goods'. Overall, Grassby suggested that in the period after 1650 'the average returns of a working life in trade probably ranged from 6 to 12 per cent'.[57]

Grassby's examples nearly all refer to overseas traders. Other occupations provide much less information since hardly any of their account books have survived and contemporaries were much less interested in the profits of publicans and shopkeepers than in those of merchants. One suspects, however, that the normal profits of such lesser men must have been much greater than those of merchants; indeed, if they had not been, it seems unlikely that they could have accumulated at all, since their living expenses would have absorbed all their profits. This can be shown by examining the articles of agreement of five partnerships – two goldsmiths' businesses, a grocer, a mercer and a saddler. These all provided for individual partners to draw 'for their owne private and particular expenses' sums ranging from £78 to £234 a year. If these businesses had only been making profits of 12 per cent, at the top end of Grassby's range, then the partners' drawings would have exceeded the profits in three cases and only in one, the mercer's business, would there have been as much as £100 a year addition to the joint stock.[58]

The stock of these businesses did in fact grow over time, so it must be assumed that their profits were considerably higher than those of the average merchant, perhaps in the range of 15 to 30 per cent. Some indication that this is roughly the right range is given from evidence provided by pawnbrokers in 1745. They claimed that their profits were 'not superior, if equal, to those of other middling tradesmen' and with remarkable unanimity stated that their gross profits on their 'whole capital' were 16 or 17 per cent per annum. However, living expenses would have taken a higher proportion of profits for most 'middling tradesmen' than for merchants, since these expenses were income inelastic, the result being that it was easier for a rich merchant to accumulate than it was for a poor shopkeeper, even though the latter's profits might have been considerably higher.[59] For example, a merchant with a capital of £10,000 who made profits of 10 per cent and spent £500 per annum would have accumulated another £8000 in ten years. A shopkeeper with a capital of £1000 who made profits of 25 per cent and spent £200 per annum would accumulate faster but would still only be worth £2650 after ten years' trading. He would be dead long before he caught the merchant up.

It was of course possible for our hypothetical shopkeeper to pinch and scrape and spend much less, and this is what the writers of contemporary treatises urged him to do. If, for instance, he only spent £50 a year instead of £200, he would be worth £2650 in five years instead of ten. However, it was difficult to keep this sort of thing up, since the acquisition of riches nearly always tempted people to use them to improve their image in the eyes of the world. 'The hope of rising in life makes a man a mighty producer and accumulator of riches', as Alfred Marshall wrote, but the passage continues, 'unless indeed he is in too great a hurry to grasp the social position which his wealth will give him.'[60] Most men in Augustan London were in too great a hurry and so the pace of accumulation was not particularly rapid.

It follows that most rich men must have been already rich or at least reasonably well off when they were 'young beginners', though there were exceptions such as Sir Dudley North, who

TABLE 4.7: Influence of Age at Death on Fortune

	Age at Death				
Fortune at Death	Under 30 %	30–39 %	40–49 %	50–59 %	60 & over %
Less than £2000	88	73	56	46	19
£2000–£4999	12	20	26	23	35
£5000 & over	0	7	18	31	46
	100	100	100	100	100
Number of cases	17	107	131	83	37

Source: Linked sample.

turned £100 into a fortune of £40,000. However, North is in many ways the exception which proves the rule since his overall trading profit in the prosperous 1680s was only 3¼ per cent and he 'made his initial fortune by usury and earned more by his marriage than from a lifetime in trade'. Many other great fortunes were acquired by usury, either by lending to government and courtiers at exorbitant rates or by taking advantage of the absence of an effective loan market in a foreign country, as did North, whose profits from usury were made in the Ottoman Empire where rates of interest were from two to four times those in England. Marriage was an even more effective agent of accumulation for the generality of middling people, most marriages being based on 'equality of fortune', an expression which meant that in many cases the dowry would double the citizen's wealth.[61] However, once again, it was usually rich young men who attracted rich dowries and so one has to conclude that the best way to wealth in Augustan London, as in most places, was to have a rich father.

The other important thing was to stay alive. Whether the businessman accumulated at 5, 10 or 25 per cent, it is reasonable to assume that he would accumulate more the longer he lived. This principle is illustrated in Table 4.7 above by cross-tabulating the age and fortune at death of the sample. The distribution satisfies the common sense hypothesis above; on average, businessmen got richer as they got older. Such a process was cumulative, since those who died older and richer could provide larger portions for their sons, who would then start the accumulation process at an advantage. It will be seen later that middle-class Londoners lived longer in the eighteenth century than in the seventeenth and, as a result, they got richer and provided their children with bigger portions which enabled them to get richer still. Since these children were also more likely to follow their fathers into business in the eighteenth century than in previous times, it is easy to see how even modest rates of profit and accumulation enabled London to become the immensely wealthy city that it was in the second half of the eighteenth century.[62]

5 Investment

Money-making has so far been considered in terms of the active conduct of a business. However, running a business was only one way in which to make a living and accumulate property. Many people lived entirely on income from loans and other investments, while many others placed varying proportions of their capital into investment assets. Investment required less management and was an attractive way to employ one's wealth, since the returns could well be comparable to those earned running a shop and might exceed the profits from a mercantile business. They were certainly more easily earned. In this chapter, the role of investment in the affairs of the middle station is examined, starting with investments recorded in inventories of personal estate.

i Personal Estate

When the inventories of the sample were analysed in the last chapter, it was found that just over a third of all assets were in the form of investments, a fairly high proportion, which suggests that passive investment as opposed to active business was an important feature of the monetary activities of the middling people. This proportion was also seen to vary considerably between different occupational groups. Rentiers and money-lenders invested the most, as one might expect, investing on average over 88 per cent of their assets. Another group investing well above the average were apothecaries, with over 46 per cent, and other professional people probably came somewhere in between these two high investing groups. Merchants were the richest occupational group in London, and so were important in investment as they were important in everything else, but the proportion of their assets invested was the same as the sample as a whole, just over 35 per cent. Finally, two groups were identified who were investing considerably below the average, textile retailers and textile wholesalers, both of whom invested less than 20 per cent of their assets. This low proportion was probably true of most other wholesalers and retailers, whose need to have much of their assets tied up in stock in trade and trade credit meant that they had little available to invest until they decided to retire from active business.[1]

Age as well as occupation had an influence on investment. Table 5.1 opposite shows that people tended to invest more as they got older, and this is explored further in Table 5.2 opposite. For young men the relationship is fairly clear cut. About two-thirds of all those who died in their twenties and thirties have 20 per cent or less invested and very few people in these age groups have large percentages invested. For older men the situation is more complex. About a third of those who died in their fifties and sixties have over 60 per cent of their assets invested, but roughly the same proportion have only 20 per cent or less invested. Nevertheless, it is clear that men tended to invest more as they got older. They also tended to borrow less as they built up their capital. There was then something which might be called an investment cycle. Young men tended to be net borrowers. As they grew older, they tended to become net lenders and to invest a higher and higher proportion of their assets outside their business. This process of accelerated investment seems to begin when the businessman is in his forties, after some twenty years of business activity.[2]

Such an investment cycle implies that, other things being equal, the volume of investment is likely to be affected by the expectation of life of the business community. If businessmen tend to die young, as they did in the 1670s and 1680s,[3] then fewer men will pass from the borrowing to the lending stage of the investment cycle and fewer will live to become retired men lending all or a high proportion of their assets to other businessmen, the general public or the government. Improvements in life expectancy were to change all this and are an important factor to remember when one tries to understand the ease with which money was raised for war, economic improvement and general business activity in the 1690s and the eighteenth century. It was, quite simply, a period when far

TABLE 5.1: Investment Proportions and Age at Death

% of Gross Assets Invested	No. of Cases		Ave. Age of Case	
	No.	%	Mean	Median
None	84	22.4	40.5	38
1–20%	98	26.1	42.8	41
21–40%	70	18.7	44.3	45
41–60%	51	13.6	48.8	48
61–80%	37	9.9	49.4	48
81–100%	35	9.3	50.3	50
	375	100.0		

TABLE 5.2: Percentage of Assets Invested by Age Groups

% of Assets Invested	Age at Death				
	Under 30	30–39	40–49	50–59	60 & over
None	47	33	18	10	10
1–20%	18	36	33	19	22
21–40%	24	17	16	25	8
41–60%	6	7	14	16	27
61–80%	5	4	8	16	11
81–100%	0	3	11	14	22
	100	100	100	100	100
Number of cases	17	107	131	83	37

Source: Inventories of sample. Assets do not include domestic goods, jewellery and plate.

more businessmen were reaching those ages when they were accustomed to invest a higher proportion of their assets outside their own immediate business.

What sort of investments did the middle station make? Table 5.3 overleaf shows the distribution of investments between a number of sub-groups before and after 1690. The first thing to note is the dominant position held by loans throughout the period, two-fifths of all investment taking this form.[4] Historians have concentrated on change rather than continuity in studies of investment and, as a result, have tended to neglect the more prosaic forms of finance. However, the results in the table should not be a surprise. Lending to relatives, fellow citizens

TABLE 5.3: Distribution of Investment Assets

Type of Investment	1665–89 %	1690–1720 %
Loans and mortgages	44.4	40.5
Leases	22.2	8.7
Government debt	3.4	12.0
Company stocks and bonds	24.0	35.6
Shipping	6.0	3.2
	100.0	100.0
Number of cases	211	164

Source: Inventories of sample.

and the West End gentry is very much what one would expect the middling people to do with their savings. The assessment of other people's credit status was one of the first things a tradesman had to learn and to move from giving trade credit to lending as a rentier would have been a natural progression for him.

The second feature which stands out in Table 5.3 is the rising share of investment taken by government debt and company stocks and bonds in the period of so-called Financial Revolution after 1690.[5] Government debt nearly quadruples, while the two types of investment together rise from 27.4 to 47.6 per cent, an increase sufficiently dramatic to allow the revolutionary label to stand. This proportionate increase naturally affects all the other groups, but is mainly at the expense of investment in shipping, which was no doubt less attractive in wartime, and investment in leases, which had been particularly high in the earlier period when a property boom involved not only rebuilding after the Great Fire but also development of both the East and West Ends.

It would be wrong, however, to adopt the convenient hypothesis that it was money previously invested in leasehold property which was available after 1690 to fund the Financial Revolution.[6] There were in fact two separate investment markets and two separate types of investor in London, a distinction which survives throughout the period. The first comprised the great bulk of the citizenry and concentrated on loans and leases. The

TABLE 5.4: Numbers Investing in Different Types of Asset

Type of Asset	Number	% of Sample
Loans and mortgages	221	58.9
Leases	173	53.9
Government debt	62	16.5
Company stocks and bonds	55	14.7
Shipping	52	13.9

Number in sample = 375

TABLE 5.5: Percentage Investing in Different Assets by Wealth Groups

Wealth	Any Asset	Loans	Leases	Govt	Co.	Ships	Sample Size
Under £500	52.9	36.5	30.8	2.9	1.0	1.9	104
£500–£999	91.5	55.3	70.2	6.4	2.1	6.4	47
£1000–£1999	85.2	65.6	49.2	11.5	6.6	4.9	61
£2000–£4999	90.0	72.2	48.9	18.9	13.3	15.6	90
£5000–£9999	94.7	71.1	44.7	42.1	26.3	36.8	38
£10,000 & over	94.3	71.4	48.6	45.7	74.3	45.7	35

Source: Inventories of sample. The percentages are those of each wealth group who had any amount of a particular asset listed in their inventory, i.e. 52.9 per cent of those worth under £500 had some investment listed and 74.3 per cent of those with £10,000 or over had company stocks or bonds listed.

second consisted of what Dickson has called the 'mercantile bourgeoisie', who concentrated on government debt, company stocks and bonds and shipping, this group remaining distinct well into the Victorian age, by which time they had become 'the City'. These two investment markets can be shown in two ways. Table 5.4 above presents the number of people investing in the five different types of asset. It can be seen at once that there is a striking difference between the numbers investing in loans and leases and in the other three types of asset. Table 5.5 takes this distinction further by tabulating the proportion in different wealth groups who held some of their assets in each of the different types of security. This shows that few people worth less than £1000 held any other asset but leases and loans and

that the wealthy invested in everything but completely dominated investment in government debt, shipping and company
stocks and bonds, especially the last.

The relative lack of interest of the wealthy in leasehold
property is surprising, since it was potentially a profitable field,
giving gross returns of between 8 and 13 per cent.[7] Three main
groups of leaseholders can be distinguished. The first and most
numerous were those whose only leaseholding was their own
dwelling-house, together with adjacent property relevant to
their business, such as warehouses, breweries, yards, etc. The
second group were those who invested in property which they
sublet to provide a rentier income. This, together with money-
lending, was the favourite investment of the small shopkeeper,
though all types of businessmen and many women were represented in this market. The third group were the developers and
speculators, the typical developer being a member of one of the
building trades, though property speculation also attracted
many people unconnected with building. The two biggest
leaseholders in the sample were Levant merchants, James
Birkin who had £7797 invested, mainly in Mincing Lane, and
George Treadway who had £13,599 laid out in an estate in
Hammersmith in partnership with his father-in-law. Other big
developers include a cloth-finisher with £3000 invested in
'several tofts of ground in Lothbury with several houses built
and some ground unbuilt', a cabinet-maker who built ten
houses in the area of the Strand and Fleet Street, a grocer with
thirty-eight houses in the East End and many others. Anyone
with money or credit and the optimism engendered by a
booming property market might plunge into the development
business. Most flourished, even if some struggled a bit, like the
button-seller Gilbert Savill, whose investment of £1200 in the
rebuilding of Wood Street was nearly swallowed up by outstanding mortgages on the newly erected property. But, with a
potential profit of twice the rate of interest, no one minded
borrowing to develop and the market in mortgages of London
leasehold property was a very active one in the second half of
the seventeenth century.[8]

While men of any occupation could be found in the loan and
lease markets, the same could not be said for the other main

types of investment. Shipping shares were held almost exclusively by merchants, mariners, shipbuilders and suppliers of equipment for ships.[9] Investment in company stocks and bonds was also fairly exclusive, being reserved mainly for the wealthy, particularly wealthy merchants, though more people were drawn in as a wider range of joint-stock securities became available. Before 1690, only fifteen men in the sample (7 per cent) held investments in company stocks and bonds, and they were very rich indeed, with a median fortune of over £19,000 compared with a median of £1353 for the sample as a whole in this period. After 1690, the scene changes a bit. Forty men (24 per cent) had investments in company stocks and bonds and, although they remain rich, their median fortune comes down to £7850 compared with £2076 for the sample as a whole. The increasing spread of investors is particularly marked after 1700, when the New East India Company and the South Sea Company drew new men into the joint-stock investment market.

Investment in the Bank of England, however, reflects very much the old type of mercantile bourgeoisie. Just over 10 per cent of those who died after its foundation in 1694 held Bank of England stocks and these included seven merchants, three rich rentiers, a mercer, a jeweller and an upholsterer. These last three relatively humble men are the only investors with stakes of less then £1000. Investment in the Bank and the East India Company was characterized by a few very big holdings which dominate the total. In the whole sample, there were twelve investments in companies of over £5000 – seven in the East India Company, four in the Bank of England and one in the South Sea Company. Together these twelve holdings, which were held by nine men, all merchants or rich rentiers, accounted for 63.5 per cent of all investments in company stocks and bonds.

Finally, there are the investors in government debt, and here it is necessary to distinguish between short-term debt (60 per cent of the total) and those who invested in the lotteries and annuities which formed the innovatory long-term debt (40 per cent).[10] Short-term government debt was clearly perceived as a branch of the normal loan market. In the period after 1690, there were twenty-nine men (17.5 per cent) who invested in the wide range of short-term government paper. They tended to be fairly well off, but otherwise reflect the general run of the sample. A paper-seller with £157 in Exchequer Bills and £54 in Malt tickets or a grocer with £500 in tallies would be typical examples, though there were also some very big investors in this field, such as Peter Vansittart, who had over £15,000 invested in a variety of government short-term debt.

While the short-term debt tended to be held by a wide variety of citizens, the long-term debt remained a prerogative of the mercantile bourgeoisie until the very end of our period. One would have thought that government annuities carrying interest of up to 14 per cent for ninety-nine years would have been an attractive investment for the citizens in general, a group who were certainly very interested in providing for their children. The sample, however, suggests that such was not the case. The first man with government annuities in his inventory was Francis March, a Levant merchant who died in 1697. There were nine others, 8 per cent of the remainder of the sample. They were all rich, mainly elderly, and were all either merchants or rentiers except Benjamin Boultby, a soapmaker worth over £8000, and Richard Blundell, a surgeon who died in 1718 worth just under £10,000.

The same pattern is found initially amongst the holders of government lottery tickets, again rather surprisingly since the terms were very attractive.[11] The Million Lottery of 1694 entitled all those who purchased one of the £10 tickets 'to an annuity of one Pound or (by chance) to a greater yearly sum for sixteen yeares'. In other words, you were bound to get £16 back for your £10 investment and the holders of 'fortunate' tickets got from £10 up to £1000 a year for sixteen years, though these annuities were difficult to collect as the government ran into financial troubles later in the 1690s. However, the citizenry as a whole seem to have been suspicious of the innovation and there are just six men whose inventories mentioned Million Lottery tickets, roughly one in ten of those who died between 1694 and 1703, when the last holder of a ticket in this lottery died. All six were merchants and only one had a fortune of less than £10,000.

However, the picture changes with the lotteries in the latter years of Queen Anne's reign. Starting with Edward Hancock, who died in 1710 with lottery tickets valued at £35, it is found that one in three of the rest of the sample held lottery tickets. This group included a wide range of occupations, such as apothecary, leather-seller and printer, as well as merchants and rentiers. One man, Caleb Booth, a soapmaker who died in 1713, had nearly a third of his total assets invested in the Lotteries of 1712 and 1713. It is clear that by this date the government lotteries had become well established and very popular, and one often comes across anxious enquiries about the results of the draws in the correspondence of the period. Winning could set you up for life. The first prizes in the 'First Classis' and 'Second Classis' lotteries of 1711 and 1712 were £20,000, which were won by a merchant of Gray's Inn and a widow of St Bride's respectively.[12]

It seems reasonable to conclude that there was a tendency for investment in both joint-stock companies and long-term government debt to filter down slowly from the 'mercantile bourgeoisie' to the citizenry as a whole, but that this process had not gone very far by the end of our period.[13] Most investment in these fields remained the preserve of the élite members of the middle station, many of whom by the end of the period had well-balanced portfolios of what were increasingly seen as very attractive investments. John Brookes, a merchant who died in 1712, is a good example of such men of the Financial Revolution. Brookes rented a town house in Cheapside and a second home in Hackney, but he owned no real estate nor leases. About 30 per cent of his assets were in domestic goods, jewellery and plate and in the mercantile business which he ran in partnership with his brother. All the rest of his assets (£23,384) were invested in government debt and in company stocks and bonds. He had capital stock worth a total of £12,642 in the Royal African Company, the Sword Blade Company, the United East India Company, the Bank of England and the South Sea Company. He owned bonds of the Sword Blade Company and the East India Company worth £3500. He had lottery investments worh £2076 and annuities worth £4600. He had £239 in Exchequer Bills, £138 in the stock of the Russia Tobacco Company and a share in a lead mine which was valued at £189.[14] No one else in the sample had quite such a wide range of securities, but the inventory of John Brookes is a pointer to the future. The days of stocks and shares had arrived. Nevertheless, investment in ordinary loans and leases still accounted for nearly half of all investments made by men in the sample who died after 1690, and such investments continued to be the only investments made by the great majority of small businessmen.

ii Real Estate

One would not expect to find all of the investment made by the London middle class in an inventory of personal estate, for the citizens in general and merchants in particular have traditionally been thought of as major investors in real estate. Indeed, the dream of owning a landed estate and becoming a country gentleman has been seen as one of the major motivations of the middling sort of people. Contemporaries certainly emphasized this sort of behaviour. Sir William Coventry observed in 1667 that as soon as an English merchant 'has a good stock of money, he presently buys an estate', a remark echoed by B.L. de Muralt, who was in England in the 1690s: 'No sooner do they [English merchants] acquire wealth, but they quit traffick, and turn country gentlemen.' Such behaviour was approved in the 1720s by Defoe, who thought that those who became rich should quit business to make room for younger men: 'When a rich tradesman leaves off with say £20,000 he should buy rents, save half his income of £1000 and thus grow richer.'[15]

Here Defoe assumed, as did most of his contemporaries, that the return on investment in land was 5 per cent, which by the 1720s was the same as the maximum interest allowed on loans. However, this was a gross return. The net return was much lower and compared unfavourably with almost any other form of investment, as Lord Hervey noted in 1707: 'How much better money yields than land, which after taxes and repairs allowed never answers above three per cent.'[16] This observation must make it questionable whether there was quite such a massive investment in land by the business community as contemporary comment suggests. In this section, then, an attempt will be made to estimate the value and type of real estate held by the sample and to compare this with their holdings of other types of investment.

This exercise poses problems since real estate was not of course included in listings of personal estate. However, sufficient clues can be got from inventories, wills and other sources to obtain a fairly good idea of real estate holdings.[17] These make it possible to say that, at a minimum, ninety-four men in the sample (25 per cent) had some real estate; these holdings are listed in Appendix B. The sources provide a valuation or a rental only in a minority of cases; for the rest, there is simply a very general description of the property involved. In order to get some idea of the type and value of real property owned by Londoners, these descriptions and such valuations as exist have been used to grade all the holdings on a five-point scale. This procedure is fairly arbitrary, but it does enable a distinction to be made between a couple of houses in Southwark and a major landed estate in Lincolnshire, to take two examples which were graded 1 and 5. The distribution of real estate on this basis, together with the valuations attached to each grade, is shown in Table 5.6 overleaf. The main point to make here is that there were not many really large holdings of real estate; only eighteen men were estimated to have property worth £2000 to £5000 and only eight had estates worth more than £5000. Since there are seventy-three men in the sample with personal estate worth over £5000 and thirty-five worth over £10,000, one can conclude that the acquisition of a large real estate was not an all-consuming passion for the business community.

The valuation process was taken a stage further by attaching a single value to each grade of real estate. This enables a valuation of real estate to be compared with the other five types of investment asset, as is done in Table 5.7 overleaf. The estimation process used here is very rough and ready but is sufficiently robust to enable one to get some idea of the importance of real estate to the London investor. It was clearly of considerable significance, coming third in importance after loans and mortgages and company stocks and bonds. However, it hardly dominates investment; even if some of the real estate has been missed or undervalued, it is unlikely to exceed a quarter or at most a third of all investment.

Owners of real estate were a little older than the average of the sample and they tended to be a little richer. Nearly half the merchants, for instance, owned some real estate but only a

TABLE 5.6: Distribution of Real Estate by Estimated Value

Valuation of Real Estate	Number	%
Grade 1 (less than £300)	9	9.6
Grade 2 (£300–£999)	36	38.3
Grade 3 (£1000–£1999)	23	24.5
Grade 4 (£2000–£5000)	18	19.1
Grade 5 (over £5000)	8	8.5
	94	100.0

Total in sample = 375

Source: See note 17, p. 368, and Appendix B, p. 405.

TABLE 5.7: Distribution of Investment Assets (inc. Real Estate)

Type of Investment	% of All Investment
Loans and mortgages	33.3
Leases	11.2
Government debt	6.8
Company stocks and bonds	24.4
Shipping	3.4
Real estate	20.9
	100.0

Source: For other investments see Table 5.3 (p. 146) for real estate see Table 5.6 above. The five grades were valued as follows: 1 = £200, 2 = £750, 3 = £1500, 4 = £3500, 5 = £7000.

quarter of the whole sample. But one should not exaggerate such patterns, which were true of investors overall, whatever the asset. Since many Londoners were of country origin, much real estate was acquired by inheritance as the family farm or part of the family lands descended to them. Other land was acquired as a wife's dowry or was purchased to provide her with a jointure and the owners of such land were likely to be young men when they acquired it. Nor is the value of personal estate a particularly good indication of who will or will not own real estate. Several very wealthy merchants had no real estate at all, as far as can be told from the sources. On the other hand, there were men who were insolvent on personal account but had more than enough real estate to cover their liabilities. Other men who seemed quite poor from the inventory of their personal estate turned out to be wealthy when real estate is taken into account, such as the salter Richard Langhorne, whose personal estate was valued at £324 but whose real estate in Lincolnshire was worth at least £3000.[18]

Table 5.8 overleaf provides some statistical clothing for these generalizations about the ownership of real estate. The table certainly shows that the rich owned more real estate than the poor, but it also shows that three out of five men in both the highest wealth groups had no real estate at all. The diversity of ownership can be seen by looking at the twenty-six men who are estimated to have had real estate worth over £2000. They include ten merchants, six haberdashers and drapers, two men in the book trade, a silkman, a builder, a salter, a tavern-keeper, a trunk-maker, a druggist, a money-lender and an elderly rentier. They do not include ten of the twelve men with over £20,000 in personal estate, eight of whom had no real estate at all. By this date, there was no need for a wealthy Londoner to invest in low-yielding real estate, if indeed there ever had been.

Table 5.9 overleaf provides some clues to the type of real property owned by Londoners, the item 'Suburban or villa estate' referring to the growing rash of small estates in places just outside London, such as Tottenham, Highgate and Leyton.[19] It can be seen that much real estate was really no more than an extension of the leasehold market which has already been discussed. Any one of the top three types of estate listed might be held either as real or personal estate, a fact which makes the distinction between them rather unrealistic. It can also be seen that much real estate was urban or suburban and had little to do with the conventional view of Londoners buying country estates and setting up as landed gentlemen. In fact, about one-third of the real estate was in London and Middlesex and another third in the other south-eastern counties. Where citizens did own property further afield there were quite often special reasons which help to explain the investment. Peter Short was the son of a Doncaster clothier and his own huge business as a wholesale haberdasher was concentrated in Yorkshire and the East Midlands. His regional interests help to

TABLE 5.8: Distribution of Real Estate by Wealth Groups

(Percentage of Sample)

Wealth	Any Real	Real over £2000	Real over £5000	Number
Under £1000	16.6	0.7	0.0	151
£1000–£1999	21.3	1.6	0.0	61
£2000–£4999	28.9	7.8	0.0	90
£5000–£9999	42.1	21.0	10.5	38
Over £10,000	40.0	25.7	11.4	35
				375

Source: Real estate as in Table 5.6 (p. 154). Wealth from inventories.

TABLE 5.9: Types of Real Estate

Types of Property	Numbers owning	%
A. London property	39	33.3
B. Suburban or villa property	16	13.7
C. Provincial urban property	4	3.4
D. One or two farms	23	19.7
E. Larger country estates	35	29.9
	117	100.0

Source: See note 17, p 368, and Appendix B, p. 405, for brief descriptions of the real estate included under these five headings. The total of properties is greater than the number of real estate owners, since several men owned more than one type of property.

explain his decision to purchase a large real estate based on Easter Keale in Lincolnshire, where he died in 1680. Another fairly large estate in Lincolnshire was owned by Richard Langhorne, who was born in the county and acquired his estate by dowry and inheritance. Sir William Hedges, East India merchant and director of the Bank of England, was born in Cork, which explains his ownership of 'my land and estate called the Plowlands of Cloyne Preist, County Corke and Signiorie of Inchequine'. Such examples do not mean that nobody used their London wealth to transform themselves and their descendants into landed gentry. Many citizens did just that and Defoe, among others, has lovingly documented examples of such upward social mobility by successful Londoners. However, the findings of this study suggest that such behaviour was unusual.[20]

Real estate played an important part in investment behaviour but it was investment in London itself, the suburbs and the home counties which was of most interest to the London businessman. Such findings mirror those made by the Stones in their recent book *The Open Elite*.[21] It should, in fact, be expected that a profit-conscious group would invest less in land in the late seventeenth and early eighteenth centuries than they may have done in earlier periods. The later period was one in which the return on land, even including the possibilities of capital gain, must have looked very unattractive compared with the other opportunities open to the investor. It was also a period when there were new and attractive investment assets to be acquired, such as the stocks of joint-stock companies and the long-term government debt, and when the law relating to older types of investment, such as bills and mortgages, had been put on a more secure footing.[22] Land remained an attractive investment, especially if it was in Middlesex, Surrey, Kent, Hertfordshire or Essex, but other assets looked even more attractive to a group who were certainly not blind to the rates of return on their investments.

6 Women and Business

The impression may well have been gained from the previous chapters that business was something that only concerned men. This was by no means entirely true. Men certainly predominated in business, but there was a role for women too, both as a helpmeet to their menfolk, first to their fathers and then to their husbands, and also as the proprietors of independent businesses. Before this is discussed the legal position of women will be briefly looked at in relation to property ownership and trading.

i The Legal Status of Women

By the act of marriage, a woman completely lost her financial independence under English common law, a system which was harsher to the married woman than that of any other European country.[1] In this respect, the legal status of a married woman was in striking contrast to that of a spinster or a widow. A single woman was a *feme sole* and was able to trade, make contracts, sue and be sued in the same way as a man. Many spinsters of the middle station were in a position to benefit from their legal independence, since it was normal for legacies and orphanage portions to be paid to daughters either at marriage or at the age of twenty-one, whichever was earlier. A single woman of twenty-one was thus quite capable, both financially and legally, of setting up in business, and many did so. Some women remained single and thus retained this independence, but the majority married and so became *femes coverts*, a change of status which, as Roxana put it, meant 'giving up liberty, estate, authority, and every-thing, to the man, and the woman was indeed a meer woman ever after, that is to say, a slave'.[2]

Roxana was hardly exaggerating. The legal position of married women in common law was based on the doctrine of conjugal unity, a doctrine neatly summarized by Blackstone when he wrote that 'the husband and wife are one, and the husband is that one'.[3] A woman's property passed to her husband at marriage and she could own no goods, not even her own clothes and jewellery; even the wages earned by working women were by law the property of their husbands. A wife could not sue or be sued, nor could she make a contract as an individual since she had no full legal personality. She could, however, make a contract as her husband's agent or servant – shopping in a world of retail credit would have been difficult otherwise – and the law interpreted this fairly widely. Contracts entered into by a wife for her 'necessary' apparel, diet and lodging were assumed to have been made as her husband's agent, even if he had not explicitly instructed her to make them, a necessary extension of the very limited powers of a *feme covert* if husbands were to be prevented from refusing to pay their wives' shopping bills.[4]

Under common law, it would thus clearly have been impossible for a wife to run a business independently of her husband; the most that she could do was to assist him in his own business as his servant. However, some married women did run their own businesses, despite the common law, for there were two important ways in which wives were able to circumvent its rigidities. The first involved the equitable doctrine of the wife's 'separate estate', which was introduced by the Court of Chancery in Elizabethan times and had become fairly widespread by the Civil War, one authority stating in the 1630s that it was 'no uncommon thing for a wife to have separate property, independent of her husband'. The wife's separate estate was normally created either by a contract entered into by the prospective husband and wife before marriage or by conveying property to friends of the wife, who would hold it in trust for her use. In both cases, it was necessary to gain the consent of the husband, though, by the eighteenth century, a trust set up without consent would stand in equity if it could be shown that it was 'fair and reasonable', on such grounds as the wife being separated from the husband or the husband being a wastrel.[5]

Separate estate enabled at least some wives to own property.

It also presumably meant that they were able to trade independently of their husbands, though in fact there was no need for an innovation in Chancery to allow them to do this, since the custom of London already made provision for married women to trade as individuals and had done so since the middle ages. The custom converted the wife of a freeman from the servile status of *feme covert* into a '*feme sole merchant*' with the legal rights of an independent trader. This privilege was only open to a wife who practised a separate trade from her husband, 'a trade with which her husband does not intermeddle'. Most legal handbooks interpret this as meaning that the wife must practise a distinct trade in the sense that they could not both be vintners or haberdashers, though Bohun says that 'if they both exercise the same trade distinctly by themselves, and not meddle the one with the other, the wife is sole merchant'.[6]

It was, then, possible for a citizen's wife to own property and trade independently of her husband. She would, however, still be a wife and thus liable, both in law and practice, to other constraints. Real independence only came if her husband was dead and it is the rich London widow who has most often caught the attention of historians, just as fortune-hunters sought to catch her attention in the past. A widow, like a spinster, was a *feme sole* and the widow of a successful London businessman was likely to be rich, for common law was much more generous to widows than it was to wives, guaranteeing them one-third of their former husband's personal property, a provision also made by the custom of London. Widows were also allowed to carry on their former husband's trades, the period of marriage being seen as the equivalent of an apprenticeship. The widow as rentier and businesswoman is discussed in the third section of this chapter, but first a look will be taken at the role that wives played in the running of their husband's businesses.

ii Women as Helpmeets

The traditional role of the wife in the English household was as a friend and partner, albeit a junior partner, of her husband. Some tasks, such as running the household, doing the shopping and bringing up young children were more the function of the wife; others, such as running the family business, were more the function of the husband, but this did not mean that the wife should not play an important part in the business side of family life. One reason that Defoe opposed the marriage of young tradesmen was that their savings would be so small that their wives would be forced to do the housework, as they would not be able to afford servants, and so would not have time to learn the business and help in the shop. This was the place for the wife of a shopkeeper, not upstairs dispensing tea to her friends or gadding around town turning over the stock of other shopkeepers.[7]

Most authors who wrote on this subject emphasized that women should learn their husband's business not simply to provide assistance on a day-to-day basis but also so that they could take over in such regularly occurring situations as his visits to the fairs and country traders or in emergencies, such as a husband's illness or flight for debt. The greatest emergency was the husband's death. As already mentioned, the widows of Londoners could be in an enviably independent legal and financial situation. However, none of this was likely to be enjoyed if the woman was ignorant not just of her husband's business but of business in general, since there were plenty of people around who would be only too happy to take advantage of a widow's ignorance.

Defoe repeatedly stressed this point in his chapter on the role of the wife in business in the *Complete English Tradesman*, where he points out that women who do not understand business are frequently cheated as widows, find it difficult to recover their husband's debts, cannot get a good price for the goodwill of the business and, far from being able to maintain their former pretensions of gentility, are reduced to beggary. Other writers echoed Defoe, the lengthy subtitle of *Advice to the Women and Maidens of London* giving the advice away by saying that, instead of learning needlework, lace and pointmaking, women should 'apply themselves to the right understanding and practice of the method of keeping books of accompts, whereby either single or married, they may know their estates, carry on their trades, and avoid the danger of a helpless and forlorn condition, incident to widows'.[8]

Very few girls did learn book-keeping, or anything else which might have helped them fulfil their role as the partner of a businessman. The provision of education for girls certainly improved in the seventeenth century, and so did their general standard of literacy,[9] but the emphasis for middling girls was on acquiring social graces, domestic skills and perhaps a smattering of French. Girls of this class married quite young and most would probably still be living at home when they got married, so they were devoid of independent work experience and their knowledge of business would depend on how much responsibility or instruction they had been given by their parents. Girls of a rather lower class tended to leave home earlier and marry later. In the meantime, they would have had work experience, but this was unlikely to be particularly relevant to the understanding of business. Much the commonest employment of girls before marriage was domestic service, good experience for a future housekeeper but not of much value for the junior partner of a businessman. Few girls in London were apprenticed to trades and those that were tended to be concentrated in a few 'feminine' occupations such as millinery, mantua-making, lace-making, various branches of the silk industry and some shopkeeping trades. Such girls tended to be poor and remain poor as married women, though some were able to set up as independent businesswomen, as will be seen in the next section. However, the great majority of girls destined to become wives of London businessmen, especially those who were at least moderately well off, had virtually no experience or knowledge of business except what they might have picked up from their parents or brothers. If they were to be of use as business partners, it was up to their husbands to train them to their new responsibilities.

It would certainly be worth the while of husbands to do this, for, quite apart from learning the business as an insurance against widowhood, there was an important role for women to play in many of the businesses that have been discussed. The wives of tavern-keepers, innkeepers or coffee-house-keepers played a fundamental part in attracting and serving customers, and all these catering businesses had a role for daughters to play as well. The same was true of most shops, particularly those which dealt in textiles, clothing, small-wares and food. 'Not one grocer in twenty employs a regular bred journeyman,'

wrote Campbell. 'Their wives, daughters, and perhaps a servant-maid does all the business of the shop.'[10] The manual side
of manufacturing was much more dominated by men, but
selling goods from the front of the workshop, supervising
journeymen and apprentices, and buying raw materials might
well be the job of the master's wife, while in some industries,
particularly in textile manufacture, it was absolutely normal for
the wife and daughters to work alongside the master. It might
be rather more surprising to find women working in the realm
of 'big business', in a merchant's counting-house, a wholesaler's
warehouse or a bank, but it was in just these types of business
that writers thought that wives should make the greatest effort,
learn the business, study accounting and work as the book-
keeper and close partner of their husbands in preparation for
the possibilities of widowhood.

There was, then, a wide range of occupations where a sensible
master might have been expected to employ his wife and
daughters, if only to save himself paying wages to someone else,
and where a sensible wife would insist on being admitted to all
the secrets of the business. However, it is the thesis of Alice
Clark, one of the pioneers of the study of women's work in this
country, that such expectations were increasingly not being
fulfilled in the course of the seventeenth century. She found this
to be a period when the concept that women should be 'kept'
by men was growing, as wives became either unpaid domestic
servants or, if their husbands were rich enough, decorative
ornaments.[11] She explained this fundamental change in the life
experience of women by the rise of 'Capitalism', a stage of
economic development which still warranted a capital letter
when she published her book in 1919. Capitalism led to an
increase in the scale of business, with the result that fewer
journeymen could afford to set up in business for themselves
and so had to leave home each day to work on a master's
premises where there was no place for their wives to work.
Capitalism also made the capitalists richer and placed them in
a position where they could not only afford to have an idle wife
but would positively want one as a sign of their rise in the world
and a recognition of their newly genteel status – idleness and
gentility being closely connected in the English mind.

A steady stream of social comment certainly suggests that

good sense was indeed giving way to vanity and extravagance, producing a new breed of idle middle-class women whose husbands and fathers did not make them work. They preferred to see them as the means of displaying their own economic success, thus foreshadowing those very negative attitudes towards women's work which are often seen as a product of the social ethos of Victorian times. As has been mentioned, daughters were in fact educated in needlework and French and not in accounting and, when they were married, they continued to engage in purely decorative activities rather than playing their part in the business. 'The tradesman is foolishly vain of making his wife a gentlewoman, forsooth,' complained Defoe. 'He will ever have her sit above in the parlour, and receive visits, and drink tea, and entertain her neighbours, or take a coach and go abroad; but as to the business, she shall not stoop to touch it.'[12]

Some writers suggested that women disliked this new idleness and wished that their husbands would treat them as something more than ornaments. Lucinda in Bernard de Mandeville's *The Virgin Unmask'd* of 1709 rebuked her niece, who praised the respectful and tender way in which Englishmen treated their wives. ''Tis that respect and tenderness I hate, when it consists only in outward show. In Holland women sit in their counting houses and do business, or at least are acquainted with everything their husbands do.' Holland was the Japan of the day, the place where critical Englishmen looked for evidence of excellence with which to berate their fellow-countrymen, and Sir Josiah Child also made this distinction between the wives of Englishmen and Dutchmen. In Holland, both boys and girls studied accounting and arithmetic, and showed 'not only an ability for commerce of all kinds, but a strong aptitude, love and delight in it; and in regard the women are as knowing therein as the men, it doth incourage their husbands to hold on in their trades to their dying days, knowing the capacity of their wives to get in their estates, and carry on their trades after their deaths'. In England, on the other hand, the family was likely to lose one-third of the deceased businessman's estate, 'through the unexperience and unaptness of his wife to such affairs'.[13]

However, Defoe's *Roxana* suggests that, by the 1720s, even frugal and sensible Dutchmen were beginning to treat their wives like the frivolous English, Roxana complaining of the 'life of perfect indolence' which she would live if she married her Dutch merchant. 'The woman had nothing to do, but to eat the fat, and drink the sweet; to sit still, and look round her; be waited on, and made much of.' But such examples of English women complaining of their leisure are rare in the literature of the time. Most writers, admittedly nearly all men, were scathing in their criticism of the mindless pleasure in which middle-class women indulged and the vices to which this led. They castigated them for the endless visits in which idle woman chatted to idle woman, the hours spent in scandal and gossip at the tea-table, the masquerade and the assembly-room, for going to bed late and getting up late, for gambling at backgammon and basset, for window-shopping, extravagance and for their general silliness.[14]

What is one to make of all this comment, much of which suggests that the idle woman is a new phenomenon and one little known in earlier times? Social comment is not necessarily true but, when there is so much of it pointing in the same direction, the historian is bound to take notice. There is also much circumstantial evidence which suggests that there may well indeed have been a growth in the number of idle and frivolous women. Who bought all those silk fabrics being turned out by the rapidly expanding Spitalfields industry and had them made up into garments which were certainly not designed for working? Who sat in all those comfortably upholstered and attractively covered chairs and sofas which will be discovered when the undoubted improvements in domestic comfort are looked at in Chapter 10? Who peered at themselves in the larger and larger mirrors which appear in middle-class homes? Who went to the masquerades, the assemblies and the tea-parties? Who had the time to read the translations of French romances, the play-books, the periodicals and later the novels which were poured out by English publishers for a predominantly female reading public? Much of the demand for all this extravagance and frivolity did of course come from the wives and daughters of the gentry and near gentry of the West End, people who had been idle and frivolous for a long time, but there was just too much feminine luxury around for them to have absorbed it all. There does seem to be little doubt that many citizen's wives had translated their pretensions to gentility into a fairly reckless round of pleasure which, if not quite genteel, at least appealed to them more than sitting in a shop.

All this does not mean that women completely deserted business. Some of London's business continued to be run independently by women, as will be seen in the next section, and some women continued to be helpmeets in their husband's businesses. There does, however, seem to be a *prima facie* case for a decline in this role. It is difficult, for instance, to find women of this class playing much part in their husbands' businesses from the many vignettes of everyday life which provide such an important source for social history. The records of the Mayor's Court, which were used extensively for the chapter on apprenticeship, have masses of depositions describing the ordinary situations in which an apprentice might find himself in his master's household.[15] One meets many master's wives in these depositions but one nearly always meets them in their role as housekeeper, maybe bullying an apprentice into doing housework, maybe looking after him when sick or locking up the food and drink. It is rare to find the mistress of the house working behind the counter or keeping the books, the roles which contemporaries thought that they should perform.

Vignettes provide attractive source material, but are difficult to quantify, and alternative methods of analysis are hard to find. However, it is the impression of this author that Alice Clark and the social commentators of the day were more or less right and that the majority of middle-class wives played little or no part in the running of their husbands' businesses, especially if those husbands were reasonably well off. However, this did not mean that there was no role at all for women in the London business world.[16]

iii The Independent Businesswoman

Married women may have played a diminishing part in their husbands' businesses, but many widows and spinsters ran their own businesses and virtually any type of record will throw up the occasional female shopkeeper, victualler or clothing manufacturer. The problem is to determine just how sizeable a minority of all businesses were run by women, what sort of businesses these were and the relative success of women in business compared to that of men.

There were certainly large numbers of women who, as heads of households, were in a position to be independent business-women, contemporary data suggesting that some 10 to 20 per cent of London households were headed by widows, while many spinsters lived independently as well. All these women had to make a living somehow, but the records show that for most this living was not a very good one. Of those who paid the 1692 Poll Tax, only 19 per cent of widows but 65 per cent of widowers paid more than the basic 1s. per quarter, while the disparity was greater still for single people living alone, with 13 per cent of bachelors and less than 2 per cent of spinsters being assessed above the basic rate. Women were also over-represented in that majority of people too poor to pay any tax at all.[17]

These figures suggest that only a small proportion of widows and single women were living well, a fact that is no surprise, despite the literary emphasis on the wealthy widow. What the figures do not tell us is how these women acquired their living. There was a wide range of possibilities, quite apart from the poor relief or charity which supported many London women. Both widows and single women might have rentier incomes derived from legacies or the realization of their former hus-band's businesses, while an income made up of rent paid by lodgers was another common scenario. They might be living off wages or piece-rate earnings or, possibly, off immoral earnings as a bawd or a prostitute. They might be living from the profits derived from running a business which they had either built up themselves or taken over after their husband's death. Finally, they could of course be deriving an income from any combina-tion of the above.

It would be impossible to determine accurately how many women fell into any of these categories and the best that can be done is to look at a variety of sources to see what they can tell one about the business life of women. To start, there are the bankruptcy records for the years 1711–15, which have been analysed for other purposes elsewhere in the book.[18] There seems little doubt that, if women were substantial traders, they would appear in these records, since there is no reason to assume that they were either more careful, more competent or more lucky than men or that the male creditors of women were particularly chivalrous. One finds in fact that in these five years that were just eighteen women bankrupts from London, who formed 2.8 per cent of the total of metropolitan bankrupts. This is a small number but, in order to place it in context, one should perhaps think more carefully about just what was the population at risk. It seems a reasonable assumption that most potential bankrupts would be drawn from those liable to pay more than the basic rate on the Poll Tax. If this is true, then the 2.8 per cent of female bankrupts should be compared with the 7.7 per cent of heads of households paying surtax in 1692 who were women,[19] a comparison which suggests that just over a third of such women were in 'business' and so liable to become bankrupt. It can finally be noted that the eighteen women bankrupts included six people described as 'chap-women', probably shopkeepers, four vintners or tavern-keepers, two milliners, a woodmonger, a coffeewoman, a mercer, a barber-surgeon, a silkwoman and a periwig-maker, the last three being the partner of a man.

One gets a rather different picture when one analyses those London creditors who sued bankrupts, fifty-three of whom, or 6.4 per cent, were women whose debtors covered the whole gamut of the London business world. Women were thus more than twice as likely to be a creditor as a bankrupt. Only three of the female creditors were given an occupational label: two merchants, who were the partners of men and the only two partners amongst the women creditors, and a silk-weaver from Southwark. The remainder of the sample included one infant, eight spinsters and forty-one widows, some of whom possibly had occupations but most of whom probably did not. This analysis provides some clues to the role that London women played in business. Some, but not very many, were independent traders. A much higher number, perhaps twice as many, were investors in metropolitan businesses run by men but most of these women played no part in such businesses except to draw a quarterly interest payment.

Rather more light on women in business can be obtained from the policy registers of the Sun Fire Office. The analysis below is based on seven registers covering the years 1726 to 1729, which record a total of 3531 London policies, of which 317 or just under 9 per cent were taken out by a woman.[20] In

TABLE 6.1: London Women's Fire Insurance Policies

| Marital Status | Type of Property Insured | | | Total |
| | 1 | 2 | 3 | |
	No.	No.	No.	No.
Widows	19	62	46	127
Wives	0	2	1	3
Spinsters	11	11	10	32
Unspecified	10	14	131	155
Total	40	89	188	317

1 = Household effects and furniture only
2 = Houses and other buildings (may also insure 1)
3 = Stock in trade (may also insure 1 and 2)

Source: GHMS 11936/23–29.

Table 6.1 above, this sample of women property-owners is divided into three groups, those who insured household goods and furniture only, those who in addition insured houses or other buildings and finally those who insured stock in trade, the rather bold assumption being that women in the first group lived mainly off wages, annuities or paper securities such as stocks and bonds, those in the second group off rents and those in the third off the profits of a business.[21]

The table also subdivides the sample by marital status but, as can be seen, the clerks in the insurance office were not very consistent in recording this, which is unfortunate for our purposes. This is particularly true of those who insured stock in trade, presumably because one tended to think of such women as innkeepers or milliners rather than as widows or spinsters. Nevertheless, one or two points can be made from the table. First, the ownership of property by wives does not seem to have been very important, unless they dominate the unspecified insurers of stock in trade, which seems unlikely. Secondly, spinsters had a rather more important role in the London business world than one might expect, being over 10 per cent of the sample and probably much more, as many of the unspecified businesswomen were probably spinsters. Finally, widows quite clearly dominate the female property market, especially the ownership of houses, from which they could draw a rental

TABLE 6.2: Occupations of Businesswomen

Occupation	No.	%
Food, drink and entertainment	76	37.6
Textiles and clothing	62	30.7
Pawnbroking	23	11.4
Other retailing	14	6.9
Miscellaneous	22	10.9
Unspecified trade	5	2.5
	202	100.0

Food, drink and entertainment: Victualler (14), distiller (14), tavern-, inn- or alehouse-keeper (11), tallow-chandler (5), grocer (5), butcher (3), baker (3), coffee-house-keeper (3), cheesemonger (3), dealer in tea and chinaware, pastrycook, tobacconist, bagnio (2 each), gingerbread-baker, soap-seller, sutler, dealer in rum, dealer in brandy, poulterer, show-woman (1 each).

Textiles and clothing: Linen-draper (11), milliner (10), child's coat-maker (4), haberdasher (4), hosier (4), shoemaker (3), coatseller, weaver, woollen-draper, mercer, glover, mantua-maker, slopseller (2 each), skinner, dyer, pinker, clothdrawer, indigo-maker, cap-maker, gown and habit maker, packer, throster, sempstress, hat-seller, robe-maker (1 each).

Other retailing: Glass-seller (4), shopkeeper (4), colour shop, oilshop, book-seller, perfumer, toywoman, dealer in musical instruments (1 each).

Miscellaneous: Merchant, apothecary, coachmaker, coal-seller, upholsterer (2 each), pewterer, cutler, clockmaker, farrier, warehousekeeper, coffin-maker, ironmonger, potter, chemist, turner, cork-cutter, wheelwright (1 each).

Source: GHMS 11936/23–29.

income possibly supplemented by catering for lodgers, a role which made good use of those household skills which they had acquired as wives.

One can now look at the sorts of business run by women who insured their stock in trade or who can be identified by a trade description. In Table 6.2 above, these businesses are analysed by broad categories. This shows that the typical business for a woman was exactly what might be expected: running a catering establishment selling food or drink, or running a shop selling food, textiles, clothing or such fancy goods as toys, glass, china or perfumes, while pawnbroking was another occupation with a fairly high proportion of female participants. All these businesses might be run by spinsters as well as by widows, such as the milliners' shop run by Alice Hall and Mary Plume in Exeter Exchange or the cheese shop run by the sisters Ann and Sarah Woodman in St John Street.[22] Where widows did dominate was in the group of occupations headed 'miscellaneous', nearly all of which are really 'male' trades taken over by widows after their husbands' deaths.

This analysis can be continued by looking at post-mortem inventories, starting with the estates of the first fifty London widows whose inventories are kept in the series PROB4 in the Public Record Office, all of whom died between 1660 and 1700.[23] Five of the fifty women had no assets except their clothes, a few household goods and perhaps a little cash, so that no idea is given of how they had supported themselves; maybe by wages, charity or an annuity which died with them. Nine of the women were definitely running a business when they died, since their stock in trade is listed. Two had shops selling mainly muffs and tippets and similar goods. Then there was a shop with the typical stock of the haberdasher/milliner type of business, an alehouse, a carter, a plumber and a glazier, the last being the most valuable business with nearly £2000 worth of assets. Finally, there were two women who were definitely running some sort of business, the exact nature of which cannot be determined from the inventory.

Next, there is an intermediate group of twelve women whose estate consisted of clothing, jewellery, household goods, cash and an item simply described as 'sperate debts', 'debts sperate and desperate', 'debts due to deceased' etc. None of these twelve inventories mentions any stock in trade or a shop, but it is possible that they are small businesses whose stocks have been sold before valuation. On the other hand, these widows might have been money-lenders, quite a common role for women, as has been seen, or they might have been pure rentiers, as were the remaining twenty-four women in this small sample, whose assets, apart from their household goods and other personal belongings, consisted entirely of bonds, bills, leases and unpaid rent or interest. Nine relied mainly on an income from houses and fifteen on an income from loans secured by bonds or bills. The business life of some of these widows could hardly have been simpler – just one piece of property or one bond representing virtually all their assets – such as that of Elizabeth

Dallender, who owned the lease of a property in Buckingham-shire worth £1200 and had total assets of £1250, or of Joanna Stratfold of Shoreditch, who had £168 'oweing on a bond' out of total assets of £173.[24]

A similar pattern can be found in the inventories of widows in the records of the Court of Orphans, though there tended to be rather more businesswomen and rather fewer pure rentiers in this source. Nonetheless, the businesswomen conformed to type and nearly all engaged in 'women's' businesses, in those small businesses concerned with food and drink, textiles, cloth-ing and pawnbroking, which were seen when the fire insurance records were analysed. There is, for example, Rebecca Heatley, whose 1670 inventory reveals a small shop with a wide range of ready-made clothing, such as stockings, drawers, frocks, shirts, shifts, aprons and petticoats; Mary Lee, a small tallow-chandler with thirty-seven dozen candles in stock; Grace Bartlett, who had kept on her husband's business as a poulterer and had sixty-nine chickens and nine ducks in her yard in St Andrew's, Holborn, and twelve rabbits, three pullets, three partridges and over 8000 rabbit skins in the shop within. Then, there were a dyer, a mercer and an upholsterer, silkwomen, haberdashers, hosiers, mealwomen, chandlers, distillers, coffee-shop- and dramshop-keepers, as well as two pawnbrokers, for one of whom an excellent inventory survives.[25]

Anne Deacon, who died in 1675, kept her shop in Limehouse and in the list of goods in the garret and in 'the little roome below the garrett', were fifty-three small and not so small bundles of pawned goods, mostly bedding and clothing, odd assortments of goods bundled together to raise the wind, such as the 'pair of calico sheets, child's coat, calico shirt, tufted holland mantle, shirt, cap, piece of stuff, thimble, pillow and pillow-beer' that were valued at thirty shillings. Furniture and kitchen goods also found their way to Mrs Deacon's shop, as did a large number of rings. One can see a pattern here, similar to that of Victorian and Edwardian England, by which poor families acquired such goods as linen sheets, high-quality clothing and gold rings, which could be admired in times of prosperity and pawned in the times of austerity that would inevitably follow.[26]

Other widows made a perhaps more respectable living by lending money to the prosperous or by renting out apartments in the houses which they owned. Mary Greene drew £24 per annum in interest from a loan to John Dennett and Co., and she got a further £143 a year from the rents of two houses in Crane Court, Fleet Street, one of which was occupied by the Earl of Suffolk. Hester English drew a similar income from her investments, £135 in rents and over £50 in interest from bonds, bills and mortgages, her business affairs being managed in the traditional way by Mr Walton, a scrivener. These were good solid incomes, sufficient to live a respectable life as a middle-class widow and still accumulate for the sake of the children. Such incomes could be supplemented if need be by selling household skills. Many of these widows had a room in their house called 'the lodgeing roome' and such people often have an unpaid debt listed for the 'dyett' provided for their lodgers. There was also a wide range of other possibilities, apart from running a regular business. Margaret Holloway, for instance, was able to add to the £55 a year which she got from the rents of three houses in Crown Court, Threadneedle Street, by taking in laundry, £5 being owed to her at her death 'by Mrs Smith and severall other persons in small petty debts for washing'.[27]

What can be said in summary about women in business? There certainly was a female presence in the London business world. The bankruptcy records suggest that possibly a third of all women of property ran a business and the fire insurance records indicate that these businesses were some 5 to 10 per cent of all businesses in London. They also show, however, that women concentrated very heavily on particular female types of business and that not many widows carried on their husband's business if it was not suitable to their sex. There were, however, many exceptions to this rule and the occasional woman can be found running practically every kind of business, as merchants, ironmongers, coopers, glaziers, even in the armaments industry, two women's fire insurance policies covering a saltpetre refinery and a sword cutler's business. Nevertheless, most women ran feminine businesses, not many of which were likely to lead to massive accumulation.

The other point that is obvious from this chapter is the enormous importance of women, particularly widows, in the London investment markets. Women must have owned a sizeable proportion of the London housing stock (or at least of the long leases of that stock) and a woman as landlady must have been a common experience, many such women coupling their simple rent-taking function with the provision of meals, the washing of clothes, nursing and other similar services. Women, too, played a vital role in the provison of loan capital through the bond and mortgage markets, one man's accumulation of business capital being realized by his widow to provide another man with that vital loan which would enable him to build up his business in his turn. It is no wonder that people with such liquid assets should have been so sought after as marriage partners, since marriage enabled the new husband to acquire the assets without paying the 6 per cent interest, and of course to acquire an unpaid housekeeper into the bargain.[28] These material considerations were important aspects of marriage but, as will be seen in the next chapter, there were other aspects, even love and romance, which have to be considered.

Three

Family and Social Life

7 Marriage

This chapter concerns courtship and marriage, subjects which have provoked a lively debate amongst historians in recent years. One writer, Lawrence Stone, sees our period as one when a more companionate and affectionate type of marriage developed and he claims that it was the London bourgeoisie who were the innovators in the development of this 'modern' marriage. However, Stone's numerous critics find little change in marriage and plenty of love and affection long before the late seventeenth century.[1] Our period is far too short for any real contribution to be made here to a debate on long-term changes in the nature of marriage, but some comment on the relations between the sexes will be attempted. The first consideration, however, is just what did constitute a marriage in Augustan London.

i The Marriage Ceremony

There were four different ways in which Londoners could get married. The cheapest and most private was simply 'a full, free and mutual consent between parties'. No public ceremony was necessary; all that the couple had to do was to say to each other some such formula as 'I take you Margaret to and for my wedded wife' or 'with this ring I thee wed my dear Peggy'. This elementary but perfectly legal type of marriage required no parental consent, nor indeed were witnesses necessary, though it was politic to make sure that someone else was present in case of future dispute.[2] Such marriages were common in the middle ages and were probably still fairly common in our period. However, although accepted as a complete marriage by canon law, they were increasingly not thought good by the common lawyers, who held that a marriage must be solemnized according to the rites of the Church of England if the parties were to be able to have 'any interest or property in the other's lands or goods or to legitimate their issue'.[3]

Since such matters were important to middling people, it seems probable that most got married in a rather more formal way. There was still plenty of choice. One common, cheap and private method was to undergo a 'clandestine' marriage. These took place in parts of London claiming exemption from ecclesiastical jurisdiction, such as Holy Trinity in the Minories or St James's Duke Place, a parish of 160 households which was celebrating nearly 2000 marriages a year in the second half of the seventeenth century. Clandestine marriages at these two churches were brought to an end in the 1690s but they were replaced by the 'Fleet' marriages, which were held in the area round the Fleet Prison known as the Rules. Such marriages required no publication of banns, no parental consent nor any other formal interference from outsiders.

Fleet marriages were normally celebrated in inns and taverns, and the ceremony took the form of an abridged version of the Anglican marriage service conducted by someone who at least appeared to be a priest of the Church of England. Nearly everything to do with such marriages had a sordid and semi-criminal reputation – the 'marriage houses' whose main interest was in selling drink, the 'pliers' who touted for particular houses, the dissolute parsons and the dubious registers which recorded the marriages – yet they remained amazingly popular. A recent study estimates that there were between 3000 and 5000 Fleet marriages a year between 1694 and 1754, when the practice was ended by Lord Hardwicke's Marriage Act. These numbers were swelled by people from outside London but they still must represent a large proportion of all marriages in the metropolis, mostly those of artisans and other working people but including a substantial minority of middling people.[4]

The attractions of Fleet marriages were their cheapness, about 7s.6d. before the drink, and the fact that they could be had 'without loss of time, hindrance of business, and the knowledge of friends'.[5] However, it was not very respectable to be married in a Fleet tavern and hardly accorded with the genteelness of most of the middle station. Nevertheless, most people in this class still valued a private and fairly secret

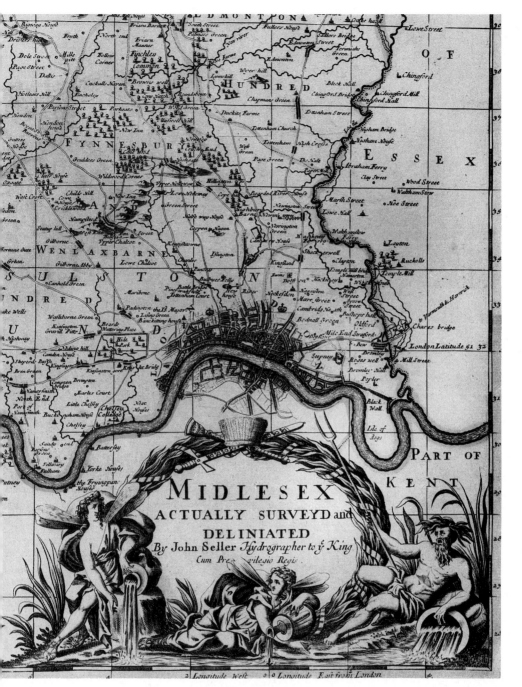

1. London was the biggest city in Europe
but it was still small and compact by modern standards,
as can be seen in this detail from John Seller's
1733 map of Middlesex.

2. 'Custom House Quay', by Samuel Scott.

3 & 4. The heart of commercial London: Cornhill (*below*) and the Royal Exchange (*above*). The houses on the left of the engraving are those shown on the south side of Cornhill in the street plan.

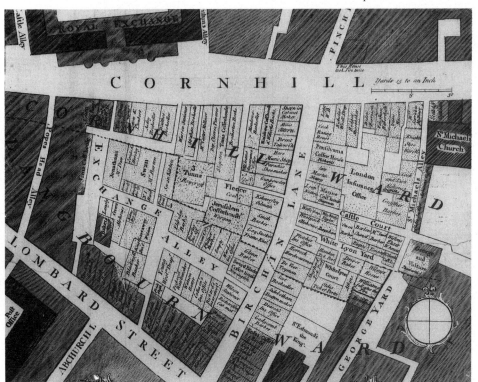

5 & 6. River and road traffic: 'The Entrance to the Fleet River'
by Samuel Scott (*above*) and an engraving of Cheapside, with the
Church of St Mary le Bow (*below*).

7 & 8. Two ways of doing business: 'Covent Garden Market', c.1726–30, by Joseph van Aken (*above*) and a London coffee house, c.1705 (*below*).

The Faces of the Middle Class

9. Thomas Sydenham, physician,
by Mary Beale, 1688.

10. Samuel Pepys, civil servant,
by J. Hayls, 1666.

11. Thomas Guy, bookseller and
philanthropist (1644–1724);
artist unknown.

12. Thomas Britton,
'the musical small-coal man',
by John Wollaston, 1703.

13. Sir Gilbert Heathcote,
merchant and financier (1651–1733),
by Michael Dahl.

14. Jacob Tonson,
bookseller and publisher,
by Kneller, 1717.

15. Thomas Tompion, clockmaker (1639–1713),
by John Smith after Kneller.

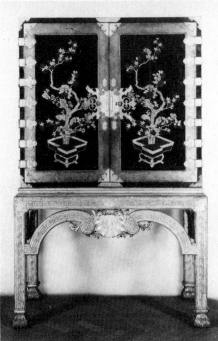

16 & 17. The influence of the orient on domestic life: 'A Family at Tea', attributed to R. Collins, c.1730, (*above*); lacquered cabinet and stand made in London, c.1715 (*left*).

marriage and so got married by licence from the diocese of London. Marriage by licence avoided the publicity of having the banns called in church, most people with 'the slightest claims to gentility' objecting to the public theatre involved, the giggling and the nudging, not being 'willing to have their affairs declar'd to all the world in a public place, when for a guinea they may do it snug and without noise'.[6] Middling people also objected to the expense created by a wedding proclaimed by banns; the publicity led to pressure to invite large numbers of guests; it also advertised the wedding to the poor who had a habit of making a filthy row outside the house in which the couple were consummating their marriage until they were paid off.

A licence required a sworn statement that, if either party was under twenty-one, they had the consent of their parents or guardian, but this was seldom a problem. The marriage itself was held in church, but as quietly as possible according to Misson, who saw such weddings as typical of 'people of a middle condition' in London. The party would consist of bride and groom, their parents, two bridemen and two bridesmaids who 'go early in the morning with a licence in their pocket, and call up Mr Curate and his clerk, tell him their business; are marry'd with a low voice and the doors shut'. They then 'steal softly out' to a tavern or the home of a friend for the wedding dinner and then home for the formal undressing and bedding of the bride and groom, this *prima facie* proof of consummation being seen as very important.[7]

The fourth type of marriage, and the commonest, was the normal marriage of the Church of England in which banns were called on three occasions and the ceremony held in open church. This cost more than a Fleet marriage and less than marriage by licence, but was open to the objections mentioned above of greater publicity. In the early seventeenth century, some five out of every six marriages in the diocese of London were celebrated by banns, but this proportion was dominated by the marriages of artisans and the poor.[8] Marriage by banns remained important during our period, but its proportional significance fell as the number of licences increased and as the trickle of clandestine marriages became a flood in the early eighteenth century.

What significance should one attach to the middle-class
predilection for a private and often secret wedding? The actual
wedding by licence cost more than a wedding by banns, but the
total cost of the celebration would have been less and this was
certainly a consideration for young people at an early stage in
the accumulation process. A distaste for publicity and a desire
to distance themselves from the common people are also
apparent and this could well reflect a growing understanding of
what was seemly and genteel. A desire for privacy can be seen
in other aspects of middle-class life, though it was often
thwarted by the fact that much of such lives was acted out
before an avidly curious audience of servants, lodgers, customers and neighbours. It should finally be noted that the
desire for private weddings may well provide a clue to the
grounds on which middling people chose their marriage partners. This will be discussed later, mainly in terms of the relative
importance of love and money. Without prejudging the issue, it
can merely be noted here that, if marriage was a rather sordid
business transaction with little love involved, the partners
would probably prefer it celebrated in the stealthy and self-
effacing way described by Misson, rather than before the eyes
of the whole parish.

ii Age at Marriage

It has been drummed into historians in recent years that
England belonged to something variously called the 'Western'
or 'Malthusian' marriage system, one of whose characteristics
was that both sexes got married much later in life than was
normal in the rest of the world, where most people married
soon after puberty. A recent study has provided some statistical
precision for this observation by showing that, in the late
seventeenth century, the median age of a sample of English
brides was twenty-six at their first marriage and their husbands
were two or three years older.[9] However, this sample was drawn
from villages and small country towns. What one needs to know
is whether the metropolitan middle class conformed to this
general pattern.

In answering this question, it is fortunate that large numbers
of middling people got married by licence since the age of the

parties was entered in the licence applications. Vivien Brodsky Elliott has studied the applications for the period 1598 to 1619 and her work shows that the average age of London-born women married by licence was only 20.5, nearly four years younger than women who were immigrants to the metropolis and nearly six years younger than the small town and rural women mentioned above. So, although London women did not marry at puberty, they married much younger than was normal in England, a high proportion marrying in their teens. Another interesting finding of Elliott's analysis is that, generally speaking, the higher the social status of the groom, the younger was the bride and the greater the difference in age between the bride and groom.[10]

The patterns discovered by Elliott are reflected amongst middling people in our period. Table 7.1 overleaf sets out the ages at first marriage of those members of the sample and their wives for whom there is sufficient information to make this calculation. These figures allow us to say with some confidence that middle-class wives in London married young by contemporary standards, over 80 per cent being under twenty-five and over 40 per cent under twenty-one at their first marriage. There was also a fairly big age difference between bride and groom, five years on average, with the result that middle-class men typically married at a similar age to men in other classes and other parts of the country. When this age difference is broken down, as in Table 7.2 overleaf, the same relationship is found between wealth or status and age difference between bride and groom as Elliott found for London generally. If fortune at death is taken as a proxy for comparative wealth at marriage, then the wealthier the husband the older he was when he got married and, in the case of the richest group, the younger his bride. The same pattern can be found when age at marriage is broken down by various occupational groupings with different social status. Wealthy young men and those of high status tended to marry when they were thirty and chose girls on average ten years younger; poorer men and those of lower status tended to get married at twenty-five to a girl only two or three years younger than themselves.[11]

Economic considerations normally govern discussion of the ages at which people got married in the past. Men are thought

TABLE 7.1: Age at First Marriage

| Age | Husbands | | Wives | |
	No.	%	No.	%
Under 21	0	0.0	89	41.2
21 to 24	59	21.5	86	39.8
25 to 29	137	49.8	37	17.1
30 to 35	59	21.5	4	1.9
Over 35	20	7.3	0	0.0
	275	100.1	216	100.0
	Median = 27		Median = 22	

Source: Linked sample; no information was found on the other 100 husbands and 159 wives.

TABLE 7.2: Age Difference between Husband and Wife

| | Median Age at First Marriage | | | |
Fortune at Death	Husbands	Wives	Difference	No. of Cases
Less than £1000	25	22	3	85
£1000–£1999	26	22	4	38
£2000–£4999	28	22	6	51
£5000 and over	30	20	10	37
Occupation Groups				
Artisans	25	23	2	18
Haberdashers	27	22	5	26
Merchants	30	20	10	29
All cases	27	22	5	211

Source: As for Table 7.1, which includes the age at marriage of some wives and some husbands without their corresponding spouses. Table 7.2 includes only actual couples.

to have deferred marriage in order to 'save up' to pay for the establishment of a new household and the expense of children. They chose wives in their mid- or late twenties, partly so that their brides would also have had a chance to save up and acquire economic skills and partly in order to limit the number of children they might have in the absence of effective contraception.[12] Such hypotheses have been developed to explain the behaviour of the population as a whole, who were on average relatively poor, and one would not expect exactly the same considerations to be relevant for middle-class Londoners.

Middling people certainly shared the view that marriage would be costly. Thomas Tryon, for instance, stated in 1691 what to his contemporaries was obvious when he started his list of the 'cross accidents attending married persons, as encrease of charge, the uncertain gains and the certain expences', his 'uncertain gains' being emotional and not financial ones. For this reason, men were always advised to wait until they could afford to get married without the 'certain expences' dragging them back down the social and economic ladder they had been patiently climbing as a bachelor. The bookseller John Dunton put it rather nicely when he wrote that he decided to postpone the 'experiment' of marriage until he had discovered 'whether my trade wou'd carry two, and then to proceed upon a safe bottom'. Such considerations probably explain why most of the middle class deferred their marriages until at least their mid-twenties and also why richer or potentially richer men married later, since it would take them longer to acquire a 'bottom' safe enough to support their larger and more substantial households.[13]

So far, middle-class behaviour is little different from that of the population as a whole. Where middling people did differ was in marrying wives much younger than themselves, in their early twenties or late teens. From the man's point of view, the explanation for this is probably that the economic considerations governing the choice of the poor were not particularly relevant to this class. The bride's monetary contribution to the marriage was normally 'saved up' by her father rather than by the girl herself and a dowry was usually no lower if a girl married at nineteen rather than at twenty-five. Nor, as has been seen, was work experience of much relevance, since few wives in this class actually did work. Finally, the cost of young children was not particularly crippling, since middling people would already have servants to look after them and would usually lose no income as a result of their wives' pregnancies and attention to childcare. When children grew older, they were of course an immense expense to the middle class, requiring as they did outlay on education, apprenticeship and portions, but by then the parents would have expected to have accumulated sufficient to cover such expenses.

In principle, then, there was no very strong economic barrier to middling people marrying young wives and indeed such barriers would be less the richer the husband, since he would have more servants and less reliance on the economic assistance of his wife. If one assumes that what a husband wanted in a wife was some combination of physical attraction and health, good company and conversation, the ability to run a household and a handsome dowry, then such attributes were as likely to be present in a well brought up girl of eighteen or nineteen as in one of twenty-four or twenty-five. There were, in other words, no strong reasons against marrying a young wife.

So far the age at marriage has been discussed from the point of view of the husband, what can realistically be called the demand side of marriage. But what about the supply side? What was the attitude of potential brides and their parents? Here, an imbalance must be noted between the numbers of men and women in London, which Gregory King put at a ratio of 10 to 13, reflected both in a surplus of spinsters to bachelors and of widows to widowers.[14] This female surplus was aggravated by a lack of enthusiasm on the part of many men to marry in a world where the financial benefits of bachelorhood and the easy availability of alternative sources of sexual gratification and of housekeepers made a single life an attractive option. The result, as Moll Flanders pointed out, was that 'the market is against our sex just now'.[15]

In such circumstances, young girls found themselves in a rather desperate race to get the best husbands and avoid being left on the shelf, since a single life for women was not regarded in the same light as it was for men. Contemporary writers advised girls and their parents to be extremely careful in their choice of husband but few advised them to let such care delay their marriages for very long. As a result, middle-class girls who could tended to marry young and it is the attitudes of these girls and their mothers, portrayed in literature and particularly plays, which have been remembered and carried down into our own times, despite the fact that the great majority of English girls deliberately delayed both their sexual initiation and their marriages until their middle or late twenties.[16]

Some reasons have been suggested why middle-class men might marry quite late and middle-class women quite early by the standards of the day. The problem of how men and women chose the particular partner with whom they would have to live 'till death us do part' has not, however, been resolved. Did men choose their brides for love or was Moll Flanders right when she claimed that 'money only made a woman agreeable . . . for a wife, no deformity would shock the fancy, no ill qualities the judgment; the money was the thing'?[17]

iii Choice of Partners

Historians have normally addressed the subject of choice of marriage partners with two questions in mind: the degree to which parents and friends influenced or controlled their children's choice, and the degree to which love or affection or some other, usually materialistic, influence affected the choice made by children. Such questions obviously cannot be resolved statistically in the way that age at marriage can and no more than probabilities can be suggested here.

It now seems to be generally agreed that, by the late seventeenth century at least, the ultimate choice was made by the young people but that this choice was normally very much affected by parents and friends, who suggested and actively promoted possible partners and who would go to considerable lengths to try to break off a match which they thought unsuitable.[18] Most contemporary writers thought that children should follow their parents' advice if they possibly could, though they would normally accept an ultimate right of veto by the children. John Dunton, for instance in the *Athenian Mercury*, an early example of an 'agony column', thought that children 'ought to endeavour as much as possible to submit to their parents' choice; unless where 'tis a plain case that t'would make 'em miserable'.[19]

Many factors must have affected the actual significance of parental consent, one of which was the sex of the child. Hardly any men in the middle class married under the age of twenty-one when consent was necessary and those over age seem to have had very considerable freedom to marry whom they wished, subject of course to advice. Middle-class parents had a much greater proprietory interest in daughters, over 40 per cent of whom married under the age of twenty-one and so would require consent unless they married clandestinely. Licence applications suggest that this parental authority often continued long after the age of majority, since consent was often recorded for daughters well over twenty-one and even for some over thirty. Over age widows also often recorded their parents' consent to their second or subsequent marriages. However, no consent is mentioned for the majority of over age brides, who were normally described as 'at their own disposal'. This was often explained by a note that their parents were dead, an important consideration, since in these days of low expectation of life the chances of even one parent being alive at their children's marriages was not all that high.[20]

Another important factor would be the whereabouts of parents if they did happen to be alive when their children were courting. Only a minority of middle-class brides and grooms would have had parents living in the metropolis, since so many were immigrants, and this would surely affect the impact of parental consent. Some of the London middle class married girls from their region of origin and such marriages were probably not only consented to but largely arranged by their parents. The majority, however, married girls resident in the metropolis about whom their parents would have little but hearsay knowledge. This would not necessarily stop them taking a great interest but it would certainly affect the possibilities of strong parental control over the courtship process. Indeed, it is more likely that 'friends' rather than parents would be the main advisers in such cases.

There were, then, a number of factors tending to minimize the significance of parental consent to marriages, especially for young men. For girls, consent was more important, since they were younger when they got married. Girls were also thought to be wilful creatures, ignorant in the ways of the world, who, if left to make their own choice, were likely to pick badly. Parental objection to a girl's choice of marriage partner might be based on virtually any grounds but the two commonest were recorded by the merchant George Boddington in his autobiography. His daughter, Sarah, was at boarding school in Hackney where she fell in love with one Ebenezer Collier, 'whose circumstances being not correspondent with what I had to give her and an inquiry having had a miserable bad carracter of him I would not consent he should address her'. Things looked bad for Sarah, for she would not marry Ebenezer without her father's consent nor would Ebenezer marry her without such consent 'lest I should give him nothing'.[21]

This was, of course, the ultimate sanction of the authority of a middle-class father and a powerful sanction it was, for the attitude of Ebenezer was typical of young middling men, who would be extremely reluctant to marry a girl with no portion. Nor was it realistic to defy the father in the expectation that, when he died, the girl would receive her portion by the custom of London, which provided for the equal division of one third of a deceased citizen's estate between his children. The custom was firm on this point: 'If the daughter of a citizen of London marries in his life-time, against his consent, unless the father be reconciled to her before his death, she shall *not* have her orphanage share of his personal estate.'[22]

The wrath of the father could therefore extend beyond the grave. Nevertheless, one's impression is that the sanction of disinheritance, although often threatened, was rarely carried out. The mere suggestion that there might be no portion or that a portion might be reduced to a beggarly size was enough to drive away a faint-hearted suitor and bring most recalcitrant girls to heel. Persistence could, however, pay off, as it did in the case of George Boddington, who finally agreed to his daughter's marriage 'with great regret . . . and since to my great trouble' after being besieged by the friends and relations of both parties as well as flooded with the tears of his daughter herself. Some fathers may have been adamant to the end, but not a single example has been found of such adamancy affecting the division of estates by the Common Serjeant, the city official whose task it was to implement the custom of London in this respect.[23]

Further evidence that fathers were not as harsh in fact as they might be in fiction can be found in wills. The normal, indeed almost universal, provision in middle-class wills was for legacies and orphanage portions to be paid to daughters at marriage or at the age of twenty-one, whichever was earliest. In 181 wills made by the sample, only 14 have any comment at all to make about their daughters' marriages. Three fathers merely put in writing what most fathers probably felt. The banker Thomas Williams, for instance, wrote that 'my will and desire is that my children do cohabit with my wife and give due obedience to her and to be advised by her in all matters, more particularly in their respective marriages', but there were no penalties for disobedience. Another eight fathers willed that either a separate legacy or an orphanage portion or both would be void if their daughters married under the age of twenty-one without the consent of their mother or guardian, but there were no sanctions against daughters who married over twenty-one without consent. One man made a legacy, but not the orphanage portion, void for ever if the girl married at any time without her mother's consent. Finally, the brazier Robert Sellers left £600 to his only daughter Mary on condition that, if she married without her mother's consent, she was not to be paid till she was twenty-four and, tougher still, the merchant John Cary willed that 'if any of my [three] daughters marry without consent of my wife and my son Thomas Cary before the age of 30', they were to lose a legacy of £500, which would be shared amongst his other children. However, Cary, who left nearly £30,000, also bequeathed an unconditional £1000 to all his children on top of the £500 legacy.[24] To summarize, the vast majority of fathers provided no sanctions at all against daughters who married without consent, even though they were under age, and hardly any provided sanctions against those who were over age.

It seems reasonable to conclude that, where parents were present, they felt it their duty to advise, warn and cajole their children, particularly their daughters, but only very rarely to the extent of punishing them financially for disobedience. Children certainly seem to have accepted the role of parents and friends as advisers and were unhappy to marry without consent. The need for consent could also be used as a valuable delaying weapon in the process of courtship, giving daughters time to think, providing a handy excuse to get rid of or put off a suitor for whom they had little taste. Sons used the same excuse to avoid or postpone marriage to girls whom they had got pregnant.[25] It is often convenient to have some shadowy and older outsider who can be blamed for your not doing something that you in fact have no wish to do.

Who did the sons and daughters of the middle class marry

and how did they make their choice? Moralists emphasized that marriage should be based on love, or at least on affection, and warned young people against tying themselves for life to someone in whom they only had a material interest. The ideal of love and the 'home' was a strong one and is attractively recorded in the diary kept by the law student Dudley Ryder, who wrote that he had a strong inclination towards marriage, 'not from any principle of lust or desire to enjoy a woman in bed but from a natural tendency, a prepossession in favour of the married state. It is charming and moving, it ravishes me to think of a pretty creature concerned in me, being my most intimate friend, constant companion and always ready to soothe me, take care of me and caress me.'

It can be seen that Ryder's emphasis was not so much on passion, which most contemporaries regarded as 'the rash intemperance of youth', a dangerous state likely to blind people to reality, as on friendship and companionship. When describing a happy engaged couple, contemporaries sometimes said that they were 'in love', but words like 'kindness' and 'affection' were much commoner. 'They were kind and familiar together', 'he had a great kindness to her' or, alternately, 'she had no kindness for him' are the sort of expressions that appear again and again. One should also note that Ryder has a rather selfish view of marriage in that he assumed that it was to be his future wife who soothed, took care of and was concerned in him rather than that such matters should be truly mutual. This was certainly a common attitude in an unequal society. Men were expected to be kind, but they in turn expected to receive rather more than they gave in emotional terms.[26]

Although contemporaries emphasized the necessity of affection, very few would have thought that this was sufficient grounds for the choice of partner in the middle station of life. Material interest, character, social position and often religion had to be taken into consideration as well and the real problem was to balance such factors against affection. The ideal was equality of fortune, rank and religion, together with mutual affection, but in a society not blinded by passion, most were realistic enough to assume that such an ideal was not easily reached and that marriage in reality involved a trade-off between affection, material interests and social ambition.[27]

Most young men of the middle station desperately needed the money which would come as their wife's portion. For some, a dowry was the only way in which they could set up independently in business; for others, it was a very valuable second injection of capital, which would enable them to develop the business already started with capital provided by their parents. In such circumstances, another £100 of capital was a very important consideration and one that had to be carefully weighed against an attractive, affectionate but poorer girl. The same Dudley Ryder, who has just been quoted on the delights of the companionate marriage, was quite clear in his mind on this subject: 'Cousin Billio said for a young man not in business that had 2 or £3000 to marry a woman of perhaps 1 or £2000 it would keep him low all his life. This I must confess gave a great turn to my thoughts with respect to Mrs Marshall. Why should I think of having her when it would expose us both to want?'[28] Why indeed, and of course Cousin Billio's advice was in fact just as applicable to young men who were 'in business'.

The same considerations applied to girls, most of whom were brought up with a realistic idea of marriage and were discouraged, not always successfully, from filling their heads with romantic ideas derived from playbooks or novels. They knew that their choice of marriage partner would govern not only their future happiness but also their future position in the social and economic hierarchy and, since middle-class girls were bred to believe that to improve oneself was a good idea, they were usually happy enough for parents and friends experienced in the world to vet their suitors. Nonetheless, girls wanted affection too and felt that they themselves were most likely to be the best judges of the possibilities of this, though not all parents agreed with them.

If affection was too much to ask for, then they would at least want to like their husband, as the eldest daughter in Defoe's *Religious Courtship* said when asked what would be the basis of her choice. 'O! I'll explain it in a few words; a good estate, and a man you like.' Her younger sister had a rather more cynical view. 'Nay; you might have stopt at the first; it's no matter what the man is, if the estate be but good.' Few girls were quite so worldly and the courtship process was one in which conflicts of interest, emotion and duty to parents often gave rise to stress but, in the end, girls had to make the same trade-offs as men, though, as we have seen, the market was against women and so they more often got the worst of the bargain.[29]

One is in no position to analyse this internal bargaining process, to weigh the money against the emotion, nor indeed to see how it worked out in practice. One simply has to assume that some people were happy and some were not, that some were satisfied with their bargain and some regretted the calculus of courtship and would rather have had more money or more affection. Contemporaries tended to be cynical about marriage and to assume that most marriages were or would be unhappy; 'the greatest plague of human life', according to Thomas Tryon. The Rev. Richard Baxter was very pessimistic: 'There are scarce any two persons in the world, but there is some unsuitableness between them. . . .Some crossness there will be of opinion, or disposition, or interest, or will, by nature or by custom and education, which will stir up frequent discontents.' People are still cynical about marriage today, with some justification, but they still get married. Perhaps Dudley Ryder best explains why: 'At length we came to talk of matrimony, and I said though I had often upon consideration thought that the miseries and inconveniences that attended that state were much greater than the advantages of it and a man runs a vast hazard in entering upon it, yet at the same time I could not suppose myself capable of being completely happy here without it.'[30]

One can never really tell just why a particular man married a particular woman in the past. Nevertheless, patterns can be seen and they are those one would expect. Roger Pocock was the son of a yeoman who became a wealthy Hamburg merchant and married the daughter of a knight. When his only child Elizabeth was eighteen, she too was married to a knight. One has no idea whether Elizabeth was or believed that she was in love with Sir Thomas Travel; but it seems a reasonable assumption that the marriage choices were governed by the fact that the Pococks were moving up in the world, translating money into status, a common enough process which aroused the interest, envy or admiration of contemporaries, depending on their view of the world or their place in it.

William Melmoth was the son of another yeoman. In 1655,

he was apprenticed to George Johnson, an apothecary and, in 1662, he paid £4 to be released from his indentures four months early 'because he hopes to be partner to his master'. It is not totally surprising to discover that, shortly afterwards, he married Anne Johnson, his master's daughter, for this too was a common scenario, though not quite as common as the story books would tell us. Again, we do not know if Anne and William loved each other, but they would certainly have known each other very well since they had been living together in the same house for over seven years.[31]

William presumably had a business as well as an emotional interest in marrying Anne and such interests are obvious in most of the marriages on which there is any information. A merchant marries the daughter of another merchant; a bookseller the daughter of another bookseller; a mason marries the daughter of a plumber.[32] There is not space here to unravel the details of these relationships, though it would be interesting to do so. Nevertheless, enough hints are given to be sure that the London business world was meshed together by a honeycomb of kinship and particularly marriage relationships, just like the world of the gentry with which it was so closely connected.

Even when a business interest was not in the forefront of the relationship, sons and daughters were likely to marry the sons and daughters of business friends and acquaintances or at least of people of the same economic status. For these were the people whom they would meet or their parents would arrange that they would meet. London was a big place and one where women were not 'mewed up as in Italy or Spain', so it was easier for young people to play the field than it was in most countries.[33] Nevertheless, like tended to marry like and the ideal of equality of fortune and status was the one which most often governed the actual choice of partner. Disparities in status make for good stories and good drama, but good drama does not necessarily mirror social reality.

iv Courtship and Contract

Women and girls might not be 'mewed up', as they were abroad, but their accessibility to predators, lovers and suitors varied enormously. Many controlled the situation themselves since they lived on their own, 'at their own hands' in the contemporary phrase. Such women – girls from country famil- ies, orphan girls 'at their own disposal' and of course widows – might receive suitors, but they would be wise to find themselves some chaperone, such as a sister, a landlady or a 'friend', for people were always ready to think the worst of single women. It was only too easy to get the reputation of being 'a person of a lewd life and conversation'.[34] Women also seem to have had considerable freedom to move alone about the city and go to public places where they were likely to meet men. There is ample evidence of such meetings – in the streets, in shops, in the park, at church, in taverns and coffee-houses, at Mr Dawson's Dancing School where John Dunton played truant from his master during his affair with the 'beautiful Rachel Seaton', at a milk-woman's where the apothecary's apprentice Simon Mason drank glasses of syllabub in the company of Miss Weston, whose 'charms were chiefly in her father's long baggs, who was computed to be a twenty-thousand pound man'.[35]

Women certainly had more freedom than one might expect in a society whose laws and customs seemed designed to hold them down, but this freedom should not be exaggerated. It seems probable that access to most young girls of the middle station, especially those living at home with their parents, would have required rather more formality, though the degree of formality varied from family to family and there seem to have been few strict rules. Some fathers with marriageable daughters were very free and easy, inviting potential suitors to dine, encouraging them to come regularly to the house, allowing them to be alone for long periods with their daughters. Others kept their daughters much more closely 'mewed up' and it might take much ingenuity, time and argument for a suitor even to be given permission to make his addresses.[36]

Go-betweens and matchmakers might play a part in this courtship process. If you had decided on the girl you wanted to court, on the grounds of her attractions or her father's 'long baggs' or whatever other reason, it was often good policy to find someone to introduce you to the household as a young man 'of estate and of sober conversation'. Thus, in 1677, the courtier John Mazine used his acquaintance with a respected relation to get permission to court Mary Rawlinson, the daughter of a tavern-keeper 'with whom he intended to give a considerable portion'. Sometimes, there was a price to pay for such an introduction. In 1658, the Londoner Daniel Wright told a Leicestershire country gentleman that he was sure that he could make a match between him and Jane Cheeke, who 'had a considerable portion, . . . by reason of his intimacy' with her widowed mother. However, 'if the said marriage by his meanes did take effect', then he was to receive £200. How common such brokerage fees were one does not know, but given the mercenary nature of much of the London marriage market it seems probable that they were far from unusual. Some people certainly made a business of marriage broking. One went to a scrivener, for instance, not just to borrow money or to draw up a deed but also 'to find out a rich widow'. 'Experienc'd matrons' also played an important role and a young man who 'has not courage enough to trust his own judgment' would be well advised to apply 'to the next matchmaker in the neighbourhood who knows to a tittle the exact rates of the market and the current prices of young women that are fit to marry'.[37]

Mention of the market brings one to the serious side of courtship, the drawing up of 'a treaty of marriage', a business requiring such preliminary work as the investigation of the young man's claims of character, fortune and expectations. Too many people were like Thomas Burton, who, 'pretending himself to be seized . . . of £170 per annum and a personal estate of £1500 . . . was permitted to have recourse to Hannah Southwood', the daughter of a wealthy merchant. Since this quotation comes from a Chancery case, it is no surprise to learn that young Thomas was worth rather less than he pretended. Once both sides were satisfied with the other's credentials, it was time to get down to the details of the marriage contract, a process of negotiation and haggling like any other bargain, which can be illustrated by the 'communication' between John Austen and Hannah Hastings. John's father asked for £200 as Hannah's portion, in return for which he would settle lands of the value of £16 per annum for her jointure. This was a poor bargain and Hannah's father 'did refuse to give so great a marriage portion', offerring £60 instead. John's father 'did then refuse to accept this as not competent to ye condition and way of trade of him' and they finally settled for £85.[38]

These were the two main elements of a marriage contract, the portion brought by the girl and a settlement to provide for her maintenance if her husband died before her. A settlement in the form of a jointure, as in the example above, was the usual practice amongst the landed classes and was employed by some, but not very many, people in the London business world. It had the advantage of being fixed and settled in advance, a guarantee that the girl would not starve in widowhood. However, a jointure was far from attractive to a young businessman since it tied up so much capital in land, an asset unlikely to bring in much more than 4 or 5 per cent. For this reason, many men did not actually buy the land during their lifetime, or at least not until they retired, either promising their wives or binding themselves formally to make the purchase of lands of the agreed capital value a first charge on their estates when they died. Thus the Levant merchant Francis March covenanted to lay out £6000 on lands for the jointure of Mary Dunster when he married her in 1680. At his death in 1697, he had still not bought any land and he clearly continued to think that land was a bad investment, for he bequeathed the £6000 to trustees 'to place out at interest upon security'. A debt in his 1699 inventory reads 'To Mary March, relict . . . by her marriage articles for principle and interest from Christmas 1697 to Midsummer 1699 – £6540', that is £6000 plus eighteen months' interest at 6 per cent, a sum which amounted to 58 per cent of Francis March's net assets.[39]

Another way of providing a settlement of a fixed value was to bind oneself before marriage to bequeath a certain sum to one's widow, this being a first charge on the estate. Sir John Fryer, for instance, gave a bond to his future wife's father to leave her worth £1500, a sum three times her original portion of £500, though 'sometime after her father observing my industry and ye increase of my buisness added to it and made it up in all £1000'. There is not enough information available to know if such a ratio between portion and bond was typical but, if the normal ratio was some two or three times the portion, it was a real gamble on the husband's accumulation and life expectancy. Even at a 10 per cent rate of accumulation, it takes nearly eight years to double a fixed sum and nearly twelve years to treble it. Such gambles could leave all members of the family, except the widow, in a desperate situation. The draper John Ewens, for instance, covenanted to leave his wife Winifred £2000 but, when he died twenty-two years later, his net assets were only valued at £694. By contrast, James Tandin agreed to leave his wife Hester '£1000 and such jewels and wearing apparel as she had before marriage'. However, Tandin 'had a peculiar art as a pewterer' which enabled him to accumulate so rapidly that when he died he was worth somewhere between £6000 and £10,000, depending on whether one believes his widow or his executors, who were in dispute in Chancery as to whether the original bond disbarred the widow from her customary thirds, which would have doubled or trebled her inheritance. Of course, some people got such things exactly right. John Skrine married Esther Crosley when he was twenty-four and agreed to leave her £700. When he died just eight years later, he was worth £2144, making her pre-contracted £700 almost exactly equal to her widow's rights to a third of the estate.[40]

Only about 15 per cent of our sample made any provision to leave their widow a fixed capital sum, either by jointure or bond. The wives of all the rest had to take their chances that their husbands would prosper so that their customary thirds would provide them with decent security in the event of widowhood. This was one good reason to marry an older man, as Lucinda explained when her niece asked 'why must I be confined to aged people'. 'That reason is plain, because you don't know what the young ones may come to.' A marriage contract with no settlement was a much simpler document since it normally required no more than a statement of the dowry and the terms on which it would be paid. Sometimes there would also be provision for the wife's 'separate estate' if she had property of her own, for the payment to her of a fixed income as 'pin money' or for the wife to be allowed to bequeath a fixed sum from her portion as she wished. However, such provisions were fairly unusual amongst middling people and most marriage contracts were about portions. 'The money', as Moll Flanders said, 'was the thing.'[41]

There must have been rules and conventions, as well as market pressures, which determined the approximate size of the portion a girl would have to bring to her marriage with men of different fortunes and expectations and so determined in turn the parameters of the bargaining process. Such patterns have been discovered in aristocratic bridal portions, which increased fairly continuously in value through the seventeenth and eighteenth centuries.[42] The data are not sufficient to analyse middle-class marriage contracts, but it seems probable that if aristocratic portions were rising, this would affect the market for gentry and middle-station portions as well. The middle-class ideal was 'equality of fortune', which appears to mean that a girl should bring a portion roughly equal to the fortune of the man she was marrying. This would make good sense, since, under the custom of London, the orphanage portion of a girl was exactly the same as that of her brother and it would be someone of the same status and fortune as her brother that she would be likely to marry.

However it was calculated, the portion was a substantial sum and was a very important factor in the process of accumulation which lay at the heart of middle-class life. The merchant George Boddington, for instance, got £2000 with his first wife Mary Steele, who died two years later in childbirth. 'Her father and mother manifested a great love and kindness to me after her decease and . . . advised me to marry agayne being young', advice which Boddington took seven months later when he married Hannah Cope, who brought him £3000, a process of multiple accretion to his personal fortune which was not unusual in a city which had very high rates of adult and particularly maternal mortality.[43] Lesser man naturally attracted much smaller portions but, if our interpretation of 'equality of fortune' is correct, nearly everyone could expect to double his original capital by marriage, a fact which might make even the most ardent misogynist a supporter of the institution.

Portions were not always all paid at once; a large sum down and the balance in six months or a year was a common practice. Sometimes, the balance was paid in instalments at the birth of each successive child or on an annual basis. Richard Mackernes, for instance, a London brickmaker, agreed to pay a certain sum down to Mintham Robinson, a carpenter who married his daughter Christian in 1652, and then to pay £13 per annum for the first seven years of the marriage and £3 per annum for the next nine. It was even agreed that some portions be paid posthumously, such as that of Thomas Robinson, an innkeeper who 'not having ready money' for his daughter's portion, entered a bond to pay his son-in-law £50 after his death.[44] Many other portions had to be claimed posthumously since fathers-in-law did not always pay up what they had promised. Whatever the particular arrangement, the portion was an essential feature of middle-class marriage and it would be very unusual to find one in which the bride brought nothing into the new household. Such considerations take us a long way away from the love and affection which was supposed to be the basis of marriage, even for middling people in Augustan London. However, the emphasis is not misplaced. Moll Flanders was right; money really was rather important in the marriages of this class.

v Relations between the Sexes

What was marriage actually like in Augustan London? Here, one moves into a field which historians have turned into a jousting-ground where they tilt at each other with quotations proving that there was more or less love, companionship and other desirable qualities of matrimony in the relationships of our ancestors.[45] The lists will not be entered here, for there are no answers to such questions. It would be easy to string together quotations illustrating a close and even passionate relationship between married people. It would also be easy to illustrate relationships in which hate, disgust, despair or total indifference seem to be the main emotions; no wonder, since the records of divorce have been used for much of the evidence. This material will be used in this section to illustrate how contemporaries expected husband and wife to behave towards each other, but first some factors will be set out which suggest that relationships between partners in middle-class marriages of our period would be different, but not necessarily worse, than they are today.

Although no one would claim that there was equality between the sexes in the 1980s, there was certainly much less equality in the 1680s. As has been said, a wife was treated in law as a *feme covert*, a minor almost totally under the legal subjection of her husband, an upper servant rather than an equal. Law was mirrored by custom, which supported a 'double standard' of morality in which, for example, adultery by a husband was considered a mere trifle compared with adultery by a wife. Law and custom were supported by even liberal conduct books, which emphasized partnership, love and mutual respect as the basis of marriage, but still made it clear that the husband was the senior partner.[46]

Law and custom, then, were on the side of male dominance, wifely obedience and paternalism in marriage. All these were surely reinforced by the age differences between husband and wife in middle-class marriages. Most girls in this class were married from homes in which they had been brought up to respect and obey their parents in particular and their elders in general. If they then married a man considerably older than themselves, is it really likely that they would be able to consider themselves his equal in any meaningful way? Conversely, would one expect a merchant of thirty who had spent some ten years travelling abroad and trading on his own to treat a girl of twenty as his equal? He would certainly treat no one else of that age as an equal, the age of his servants, apprentices and youngest siblings. This is not to say that our hypothetical merchant might not be very fond of his young wife, even in love with her, but that he would be unlikely to find her 'a person capable of advising with and consulting upon any difficulty or occurrence', qualifications which Dudley Ryder thought would be 'very good' in a wife.[47]

The third point distinguishing middle-class marriages of our period from those of today is the question of money. Whatever one may say about the relative significance of love and money in choice of partners, there is absolutely no doubt that money played a very important, if not predominant, part in the process. Marriage has always been a lottery, whatever the basis of the choice of partners, and a choice based on money may well lead to as good a marriage as one based on love or affection. Nevertheless, it seems reasonable to argue that the emphasis on money was just one more factor making the likelihood of a happy marriage even less than today, that is if we use today's criterion of what constitutes a happy marriage. Our ancestors seem to have been less optimistic and perhaps more realistic in their expectations of what one was likely to get from marriage.

The last point to be made is that the state of marriage was even easier to enter in our period than it is today, but was almost impossible to get out of again if the marriage turned out to be unhappy, except through the very common event of one of the partners dying. Divorce, as we know it, with the possibility of remarriage, was virtually unknown. Mutual agreements to separate were quite possible and a complacent husband might make a generous settlement to support a wife with whom he no longer wished to live. Where such collusion was impossible, an injured wife could sue for divorce in the church courts on the grounds of desertion, cruelty or her husband's adultery. These were divorces 'from bed and board', that is, legal separations with no provision for remarriage. Such cases could be difficult to prove and, when the court did find in favour of the wife, the alimony awarded was rarely attractive to a middle-class wife, the normal rates at the end of the seventeenth century being between 5s. and 10s. a week, the wages of a working woman, enough to live on but hardly enough to support the genteelness of the middle station.[48] A wife who left her husband without sufficient cause or eloped with someone else had no financial claims and was therefore bound either to descend into poverty or be dependent on a lover who had no legal necessity to support her. Better, then, to stay at home, for 'although a wife is very lewd, if she lives with her husband, he is chargeable for all necessaries for her, because he took her for better or worse'.[49]

Contemporaries knew that marriage was unlikely to be perfect, but they had a fairly clear idea of what was or was not conducive to a reasonable degree of harmony in the household. This can be illustrated from the evidence given in divorce cases. The witnesses were giving evidence for or against one of the parties and it can be assumed that they were often exaggerating, if not downright lying. However, their assumptions about what makes for harmony are still quite clear.

It can be said at the outset that they disapproved of what one might expect. They disapproved of 'the foul crime of adultery', but both men and women witnesses applied the 'double standard' to this and disapproved more of women who committed adultery than men and especially of convinced and repeated adulteresses, such as the one reported as saying 'I would damn my soul to make my arse merry'. Where men attracted particular opprobrium was when they contracted pox from their infidelity and so infected their wives and unborn children, a state of affairs which seems to have been regrettably common. Witnesses also disapproved of cruelty and none of the condonement of physical chastisement of wives has been found, which one might expect from literary evidence of the period. Defoe, for instance, thought that the beating of wives was on the increase, so much so that their screams did not even bother the neighbours. 'The common answer to one another is only thus; "'tis nothing neighbour, but such a one beating his wife"; "O dear", says the other, "is that all?", and in they go again, compos'd and easie.' However, such scenarios do not appear in the legal records; on the contrary, neighbours came right into the house to stop husbands beating their wives and such behaviour was never implicitly condoned by saying that, in this particular case, the beating was done 'without cause' or some similar expression. It seems that husbands were not expected to beat their wives and wives, of course, were not supposed to beat their husbands or 'fly in their faces and tear their hair'.[50]

An idea of how wives and husbands were expected to behave can most easily be gained by quoting adjectives and phrases which describe good or bad behaviour.[51] To start with the bad, or at least not very good, wife: she was likely to be 'very perverse and morose' or perhaps 'proud, ambitious and passionate', to call her husband 'opprobrious names' and use 'undutifull' language. She might well be 'a person of a very turbulent spirit', almost daily disturbing and disquieting the household, perhaps so much so that by her 'disturbance and noise' she drove her husband away from the warm fire in the dining room to find quiet but freezing cold in another room. She was likely to go to taverns and keep lewd company and her 'goings abroad' and 'stayings out late' and 'keeping of loose and strange company' would be 'without the consent, well likeing and contrary to the desires and admonitions' of her husband. Such a wife who 'would not keep at home' would also probably be 'a very extravagant wife' who 'wore more new cloathes than became her condition . . . and hath wasted and mispent a great deal of money'. Wives like this quite often stole from husbands or took goods from his shop to support their extravagance. Bad wives also damaged the husband's business more obliquely by shouting at him in his shop, being 'perverse' or 'proud' towards the customers or calling the female customers 'whore' when their husband shook their hands to seal a bargain. Some wives might take a perverse pleasure in such destructive activity, glorying in their husband's failing business and swearing before witnesses that 'she would ruin him and make him rot in a jayl'. Finally, a bad wife would not only lose her husband business but would destroy the good name of the family by making herself 'the town talk' or by using such 'horrid oaths and imprecations' that she caused 'a mobb to come about his house to his great disgrace and the disturbance of the neighbourhood'.

The good wife would do none of these things. She would be 'a person of a modest and civil behaviour and demeanour' who 'carried and behaved herself towards the said George her husband as a loving dutifull and observant wife'. She would be 'an honest woman and as vertuous as the Virgin Mary', 'very obedient and loving', 'sober', 'affectionate' and 'obliging'. She would cause no trouble in the family nor amongst her neighbours, who would describe her as 'a person of good creditt and reputation' of whom they had 'never heard any ill'.

These epithets, from men and women, rich and poor, servants and householders, make it clear what the world expected from a wife. She should be obedient, dutiful, affectionate, modest and self-effacing, frugal in her household management, and should be careful to control her temper and not allow herself to be proud, ambitious or passionate. She was, in short, expected to know her place and to behave accordingly. She should give her husband no cause to treat her badly and she should love him or at least be affectionate to him. Nothing much is said about marital sexual relationships in these depositions, but it is clear that the wife was expected to sleep in the same bed with her husband and be available for his embraces, though under some circumstances, such as his catching the pox from his whores, it was accepted that a wife might well want to 'part beds'.

What did a husband have to do to deserve such a paragon of a wife? He should first of all be 'a person of a sober and chaste life and of very civill conversation . . . and of very good character and esteem amongst his acquaintance'. He should 'behave and demean himself very kindly and affectionately' towards his wife, 'as a kind and loving husband'. 'No angry word or frown', let alone a blow, a kick or the threat of a 'naked sword' should 'proceed from him to his said wife'. 'Mildness and gentleness' were praised, in addition to 'a great deal of affection and respect'. He should 'provide for and furnish . . . all things that were necessary and convenient for her and suitable to his condition and circumstances'. Indeed, he should also think of her 'condition' and would acquire praise if he did 'att all times and upon occasions with great readiness and willingness of mind allow [his wife] all necessaries and conveniences suitable to her quality and estate', though in doing so he should not go 'beyond his circumstances', 'a frugall saveing man' being an object of praise in the accumulative world of the middle station.

Needless to say, the sort of husband who appears in the records of a divorce suit rarely behaved with such generosity, consideration and affection. He tended to be 'an extravagant man in his expenses and much addicted to drinking' or 'a person of a harsh temper and disposition' who would call his wife 'severall opprobrious names as bitch and whore', without cause. He might well treat his wife 'in a very unkind and cruel manner and often quarrell with her . . . without any cause . . . in a violent passion'. He was likely to be described as 'surly', 'morose', 'inhumane' and 'debaucht', but much the commonest epithet used for a bad husband was that he was 'unkind' to his wife, the sort of man about whom a servant might say that she 'seldom or never observed him to be any wayes loving or tender to . . . his wife'.

What do these brief extracts tell us about relations between the sexes? Most of them, in different language, could be found in any manual on how to conduct a marriage. People then, as now, expected couples to try to conduct their relationships in a harmonious manner, giving no pain to each other and offering no disturbance to the rest of the household or the neighbourhood. Couples were also, as one might expect, supposed to be affectionate to each other. However, there are some aspects of marriage in our period which distinguish it from modern marriage. The emphasis on wifely obedience, duty and respect

is an obvious example, but there are other slightly more subtle
aspects of the same thing. The wife more often has to have
'cause' if she does anything out of the ordinary, such as the wife
who was said never to 'call her husband any opprobrious names
or use any undutifull language saving that once upon [her
husband] calling her . . . whore, shee did . . . call him pitifull
fellow'. The wife has to be much more chaste and in general
has less latitude in behaviour. She was more confined, less able
to go out and about as she wished, 'without the consent' of her
husband, though she was certainly not so much confined as
most European wives of the same period. There is also a subtle
difference in the quality of the affection expected between the
sexes, with the wife being expected to be more 'loving' and the
husband more 'kind', an emotion which could be interpreted as
slightly patronizing or paternalist.

Nevertheless, despite these rather different expectations of
the behaviour of husband and wife, the records do make it clear
that the wife is not a downtrodden creature whom a husband
can treat as he likes. What is striking in the depositions is the
fact that wives so often gave as good as they got, or better. They
were independent individuals who would strike and abuse a
husband they did not like or who treated them badly. They
would say that they would do as they please and then proceed
to do as they pleased. Mild and meek they were supposed to be,
but in reality the women of the middle station were quite
capable of holding their own on the battlefield of marriage.

8 The Household

It was normal practice in England, as in most regions where the Western marriage system held sway, for each new marriage to create a new household and middling Londoners were no different from their fellow-countrymen in this respect. In the early years of marriage, a couple might share a house but not a household with some other family or families, as lodgers in two or three rooms or as joint-occupiers of a house with a senior partner. But nearly everybody aimed to have a house of their own eventually, once sufficient accumulation had taken place. This chapter will look at the houses of the middle station and at the people who lived in them together with the master and his wife, but first it is necessary to say a few words about where these houses were.

London was not yet a city with the rigid class segregation that was to develop in the late nineteenth and twentieth centuries. There were 'rich' areas, such as the central City and the West End, while most of the rest of the metropolis was relatively 'poor'. However, no area was totally rich or poor, so that 'the parish was more like a microcosm of the city as a whole than a social quarter'.[1] In an age when what public transport was available was both slow and expensive, it was necessary for the rich to be surrounded by middling and poor people to serve them. Nor were the poor areas all poor, for the densely packed, small, low-quality housing of the 'proletariat' was interspersed with individual houses of high quality in which lived the manufacturers who employed them and the shop-keepers who sold them their necessities.[2]

It is, then, no surprise to find middle-class people scattered throughout the metropolis, the 375 men in the sample living in no less than 118 different parishes.[3] However, there was a heavy concentration of the wealthier middle class in the central parishes of the City, where most of the merchants and whole-salers and many of the richer shopkeepers lived. Other smart shopkeepers and people providing high-class services lived in the West End near to their upper-class customers. Most manu-facturers lived either on the borders of the City proper or beyond the City in the so-called 'extramural' parishes, the product of London's first expansion outside its ancient walls, or beyond that in Clerkenwell, Shoreditch, the East End and Southwark. These areas were also the homes of small shop-keepers serving the manufacturing population, whilst such people as builders and the various sorts of caterer and victualler might be found anywhere in the built-up area.

It should finally be noted that some members of the 'London' middle class chose not to live in London at all. There were, for example, fifteen men in the sample who illustrated a developing trend of city life by living in a villa or farm just outside the metropolis, their homes being in such places as Leyton, Totten-ham, Islington, Hammersmith and Wandsworth. Nearly all these men were either rentiers or retired or, if they were still active, were merchants, men who reflect the truth of Defoe's remarks on the fine buildings of Tottenham, which generally belonged 'to the middle sort of mankind, grown wealthy by trade, and who still taste of London; some of them live both in the city and in the country at the same time'.[4]

i The Middle-Class House

Londoners have always been famous for 'the agility, the ease and the quickness' with which they climb up and down large numbers of stairs and the people of our period had already adopted that vertical way of living which distinguishes the London living space from that in most other continental capitals.[5] The typical middle-class house was similar to those which estate agents today call Georgian or Early Victorian, a narrow-fronted tall house with three, four or five storeys with two or sometimes three rooms to each floor. Most houses had a yard at the back, sometimes with access to warehousing or stabling and so through into a narrow back lane, while a few had proper gardens, mostly those in the suburbs but including a few of the grander houses in the centre of the City. Most houses had a cellar, normally not as high-ceilinged as the modern 'basement', with storage for business purposes or for coal, beer and other things belonging to the household. Nearly all houses also had a garret floor set in the roof, which was used for servants' bedrooms, storage and occasionally for work purposes, the looms of weavers often being set up in garrets with large windows to catch the light.[6]

Most of the houses in which the middling people lived were comparatively new, either because they were in areas which had only been recently built up or because they were City houses rebuilt after the Great Fire. The Rebuilding Act of 1667 had laid down strict rules of standardization which reflected the best practice already existing and so reinforced the tendency to uniformity of London houses. There were to be four classes of house: those of four storeys (not counting garrets) on the 'high and principal streets', three storeys on 'streets and lanes of note' and two storeys on 'by-lanes', while provision was also made for houses 'of the greatest bigness', 'merchants' houses' of a maximum height of four storeys which generally stood back from the street with courtyards and gardens. The thickness of walls and ceiling heights on different floors were specified and builders were required to use non-inflammable materials such as brick, stone and tiles.[7] Such provisions meant that most London houses would have looked almost exactly the same had it not been for the individuality of builders, which was reflected in the use of different colours and patterns of brickwork, elaborate cornices and balconies, mean or magnificent doorways and windows and the like.

Not very many middling people owned the freehold of their houses, most freeholds in the City belonging to public bodies, such as the Corporation, parishes, hospitals and Livery Companies, or to ground landlords who tended to be absentee and aristocratic. This latter group also owned most of the land in the West End and the suburbs, which they developed by selling long leases to builders and other speculators or to potential occupiers who wished to build on their land. Owners of City freeholds also sold long leases and over a third of our sample owned a lease of their dwelling-houses for which they paid a quit or ground rent to the landlord. The amount paid ranged from the full commercial rent or rack-rent to a fairly nominal sum and valuations varied accordingly, the valuation of a lease on a rack-rent normally being zero and of a long lease with a small quit-rent being between eight and twelve times the computed rental income which could have been earned had the property been let out. Such valuations obviously fell as the date approached when a new bargain had to be struck with the ground landlord and a fresh capital sum (known as a fine) laid out to extend the lease.[8]

Leases tended to be very long. An average of twenty-seven years remained on the leases of dwelling-houses occupied by our sample when they died and, of course, such leases would have been considerably longer when first negotiated. Most corporate bodies had had financial difficulties during the Civil War and Interregnum, and had decided to solve these embarrassments by sacrificing long-term annual rental income in return for selling long leases for as large a fine as they could get. This process was intensified by the Great Fire. Landlords were desperately keen to rebuild but few had the capital to do the job themselves. The easiest solution was to get the occupier or some other person to rebuild at his own expense in return for a further extension of the lease, often to sixty years or more, and a reduction of the ground rent.[9]

Investment in long leases tied up capital, several hundred pounds in the central City area, which could have been invested in a business.[10] It is not surprising, then, that the majority of our sample rented their shops and dwelling-houses, either from the owners of long leases or directly from the ground landlords. In 1776, Adam Smith thought that house rent in London was greater than in any other European city, partly 'from those causes which render it dear in all capitals, the dearness of labour, the dearness of all the materials of building . . . the dearness of ground-rent', but also because of 'the peculiar manners and customs of the people which oblige every master of a family to hire a whole house from top to bottom'. Such conditions already existed in our period and rents were high, especially in the major shopping streets. The highest rent that has been found in an inventory was £80 a year paid by a jeweller in Cheapside; typical high rents in the central City area or the Strand were £50 to £60 a year; while off the main streets in the City or in meaner areas, rents for middle-class houses were about £20 to £30.[11]

These were major fixed costs to set against a business, the equivalent of the wages of one or even two journeymen for a year or of three or four domestic servants and their keep. One way to make sure that one could pay the rent even when trade was poor was to take in lodgers, particularly high-class lodgers who could pay a good rent, and this was a common practice. Adam Smith thought that competition between shopkeepers in this respect explained the low rates paid by lodgers compared with the high rents paid by shopkeepers for their houses, although in fact the rates paid by lodgers do not seem to have been particularly low. Jonathan Swift was paying 8s. a week or £20 a year for the first floor (a dining-room and bed-chamber) of a house in Bury Street in 1710, a rent which he thought 'plaguy deep' but was about the norm for lodgings suitable for gentryfolk during the reign of Queen Anne. In 1706, Francis Tallents reported to a friend in Derbyshire that 'you can not expect to board at London under £20 a year at least for yourself, and proportionately for your maid'. The poor, few of whom earned £20 in a year, obviously paid very much less and de Saussure said that weekly rates for rooms in London ranged from 'sixpence to half a guinea a head'. However, most lodgers in middle-class houses, who tend to be described by such labels as 'Mister' or 'Captain', were paying nearer half a guinea than sixpence and such payments could be a useful income for a shopkeeper.[12] It was, however, a considerable nuisance to have your first floor occupied by strangers, as can be seen when the lay-out of houses is considered.

The number of rooms and their distribution within the house obviously varied, depending on the number of storeys, on whether a back extension had been built, and on the idiosyncrasies of particular builders. Nevertheless, the structure of London houses led to some uniformity in the way that they were laid out.[13] A common arrangement was to have the shop or work-shop on the ground floor, with cellar beneath and yard behind, the kitchen and dining-room on the first floor, two bedrooms including the best bedroom on the second floor and then either a third floor with two more bedrooms with garrets above or straight up to the two garret rooms, which were most commonly used as servants' bedrooms.

Another arrangement was to have the kitchen on the ground floor. This was sometimes because the house was small, such as that of William Justice, a comb-maker in Whitechapel, who had his workshop at the front and his kitchen at the back on the ground floor, a dining-room and one good bedroom on the first floor and two garret bedrooms above. People who needed no shop were also likely to use the ground floor as living space. Joshua Marshall, who built many houses for other people, showed his own preference with a front parlour and kitchen on the ground floor and a large yard behind where he stored building materials. Many merchants and professional people needed only a counting-house at street level and would use the back of the ground floor as a large kitchen which could be extended out into the yard in the form of a buttery or wash-house.[14] This made access to piped water easier and gave servants plenty of work space, but it also meant that all the food had to be carried up 'one pair of stairs' since most people had their dining-room on the first floor, normally the grandest floor of the London house.

Not everyone occupied a whole house, even in the middle station. Some people only rented one or two floors in somebody else's house. Some managed with even less, such as the Levant merchant William Edwards, who died worth nearly £6000 but was living with his wife and small baby in only two rooms. However, Edwards was only thirty-one and had been married less than a year when he died and he would probably have moved into something more fitting to his status if he had lived longer. Many other people rented or owned the lease of a whole house, but did not fill every room with their family, servants and goods. The other rooms would have been occupied by lodgers, some in furnished rooms, which appear in inventories since the furniture was the property of the deceased citizen, and some in unfurnished rooms, which usually do not. This can lead to some confusion since rooms or whole floors will be missing from the inventory and one can easily get a false impression of the lay-out.[15]

Thus the number of rooms used for domestic purposes might vary quite considerably. The smallest living space in our

TABLE 8.1: Number of Rooms in Houses

Number of Rooms	Number in Sample	
	No.	%
4 and under	37	11.5
5 to 8	209	64.7
9 to 12	64	19.8
13 and over	13	4.0
	323	100.0

Average number of rooms = 7.2
Median number of rooms = 7

Source: Inventories of sample. Inns and taverns and inventories where rooms are not listed separately have been excluded. Rooms are defined as in note 16.

TABLE 8.2: Number of Rooms by Wealth Groups

Wealth Group	Average	Median	No. of Cases
Less than £500	5.7	6	81
£500–£999	5.8	6	41
£1000–£1999	7.1	7	60
£2000–£4999	7.6	7	80
£5000 and over	9.5	9	61

Source: As in Table 8.1.

inventories was a single room occupied by Lawrence Pinder, a rather poor widower with one child, who was probably boarded out; the largest, not counting inns and taverns, was nineteen rooms occupied by James Birkin, a wealthy alderman and Levant merchant who lived in Mincing Lane, a property which included gardens, summer-house, stables and warehouses and whose lease was valued at over £5000.[16] Houses can be found with every number of rooms between these extremes, but for most people there was considerable uniformity in the number of rooms which they occupied, as is seen in Table 8.1 above. Nearly two-thirds of houses had between five and eight rooms, which were typically arranged on three or four floors (including garrets) above the shop, the standard arrangement for the median seven-room house being five bedrooms, kitchen and dining-room or four bedrooms, kitchen, dining-room and parlour.

In Table 8.2 (p. 211), it can be seen that richer people tended to have more rooms, as would be expected, but the medians do not cover a very wide range, varying only from six for the poorer members of the sample to nine for the richest, despite the fact that the latter were at least ten times as rich as the former. Rooms in the houses of the rich were no doubt larger than those of the poor, but the constraints on London houses meant that there were limits to the ostentation one could display in one's dwelling-house. There was just not enough room in good commercial areas for many urban palaces on the scale of James Birkin's house in Mincing Lane, even though there were many other wealthy men with the £5000 necessary to acquire the lease.

ii The Structure of the Household

Who lived in middle-class houses can be discovered by looking at the structure of households. Much the best source for this is the series of assessments produced for the tax on burials, births and marriages which came into force on 1 May 1695. This tax required parishes to produce a complete enumeration of their populations and these are listed in a standard form, which enables one to see not only who was living in a house in 1695, but also the relationship of most of the occupants to the householder.[17]

These assessments were first analysed by Gregory King, who found an average of six 'heads per house' in the parishes within the walls, five in the extramural parishes and four and three-quarters in the remaining parishes of the metropolis, and his first two figures were confirmed in 1935 by Jones and Judges, who found 6.1 and 5.1 persons per house in the intramural and extramural parishes respectively.[18] One would expect middle-class households to have rather more occupants than the average, so one may hazard a guess that the average middling household had some seven to eight persons living in it, a density of about one person per room, though of course some people such as the master had exclusive use of much more of this space than others, such as the foot-boy.

The variety which made up this average of seven or eight persons per household can be seen in Table 8.3 overleaf, where the members of thirty-six households are set out. It has been compiled by linking data from the sample with the tax data, a task much simplified by the excellent index to the assessments.[19] This linking exercise shows that several people must have deceived the assessors and so avoided the surtax paid by those worth more than £600. The most blatant example was Samuel Palmer, a cheesemonger who was also a collector for the tax. He was taxed in 1695 as a man with less than £600 but died in 1701 with a fortune of £3603, a remarkable rate of accumulation.[20] There were also several people alive in 1695 who were not listed as resident in the family home. The merchant Daniel Wigfall was listed as living with his son and one female servant, but had a wife and no less than seven other children alive in 1695. The assessment for Francis Levett lists his wife, a footman and a maid; none of his six children alive in 1695 is mentioned. Both these men had country houses, one in Woodford and one in Enfield, and, since the assessments were supposed to be made on or before May Day, it seems probable that the missing members of their families were enjoying the spring air.[21] Since these and other similar cases rather distort the 'families' of our sample, they have been left out of the table.

The table shows that middle-class households took on a variety of forms, as might be expected, but a few general points can be made. First, virtually all the families had servants; indeed, they are so regular a feature that one suspects that a servant or servants have been overlooked in the assessment of John Rouse (No. 11), a wealthy cheesemonger and the only household without a single servant. Only a few assessments distinguish between apprentices and domestic servants, lumping them together under 'servants'. However, it is a reasonable assumption that, in most cases (except Nos 35 and 36), the male servants were either apprentices or, if they were over twenty-five, journeymen, clerks or book-keepers – in other words, the 'service' they performed was connected with the business side of household life. Most of the female servants, who appear in every house but two, would have been true

TABLE 8.3: Households in 1695

Key: Numbers in brackets represent ages in 1695, if known; m. = date of marriage if known; (1 = first, 2 = second marriage); M = Male, F = Female.

Head of Household	Wife	Children	Servants	Others	Total
1. Edward Osborn(30) Tavern-keeper	Yes(26) 1m.1693		Male Female		4
2. Francis Grevill(32) Rentier/banker	Yes(24) 1m.1693		Male Female		4
3. Thomas Penford(34) Ironmonger	Yes(22) 1m.1693		Male Female		4
4. Lancelot Baker(42) Jeweller	Yes 1m.		Male Female		4
5. Gilbert Lancaster(24) Victualler	Yes 1m.1693	Gilbert(2)	Female		4
6. Thomas Barber(40) Cook-shop	Yes(39) 1m.1682	Matthew	Male Female		5
7. Henry Winston(30) Cooper	Yes(30) 2m.		Male Male Female		5
8. George Fryer(35) Haberdasher	Yes(32) 1m.1688	George Priscilla	Female		5
9. Alan Hackshaw(42) Grocer	Yes(40) 1m.1677	Elizabeth	Male Female		5
10. John Barrow(28) Tavern-keeper	Yes(26) 1m.1692		Male Male Male Female		6
11. John Rouse(35) Cheesemonger	Yes(36) 1m.1687	Nathaniel Susanna(5)		Lodger(M) Lodger(F)	6
12. Samuel Hayward(40) Grocer	Yes 1m.1681	Mary(10) William	Male Female		6
13. John Sherwood(29) Drysalter	No		Male Male Male Female	Brother(25)	6
14. Richard Harrison(28) Cloth factor	Yes 1m.1688	Richard	Male(25+) Female	Lodger(F) Lodger(M)	7
15. Samuel Palmer(43) Cheesemonger	Yes 2m.	James(10) Samuel(7) Joseph(2)	Male Female		7

Head of Household	Wife	Children	Servants	Others	Total
16. Thomas Wise(30) Clockmaker	Yes 1m.1689	Thomas	Male Male Female	Lodger(M)	7
17. Luke Meredith(34) Bookseller	No 1m.1687	Elizabeth(7) Royston(3)	Male Female Female	Lodger(M)	7
18. Henry Waller(41) Horner	Yes(27) 2m.1694	Edmund William(7) Susan	Male Male Female		8
19. George Carew(58) Merchant	Yes(50) 1m.1666	Thomas Richard Alice Penelope	Male(25+) Female		8
20. Richard Lillie(33) Coal merchant	Yes(32) 1m.1688	Sarah(7) Abraham(5) Anne(3) Mary(0)	Female Female		8
21. John Broadhurst(44) Draper/outfitter	Yes 1m.1686	John Sarah Dorothy	Male Male Female		8
22. Peter Vansittart(45) Merchant	Yes 1m.1678	Robert(16) Susanna Peter(15) William	Male(25+) Male Female		9
23. Thomas Jones(43) Apothecary	Yes(39) 1m.1677	Thomas(16+) Katherine(10) James(8)	Male Male Female Female		9
24. William Fitzhugh(48) Paper-seller	Yes(36) 2m.	Elizabeth Robert Anthony Mary Hannah	Male Female		9
25. Philip Scarth(52) Druggist	Yes 1m.	Philip William Thomas Margaret	Male Female Female		9
26. John Aldersley(56) Leather-seller	Yes(42) 1m.1680	Robotham Thomas Anne	Male Female Female Female		9

Head of Household	Wife	Children	Servants	Others	Total
27. Nevill Lemon(38) Mercer	Yes(38) 1m.1684	William Anne Lucy	Male Male Female Female	Lodger(M)	10
28. Abraham Cullen(31) Haberdasher	Yes(27) 1m.1693	Jane Sarah	Male(25+) Male Female Female	Father Lodger(M)	10
29. John Carter(47) Tavern-keeper	Yes(42) 1m.1673	Edward(14) Martha(11) Elizabeth(7)	Male Male Female Female Female		10
30. Robert Maddox(44) Distiller	Yes(31) 2m.1686	Francis Joseph Jane Elizabeth	Male(25+) Male Male Female Female		11
31. John Hicks(34) Tobacco-refiner	Yes(29) 1m.1689	John(5)	Male(25+) Male(25+) Male Male Female Female	Lodger(M) Lodger(F)	11
32. Francis Minshall(56) Orange-merchant	Yes(37) 1m.1681	Mary(13) Elizabeth(11) Chris(10) Margaret(9) Francis(6)	Male Male Female Female		11
33. John Mumford(55) Tobacconist	Yes(42) 1m.1673	Edmund(20) John(18) Mary(15) Augustin(13) Elizabeth(10) Anne(8) Samuel(5)	Female	Brother	11
34. Thomas Lawrence(47) Bricklayer/builder	Yes 1m.	Mary Jonathan(14+) Sarah Anne	Male Female	Lodger(M) Lodger(F) Lodger(F) Lodger(F)	12

Head of Household	Wife	Children	Servants	Others	Total
35. Sir William Hedges(63) Merchant/rentier	Yes 2m.1687	William(19) Susanna(17) Robert(14) John(7) Charles(4)	Male Male Male Male Female Female Female		14
36. John Cary(51) Merchant	Yes 2m.1672	Thomas(28) John(18) Mary(17) Elizabeth(15) Richard(14) Hannah(9) William(6) Peter(1)	Male Male Female Female Female Female	Kin(F)	17

Source: CLRO Marriage Assessments were linked with members of the sample. Ages of husband and wife are mainly from marriage allegations. Ages of children are calculated from ages in the Common Serjeant's Book given at the time of the citizen's decease. Bachelors over 25 were distinguished by the tax. The following children known to be alive in 1695 are missing from the assessments: No.11 (Ann, aged 1); No.18 (Grace, aged 1); No.19 (George, John and Catherine, all at least in their teens by 1695); No.22 (Emma, probably already married, and Jacob, in teens); No.25 (John, aged 11 and Richard, aged 8); No.36 (Callow, over 18, and Robert, between 1 and 6). There may be many reasons for these absences, including carelessness on the part of the assessors, but one could put forward the hypothesis that the very young children were at nurse, the two boys aged 8 and 11 were at boarding school and the older children were either apprentices if boys or married if girls.

domestics, though it is probable that some served in the shop as well or in the bars of the two taverns. The next point to note is that lodgers, although not uncommon, were hardly as ubiquitous as Adam Smith suggested, less than a quarter of the families having any lodgers at all.[22] Finally, it can be noted that resident kinfolk outside the nuclear family were unusual, there being only two brothers, one father and one unspecified 'kinswoman' in the thirty-six families.

It is, then, the number of resident children and servants who determine the size of the household in the majority of cases. Nearly all the small households were those of comparatively young people who had only recently married and so were likely to have no or few children and less need for many servants. It is less easy to generalize about large households since their composition varied so much. Some resulted from large numbers of children (e.g. No. 33), some from large numbers of children and great wealth, which enabled a staff of six or seven servants to be kept (Nos 35 & 36). Other large households might result from the residence in the family home of an industrial labour force, such as seems to be the case in the home of the tobacco-refiner John Hicks (No. 31), whose two lodgers may also have been workers in his business, while the builder Thomas Lawrence's household (No. 34) is swelled by the presence of four lodgers.[23]

There were in all 286 people listed in these 36 households, of whom 91 or 32 per cent were children of the householder, 54 or 19 per cent were his male servants and 52 or 18 per cent were his female servants. Children and servants thus made up over two-thirds of the residents in middle-class households, and these two groups will be discussed in the next two sections, concentrating on the female domestics since the male servants were mainly apprentices, who have already been considered.

iii Relations with Servants

The employment of domestic servants was virtually universal amongst the middle class and indeed went right down into fairly lowly strata of the artisan population of Augustan London.[24] Some households employed huge numbers of servants, especially in the West End, but the typical staff was modest, as can be seen in Table 8.4 opposite, where the servants in two wealthy City parishes are analysed. The table shows the dominance of female servants, who represent four out of every five domestics and were the only domestics in over three-quarters of the households. It can also be seen that over half the households had only one servant, nearly always female, and that nearly 80 per cent had only one or two. One or two servants, usually female, was therefore the normal domestic staff, this being all that most households had space for or could afford. A staff of three or more, ideally with at least one man or boy, was, however, something to which most middling people aspired, since a larger staff freed wives from virtually all menial tasks and a male servant gave the household distinction in the neighbourhood. Such aspirations ensured that London's servant

TABLE 8.4: Distribution of Domestic Servants						
Size of Staff	*No. of Households*		*No. of Servants*			
	No.	*%*	*Female*	*Male*	*Total*	*% Female*
One servant	100	56.8	96	4	100	96
Two	37	21.0	62	12	74	84
Three	20	11.4	54	6	60	90
Four	7	4.0	16	12	28	57
Five	7	4.0	21	14	35	60
Six and over	5	2.8	22	17	39	56
Total	176	100.0	271	65	336	81

Average number of domestic servants per household: 1.9

Source: Marriage Duties Assessments 62 and 73 (St Mary le Bow and St Michael Bassishaw) in CLRO. All households listed as having at least one domestic servant are included. The parishes were chosen because their assessments distinguish clearly between domestic servants and apprentices, clerks, journeymen etc., who are excluded.

population grew faster than the city as a whole, as more Londoners employed at least one servant and as those who already had one began to think in terms of a staff rather than a single maid. 'I believe nobody will deny', wrote Defoe in 1724, 'that people live more profusely, keep greater equipages and more servants than ever was done before.'[25]

There was always a steady flow of country boys and girls coming into London to seek a place, but this was not sufficient to satisfy demand and our period sees an increase in servants' wages, Defoe claiming that the wages of female domestics had risen from 30s. or 40s. a year to £6–8 during his lifetime. A few pounds more a year does not seem very much for employers to pay, though they certainly grumbled about it, but there were other ways in which servants could enhance their incomes. Many writers thought that servants could double their wages by what they got as vails, or tips, from guests. It was also claimed that servants took commissions from shopkeepers for the family business and helped themselves to some of the money given them to go shopping. Further income might be earned, with or without the employer's permission, by selling worn-out clothing, left-overs from the table and other things which might be considered perquisites and not downright thieving, though there was said to be much of that as well.[26]

Defoe also suggested that domestics were becoming much more sophisticated about job specification and the definition of what might be considered a proper work-load. The main point here was how much work might be expected from a single maid-servant working on her own, 'the useful housewifery servant, commonly called maids of all work', as Sir John Fielding described them. Defoe claimed in the 1720s that it took two servants to do the work done by one in the past. He illustrated the growth of job-specification by describing a girl who, while being interviewed for a job as a house-maid, laid down the law in no uncertain way. 'If you wash at home, you should have a laundry-maid; if you give entertainments, you must have a cook-maid; if you have any needlework, you should have a chamber-maid; for such a house as this is enough for a house-maid in all conscience.'[27]

It seems then that our period was generally a good one for servants, who were becoming better paid and more independent. Servants made the best of the good times. They dressed well, enjoyed themselves in the myriad ways offered by London and regularly changed jobs to make the best of their excellent bargaining position. It need hardly be said that such behaviour made the employers think that the 'servant problem' was more than usually intractable. They moaned and wrote pamphlets complaining about servants or manuals directed to potential servants which were designed to improve their characters by telling them that they should be pious, faithful, diligent, submissive, humble, honest, modest, early-rising, neat, clean, housewifely and a large number of other things which it seems clear that many girls were not.[28]

Such didactic literature gives very little idea of just what servants actually did or of the nature of their relations with their employers. For these subjects, one can turn to the diary of Samuel Pepys, which provides a marvellous running commentary on domestic servants in the household of an upwardly mobile public servant.[29] When he started his diary in 1660, Pepys had just one female servant, but he was soon to learn 'the inconvenience that doth attend the increase of a man's fortune, by being forced to keep more servants, which brings trouble'. The first addition to his family was a footboy, engaged in June 1660, whose main duties were to wait on him as he went about the city, sometimes lighting him home with a link, go on miscellaneous errands and do odd jobs about the house. In 1661, Pepys took on a second maid, one girl now being cookmaid and the other chambermaid. In 1663, a third maid was engaged as a 'little girl' or under-cookmaid and in the same year his household reached its maximum size during the diary period with the appointment of a waiting-woman or companion for his wife. Although there was sometimes no companion or only two maids, this establishment of four women or girls and a boy was the normal arrangement till 1669, when the diary closes. Pepys was a man in a hurry, with no children to drain his purse, but his pattern of household building was typical of the more successful of middling Londoners.

In order to maintain their household at the requisite level, Samuel and Elizabeth Pepys had to engage at least thirty-eight servants in just over nine years, and the service of thirty-one of these can be analysed. The longest service was given by Jane Birch, 'our old little Jane', the only servant when the diary starts, who stayed in all for seven years in three separate periods. The next longest service was that of Tom Edwards, who doubled as a junior clerk in the Navy Office and a footboy in the household, his wages being paid by the government.[30] He stayed four and a half years, eventually leaving to marry his fellow-servant Jane Birch, much to the delight of the Pepys, who gave them £40 each as a marriage portion. Long service was also given by Jane's younger brother Wayneman, as footboy, and 'our little girl Susan', under-cookmaid, both of whom stayed nearly three years, and Mary Mercer, the longest lasting of Elizabeth Pepys's five companions, who stayed for two years.

There was much greater turnover among the other twenty-six servants. Six stayed between a year and eighteen months, seven between six months and a year, five between three and six months, and eight did not even last a quarter. Such lack of continuity in a household was by no means unusual. Six former servants of a scrivener who gave evidence in 1698 had lived in the household for thirty-six, twenty-one, twelve, ten, six and four months, and their service with other employers showed the same pattern with periods of from three to eighteen months with each.[31] Turnover of servants caused continuous disruption in middling households as new girls had to be found, trained and hopefully moulded into becoming members of a happy and well-ordered family. Most of Pepys's servants were acquired through personal recommendation, though agencies already existed, a service to householders which became more important in the eighteenth century. Nell, for instance, who was taken on in October 1661, was chosen from several maids who arrived to be interviewed. She insisted on being hired for six months, though the normal arrangement was for a month's notice by either side, servants who were dismissed or discontented being given time off to find a new place.

Houses were kept to a high standard and the work of servants was accordingly arduous. César de Saussure reported that well-kept houses were washed twice a week 'and that from top to bottom; and even every morning most kitchens, staircases and entrances are scrubbed. All furniture, and especially kitchen utensils, are kept with the greatest cleanliness.' Our sources provide much evidence of the effort that went into such work. Floors and stairs were sprinkled or scrubbed with sand to soak up grease and droppings before sweeping and saucepans and kettles were regularly scoured with sand. Wainscots had to be washed down, walls white-washed, hangings, mats and carpets brushed and beaten, and the house searched regularly for bugs, one of the curses of the age. Then there was the washing of clothes and household linen, a task done once a month 'in good citizens' houses'. Wash-day was a terrible day for servants, who, in Pepys's house, were got up at two in the morning and might still be at it when he returned home late in the evening.[32]

The work of the kitchen was equally arduous – boiling, baking and spit-roasting on an open coal fire, making pies and pasties, salting and preserving, maybe brewing and baking, and then serving the food 'neatly' to the master and mistress. When there were guests, the work-load was appalling. Hannah, the best cook ever employed by the Pepys, once prepared a feast of nine different dishes, served it to eleven diners and then cleared the whole lot up whilst the Pepys and their guests were taking the air in the park, returning to 'find the house as clean as if nothing had been done there today from top to bottom'. It is gratifying to learn that Hannah's efforts were appreciated and she was well rewarded, receiving a shilling from 'each of us'.

Nearly all work in middle-class homes was made more difficult and tiring by their lay-out. Fire and water were needed in every room, but the coal and wood were kept in the cellar and water was only piped to the yard. The kitchen was often at ground level but the dining-room on the first floor, so all food had to be carried up one pair of stairs. Close-stools and commodes were kept in bedrooms but the house of office or privy where they had to be emptied was in the yard. And when the privy itself was emptied, it was not only the nightmen who had to work. Pepys got home at eleven one evening to find the nightmen at work and, when he got up the next morning at six, he found 'the people to have just done; and Hannah not gone to bed yet, but was making clean of the yard and kitchen'.[33]

Such dirty, nasty work was interspersed with work involving cleanliness, neatness and very close and personal attendance on the master and mistress. Much time was spent ironing, mending and altering clothes, making night-caps and shirts, cutting out and hemming sheets, pillow-cases and towels from rolls of linen. Chambermaids had to keep the clothes of the master and mistress in order, help them dress and undress, and be clean enough and sufficiently well dressed themselves to escort their mistress around the town – to shops, to friends, to the theatre, even to her adulterous liaisons, as one can learn from the records of the Consistory Court.[34] Any servant of Pepys might have to cut or comb her master's hair, search it for lice or wash his feet or ears. Most middle-class households would have one or two, possibly·more, small children, who created more work. Sometimes girls were hired specifically as nursemaids but, in most households, minding children, washing and feeding them, making and mending their clothes and similar jobs were part of the duties of the maids or the single maid-of-all-work. On top of all this, many girls had to help out in the shop or other business premises of their employers. The range of duties obviously varied, but there is little doubt that a servant's life was not quite as easy as contemporary commentators often made out.

Samuel Pepys took all this work for granted, as would any member of the middle class. Servants were not hired, paid, fed and clothed in order for them to be idle. The childless Pepys seems to have been genuinely fond of many, indeed most, of the servants who made up his 'family' over the years, and evidence can be found of kindness and affection from many other employers. Pepys was amused by the antics of his adolescent footboys, enjoyed a chat with servants in the kitchen, took servants on outings, was interested in their problems and normally genuinely upset when they were ill, so long as he was sure that they were not malingering, and was nearly always sorry and often very sad when they left. He was probably not unusual in preferring attractive servants and in grumbling when his wife hired girls like Doll or Luce, both of whom were 'very ugly'. Pepys, of course, is notorious for his loose ways with women and two of his wife's companions and three of the maids had to put up with his groping hands on their 'mamelles', their belly or even their 'thing'. Just how common such behaviour was one cannot tell, but the opportunities were certainly manifold. Judging from the diary, most of the girls seemed to regard Pepys's exploration of their person as just part of the job, though some were certainly more willing than others. And, just for the record, one might perhaps note that Pepys employed twenty-four female servants who do not seem to have been subjected to such indignities and not all of them were ugly.[35]

Pepys certainly liked a pretty face or a well-shaped bosom, but he also appreciated good service and was generous in his diary and no doubt in person when he thought he was receiving it. Such comments enable us to determine what was expected. The first quality to look for in a servant was that she should 'do what she is bid', be modest, humble, well-meaning and faithful. She should be ready to take criticism without argument and be duly remorseful if she did something wrong, such as the servant who fell on her knees and asked pardon for running away after being struck by Elizabeth Pepys. Willingness to work hard was obviously an important asset and a servant who was 'a drudging, working wench' would receive due praise, as did Susan, who was described as 'a most admirable slut', not at all an opprobrious term, when she did 'more service than both the others' on a wash-day.

Another great bonus in a servant was that she should be good-natured, quiet and not liable to burst into tears, tantrums or arguments either with her employers or her fellow-servants. In the whole of the diary period, the best time was August 1664: 'Never since I was housekeeper I ever lived so quietly, without any noise or one angry word almost, as I have done since my present maids, Besse, Jane and Susan came and were together.'[36] Finally, it was of course useful if a servant was particularly skilled at her job. The ability of a chambermaid to dress the mistress's hair really well, of a cook to 'dress meat' and serve meals with some style or, in the case of the companions, to talk, sing and play musical instruments with unusual talent, were all valuable assets. However, a servant was never dismissed for a lack of innate skills and Pepys was always ready to put up with less quality if a servant was willing and well-disposed. Harmony and quiet were the keys to a happy household, just as they were to happy relations between husband and wife.

A bad servant was likely to be proud and would not show that proper humility, respect and gratitude which her employers expected. She would be lazy, sleepy and forgetful, with 'no care nor memory of her business at all'. She might be dirty and was almost certain not to do things 'as they should be'. She would lie, answer back, speak boldly and be 'apt to scold'. She was likely to go out visiting without permission and, worse still, gossip about the household when she was out, a terrible crime in the small world of London. Pepys expected his servants to be silent when they were 'abroad', but to keep their ears open and report back any criticism of his household which they heard. One can understand his paranoia, since the servants of a household knew everything that was going on within it and indeed everything that their employers did elsewhere, as is made abundantly clear from depositions in the Consistory Court. High turnover made such silence impossible, however, and one can appreciate Pepys's annoyance when his maid Sarah left and almost immediately got a place with his *bête noire*, Sir William Penn, where inevitably 'all our affairs of my family are made known of and discussed of there, and theirs by my people'.[37]

Just as bad as gossiping abroad was asking people into the house without permission, such visitors being liable to gossip in their turn, steal or provide thieves with useful information.

Susan felt the full weight of Pepys's anger when she let in 'a rogueing Scotch woman . . . to help them to wash and scour'. Pepys made his wife 'beat our little girle, and then we shut her down into the cellar and there she lay all night'. This was a savage punishment and out of character, for the maids were rarely beaten, a cuff or a box on the ear or a serious and angry talking to being the normal method of maintaining discipline. Boys were beaten more, especially the incorrigible Wayneman, who was beaten at least eight times with a cane, a whip or with rods, and sometimes very savagely. A master or mistress could, if necessary, call in the law to punish troublesome servants. In a defamation case of 1697, for instance, we learn that the nursemaid Mary Fawden was taken up by the constable 'for abusing and calling her then mistress . . . ill names'. She was brought before a magistrate who sent her to Bridewell 'and she was there whipt and lashed', her mistress adding insult to injury by kissing her at the whipping-post and saying, 'Mary, God forgive you, I do.' The only time that Pepys sought assistance was in the case of the parish-child Jinny, who arrived in August 1663, was deloused and dressed in 'good new clothes' and then immediately ran away. She was captured by the parish beadle, stripped of Pepys's clothes and then sent away to be whipped. Employers were no doubt glad to have the force of law behind them, but the usual final sanction was dismissal, the eventual fate of the naughty Wayneman.[38]

Pepys saw his household as a family, but it was a family where nobody was equal to anybody else and Pepys was often troubled lest the strict hierarchy be disturbed. This was most obvious amongst the five female members of his family, a hierarchy headed by his wife Elizabeth and then, in descending order, her waiting-woman or companion, the chambermaid, cookmaid and under-cookmaid. The companions, who were usually poor members of respectable families, were treated as gentlewomen and sat down to table with their employers and spent their evenings with them. They were, however, still expected to show a due respect and this was a difficult relationship to maintain. Pepys's fears that Winifred Gosnell 'hath been bred up with too much liberty for my family' proved to be correct, while the problem with Barker was exactly the opposite, 'because she will be raised from so mean a condition to so high, all of a sudden'. Mary Ashwell was 'not proud, but will do what she is bid; but for want of being abroad, knows not how to give that respect to her mistress as she will do when she is told it'. On the other hand, she also had to be told 'not to make herself equall with the ordinary servants of the house'. Barker's problem was that she really wanted to be an ordinary servant and 'did always declare that she would rather be put to drudgery and to wash the house than to live as she did, like a gentlewoman', an attitude which Pepys found incomprehensible.[39]

Chambermaids also gave trouble. They might be upset at the appointment of a waiting-woman above them, thus effectively pushing them down one rank in the domestic hierarchy. They might think that they were too 'high' for the job, like Pepys's sister Pall, whom he introduced into the household as a chambermaid, not thinking her 'worthy of being Elizabeth's waiting-woman'. Pall had to stand in Elizabeth's presence and was not allowed to dine with her brother and sister-in-law and, not surprisingly, turned out to be too proud and idle to retain for long. Pall was Pepys's first chambermaid and she had a bad effect on Jane Birch, who had previously been the only maidservant, but who now became 'lazy and spoiled'. Chambermaids might be proud because they thought themselves of good birth or because they had previously served in a higher class household. However, the very condition could make a girl 'high', since the chambermaid's personal service to her employers was considered superior to service in the kitchen and was rewarded by higher wages. This made promotion a tricky problem since the glory involved might turn a girl's head. Should Bess be raised to chambermaid? 'We have both a mind to it, but know not whether we should venture the makeing her proud and so make a bad chambermaid of a very good-natured and sufficient cook-maid.' Even in the kitchen itself there were problems of hierarchy and status. Pepys was worried about a new cookmaid who had formerly been a chambermaid and 'holds up her head'. He also worried about hiring a new 'little girl' under the long-serving Susan. 'I am a little disatisfied that the girl, though young, is taller and bigger then Su, and will not I fear be under her command.'[40]

Why did servants leave the Pepys's household? Some were dismissed, like the rogue Wayneman, whose crimes included lying, fighting, stealing and dawdling on errands. Two other servants were dismissed for theft, two cooks for drunkenness and one servant for telling stories about the household in the neighbourhood. Most dismissals were, however, for less obvious reasons. What tended to happen was for there to be a honeymoon period in which a new servant received praise or at least was given the benefit of the doubt and then, slowly, the relationship began to deteriorate. Sometimes this was clearly the result of the servant's own personality but, very often, it was the product of Elizabeth Pepys's awkward character, which caused her to turn against her servants and begin to dislike or even hate them. She obviously had some justification for jealousy of her husband, but her contrariness went far beyond this and time after time one finds her picking quarrels with servants and accusing them, usually falsely, of lying and stealing. The end product of such relationships was that the servant was either dismissed, being described as proud, negligent, quarrelsome or some other opprobrious epithet, or she could stand it no longer and handed in her notice.

However, there did not have to be any unpleasantness for a servant to leave. Some girls left to get married or because they were sick. Many left simply because they wanted a change or because they wanted a different sort of job. Mary, a cookmaid, for instance, left after a month's trial because she wanted 'to live in a tradesman's house where there was but one maid', a situation in which she might have to work even harder than in Pepys's household but in which she would be the boss below stairs. Servants who left, even those who were dismissed, do not seem to have borne any grudge. Nor did they necessarily vanish. Many came back to visit, to chat with their fellow-servants or to call upon their former employers. The household had after all been their home, almost their universe, for several months and sometimes for several years.

All these reasons for leaving are, of course, a matter of Pepys's own interpretation of events and do not necessarily reflect how the servants themselves saw the situation. Nevertheless, when servants did give reasons for leaving their places, as they often did when giving evidence to the Consistory Court, one can see that Pepys's household is not atypical. Nearly all the servants whom he employed had been, or were to be, employed in other London households and they simply reflect the range of servant personalities and experiences which could be found in the metropolis. Even Elizabeth Pepys is by no means unusual as an employer; indeed, she could almost be taken as a prototype of the idle, spoiled and discontented wife of contemporary literature. Give a woman like her a servant or servants and she will quarrel with them for no particularly good reason. Deborah Coleman, for instance, left the service of a scrivener's wife 'because of some difference betwixt this respondent and . . . her mistress', and such a vague reason for leaving was common enough. Another common scenario, likely to be interpreted differently by mistress and servant, is illustrated by a servant in the household of Elizabeth Nowes, the wife of a barrister. She left because her mistress 'and shee could not agree in their bills and reckonings about money laid out', a constant source of disagreement when innumerate but not necessarily dishonest servants went out shopping. Other servants in these depositions left because they were sick or wanted to get married or had found a better place or wanted to visit their relations in the country. Service in London was not exile and many girls spent long periods at home, interspersed by periods of service in London or elsewhere, before eventually getting married.[41]

Samuel Pepys's diary has been used as the main source for this section because nowhere else can one get the same detail on the relations between master, mistress and servants in a London household. His became a large household by middle-class standards and one must expect that, in the typical single servant household, relations would have been rather different, with the mistress doing far more work in the house, as indeed Elizabeth Pepys did in the early months of the diary. However, the general impression is that Pepys's household was not untypical of his day and it seems legitimate to use examples from his diary to make general points about the life of servants. Where Pepys's diary is of no use is in discussing relations with children, the subject of the next section, for which different sources will have to be found.

iv Bringing Up Children

One tends to think of the families of the past as teeming with children, and if we go back a mere hundred years this was certainly true. In our period, however, although there were some very large families, most were relatively small. Table 8.5 opposite sets out the numbers of children in the families of the sample who were alive when their fathers died. Nearly half the families had only one or two children, while the average was just over three, a figure which takes no account of families with no children at all. Vivien Brodsky has shown that nearly a quarter of marriages were childless in late Elizabethan London and that there was an average of only two surviving children per family, and one suspects that the figures would have been similar for our period.[42]

Such numbers seem remarkably small when it is remembered that most middle-class mothers got married in their early twenties or even younger, and one might assume that birth control was providing at least part of the explanation. Contraception certainly existed and was condemned by moralists, who regarded it as murder and normally assumed that women were responsible, such practices being seen as yet another example of the frivolity of the modern woman. 'She would have the pleasure of lying with a man, but would not have the least interruption from her usual company keeping.' There is, however, no evidence that contraception had any effect on the birthrate, fertility being exceptionally high in London and even higher in parishes with a high proportion of middle-class mothers than in poorer parishes. There seems little doubt, then, that the small numbers of children shown in Table 8.5 were predominantly the result of the appallingly high levels of infant and child mortality in the metropolis. Middle-class mothers gave birth to many children, on average one every twenty-three months in the early years of marriage, but comparative wealth, clean homes and plentiful food were no guarantee that these children would live for very long. Infancy was the worst period, but all of childhood was dangerous and Finlay has estimated that only three out of five of those born even in wealthy parishes would survive to the age of 15.[43]

High rates of infant and child mortality were a sad fact of the

TABLE 8.5: Number of Orphans

No. of Orphans	Number of Cases	
	No.	%
One	76	23.1
Two	83	25.2
Three	49	14.9
Four	49	14.9
Five	32	9.7
Six	18	5.5
Seven	15	4.6
Eight and over	7	2.1
	329	100.0
Unknown	46	
Total	375	

Average orhpans per case: 3.1

Source: Sample; numbers and often ages of orphans were normally given in the Common Serjeant's Book in CLRO. This data has been supplemented where necessary from wills, which sometimes mention children over the age of 21 who do not always appear in the Common Serjeant's Book. The missing cases are mainly those of people who died insolvent or whose assets had not yet been realized when the Common Serjeant made up his books. If there was nothing to divide, the Court of Orphans was not interested in the number of orphans.

human condition and parents had to learn to live with the loss of many of their children. Since we today would find such repeated grief almost impossible to bear, some historians believe that the parents of the past did not love their children as we do. Lawrence Stone, for example, has suggested that high mortality rates 'made it folly to invest too much emotional capital in such ephemeral things'. He claimed that parents were indifferent to their children or, at best, gave them the same sort of affection as they gave their pets. Such attitudes reduced grief when a child died but also tended to make parents unloving and sometimes extremely harsh in their treatment of children, subjecting them to savage beatings and other forms of cruelty.

This grim form of childhood began to change in the second half of the seventeenth century, at least in 'the middle ranks of the society'. Parents now began to love their children more and beat them less. Kindness and encouragement appeared in children's lives and a reasoned rebuke replaced the harsh word and the rod as the means of correction. Many parents still regarded their children as pets but they now became pets on whom they were prepared to spend large amounts of money in the form of clothes, toys, expensive outings and a much more thorough education.[44]

This thesis has proved totally unacceptable to the majority of social historians who claim, with reason, that Stone's views have been developed on the basis of unrepresentative sources and selective quotation. Such critics see childhood as changing very little between the sixteenth and nineteenth centuries or indeed today. They accept that there have always been some bad and uncaring parents, but these were very much a minority. Most parents loved their children and the fear of losing them probably made them love them even more and care for them more tenderly than parents do in our safer society.

Despite the gulf between these two schools of historians, they both agree that a decline in religious sensibility in our period led to less emphasis on the salvation of children and a greater concern with secular ambitions for their futures as adults. In particular, the decline in belief in original sin and a growing acceptance of the innocence of children had an important influence on their treatment. Even the kindest parent might accept the epigram of Cotton Mather – 'better whipt than damn'd' – if they genuinely believed that the death of an unrepentant child might take him straight to hell. In fact, as a recent study of diaries by Linda Pollock has shown, such beliefs often led to unbearable conflict in the minds of parents, torn between love for their children and acceptance that it was their duty to punish them for their own good. However, affection usually overcame duty, with the result that diary entries are often heavily laden with guilt. Even Cotton Mather was far more terrible in print than he ever was in reality.[45]

Diaries have been the main source used by these revisionist historians, Linda Pollock's work being based on 496 British and American diaries and autobiographies, a huge body of material which might be expected to silence all critics.[46] However, the number of diaries for any period before the second half of the eighteenth century is small and the number written by mothers even smaller, while the diaries which do exist often throw little light on childhood. Most diarists were much more interested in their own activities than in those of their children and simply did not mention the things that interest historians of childhood, such as methods of childcare and discipline, children's games and the early learning process.

All historians must be grateful for the efforts of Linda Pollock; her work is much more systematic and far more convincing than that of Lawrence Stone but, because of the nature of the evidence used, one should perhaps be cautious of some of her conclusions. The case that parents generally loved their children and grieved when they died certainly seems proven, especially for those children who survived infancy. There also seems little doubt that parents were interested in the development and education of a child and had hopes and fears about its future. However, it is much harder to generalize on such subjects as discipline in the home. Only a third of Pollock's diaries for the seventeenth and eighteenth centuries have any information at all on this subject and one wonders just how thorough this information is.[47] She wishes to minimize the physical chastisement of children in the past, as a counter to the habitual brutality claimed by other writers, and the fact is that not very much evidence of chastisement and very little of brutality appears in the diaries that she has read. But does such silence mean that children were only very rarely beaten? Would people necessarily comment on this subject?

Everything else that is known about the society of Augustan London would suggest that young people, and especially boys, were likely to be beaten quite a lot. Conduct books nearly always mention beating as a final sanction; one can hardly read about a school without being told of the savage beating of boys, not just for naughtiness but for what seem to us trivial lapses of memory; the normal punishment for erring apprentices and servants, for unmarried mothers and for a host of other young and not so young people was a beating in Bridewell or in some other place of correction, if their master had not already provided the punishment. In other words, this was a culture where beating was quite common. Can parents in our period really have loved their children so much that they spared the rod? It does seem rather unlikely, despite the evidence from silence in the majority of Linda Pollock's diaries.

The fact is that silence surrounds every aspect of childhood. The only people with much to say about the subject, and not much even then, were those who wrote books of advice for parents. Most of these concentrate on moral issues, on the need to instil in the child a fear of God and a respect for the authority of parents. Other books discuss the practicalities of pregnancy, childbirth and infant and child care, somewhat in the manner of a modern baby book. One can learn, for instance, that 'experts' disapproved of wet-nursing throughout our period, that swaddling was approved of in the seventeenth and not in the eighteenth, and so on. All of which is interesting, but does not tell us whether parents took any notice of such books, which are generally written in a depressingly pious manner or in obscure medical jargon. Recent research has shown that twentieth-century mothers do not follow baby books, a fact which makes it unlikely that their seventeenth-century ancestors did, making any conclusions from such literature of little value except for those interested in the history of baby books.[48]

When other types of source material are looked at, one moves into areas of even greater darkness. Several hundred depositions from divorce cases have been studied for this book. Most relate either to the cruelty of husbands and thus a considerable degree of violence in the home or to the adultery of wives, which usually involved absence from home. In no case does one learn that the husband's brutality frightened or might have frightened the children or that the mother was neglecting her maternal duties by gallivanting about the town. Indeed, in very few cases would one know that there were any children of these broken marriages. Children are simply not mentioned and no attention is paid to their welfare, upbringing and maintenance. Does this mean that nobody cared about children or does it simply mean that a divorce required evidence of a husband's cruelty or a wife's adultery and nothing more, facts which could be proven without reference to the children?[49]

When inventories are looked at, it can sometimes be sensed that children lived in these middle-class houses, as it is known they did from other sources. Some houses had a room called the nursery or the 'children's room'. Others had rooms which were described by the name of a teenage child, such as 'Mrs Phoebe's room' or 'Master Gabriel's room'. Lists of furniture sometimes contain evidence of children, too. There is the occasional 'child's chair' or 'child's table', lots of clouts and child bed linen and quite a few cradles and child's baskets. However, not many inventories mention purpose-built children's furniture at all. Many list 'toys', but these were ornaments rather than what we understand by toys; others list the equipment for games such as draughts, chess and backgammon, but these were just as likely to be played by adults as by children. In short, inventories show that children often lived in comfortable quarters, but do not give any support to a hypothesis that children were a pampered breed on whom a great deal of money was spent. They may have been, but the evidence will not be found in this source.[50]

Wills are another source which might be expected to throw light on attitudes to children, though in fact most are disappointing in this respect. One thing which comes through clearly in nearly all middle-class wills is the father's desire that his children should be treated equally and equitably, older and younger, boys and girls all normally getting exactly the same amount of his personal estate. This seems to have been a fundamental difference between middle-class attitudes and those of the gentry and aristocracy, who treated their children very unevenly. However, wills provide little evidence that fathers actually loved their children, either equally or at all, adjectives such as 'loving' or 'dear' being used rarely and in fact less frequently for children than for the father's adult friends.

A frequent theme in wills is the mention of duty and obedience that the children either have not observed towards their father or should observe towards their mother in the future. Three fathers in our sample disinherited their eldest son and all mentioned disobedience, unfaithfulness and lack of duty as a reason for this, Daniel Darnelly, for instance, being described as 'a very undutifull and disobedient sonne unto mee and his mother'. Other men bequeathed property to their wife to give to such of their children 'as shall be the most dutifull to her'. The wealthy merchant John Brookes left £3000 to be distributed by his widow amongst his eight children, 'as she shall in motherly prudence see fitt thereby to engage their love and obedience . . . and also that they are most pious, dutifull and diligent may be most encouraged'. Finally, it should be noted that many wills showed much concern about the education and future careers of the children. These wills, then, present a picture of middle-class fathers behaving almost exactly as they were told to behave in conduct-books. There is little evidence here of the new-look fathers who pampered and spoiled their children or would put up readily with disobedience, a model which Lawrence Stone thinks was common amongst the members of the London bourgeoisie.[51]

Childhood is one of the few subjects covered in this book on which it has been difficult to find good sources and it is important to realize just how fragile is the evidence from which large books have been written on the subject. Despite this, I, like others, will say what I think were typical attitudes to the upbringing of children. But, first, it should be noted that children were not necessarily brought up by both of their own parents, since adult as well as child mortality was very high. A quarter of our sample, for example, had lost their fathers before they were apprenticed. Widows and widowers often continued to raise their families single-handed or with the assistance of a housekeeper, but remarriage was also common. Many families, then, were very complex, with step-parents, natural parents and children from two or more unions all living in the same house, a situation similar to that created today by high divorce rates. Such arrangements could often lead to family tensions. Some people might refuse to allow the children of their spouse's previous marriage into the house; many husbands worried that if they died their widows might not treat the children of a previous marriage fairly. No evidence of really wicked step-mothers has been found, but presumably the stereotype had some basis in reality.[52]

The care of young children was therefore distributed amongst a number of persons, of whom parents, step-parents, servants and wet-nurses were the most important, though older siblings probably played their part as well. A middle-class baby's first few months might well be spent with a wet-nurse, either at home or in the villages on the outskirts of London whose air was supposed to be good for babies. Linda Pollock has demonstrated the care with which parents chose and supervised wet-nurses, and there seems little reason to suppose that the practice illustrates indifference to the baby, as some writers have suggested, but it would presumably have reduced the strength of maternal bonding. Contemporary writers tended to criticise wet-nursing, on the grounds that it was due to idleness and vanity on the part of mothers and also because babies were supposed to absorb plebeian instincts with their nurses' milk. How common wet-nursing actually was, nobody knows, but contemporary comment suggests that it was widespread among those who could afford it.[53]

Once the baby was weaned, it seems probable that much of the everyday care of small children was left to servants, who would produce them from time to time, nicely cleaned up, for the amusement and gratification of their parents. Misson thought that the English found young children too amusing and were over-affectionate and too tolerant of them, 'always flattering, always caressing, always applauding what they do; at least it seems so to us French folks who correct our children as soon as they are capable of reason; being of opinion, that to keep them in awe is the best way to give them a good turn in their youth'.[54] The truth of Misson's comment cannot be proved but it agrees with what Linda Pollock has found in her diaries. How parents were supposed to behave, according to the conduct books, was much more in the French manner, though correction was always supposed to be tempered with affection.

In practice, it seems to have been the mother who provided most of the instruction and correction, as can be seen from two middle-class autobiographers, both of whom praised their mothers in almost identical terms for taking 'all oppertunityes to instruct and instill good principles of religion and moralls into us her children'. One also gets a hint of attitudes to mothers, a very shadowy subject, from the fact that the commonest adjective describing a mother in a will is not 'dear' or 'loving', which were used for many other people, but 'honoured'. This may simply be a convention, but it is important to remember that however much affection, however many caresses, there were in a family, children were still expected to honour, obey and respect their parents. There was always a distance, symbolized by such customs as bowing, kneeling or at least standing in the presence of parents. One also gets the impression that these middle-class houses were not places where children raced up and down stairs, screaming and shouting and constantly vying for their parents' attention. They seem rather to have been quiet, almost sombre, places where children were seen but not heard and were whisked away by servants if they began to be a nuisance.[55]

Our evidence suggests that parents took their duties towards children seriously and were chided by relations, friends and neighbours if they did not. Such duties took many forms besides the instilling of good principles of religion and morals, though this came first. Accumulation itself was one such duty, its object being not the gratification of the accumulator but the advancement of the next generation. Middle-class stock, like upper-class land, was something received on trust from parents to be improved and then handed on to children, an attitude symbolized by the frequent reference to stewardship in wills: 'And as concerning such worldly estate as God in his goodness hath made me steward of in this life, I give and bequeath the same as followeth.' Fear that one might be a poor steward, that there might not be enough money to advance one's children, was a common middle-class phobia.[56]

If accumulation was a duty, so was the education of children so that they would be able to make good use of the money when it came to them. Education was also, of course, a vehicle for social advancement, the dream of 'the meanest tradesman [who] affects to raise his family out of its original obscurity by fixing his children some degrees higher than the vulgar occupation in which he has worked himself'. Parents certainly took great trouble over the choice of schools, a choice made more taxing by the expansion of different sorts of school, which was discussed in Chapter 2.[57] Most children in this class went to school for eight to ten years, starting around the age of six and continuing till their early or mid-teens. Schoolmasters and mistresses were therefore another group playing an important part in the moulding of young members of the middle station, a group who emphasized religion, hard work, attention, obedience and duty, and thus reinforced what children were supposed to have already learned from their parents. School removed children from home all day and so reduced their contacts with parents and servants; boarding school, to which many children went, removed them for months at a time, though contact was

retained through visits and the rather stilted letters that parents
and children tend to write to each other.[58]

Both boys and particularly girls often stayed at home for
some years after they had finished school. Many sons were
apprenticed in their late rather than early teens and some were
formally apprenticed to their fathers, while others, like George
Boddington, learned their father's business in a more informal
way. When he was fifteen, his father 'set me to his business in
the packing trade and wrighting his letters and keeping his
cash'. That this was quite common is indicated by the number
of families in Table 8.3 (p. 214) who had sons in their late teens
still at home. Sir John Hedges, for example, had his nineteen-
year-old son William living at home, while John Cary had a
twenty-eight-year-old son by his first marriage and an eighteen-
year-old from his second marriage living with him. Both these
men also had girls in their late teens living at home and it seems
probable that most daughters in this class got married from
home. The influence of parents on the children of the middle
class might be broken to a certain extent by the long period of
formal schooling that most children went through, but it was
an influence which lasted much longer and was almost certainly
more pervasive than in the working classes, where children
tended to leave home in their early teens or even earlier. What
exactly this influence amounted to is difficult to say given the
paucity of the sources, but the impression is that parents' desire
for respect and obedience from their children created a rather
more formal relationship than is suggested by some historians.[59]

9 Civic Life

Middling people had interests and duties which stretched well beyond their business life and the narrow vertical world of the household. They were, as has been seen, part of a network of 'friends' to whom they could look for help and advice in matters of importance, such as apprenticeship or marriage, and who might well turn to them as they grew older and more experienced in the world. They were also very much part of the neighbourhood in which they lived and it is to this aspect of their lives that attention is now turned.

i Neighbourhood and Parish

Augustan London shared the anonymity of all great cities and it could be a lonely place to live in. Nevertheless, despite this and perhaps because of it, there was also a village atmosphere about the parishes within the city. This neighbourhood ambience meant that in the heart of the metropolis one could find some of both the best and worst aspects of the villages and small towns from which so many Londoners had originally sprung, a combination of the mutuality which saw it as a duty to look after 'our poor' with the moral determinism which saw it as another duty to tell one's neighbours how to live.

Once they had married and acquired a house, most middling people seem to have stayed in the same house and so had most of the same neighbours for a fairly long time. This cannot be proved conclusively, since there are no records of actual addresses, but some idea of continuity of residence within the same parish can be obtained from evidence provided by witnesses in the Consistory Court and figures relating to this are presented in Table 9.1 opposite. It can be seen that at all ages there must have been a considerable turnover of people living

TABLE 9.1: Continuity of Residence

| | Age of Witness | | | | | |
| Years in Parish | 30–39 | | 40–49 | | 50 & over | |
	No.	%	No.	%	No.	%
0 to 4	57	42.5	31	22.5	29	29.3
5 to 9	53	39.6	27	19.6	10	10.1
10 to 14	24	17.9	23	16.7	12	12.1
15 to 19	0	0.0	37	26.8	10	10.1
20 and over	0	0.0	20	14.4	38	38.4
	134	100.0	138	100.0	99	100.0
Average residence	5.4 years		11.0 years		15.0 years	
Median residence	5		11		14	

Source: GLRO DL/C/247–250. The four volumes of depositions cover the period 1701–9. All male witnesses aged 30 or over who were resident in London and whose depositions included the necessary information have been included. Since the table is designed to show the continuity of residence of married householders, it was decided to avoid distortion of the figures by ignoring all residence before the age of 25. For example, a man of 37 who had lived in a parish for 15 years would be counted as living there for only 12 years and a man of 44 who had been resident in the same parish since birth would be counted as living there only 19 years. Only 11 (3 per cent) of the sample analysed were in fact still living in the parish of their birth, but the inclusion of a few figures such as 76 or 68 would have made rather a nonsense of the averages, though not of course the medians.

for less than five years in the same parish. However, the length of continuous residence of the older householders is quite striking, with over 40 per cent of those in their forties and nearly half of those over fifty having spent at least fifteen years in the same parish.

Such continuity of residence meant that most middling people must have been very well known by their neighbours, whom they would meet regularly in their homes and shops, on the street or in such institutions of good neighbourhood as the local tavern or coffee-house. Such relationships could take on a certain formality, as is indicated in a *Spectator* of 1711: 'There are at present in several parts of this city what they call Street-Clubs, in which the chief inhabitants of the street converse together every night.' Clubs were indeed very common in early eighteenth-century London, there being some 2000 in all according to one recent study, such purely neighbourhood clubs as the street-clubs being well outnumbered by those catering for people with something other than propinquity in common, from bird-fancying to politics and from gardening to being Irish.[1]

The implications of neighbourhood were wide-ranging. A neighbour was, for instance, the person most likely to be asked for information on one's character and business competence, either formally in a court of law or informally in the course of casual conversation. His loose tongue and assumed knowledge of your affairs could dry up your credit and set you on the road to the debtors' prison. On the other hand, a well cultivated neighbour could be expected to show solidarity in times of trouble, by giving evidence of one's probity, business ability, generosity or virtue as the case might be. Neighbours were also often chosen as peacemakers or arbitrators, an important function in a society which usually preferred to avoid the publicity and expense of the law. It was William Hillyard, for instance, 'a near neighbour of the master', who agreed to act as arbitrator between a Holborn tallow-chandler and his apprentice, who had run away after being accused of theft.[2]

Neighbours took a great interest in each other's sexual and marital as well as business affairs. In England, it was said in 1602, 'every citizen is bound by oath to keep a sharp eye at his neighbour's house as to whether the married people live in harmony.' Such busybody interference in other people's lives had once been one of the main tasks of the ward inquest, a lowly component of the complex City government whose questmen eagerly presented their neighbours for moral and personal failings. By our period, however, the inquest normally confined itself to presenting people for such mundane failings as not maintaining their pavements or keeping shop without attaining the freedom of the City. However, this change in emphasis did not mean that the citizens had lost their previous interest in the sexual lives of those who lived around them. Case after case in the Consistory Court depended on the evidence of neighbours, who claimed to have seen a surprising amount of intimate behaviour through windows or doorways or by peeping through 'a hole or crevize' in a coffee-house.[3]

Moral vigilance often went much further than mere peeping. The outrageous behaviour of Lavinia, wife of the parish clerk of St Peter's Cornhill, 'caused a mobb to come about his house to

his great disgrace and the disturbance of the neighbourhood.'
Such a mob might simply abuse the offending person or they
might play out the crude rural theatre of the 'skimmington
ride', a ludicrous procession designed to ridicule the offender
and provide a moral lesson to the bystanders. Matters often got
out of hand and such sanctimonious mobs were a common
focus for riots and brawls.[4]

Augustan London was a fairly lawless place, teeming with
thieves and pickpockets whose main victims were likely to be
the prosperous members of the middle station. The official
protection provided by the small numbers of constables, beadles
and watchmen in each ward or parish was strictly limited and
the citizen needed to watch out for himself and his neighbours.
With no police and no public prosecutor, it was the victim of
crime himself who was expected to detect, catch and prosecute
the criminal who had robbed or attacked him, and often did so.
The opportunist nature of much crime helped in this respect,
many thieves being former servants or close neighbours of their
victims who could be recognized as they jumped out of windows
or climbed over walls. Apprehension was also not quite the
problem one might expect, for, in the circumstances of the
period, honest neighbours and bystanders were not so ready to
turn a blind eye to roguery as they are today and were quite
prepared to join in a hue and cry, as indeed it was their duty to
do. Self-reliance also meant that many citizens kept arms and
some kept small armouries, such as Edward Kingsley, carpenter
of Crutched Friars, who had two pikes, two swords, a halberd
and three muskets in his kitchen when he died in 1679. Some of
this weaponry was no doubt left over from the Civil War or was
used in the periodic musters of the trained bands, London's
militia, but much was also kept for the protection of the citizen
and his neighbours.[5]

A neighbourhood might be a street, a few streets or, in the
City, it might be contiguous with the precinct and the parish.
In medieval times, these small areas of a few hundred houses
had been the setting for a vibrant community culture. Much of
this vanished with the Reformation and, although such institu-
tions as the Ascension Day procession round the parish and the
Ward Inquest dinner survived, the local life of Augustan
London had little of the colour and pageantry of other European

cities.[6] Nevertheless, the parish church continued to provide a focus for neighbourhood life and pride and many local dramas were played out within its walls. The church, or rather the vestry, was also where the meetings of local government were held, meetings which one finds with little surprise were dominated by members of the middle station. Local office and attendance at meetings were time-consuming but they were a necessary condition of earning the respect of one's neighbours and moving up in the world. Many men paid a fine or hired a substitute to avoid some bothersome local duties, but few of the middle station, even those who were nonconformists, opted out of parish government altogether.

This can be illustrated by looking at Allhallows Bread Street, a prosperous central City parish which contained about eighty houses and five hundred people in the late seventeenth century. The business of the parish and its two precincts was supervised by a vestry open to all householders which met about ten or twelve times a year in the 1690s and normally attracted between fifteen and twenty men or nearly a quarter of the householders. The main business was to make appointments to local offices; to make recommendations relating to the parish poor, such as who should be on the pension list, how much they should be paid and whether they should suffer the indignity of wearing a pauper's badge; and to supervise the fabric and decoration of the church. Allhallows was burned down in the Great Fire and for many years the parishioners shared temporary accommodation with their neighbours from St John the Evangelist. However, in 1680, the vestry finally decided to rebuild and by 1684 a fine new church had been erected, which was improved and embellished in the 1690s.[7]

The vestry also appointed various sub-committees, some on an ad hoc basis, such as the eight men chosen in April 1698 'to wait on his Grace of Canterbury to desire him to recommend a new curate'; some set up every year, such as those which audited the churchwardens' accounts and assessed the poor rates. For the social historian, the most interesting is the committee of 'seators', who were appointed every three or four years to seat the parishioners in the various rows in the church, this important social duty even being carried out in the long interval between the burning of the old church and the building of the new one. As in many churches of the day, Allhallows seated men and women separately, 'to avoid thereby all appearance of evil', according to Sir George Wheler, though in fact this arrangement facilitated the ogling of such itinerant church attenders as Samuel Pepys.[8]

The seating arrangements provide a series of snap-shots of social hierarchy and social mobility within the parish. In 1701, for instance, the first name in 'No.1 South Side' was Sir Owen Buckingham, a prominent presbyterian alderman but nevertheless a stalwart of his Anglican parish church. Next to him were the two common councillors, while the row as a whole paid an average of 22s. to the poor rate, compared with 13s. in rows two and three, while, at the back, those who paid averaged only 9s. and most were exempt.[9] Wealth was not the only determinant of one's place in church and so, very visibly, Sunday after Sunday, in the parish. Many merchants, wholesalers and rich shopkeepers are of course found near the front and such lowly creatures as Stephen Champion, hemp-porter, at the back. However, other poor men can be found well up the church, such as the glazier Richard Joynor, who paid only 1s. in the Poll Tax of 1692 but was a regular attender of vestry meetings and clearly deserved his place in the second row, while no less than seven men paying surtax in 1695 were seated as far back as Row Five. At least five of these men were young bachelors and this helps the analysis of the seating arrangements to be refined a little further. The fact is that these reflected seniority in the parish and the holding of office, as well as wealth and occupation, so that a poor glazier could get up to the second row if he lived long enough, but would be unlikely to attain the dignity of the front row, while a rich young man had to start near the back and work his way up the church over the years.[10]

Such social progress is illustrated in the bottom half of Table 9.2 overleaf, which shows the seats given in successive years to the twelve top men in 1701. As far back as 1673, the front row was already occupied by Richard Bristow, who was born in 1630 and was to be elected common councillor eighteen times between 1672 and 1701. For the others, progress up the church was slow but steady and usually required lengthy residence in the parish to get to the top. In fact, all twelve men except Buckingham and Keeling were already resident in the parish at

TABLE 9.2: Social Progress in Allhallows Bread Street

Name and Occupation	First Year in Parish or Precinct Office				
	Aud.	Const.	S/Man	C/W	C/C
Owen Buckingham, merchant	1692			1692	1695
Richard Bristow, grocer	1672				1672
Edmund Clarke, silkman	1677	1680	1686	1687	1697
Ralph Keeling, tobacconist	1683			1684	
Thomas Tuckfield, grocer	1678	1681	1687	1688	1688
Richard Chase, grocer	1689	1682	1687	1689	1692
James Hulbert, linen-draper	1688	1688	1691	1692	
Lemuel Leppington, salter	1686	1689	1693	1694	1697
Jeremy Gough jr, grocer	1692	1694	1695	1697	1702
Robert Aldersey, salter	1677	1677	1682	1683	1688
Daniel Oley, haberdasher	1688	1679	1690	1691	
Isaac Ash, linen-draper	1691	1682	1691	1691	

Key: Aud. = auditor of churchwardens' accounts; Const. = constable, usually served jointly with scavenger; S/Man = sidesman; C/W = churchwarden; C/C = common councillor.

Name	Row in Church as Directed by Committee of Seators							
	Year							
	1673	1677	1683	1688	1691	1694	1698	1701
Buckingham					3	2	1	1
Bristow	1	1	1	1	1	1	1	1
Clarke		6	5	3	2	2	1	1
Keeling			2	2	1	1	1	1
Tuckfield		6	5	3	2	1	1	1
Chase	8	6	5	3	2	2	1	1
Hulbert		9	7	5	3	3	1	1
Leppington			8	5	4	3	1	1
Gough				7	5	3	1	1
Aldersey	6	4	4	3	2	1	1	1
Oley		7	6	4	3	2	1	1
Ash		8	7	4	3	2	2	1

Source: GHMS 5039/1 and for occupations see note 10. The method of distinguishing rows changed from a simple numerical order during the period of temporary accommodation after the Fire to No.1 South Side, No.1 North Side etc. in the new church from 1683 and to No.1, No.A, No.2, No.B etc. from 1701. Since the order of precedence is always obvious, the row order has been made consistent by maintaining the simple numerical order of the earlier period. The seators' arrangements for 1696 have been omitted, since they are identical to 1694 for these people.

the time of the 1678 Poll Tax, twenty-three years earlier; Gough as a child living with his father, Hulbert and Leppington as apprentices, and the rest as householders paying the surtax rate of 10s. Owen Buckingham lived in St Mildred, the other Bread Street parish, during the 1670s and 1680s, and Ralph Keeling came into the parish in the early 1680s, a senior man who had already served as common councillor for Langborn Ward.[11]

In the top half of the table, the office-holding of the same men is shown and it can be seen that it would be difficult to get to the top without serving all or nearly all the major offices and putting in time on committees such as that which audited the churchwardens' accounts. The vestry nearly always allowed men to be excused from office on payment of a fine, Keeling and Oley for instance paying £15 and £12 respectively after being appointed churchwardens. However, the others all served this important office, though some paid fines of £4 to avoid being questman and nearly everyone paid £1 or £2 to avoid the second year as constable. Indeed, hardly anyone served even the first year of this tiresome chore, paying a substitute instead of fining, and for much of the period the two constables were in fact Job Makepeace and Samuel Landon, paid substitutes of no social significance in the parish.

It would be foolish to pretend that Allhallows Bread Street was a typical London parish. It was small and wealthy and it was the only parish in which the arrangements for seating discussed above have been found.[12] Nevertheless, Allhallows probably illustrates in a formal way what was generally true of other parishes. It is probable that most middling people went to church at least once on Sunday and many went twice. Even many of London's middle-class dissenters went to church as well as meeting, because they wanted to see and be seen by their neighbours or hear the sermon or because occasional attendance at church and the holding of posts such as church-warden was a necessary condition both of being elected to higher offices and of being allowed by the law to hold such offices. It is unlikely that once in church people sat where they liked, a freedom which would have been contrary to the minutely observed social hierarchy of the age. Other parishes may not have had a committee which pondered these nice problems every few years, but there seems little doubt that subtle nods and hints would have ensured that the seating reflected those factors such as age, wealth, occupation and the holding of parish office which determined one's position in Alhallows Bread Street. The parish church would thus reflect the social hierarchy of its neighbourhood, however formal or informal the particular arrangements.

It would be laborious to prove, but it certainly seems very probable that nearly every middle-class householder would have had either to fine or serve at least some of the various parish offices, such chores or expenses being virtually a precondition of social progress, a rite of passage by which you were elected constable in your early or mid-thirties and sidesman or churchwarden a few years later. Naturally, the details and the willingness to undertake chores would vary from person to person and parish to parish. The Webbs pointed out many years ago that people were most keen to avoid office in the crowded parishes where there was most to do, and this seems very likely, jobs such as churchwarden or constable being a very different matter in a parish such as St Giles in the Fields, with nearly 1000 poor people supported by the rates, than in Allhallows Bread Street, which had just a handful of poor old people and orphan children.[13] On the other hand, social progress for middling people might well be faster in a poor parish where there was less competition, an acceleration of dignity which might enable them to get to the front row of the church in rather less time than the fifteen, twenty or twenty-five years that it took in Allhallows Bread Street.

The highest office chosen at parish or precinct level was common councillor and it can be seen from Table 9.2 that this was a dignity quite often achieved by the cocks of the parish, eight of our twelve men being elected to that office at least once and many of them several times. This may seem surprising since there is a tendency to see this 'lower house' of the City government as composed mainly of lowly people from the very bottom of the middle station or even below it. The Webbs, for instance, wrote that 'the common councillor would find his couple of hundred colleagues made up, almost entirely, of the retail shopkeepers of the narrow streets and lanes converging on the Guildhall; or of the old-fashioned master-craftsmen whose workrooms and sales counters still lingered within the

TABLE 9.3: Wealth and High Civic Office

Wealth at Death	Holding High Office	Not Holding High Office	Total	% Not Holding High Office
£10,000 & over	20	12	32	37.5
£5000–£9999	11	22	33	66.7
£2000–£4999	14	56	70	80.0
Less than £2000	4	113	117	96.6
	49	203	252	

Source: Wealth from inventories of sample; office from Woodhead (1965), Beaven (1908, 1913) and Ms list of common councilmen in CLRO. 123 men who died aged less than 40 without holding office have been omitted from the analysis since it was very rare to be elected before one's late thirties.

City boundaries; together with a dozen or two of the apothecaries, surgeons and petty attorneys who dwelt among them'.[14]

This comment sounds as though it is based on West End prejudice and it was certainly not true in our period or, at least, it was not true of our sample. Altogether, forty-six men were common councillors and another three were aldermen but not common councillors, a total of forty-nine men chosen for high City office. In Table 9.3 above, the wealth of those who did and did not get chosen is compared. The figures completely deny the Webbs' assertion that common councillors were selected from retail shopkeepers, artisans and other lowly groups, people who would be extremely unlikely to accumulate the £2000 or more which was left by forty-five out of the forty-nine common councilmen and aldermen in the sample. There were, of course, exceptions to the general rule, the four 'poor' men being a carman, a grocer, a 'dealer in turnery ware' and an insolvent linen-draper who, if he had run his business properly, would certainly have been in the £5000-plus group.[15]

It can be concluded, then, that neighbourhood and parish played an important part in the lives of those of the middle station. Not all achieved or aspired to the dignity of common councillor; several tried to avoid many lesser dignities as well. Nevertheless, it seems probable that most were happy enough to accept the fact that, as one got older and richer, one acquired added responsibilities and duties as well as the respect of one's neighbours and a seat at the front of the church. This was as it should be in a hierarchical society, but it did mean that one had to concentrate very hard on the serious and difficult business of maintaining one's reputation. Life was played out before an audience made up not just of one's equals and superiors but also of the poor and unsuccessful who waited avidly for the fall of the great.

ii Livery Companies

All members of the middle station belonged by necessity to a parish or a precinct, but most also belonged to parallel organizations which could offer similar social and political opportunities. These were the livery companies, some ancient, some of comparatively recent vintage, which in theory combined many of the functions of both a trade association and a trade union, as well as providing a clubbish ambience of fraternity in which the members of a craft or trade could express their appreciation of each other. Our period, however, sees the virtual demise of the livery companies as effective controllers of the City economy. They had once controlled entry to the various trades, the numbers of apprentices, the conditions and quality of work and a host of other matters relating to the social and moral as well as the economic behaviour of their members. Many were still doing some of these things in 1700 but all of them were moving, some slowly, some fairly rapidly, towards becoming the wealthy dining clubs with important charitable functions which most of them are today.[16]

The conservative and corporate nature of the livery companies was contrary to the individualist spirit of the age, a spirit which was reflected in the law courts, where those who challenged the companies found that they could often gain a favourable decision. As a result, many of the powers granted or taken for granted in Elizabethan times were to be lost in the next century. The most important power was the right of search, essential if companies were to control their trades and maintain their monopolies. The growth of the metropolis had long made such a right difficult to enforce in Westminster and the suburbs. By the end of the seventeenth century, doubts about the legality of searches meant that, even in the City, companies were increasingly reluctant to act for fear of prosecution for trespass.[17]

The loss of ancient rights was compounded for most companies by serious financial problems. They had been weakened by demands made on them by both King and Parliament ever since the 1620s, but it was the Great Fire of 1666 which dealt the hammer blow. This not only destroyed their ancient halls, which had to be rebuilt at great cost, but also much of the property on which they relied for their income and the support of their charitable obligations. The property was rebuilt, but at the cost of lowering annual rents and extending leases, with the result that for most of our period the companies had diminished incomes, which made prosecution of offenders even less attractive in the face of doubts of success in the courts. It also had a serious effect on the morale of members, who looked to their companies for extravagant pageantry and bountiful dinners. The Fire also made it necessary to relax or abandon restrictions on unfreemen, in the building trades to encourage provincial workmen to come to London to rebuild the city, in the shopkeeping and craft trades to encourage people to take up the new-built property as fast as possible. Such decisions were not easily reversed and the Fire was very much a turning point in the fortunes of the companies.

There was one last problem facing the companies. Much of their logic depended on their members having in common some particular trade or occupation; the Mercers were supposed to be mercers and the Fishmongers fishmongers. However, from quite an early date, this uniformity of occupation began to be undermined as people changed their trades or as sons acquired the freedom through patrimony but did not practise their father's trade. Attempts to regularize this situation were not very successful and were seriously undermined by a legal decision of 1614 which in essence said that anyone free of any London company could practise any trade that they wished. The result, by our period, was that a livery company label was by no means a good indication of a man's occupation, especially for members of the older, larger and more prestigious companies. Some idea of the confusion can be seen in Table 9.4 overleaf, which lists the occupations of members of the sample belonging to companies with at least ten representatives. A few companies, such as the Apothecaries, Distillers and Vintners, could still be said to represent a trade but most were so

TABLE 9.4: Livery Company and Occupation

Livery Company	Occupations
Apothecary (16)	15 apothecaries, 1 money-lender
Clothworker (22)	7 merchants, 4 cloth-finishers, 2 silkmen, 2 rentiers, 2 cheesemongers, woollen-draper, tobacco-refiner, tobacco factor, butter-seller, timber-merchant
Distiller (10)	9 distillers, 1 brewer
Draper (19)	5 woollen-drapers, 2 merchants, 2 oilmen, 2 rentiers, upholsterer, tailor, bodice-maker, silkman, hosier, bricklayer, coachman, linen-draper
Fishmonger (13)	5 merchants, grocer, silkman, linen-draper, salter, cheesemonger, hop merchant, jeweller, rentier
Goldsmith (13)	5 jewellers, 2 bankers, goldsmith, silversmith, metal refiner, milliner, merchant, rentier
Grocer (17)	7 grocers, 2 tobacconists, 2 druggists, seedsman, jeweller, milliner, cheesemonger, merchant, rentier
Haberdasher (30)	11 haberdashers, 3 merchants, 2 leather-sellers, 2 lacemen, cloth-presser, oilman, woollen-draper, silk hatband-maker, innkeeper, timber merchant, hatter, gold & silver wire-drawer, tailor, moneylender, cloth factor, rentier
Mercer (22)	7 merchants, 3 linen-drapers, 2 mercers, 2 rentiers, 2 tobacconists, money-lender, silkman, dyer, haberdasher, haberdasher of hats, sugar refiner
Merchant-Taylor (22)	4 rentiers, 3 haberdashers, 3 salesmen, 2 merchants, 2 money-lenders, linen-draper, brewer, dyer, silkman, glass-seller, map-printer, tobacconist, distiller
Salter (20)	4 salters, 4 soapmakers, 2 grocers, 2 merchants, mealman, innkeeper, dyer, haberdasher, corn-chandler, leather-seller, hardware dealer, cheese factor
Vintner (26)	19 tavern-keepers, 2 merchants, money-lender, draper, milliner, horner, rentier

Source: Common Serjeants' Books in CLRO for Livery Company; inventories of sample and occasionally Boyd for occupations. All Companies with at least 10 members have been included and those of unknown occupation have been left out.

heterogeneous in their membership that little loyalty to craft or occupation can have remained.[18]

Given all these problems, it seems amazing that the livery companies survived at all, but survive they did and most of the

London business community belonged to one, though some people opted out. Many merchants and wholesalers who required no shop premises in the City never bothered to acquire the freedom or join a livery company. Neither did an increasing number of shopkeepers in Westminster and the suburbs. Nevertheless, the number of freemen bore up quite well, declining only slowly from a peak figure of over 2000 new freemen every year in the late 1670s, when entry restrictions were temporarily relaxed, to 1250 a year in the 1740s. Relative decline was more serious, as population grew, but the decline was probably greater amongst those destined to be journeymen than in the business community itself. Prospective masters, even those in Westminster and the suburbs, continued to be apprenticed to a freeman and to become free of their companies as a matter of course, because it was the normal thing to do or because it saved trouble or the possibility of trouble.[19]

For many people, the acquisition of the freedom was the last active interest that they took in their companies. They were indifferent to company business and felt, quite rightly in most cases, that the activities of the Court of Assistants who ruled their company had no significance for them as individuals. However, indifferent or not, many of the apathetic had no choice but to move up to the next stratum of their companies by joining the 'clothing' or livery. This was because most companies had found that the easiest way to raise much-needed cash was to increase the numbers of the livery and to charge high fines, from £10 to £30, for the privilege of joining it, threatening to prosecute those who refused to comply. Many men begged to be excused, as can be seen from the Committee Book of the Grocers' Company, the most prominent committee being that which raised the livery fines and listened to the petitions of those who tried to wriggle out of them. Some got away with it on such grounds as 'inability', 'age', 'small trade and must repair his house which will cost £100'. Most did not; not even Joseph Stone whose plea that 'he has but half a trade being concerned with his mother who has losses and troubles' had no effect on the hard-hearted committee.[20]

Liverymen had no actual duties, though they had the right to vote in parliamentary elections and could attend certain dinners and processions, as well as being entitled to wear a handsome livery gown. They were, however, liable to be appointed to such posts as Steward or Gentleman Usher, which could be a heavy strain on their holder's purse, since they often involved the obligation to pay for a dinner for the liverymen and it was a nice point whether the dinner or the fine exacted for refusing the office would be cheaper. As time went on a minority of liverymen would find themselves called to the ruling body of their company, the Court of Assistants. Most companies had some twenty to thirty assistants and, although they included a few keen or politically active men in their thirties and forties, the great majority were elderly men, the 'antientest' of their company.[21]

What did these elderly members of the middle station talk about at their meetings, and what indeed was the business of the livery companies in our period? A partial answer to this question may be provided by examining the accounts and court minutes of a few companies in which our sample were well represented, concentrating on the 1690s and 1700s. A start can be made with the Society of Apothecaries, whose membership consisted almost entirely of apothecaries and whose society was the best run and most actively interested in the promotion of the trade of those whose records have been examined.[22] The apothecaries were very much on the crest of a wave in the late seventeenth century, just about to win their long running battle with the physicians and attracting new freemen at the rate of twenty-five a year. The society had only been founded in 1617 and had none of the accumulation of property which was a feature of the older livery companies, so that most of its income came from fees for apprenticeship and freedom, fines and from the two shillings a year that its members paid as quarterage. Outgoings included interest on loans and legal expenses but were concentrated on basic housekeeping – the maintenance of the hall, salaries for beadle, clerk and bargemaster, and on 'feasts and other entertainments and refreshments', such as the Midsummer's Day and Election Day dinners. A few widows and elderly members of the society were supported by pensions but there was none of the heavy involvement in charity which is to be found in other companies.

As a new company, the Apothecaries were very conscious of their dignity, very upset when not accorded what they thought was their proper order of precedence on great public occasions, keen to acquire all the paraphernalia of the older companies, such as a handsome hall, a barge and plenty of silverware. Such matters attracted considerable attention at Court meetings, as did the business of admitting members, electing officers and fining those who refused office, business which was done by all companies. However, what is striking about the records of the Apothecaries, when compared with other companies, is the impression that this was a real professional association, interested in promoting the business of its members and the education of its apprentices. In the early 1690s, the society was actively engaged in defending its members' interests against both the surgeons and the physicians, and was still using the powers given by its charter to enter premises and search for defective drugs and medicines. The search of 1695, for instance, resulted in five apothecaries being summoned before the Court for having bad medicines on their premises. However, these men were discharged without fine, which suggests that, even in this active society, the search was not the important part of its activities which it had been in the past.

Much more important in the minds of the Court were the six annual 'herbarizing' or botanical excursions, which were laid on in the summer months for the education of apprentices. These expeditions combined the attractions of a fraternal picnic with a genuine zeal in botanical matters. The party often set off to a riverside destination in the society barge, wandered through the fields identifying herbs for the benefit of the apprentices and then ended up with a dinner. Two other activities specific to the Apothecaries also engaged much of the time of the Court and its sub-committees. In 1672, the society had established an 'elaboratory' for making chemical medicines, a successful experiment run on a joint-stock basis for its subscribers, who received a dividend and were also able to buy stock for their shops at low prices. In the following year, the energetic society inaugurated the Physic Garden on its land at Chelsea, which by the 1690s had become an important botanical collection, 'very necessary for the honour and dignity of its members and the education of its apprentices', though its management was giving the Court so many headaches that some members were in favour of giving it up and letting the land to a professional gardener.

The Distillers' Company was also very active in the early 1690s in promoting the trading interests of its members, for example, by lobbying parliament for or against any legislation which might affect the trade. This company was even newer than the Apothecaries, first chartered in 1638 but not enrolled by the City government until 1658. They had no hall and, although like all companies they had plenty of dinners, one feels that business rather than ceremonial was what really interested the Court. Here, the search was still an active business, the metropolis being covered by seven search parties. Defaulters were regularly summoned before the Court, where many were fined, and the company were quite prepared to take matters further if necessary. Mr Walsingham Heathfield, for instance, was summoned 'for abusing the Master and Warden Henning upon a search and giveing them very bad language'. He was fined £3 for contempt and, when he refused to pay, was sued in the Court of Common Pleas, an action which led Heathfield to submit and declare 'himself to be very sorry for his offence', as well he might be since now he had to pay £13. 10s. to cover the company's costs.[23]

The company was also prepared to prosecute those who refused to pay livery fines or fines for avoiding such offices as steward, but it was most active in defence of its monopoly of distilling. In the early 1690s, person after person was summoned 'to show his right to the trade'. Charles Loving, summoned in April 1694, was just one of many who 'confesses he does distill fruit and molasses but hath noe right'. He was ordered to desist by midsummer or be indicted and, when he called the company's bluff, he was in fact sued in the following year. However, just a few years later, the company was beginning to have doubts about its legal position and, in 1704, a committee was set up 'to advise with Councell touching prosecuting interlopers'. Meanwhile, a profitable trade was being conducted in selling the freedom of the company to interlopers rather than sueing them, the normal price being £25.

By the reign of George I, one fears that the company was fighting a losing battle as the Gin Age encouraged the multiplication of back-street distilleries and the smuggling of French brandy became a major English industry. In 1715, the company still showed an interest in defending the monopoly, but there are few further signs of activity in succeeding years. The Court was now showing more interest in its investments in South Sea stock, the list of pensioners supported by the company was growing and it was beginning to look more and more like any other livery company, with few interests outside its property, its dinners and its charities. Early in 1723, there was a debate in the Court on 'whether the searches be continued for the future' and, although this was not resolved immediately, there do not seem to have been any more searches after that date. In the following year, the changing nature of the company is nicely symbolized by the Court's decision to invest £4000, the accumulated balance of many years of livery fines and selling the freedom, 'in the purchase of freehold lands or houses in the City of London'. The company still acted as a lobby for the spirits trade, but had abandoned most of the other activities and powers for which it had fought when it first acquired its charter in the 1630s.

A rather similar story can be told of the Vintners' Company, which as can be seen from Table 9.4 (p. 252) was largely composed of tavern-keepers. The company was of medieval foundation and its members had many important privileges, including that of selling wine without licence in the City and liberties.[24] Past members had left property which the company administered as trustee, and rents comprised 56 per cent of the company's income in the early 1690s. However, nearly all this rental income was specifically tied to charitable purposes and the Vintners shared the problems of all the ancient property-owning companies of honouring their charitable commitments in the difficult half-century following the Fire. Livery fines, very high at £31 each, were the backbone of the company's non-property income, while the tavern-keepers seem to have been better payers of quarterage than the members of most companies.

The company still carried out searches in the early years of the reign of Queen Anne. In May 1704, for instance, some wine found in the cellar of William Lewellin of Pudding Lane was 'tasted and tryed by severall members and found to be defective and not fit for the body of man to be drunk'. However, the

Vintners, like the Distillers, were doubtful about the legality of
their searches and sought legal opinion in 1704 and again in the
winter of 1706 on the subject. It is not known what advice was
given by 'eminent Councell', but matters seem to have come to
a head in 1708 when the Master was faced with a mutiny, the
majority of those summoned for the search failing to turn up.
Eventually, most of the mutineers appeared before the Court to
purge their contempt at a cost of 3s.4d. a head in the poor box
(or 5s. for late-comers) but, from this date onwards, searches
were few and far between and seem to have been give up
altogether by the reign of George I. The company continued to
lobby on behalf of its members but its main business was
property management, charity and more than usually good
dinners.

The last two companies which will be considered had reached
this position much earlier. These were the Grocers and the
Fishmongers, second and fourth in the order of precedence of
the 'Twelve Great Livery Companies', both companies having
a heterogeneous membership, as was seen in Table 9.4. In the
early 1690s, one can still find a faint flicker of the control of the
London fish trade which the Fishmongers had acquired in the
middle ages.[25] The first Monday in Lent was traditionally the
'view day for this Company's land and the search for corrupt
fish' and this was still being carried out, some traders being
fined for 'exposing to sale unseasonable salmon', but cases were
rare and the main attraction of the search day was the
'moderate dinner' laid on by the renter warden. The Court is
also found occasionally establishing a committee of 'all the
Assistants being traders in fish and others as they shall thinke
fitt' to hear the grievances of 'severall traders in fish of this
company', but this was a very pale reflection of the famous
fishmongers' hallmoot which sat once a week to settle disputes
in the fourteenth century.

References to fish are in fact hard to find in the indexes of the
court minutes and are totally overwhelmed by the company's
main business, which was managing its extensive property and
administering several important charities and trusts, such as
the free grammar school at Holt in Norfolk and St Peter's
Hospital at Newington in Surrey, which housed forty-two poor
men and women free of the company, petitions for places

forming a recurrent theme in the minutes. Every year, just before Christmas, a party of assistants went down to St Peter's to distribute doles to the almsfolk, first admonishing them 'to live in the feare of God and to avoid drunkennesse and to be helpefull one to another'.

Managing property and carrying out the testamentary wishes of former Fishmongers meant that the wardens, clerk and beadles were busy men, collecting rents (often in arrears), repairing property and paying out over a hundred separate legacies and doles to the poor of this or that parish, to hospitals and to particular individuals, many of these doles requiring a selection process to decide which particular worthy, poor and ancient man or woman should be the lucky recipient. Some idea of the problem can be seen from a typical entry in the renter warden's accounts: 'paid for coles and faggotts distributed to poore and needy fishmongers in St Michael Crooked Lane and elsewhere according to Mr Pendlebury's last will, 20s.' Collectively, the charities administered by the older livery companies must have handed out amounts of money, coal and bread which compared in total with the parallel system of poor relief provided by parishes, but it was all scattered around in bits and pieces and must have been a tiresome burden to administer.

There was still a faint odour of fish in the deliberations of the Fishmongers, but one would never know that the Grocers had any connection with sugar and spice if the company had not borne that name, despite the insistence of the historian of the company that 'the excellence and purity of foodstuffs' was still one of its primary concerns in the 1690s.[26] This statement is based on the revised bye-laws of 1690, which still provided for an inspection of grocers' shops 'once or oftner in every year . . . to search view and essay all raisins, currants, prunes, figs, almonds, sugar, pepper etc.' and included a scale of fines for 'rotten, false or counterfeit wares'. However, it is clear from the court minutes and accounts that these searches were not carried out and there is virtually no reference to business relating to the grocery trade in the excellent index to the minutes.

What interested the Grocers was their appalling financial position, they probably being the worst hit of the big companies by accumulated indebtedness before the Fire and the effects of the Fire itself. This did not stop them splashing out on two pageants for the Grocer Sir John Fleete's 'Triumph' as Lord Mayor in 1692, the money on this occasion as on others being raised by appointing a large number of new liverymen. A couple of years later, the company's financial problems were solved by Sir John Houblon, the first governor of the Bank of England and himself a Grocer, who rented Grocers' Hall for the use of the Bank in return for a fine of £5000 and a loan of the same amount. Otherwise, the Grocers' records show that their activities were very similar to those of the Fishmongers: dinners and ceremony, property management and the administration of charities and gifts, including Oundle and other schools, almshouses, scholarships and exhibitions at Oxford and Cambridge and the normal profusion of doles in kind and money.

The Grocers were already in the 1690s what all the other companies would be by the end of our period, 'a Nursery of Charity and Seminary of good Citizens', as their clerk put it in 1689.[27] Most of their income was spent on charity, though some was used 'for defraying the charge of sober anniversary festivals in moderate entertainment of the members, to maintain and increase mutual friendship and Christian conversation in the fraternity as well in ease as for encouragement of the members'. George Ravenhill's words nicely sum up the meaning of the livery companies to those of their members who actively supported and enjoyed what they did. One suspects that by our period this would only have been a minority of those of the middle station, though occasional attendance at such fraternal festivities remained an important part of civic life.

iii Tory and Whig

What one reads in court or vestry minutes was no doubt only the bare bones of what had been discussed by the worthies of parish or livery company, who would hardly have come together so many times a year for such dry business alone. One subject which would almost certainly have been aired was politics, for this was an intensely political age and nowhere more so than in what had once been described as 'the proud, unthankful, schismatical, rebellious, bloody City of London'.[28]

Political activity took many forms, but the one most likely to

pay dividends was lobbying. The practice of addressing grievances in person or in writing to parliament, the privy council or
the City government was an ancient one but it reached new
levels of intensity in our period, especially from the 1690s
onwards. Annual sessions of parliament, and sessions long
enough to ensure that bills had a fair chance of being enacted,
meant that much more legislation relating to economic affairs
could now get into the statute book. The process of initiating
and supporting such legislation, or of opposing it, was one that
might engage any Londoner, rich or poor, at some time in his
life. This might involve nothing more than waiting, cap in
hand, on one of the members of parliament for the City or it
might involve a fully orchestrated campaign with signatures
collected for petitions, a printed statement of grievances and
perhaps a well-organized procession of petitioners. Such cam-
paigns were normally conducted in a polite enough way, with
emphasis on the respectability and good standing of the petitioners. Sometimes, they were far from polite, frustration leading to violence, as in the weavers' riots of 1675 or the calico
riots of 1719-21 in which women wearing cotton had the clothes
ripped off their backs by embittered silk-weavers.[29]

The weavers of Spitalfields and the East End had a notorious
reputation for crowd violence and they were to make a threatening appearance on a number of occasions in our period,
either in pursuit of an industrial grievance or as a force
manipulated by politicians for their own ends, such as the
crowd of weavers with whom the Whigs flooded Guildhall
during the General Election of 1710, who 'caused much fighting
and quarrelling in the street'.[30] However, weavers had no
monopoly of political or industrial violence and the threat of
the crowd was a major factor in London political life.

No one could forget the pressure that had been imposed by a
well-articulated London crowd on the eve of the Civil War,
pressure which took the form of 'monster' petitions or the
physical presence of hundreds or thousands shouting slogans or
waiting menacingly outside parliament to ensure that the
members voted correctly. The London crowd was never again
to play quite such an important political role but the fear that
it might was always a factor in the political calculus, as the
respectable were to be reminded on several other occasions

during the Civil War and its aftermath – in the Exclusion Crisis of 1678-81, during the Revolution of 1688, in the Sacheverell riots of 1710 and again in the anti-Hanoverian riots of 1715 and 1716. Historians love riots and the social make-up of those arrested or indicted on these occasions has been carefully analysed. In nearly all cases, one finds that the crowd was not composed of the totally dispossessed, but was drawn mainly from artisans and from the lowest section of the middle station, who used these occasions not as an opportunity for looting and mayhem but as a means of demonstrating on some specific political or religious issue. Sometimes the crowd would generate its own leaders, but often it was orchestrated by people of higher status, most obviously in the Exclusion Crisis and in the Sacheverell riots of 1710.[31]

Political activity by large numbers did not necessarily involve riot. London had a long tradition of pageantry and processions, a form of street theatre which might be used for patriotic purposes or to reinforce the social hierarchy but which was often used as political propaganda, in much the same way as the marching days of modern Ulster. Processions were meticulously organized and could be stirring spectacles, but they were often full of menace and none more so than the savage pope-burning processions of 1673-80. Normally held on Guy Fawkes night and on the anniversary of the accession of Queen Elizabeth on 17 November, these processions became more and more elaborate and often involved several hundreds of people, a host of whistlers, bellmen and torch-bearers escorting their fellows dressed as Catholic priests, Jesuits, cardinals and, of course, 'a most costly Pope, carried by four persons in divers habits, and the effigies of two devils whispering in his ears, his belly filled full of live cats who squawled most hideously as soon as they felt the fire'. The size and importance of such processions ebbed and flowed with the intensity of political activity, but they were to reach a new crescendo in the last years of the reign of Queen Anne and the period of the Hanoverian succession, when pope-burnings, fireworks, ox-roastings and free beer laid on by the Whigs were matched by the rival displays of the Tory Jacobites, who celebrated such occasions as the anniversary of the martyrdom of Charles I or the Pretender's birthday with equal panache.[32]

Riots and processions were the noisy and sometimes exciting manifestations of street politics but, for most people most of the time, politics was a quieter business, an intermittent process of complaining about this and that, and particularly about the government. Seditious words spoken by drunks in taverns form a recurring theme in the revelations of the numerous spies employed by the secretaries of state, but the democracy and sobriety of the coffee-house was often seen as a greater danger. 'These sober clubs produce nothing but scandalous and censorious discourses and at these nobody is spared,' wrote the City Chamberlain, Sir Thomas Player.[33]

The grumbling of political discussion reached its peak, then as now, at the times of elections, democratic processes which involved virtually all the middle station and a surprising number of lesser people in this period over a hundred years before the first Reform Act. Democracy at the local level varied from parish to parish, depending on such matters as whether the vestry was open or closed, but in many parts of London all rate-paying householders had the right to vote in local government elections. Most of these were not very exciting or well attended, but a particularly fraught political situation could induce a strongly contested election for such offices as common councilman, while for many people a local election was a matter of bread and butter on whose result depended local power, office and its perquisites and lucrative contracts which could be distributed to the friends of the elected man.

Local elections happened every year, but most middling people were also able to vote from time to time in parliamentary by-elections and in general elections, the latter occurring on an unprecedented number of occasions during the middle years of our period. There were three general elections during the exciting years of the Exclusion Crisis and then a lull during the period of absolutist backlash, which was ended by the Revolution of 1688. Then came a period of electoral excitement such as the English public had never experienced before, the Triennial Act of 1694 being followed by ten general elections in twenty years, a record never since beaten. Not only were there more elections, but more seats were contested during this period than at any other time before the nineteenth century, and each contest was magnified and made more exciting by the increasingly partisan coverage provided by the newspapers. If many people had been able to ignore politics in the past, few were able to forget that they lived in an intensely partisan and divided city by the end of the reign of Queen Anne, when the two general elections of 1710 and 1713 produced the highest polls of the period, some 92 per cent of the liverymen of London voting in the 1713 election.[34]

Londoners voted for only ten members of parliament, four for the City and two each for Westminster, Southwark and the county of Middlesex. This was a minute proportion of the House of Commons relative to the population of the metropolis but the London members, especially those for the City, played a much more important role than is suggested by their numbers, for example, as key committee members on legislation relating to economic affairs. The results of London elections were eagerly awaited because the electorate was large enough to reflect public opinion rather than just the largesse handed out by the candidates. Londoners were notorious for their independence and the large floating vote reflected and indeed led the national trend in all but one of the seven general elections between 1701 and 1715. 'The countrys always take the rule from hence', observed Lord Halifax of London in 1705, 'and the true pulse of a nation is always felt at the heart.'[35]

What sort of politics was this heart interested in? This is not the place to attempt to write a political history of London, but it is possible to observe a continuity in the political structure of the metropolis which reflected the social structure and survived right through from the hectic days of the early 1640s to the comparatively quiet years of 'stability' at the end of our period and indeed much later in the eighteenth century.[36] In this scheme, one can identify five levels of political activity. The first, and usually the most active, comprised the gentry and aristocracy, who played out on a London stage the struggles of national politics, a continuing and often intense political debate which took place in their West End houses, in taverns, coffee-houses and clubs, in the street and in the theatre and, of course, in the forum of parliament itself. The nature of this debate naturally varied with time, but it was usually as much about jobs and power as about ideology, and it often reflected long-standing divisions between the great families of the counties far more than any metropolitan or even national political issues.

The fact that the seat of government and parliament was in the metropolis meant that such people, the real political nation, were always aware that what they said or did was observed and discussed, welcomed or execrated by their neighbours, the citizens and people of London. This audience at the doors of Westminster and the West End necessarily had its effect on national politics as politicians of all hues courted the electorate and placated or enflamed the London crowd, while governments kept close contacts with their natural allies in the City élite. It was the latter, the very rich, who formed the second stratum in metropolitan politics. This élite, which came to be known as the monied interest, was made up of wealthy merchants, directors of the trading companies, bankers and other financiers. Such people were usually able to control the Court of Aldermen, the effective rulers of the City, and they benefited handsomely from their close links with successive governments. These provided them with potentially lucrative positions as customs farmers or in the revenue service, with beneficial access to the subscription lists for public loans and with commercial contracts which, especially in wartime, could quickly enhance a man's fortune as supplier of victuals, naval stores or clothing or as the organizer of remittances for the support of troops abroad. Such men were natural supporters of any government in power, mainly for practical reasons, and were often quick to trim their ideology to suit the times.

Below this élite came the majority of the people considered in this book, the wealthy and fairly wealthy traders, shopkeepers and manufacturers. Such people were usually conservative supporters of the status quo, active to lobby government but not normally hostile to government, whom they expected to protect them and forward their interests. However, they were not blind supporters of the establishment and it was the antagonism of this group which ensured that London would be a parliamentary city in the Civil War, though it was also the same people who as the 'Presbyterians' eventually ensured that the revolution of the 1640s would not go too far, closing ranks to resist the radicals and welcoming the return of monarchical government in 1660.

These radicals, the 'Independents' of the 1640s, were drawn from the largest stratum of the London political world, small shopkeepers, petty industrialists, artisans and journeymen, who form a continuum in the political life of the metropolis. We are told that the 'agitation of small London master craftsmen against their growing subjection to capitalist middlemen is one of the most prominent themes of London history under the early Stuarts', but this theme is a continuous one which runs right through our period and beyond.[37] Hostile to or critical of the wealthy and almost always against the government, members of this section of the population crop up time after time under various names in the political history of London. Whenever there is a riot, one can be sure that it will be people from this group who will be prominent. However, their activities went beyond mere rioting and their politics ranged from the radical and populist to the frankly revolutionary and republican.

They were the Independents and Levellers who tried to convert an argument between gentlemen into a truly radical revolution in the 1640s and 1650s. They were the populist Whigs of the 1670s and 1680s who revelled in the great pope-burning processions. By the reign of Queen Anne, after a remarkable political sea-change,[38] they have turned into populist and radical Tories but they are still the same people, still hostile to the rich, still against the government. They are still there in the 1720s and 1730s, still mouthing the same levelling and radical maxims which they had first learned in the 1640s, and they are still there in the 1760s and the 1790s. They never enjoyed power except for a few years in the middle of the seventeenth century, but their numbers were sufficient in the outer wards of the City to ensure that the Court of Common Council, the lower house of the City government, was normally opposed politically to the Court of Aldermen and that the history of City politics would be an intermittent battle between those wanting to enlarge the populist element in local government and those who wanted to restrain it, the latter group normally but not always winning the day.

There was finally a much larger group of the dispossessed –

women, children, servants and the poor – who were considered beneath political consideration even by the Levellers. If one wanted to insult one's opponents, one described them as members of this despised breed, as the Whig newspapers did in 1715 when they depicted the Tory rioters as 'Black Guard Boys, Clean Your Shoes Your Honour, Parish Boys, Wheelbarrow-men, Butchers, Porters, Basket-women, Ballad singers, Bawds, Whores and Thieves'. But, as has been said, most rioters were not in fact drawn from such lowly people but from the next group up in London's political hierarchy, the 'petty tradesmen and craftsmen of the industrial suburbs'.[39]

London's politics can thus be depicted as class politics, with rich, middling and comparatively poor people distinguished from each other and each striving to protect or promote their interests. Needless to say, politics has never really been as simple as that; nor was it in our period, when political opportunism, ideology and particularly religion combined to confuse the politics of wealth and so create the 'fractured society' which has been analysed in a recent book.[40] In particular, a man who was a dissenter or was sympathetic to dissenters would nearly always be a Whig, the party which favoured toleration and which after the Toleration Act of 1689 was normally prepared to defend it, while a man who was an ardent Anglican would nearly always be a Tory. Dissenters could be found in all levels of London society, from very rich Presbyterian aldermen to poor Baptist craftsmen, and so religious lines cut right across the politics of wealth and status.[41]

How much politics actually affected the lives of middling people is difficult to say. They certainly voted Whig or Tory, depending on their wealth, their religion or their inclination, and it seems certain that political debate and the reading of the mass of ephemeral political literature must have absorbed quite a lot of their time. Indeed, according to Defoe, all this politics could have serious effects on the efficient running of a business. 'Never was the gazette so full of the advertisements of commissions of bankruptcy as since our shop-keepers are so much engaged in parties, form'd into clubs to hear news and read journals and politicks.' However, one does not necessarily have to believe Defoe. There is no doubt that the men, and indeed the women, of the middle station thought that politics was interesting and important and that it could sometimes be profitable, but it seems unlikely that even the excitement of the 1710 general election would have so turned their heads that they forgot that 'the main affair of life' was getting money.[42]

It can be seen that an active civic life was open to and indeed to a certain extent mandatory for the middle station. They needed to be good neighbours, both for friendship and for the sake of business, reputation and the safety of their property. They had an important role to play in local government and might be expected to play some part in the running of their livery company. They were likely to be involved in a considerable amount of political activity and discussion in their lives and, if they lived through hectic periods such as the 1640s, the late 1670s or the first half of the 1710s, they might find that the contemporary obsession with politics threatened to interfere with business. There were also many other civic or corporate activities in which they might get involved, such as active membership of a society for the reformation of manners, the management of a charity school or a directorship of a trading company. All this required time and attention, but it was unlikely to have played such a regular part in their lives as the subject of the next chapter, the spending of their money.

10 Expenditure and Consumption

Accumulation has been stressed throughout this book as a major feature of middle-class life, a thirst for greater wealth which ideally required thrift, economy and miserliness. However, although the miser is the classic image of the capitalist, one suspects that there were not very many amongst the middling people of Augustan London. For, paradoxically, this accumulating class were also great consumers whose collective expenditure was a major part of the effective demand which kept them all in business. In this chapter, the patterns of expenditure on the three main items of consumption, food, dress and domestic goods, will be examined but first the scene will be set by trying to estimate roughly how much the middle class spent altogether.

i Disposal of Income

How much did middling people spend a year? Such a question is difficult to answer, but a first approximation can be got from Gregory King's famous table of 'income and expense'. Here he estimated that the greater merchants and traders by sea had an income of £400 a year and an expenditure of £320, the lesser merchants £200 and £168, and the shopkeepers and tradesmen £45 and £42 15s. respectively. These figures, especially those for shopkeepers and tradesmen, seem far too low for London, and for more realistic data one needs to look at the estimates made by Joseph Massie in the middle of the eighteenth century. He subdivided merchants into three classes, spending £600, £400 and £200 a year; nearly all London merchants would have fallen within the two top groups. He provided for six categories of tradesmen, three of Londoners spending £300, £200 and £100 a year, and three in the country spending £100, £70 and £40 a year. He also had four classes of master manufacturers, the top two spending £200 and £100 a year. This gives a range of expenditure from £600 a year for the big merchants and from £400 down to £100 a year for the bulk of the London middle class.[1]

In another paper, Massie challenged the contemporary view held by gentlemen that merchants and tradesmen made exorbitant profits. His argument was based on the commonsense observation that, if tradesmen had really been making very large profits, they would have left much more money to their children than they actually did. He suggested that a profit of 15 per cent was as much as the average tradesman could expect and then calculated their accumulation over thirty years, first assuming that they spent two-thirds of their profits and then assuming that they spent only a third. The results suggested that the 15 per cent might have been too high and that most tradesmen spent about two-thirds of their income.[2]

If Massie's formula is applied to our sample, the results suggest that his calculations were sensible enough. The median fortune of the merchants was £9000, which at 15 per cent gives an income of £1350 and an expenditure of £900 if two-thirds of income were spent. However, as has been seen, 15 per cent is probably too high for merchants.[3] At 10 per cent, one gets an expenditure of £600 a year, which agrees with Massie's highest figure for merchants. The median fortune of the whole sample was about £2000, which at 15 per cent gives an income of £300 and an expenditure of £200 a year, in the middle of Massie's estimates for London tradesmen. The typical capital of a relatively small shopkeeper or tavern-keeper was about £1000 which, using the same formula, gives an expenditure of £100, again in line with Massie. There were of course many men worth less than £1000 – the young, the unsuccessful, small shopkeepers and artisans. Most of these people would probably have spent between £50 and £100 a year, though there must have been some whose middling existence was so mean that they could spend only the £42 15s. suggested by King as an average figure for all English shopkeepers and tradesmen.[4]

What was all this money spent on? Amongst his many other calculations, Gregory King produced a table of the 'Expence of the People of England in Dyet, Apparel and Incident Charges'.

TABLE 10.1: Gregory King's Breakdown of Expenditure

Total spent per family per year	Total spent per head per year	Diet per head		Apparel per head		Other expenses per head	
		Money	%	Money	%	Money	%
£21	£3	£2	67	£0.11s	18	£0.7s.	15
£63	£9	£5	56	£2.0s.	22	£2.0s.	22
£91	£13	£6	46	£3.13s.	27	£3.13s.	27
£122	£17.10s.	£8	46	£4.10s.	26	£5.0s.	28
£189	£27	£10	37	£7.10s.	28	£9.5s.	35
£294	£42	£15	36	£11.5s.	27	£16.5s.	37
£455	£65	£20	31	£15.0s	23	£30.0s	46

Source: Calculated from GLRO JB/Gregory King fo. 210. The total spent per family per year is calculated on the basis of a seven-person family for comparison with Vanderlint's data.

TABLE 10.2: Jacob Vanderlint's Breakdown of Annual Expenditure

Item	Expenditure	
	Money	%
Food and drink	£76.16s.	33
Clothes	60.0s.	26
Other expenses	95.4s.	41
	232.0s.	100

Source: Calculated from Vanderlint (1734) p. 141.

He divided the population into twelve groups of differing total expenditure per head and then broke this down into his three main categories of spending. The figures for the middling groups, together with the poorest group, are set out in Table 10.1 above. King's breakdown is similar to that of Jacob Vanderlint, who produced in 1734 'an estimate of the necessary charge of a family in the middling station of life', which is analysed in Table 10.2 above. Vanderlint's figures relate to a London family consisting of a man and his wife, four children and one maid and, if one ignores expenditure on rent, which King omits, he estimated that they would spend £232 a year. This puts Vanderlint's family between King's two groups spending £27 and £42 a head per year, both of which have similar percentages for each of the three categories of expenditure, the main difference being that Vanderlint allowed more for 'other' expenses.[5]

This may be a happy accident or it may reflect reality. There is not really enough other information available to be sure, though most early modern historians would be prepared to believe almost anything if they discovered similar information in two independent sources. Assuming, then, that King and Vanderlint got it about right, it can be said that middling people spent between a third and a half of their disposable income on food and drink and about a quarter on clothes, a concentration of spending which justifies exploring 'diet' and 'apparel' in some detail in the next two sections.

ii Diet

If Gregory King was right, middling families spent between £5 and £20 per head a year on food and drink, while Vanderlint's figures work out at £11 per head. It was suggested earlier that there might be some 20,000 or 25,000 middling families in London, with about seven or eight members each. If, say, £10 per head were spent on all these people, the total demand would have been between £1½ and £2 million a year, a concentration of consumption which explains why farmers thought it worthwhile to specialize in the production of good-quality food for the London market. London demand was well satisfied by this supply and middle-class Londoners ate well for their four or five shillings a week.[6]

Most people had three meals a day – breakfast, dinner and supper – but nearly all the eating was done at dinner. Breakfast might consist of beer or boiled milk, some bread, perhaps a bowl of porridge, although there were changes from the 1690s with the introduction of hot drinks into the home. Chocolate was an early favourite as a nourishing breakfast drink, and coffee had its devotees, but it was tea which was to conquer from Queen Anne's reign onwards. By the end of our period, the breakfast of toast and rolls and tea which James Boswell used to have in the 1760s would have been normal for a middling family.[7] Supper, too, was usually a light meal made up of such items as bread and cheese, cake, apple pie or jelly, but it could be much more substantial. Supper parties were quite popular and, although rarely as massive in content as dinner parties, their menus covered the whole range of food-stuffs which will be considered later. Supper was also a meal where one might have something fairly unusual or expensive, such as pheasant and woodcock, chicken with the first asparagus or lobster. However this was party fare, not everyday diet, and it was on their family dinners that middling householders laid out most of that one-third or more of their total expenditure which went on food and drink. Dinner had once been a meal eaten by all classes at noon, but our period sees the beginnings of those class distinctions in meal-times which have survived to confuse the unwary to this day. Workmen continued to dine at noon, but middling people began to eat an hour or so later and the upper class later still, perhaps as late as three or four o'clock, a change in habit which tended to make supper an even lighter meal but encouraged investment in a rather heavier breakfast.[8]

Misson provides a good description of what middling Londoners ate at dinner. 'Among the middling sort of people they have ten or twelve sorts of common meats, which infallibly take their turns at their tables, and two dishes are their dinners: a pudding, for instance, and a piece of roast beef; another time they will have a piece of boil'd beef, and then they salt it some days before hand, and besiege it with five or six heaps of cabbage, carrots, turnips, or some other herbs or roots, well pepper'd and salted, and swimming in butter: a leg of roast or boil'd mutton dish'd up with the same dainties, fowls, pigs, ox tripes, and tongues, rabbits, pidgeons, all well moisten'd with butter, without larding: Two of these dishes, always serv'd up one after the other, make the usual dinner of a substantial gentleman or wealthy citizen.'[9]

A few comments can be made on this interesting description. First and most obvious is the emphasis on meat, a fact of English life which impressed most foreign observers. The number of days on which one ate meat was an index of one's status in the world and about four or five days a week was probably about average for the middle station.[10] What is perhaps more surprising is Misson's comment on the quantity of vegetables served with the meat, since some historians believe that vegetables were only rarely eaten.[11] There was certainly a medical prejudice against them and, except when people mention the first peas, beans or asparagus of the season, one finds few references to vegetables in casual comments on food. Circumstantial evidence, however, suggests that Misson was right. Contemporary cookery books provide for a wide variety of vegetables, as a separate dish, as a salad, dished up with meat or used in a soup or stew. Even more suggestive are the data on market gardening in the London area, one estimate being that the area of garden ground expanded more than tenfold between 1660 and 1720.[12] Virtually the whole range of modern northern European fruit and vegetables was grown, though two vegetables which are the mainstay of modern cookery had no place in Augustan cuisine. The tomato was widely used in the Mediterranean but, in England, the knowledge that it belonged to the same family as the deadly nightshade was sufficient to damn it and it was hardly eaten at all. The potato, too, faced almost total prejudice in southern England till late in the eighteenth century and bread still provided the bulk in middle-class meals, though not very much of it according to Misson. 'I have known several people in England that never eat any bread, and universally they eat very little: they nibble a few crumbs, while they chew the meat by whole mouthfuls.'[13]

Medical prejudice also seems to have had little effect on the consumption of uncooked fruit. The quality, quantity and variety of domestic fruit were all much improved in the seventeenth century, many exotic varieties being grown under glass, and people were quite prepared to defy the doctors and sample the treats available. Jonathan Swift reflects both the English ambivalence to fruit and the variety available in a letter to Stella: 'The grapes are sad things; but the peaches are pretty good, and there are some figs. I sometimes venture to eat one, but always repent it.' However, such worries seem to have lessened with time. Dudley Ryder treated his brother and sister at one of the fruit shops in Stocks Market – 'it cost me 2s.' – while Vanderlint allowed 2s. a week each to the mistress of his middling household and her four children to 'buy fruit and toys'. Growing seasons were short and much fruit was preserved, to be eaten candied or to find its way into the many sweet-sour recipes which were so popular, while dried fruit was imported from the

Mediterranean – prunes and figs and astonishing quantities of currants and raisins, which arrived in whole fleets to catch the Christmas demand for puddings and pies. This was also the time for the arrival of oranges and lemons, nearly eleven million a year by the late seventeenth century, expensive luxuries which were confined to the middle and upper classes.[14]

One striking feature of English cuisine was the very liberal use of butter in cooking. Misson noted that the vegetables were 'swimming in butter' and that the meat dishes were 'well moisten'd with butter', while Constance Wilson writes that our period was 'the golden age of butter in English cookery'. This would have been very salt butter, which was rarely eaten with bread by the wealthy, who preferred cheese or cream. However, what was really idiosyncratic about English cookery were the puddings, which became a central element in the English diet in the course of the seventeenth century. Puddings came in all guises, packed with different combinations of meat and vegetables and especially dried fruit; this is the description by Misson, who positively drools over the English national dish:

'The Pudding is a dish very difficult to be describ'd, because of the several sorts there are of it; flower, milk, eggs, butter, sugar, suet, marrow, raisins, etc., etc., are the most common ingredients of a pudding. They bake them in an oven, they boil them with meat, they make them fifty several ways: Blessed be he that invented pudding, for it is a manna that hits the palates of all sorts of people: a manna better than that of the wilderness, because the people are never weary of it. Ah, what an excellent thing is an English Pudding! To come in Pudding time, is as much as to say, to come in the most lucky moment in the world.'[15]

As has been seen, the usual dinner of the middling family was two dishes, 'serv'd up one after the other'. The normal practice when giving a dinner party would be still to have just the two courses but to serve up several dishes at each course. A cookery book of 1729 suggests the following menu for a winter dinner party: for the first course, gravy soup later replaced by a dish of chicken and bacon, also 'Scotch collops, giblet pie, a fine boil'd pudding, roast beef with horse-radish and pickles round'; for the second course, 'a turkey roasted, three woodcocks with toasts, a tansey and garnish with orange, a hare with a savary pudding, a butter'd apple pie hot'. This huge feast is not merely cookery-book fantasy, as can be seen from Samuel Pepys's *Diary*. On 26 January 1660, for instance, when he was in his mid-twenties, employed only one maid and was worth only a few hundred pounds, his wife produced the following 'very fine dinner' for a company of twelve: 'A dish of marrow-bones. A leg of mutton. A loin of veal. A dish of fowl, three pullets and two dozen of larks all in a dish. A great tart. A neat's tongue. A dish of anchoves. A dish of prawns; and cheese.'[16]

Pepys has a number of interesting references to food, but he did not record what he ate every day and one can easily get the wrong impression about eating habits from his diary since it was the unusual that was likely to catch his attention. Very few diarists had such an interest in their stomachs as to allow it to be determined what they ate on a regular basis. One exception was William Byrd the Younger, who wrote down almost every day the main dish that he had for his dinner and also noted what he ate for supper, if anything. One can hardly pretend that Byrd is a typical middle-class Londoner, for, although he was the grandson of a London goldsmith, he was a gentleman from Virginia and lived the life of a gentleman while in London. Nevertheless, what he ate at dinner, as shown in Tables 10.3 and 10.4 (pp. 277 and 278), demonstrates what was available for those with few worries about the cost of their food.

As one would expect, Byrd ate a lot of meat, this providing his main dinner dish on almost exactly half the days in 1718, while he ate various types of fowl on another fifty-four days. However, what is striking is the wide variety of meat and fowl available and the fact that it seems to have been available most of the time. For example, Byrd was able to eat fresh roast beef or beef-steak in every month of the year, indicating that the farmers had largely solved the winter feeding problem, though one can still see a peak of beef eating in the traditional killing months at the end of the year and of mutton in January and February. One should note, too, that Byrd usually ate his meat dressed in the plain English fashion. French cuisine and, to a lesser extent, Spanish were becoming quite popular and one finds constant references to fricassees, ragouts, olios and other

TABLE 10.3: William Byrd's Diet in 1718

Meat

Beef (29 roast, 27 boiled, 18 beefsteak, 1 stewed)	75	
Mutton (19 cutlets, 10 roast, 4 steak, 4 boiled, 1 mutton)	38	
Veal (12 roast, 6 cutlets, 2 boiled, 2 minced, 2 veal & bacon, 1 calf's head, 1 ragout)	27	
Pork (5 roast, 5 boiled, 3 Virginia, 2 pork & peas, 1 broiled)	16	
Rabbit (3 roast, 2 boiled, 2 rabbit & onions, 1 fricassee)	8	
Tongue (4 tongue & udder, 2 boiled)	6	
Lamb (1 fried, 1 broiled, 1 lamb)	3	
Venison (1 roast, 1 haunch, 1 boiled)	3	
Ham	2	
Bacon (1 bacon, 1 bacon & eggs)	2	
Hare (1 roast)	1	
Ragout	1	182

Fowl

Chicken (12 boiled, 5 roast, 3 broiled, 2 fricassee, 1 chicken & asparagus, 1 chicken & bacon)	24	
Pigeon (5 roast, 5 pie, 1 boiled)	11	
Turkey (3 roast, 1 broiled, 1 young)	5	
Goose (3 roast, 2 boiled)	5	
Fowl (2 roast, 2 fowl & bacon)	4	
Duck (3 roast)	3	
Partridge (1 roast)	1	
Teal	1	54
Eggs (80 battered, 1 boiled, 1 eggs & fried udder)		82
Fish (28 fish, 4 saltfish, 4 mackerel, 3 stewed crab, 2 salmon, 2 herring, 1 trout)		44
		362

Source: Byrd (1958). All entries for the year 1718 have been analysed. On three occasions he mentions more than one dish and these have been placed under the separate headings. On six days he did not say what he ate. Byrd visited Oxford, Tunbridge and elsewhere during this period but the great majority of his meals were eaten in London, at his lodgings, with friends or in taverns. He almost always had boiled milk for breakfast in 1718, though in the following year he switched to asses' milk followed by milk porridge. He usually either had no supper or ate some sort of pudding (in the modern sense), cake or cheese in the evening. However, on 81 days he had a more substantial supper, including 37 meat dishes, quite often cold, 32 fowl dishes, 9 egg dishes and 3 fish dishes.

TABLE 10.4: Seasonal Distribution of Byrd's Diet

Month	Beef (roast, steak)	Beef (boiled, stewed)	Veal	Mutton	Pork	Chicken	Fish
Jan	3	1	2	8	0	2	4
Feb	3	2	2	10	2	0	1
Mar	3	1	4	4	1	2	4
Apr	3	0	2	3	1	2	4
May	3	3	4	3	0	1	6
Jun	5	2	3	2	0	5	5
Jul	3	1	2	5	2	0	4
Aug	2	1	3	1	3	4	4
Sep	3	1	3	1	2	3	4
Oct	5	5	0	1	4	1	3
Nov	6	4	2	0	0	1	3
Dec	8	7	0	0	1	3	2
	47	28	27	38	16	24	44

Source: As for Table 10.3.

dishes with rich sauces, but few Londoners would have eaten these on a regular basis.

When not eating meat, Byrd ate an astonishing amount of battered (i.e. scrambled) eggs, which provided his dinner on no less than eighty days, nearly always in his lodgings; a quick and nourishing meal for a gentleman, who often only ate at home when everyone on whom he called was out. This emphasis on eggs is not found in any other source, though they were certainly eaten widely and in many forms, various types of tansy (omelette not necessarily flavoured with tansy) being particularly popular.

Byrd also ate fish nearly once a week, probably more than most Londoners, since fish was 'dearer than any other belly-timber'. However, for those who could afford it, there was a wide variety available and, although Byrd rarely specifies his fish, there are several traditional fish meals in his diet sheet. Londoners tended to turn up their noses at the salt cod of Catholic days, which, as bacalhau or baccalà, was and is a staple of diet in southern Europe, but salt-cod boats still used to arrive during Lent and it was in March and April that

Byrd ate his salt fish. The next excitement in the fish calendar would be the arrival of the mackerel shoals, the first mackerel in late April or May often being noted by contemporary writers. Herrings provided another delicacy in September, to be eaten fresh or pickled in brine. This was also the time when 'damsels first renew their oyster cries', our forefathers like us only eating oysters when there was an R in the month, though Pepys once jumped the gun and had some on the last day of August, 'some pretty good oysters, which is very soon, and the soonest I think I ever eat any'. Oysters were cheap and vast amounts were consumed by both rich and poor, sold by the wheelbarrowmen or delivered in barrels to the homes of the middle station in barrels – 'Colchester Oysters may be supplied for this season with the largest pick't fat and green for 3s. a barrel.'[17]

The four or five shillings per head spent on food and drink by middling Londoners includes money spent on servants and apprentices as well as on the master and mistress and their children. Servants would not of course have enjoyed the magnificent spreads described above. Nevertheless, it seems probable that they ate very well in middling households, much better than they would ever have eaten with their families before going into service. It is striking that, amongst the large number of complaints about masters in the records of the Mayor's Court, complaints about poor-quality or insufficient food are surprisingly few and far between.

All the same, there were complaints and one of them is quoted here at some length since it throws some light on what was expected. 'The defendant [a merchant] and his wife . . . did usually feed very high of ye best sorts of food but as to his servants he kept an extraordinary bad house, for ye servants did very rarely eat of any of the meat which the defendant and his wife feed on but what was left at their table above stares was generally locked up and very seldom (only some few scraps) brought downe to the servants. And the food wherewith the servants were generally fed was very coarse stale mouldy bread and ranck salt butter together with some porrage made of the meat that the defendant and his wife eat abovestares and scraps of fish and sometimes dumplings very dry and with very little of any suet or other ingredients in them. And if it chanced the servants had any of the meat it was often stale and corrupt and soe stinking that they could scarcely eat it but yet were forced to eate it for mere necessity. . . . And ye bread and butter and also if there were at any time any chees (which was very seldom and but ordinary) it was imediately so soon as they had dyned constantly locked up so that the servants could not come at it. The said servants very seldome had any breakfasts or suppers allowed them and, if they had, it was of such ill food as they were not able to eate to any content . . . All the victuals were constantly lockd up and the beere kept above stares.' Whether it was true or not, one can see from this evidence that servants ate separately from the master, but expected very much the same food sent down to them. They expected, too, to get three meals a day and plenty of it, and, on top of this, they felt that bread and cheese should be kept unlocked in the kitchen and beer in the cellar, not above stairs, so that they could help themselves whenever they pleased.[18]

Beer was the main drink and houses frequently did their own brewing, many inventories listing 'beere stillings' and 'beere stands' as well as the occasional parcel of malt. Wine was also drunk quite often at home, but nothing has been found like the huge personal wine cellar which Pepys had accumulated by July 1665: 'at this time I have two tierces of claret – two quarter-cask of canary, and a smaller vessel of sack – a vessel of tint, another of Malaga, and another of white wine, all in my wine-cellar together – which I believe none of my friends now alive ever had of his own at one time.' Hardly any of our inventories list any stocks of wine at all, though many houses had large quantities of glass bottles which may well have been taken to the tavern to be filled up.[19]

It seems reasonable to conclude that, despite occasional complaints and meanness, the men and women of the middle station and their servants ate and drank well. Just how well can be seen by comparing Vanderlint's breakdown of expenditure on food and drink 'of a labouring man and his family in London' with his estimate 'of the necessary charge of a family in the middling station of life'. This is shown in Table 10.5 opposite, where Vanderlint's figures for 1734 are also compared with Gregory King's estimate of English expenditure in the

TABLE 10.5: The Diet of Middling and Labouring Families in
London Compared
(Cost in pence per head per week)

| Type of Food | Vanderlint | | King |
	Middling	Labouring	All England
Bread	5.25	5.25	3.50
Meat and fish	17.50	7.00	4.25
Butter	5.25	1.75	
Cheese	1.75	0.87	} 2.00
Milk	0.75	0.87	
Beer	9.50	5.25	4.75
Tea and sugar	7.00	0.00	0.00
Others	3.50	1.75	2.00
	50.50	22.75	16.50

Source: Vanderlint (1734) pp. 75, 141; King (1936) p. 56. 'Others' is 'roots and herbs, salt, vinegar, mustard, pickles, spices and grocery, except tea and sugar' for the middling; 'roots, herbs, flower, oatmeal, salt, vinegar, pepper, mustard, sugar' for the labouring; 'fruit, roots, garden stuff, salt, oyl, pickles, grocery etc' for King.

1690s. The results give some idea of what it meant to belong to the meat and butter eating and tea drinking classes.

iii Dress

'The people in general are well cloathed,' wrote de Muralt of the English, 'which is a certain proof of their living at ease; for in England the Belly always takes place of the Back.'[20] The latter point was necessarily true of the mass of the people, who needed to devote half or more of their income to their bellies, but for middling people the back ran the belly fairly close, contemporary experts suggesting that about a quarter of their income went on apparel. This section will try to determine how this money was spent.

The first two decades of our period were ones of experimentation, which resulted in an almost revolutionary change in the type of clothes worn by both sexes.[21] For men, the new clothing was the three-piece suit of coat, waistcoat and knee-breeches, worn with a shirt and drawers, stockings to the knee and usually buckled shoes rather than boots. Both coat and waist-coat were usually so long that they almost concealed the breeches, with a long line of narrowly spaced buttons right down to the hem. Further embellishment was provided by trimmings and embroidery to the main garments, lace ruffles at the wrist, bands and later cravats or neckcloths round the neck and on the head a wig topped by a beaver or a felt hat. Men doing dirty work and many shopkeepers wore an apron to protect themselves or as a mark of status, while the cloak was increasingly challenged as protective outerwear by the campaign coat, derived from the military greatcoat.[22]

Most middling women wore smocks and sometimes drawers next to the skin, but their shape was determined by their laced and boned stays, usually called 'a pair of bodies'. These were worn from under the armpits to below the waist and were often laced very tightly. However, from the 1670s and 1680s, women were to lead a rather more relaxed existence with the development of looser fitting outer garments in the form of the mantua and the gown. These were both one-piece garments, fastened at the waist with a sash or girdle, normally trailing to the ground at the back and open below the waist to reveal the petticoat. Long-sleeved waistcoats, buttoning up the front and often padded for warmth, were sometimes worn over the gown or directly over the petticoat. The rest of the ensemble would consist of shoes and stockings, perhaps an under-petticoat, gloves, various items to cover a low *décolletage* such as pinners, an ever-changing variety of hair-styles, caps and hats, and, for the women of our class, an apron or safeguard to protect their clothes. Decoration and embellishment were even more important than in men's dress and even quite poor women did not like to be seen without a considerable amount of ribbons, braid and cheap lace to brighten up their clothes.

Most fashion was derived from Paris and rapidly adopted in London by the fashionable of the West End. New fashions would then be taken up by middling people, but how quickly is difficult to say. One can find references to deliberate rejection of West End fashion and the loose behaviour that went with it by citizen's wives who laced themselves even tighter and disdained the bare-breasted fashions of Charles II's reign. Such women might continue to wear the high-crowned and broad-rimmed hats of the Puritan 1640s and 1650s 'as a conscious statement of middle class virtues against the whims of the fashionable world', while their shopkeeper husbands wore their own hair short à la Roundhead and sneered at the courtly foolishness of the wig.[23] However, such bourgeois rectitude seems to have withered as fashion changes speeded up and, by the reign of Queen Anne, middling people are regularly criticized for their reckless pursuit of the trivia determined each Easter by the *haut monde* of the West End. Mandeville noted that ladies of fashion were constantly sending for their mantua-makers, 'so that they may have always some new modes ready to take up, as soon as those sawcy cits shall begin to imitate those in being', and other comment on social competition in dress is rife in the first half of the eighteenth century.[24]

Such competition was made easy in England by the fact that there were no fundamental distinctions in types of dress by class or between town and country. Anne Buck has shown that, as early as the 1640s, class distinctions in dress were matters of detail, no form of dress being so different from those of lower classes 'that it shows a completely unrelated, independent style'. An indication of the depth of fashion can be found in the 1675 inventory of a Limehouse pawnbroker, whose customers were hardly likely to have been upper-class. The goods pawned included three very dressy bundles; the first contained 'two petticoats, a piece of gimp lace, a pair of silk stockings, a silver laced waistcoat and a pair of bodies', the next a 'lutestring [silk] gowne and pettycoat laced, a satin petticoat, a red pettycoat laced with gold and silver lace', and the third 'a red cloth mantle, a tabby [silk] petticoat, a black silk mohaire petticoat and a pair of laced slippers'. Not only are these the same sorts of clothing as were being worn by the fashionable in 1675; they are also made of expensive materials such as silk, 'cloth', which meant good woollen cloth, and gold and silver lace.[25]

Social distinctions were even less in the eighteenth century when differences were ones of fashion, fabric and the quality of the embellishments, rather than of type, so that it was well worth paying for the skills of high-class tailors, staymakers and mantua-makers in order to rise above the tolerable imitations made for the ready-made market. The initiated always knew, of course, and many a laugh and a sneer could be had at the expense of those aping their betters, but, for all that, the homogeneity of English dress provided wonderful opportunities for both the makers of clothes and their wearers and was a major factor in ushering in that mass market for cheap textiles whose demand fuelled the Industrial Revolution.

How many clothes did middling people own? A preliminary answer can be found in an unlikely source, the evidence given in disputes between master and apprentice. It was normal practice for parents or friends to supply the apprentice with a satisfactory wardrobe 'at his entrance' and for the master to maintain and replace these clothes at his own charge as became necessary. Since the quality or quantity of the clothes originally supplied was often in dispute, it is quite common to find them listed by witnesses in the Mayor's Court. Such wardrobes obviously varied in value and quantity, but one can still see what were the basic requirements of a young man starting service and these can reasonably be taken as the minimum wardrobe of middling men.

A typical wardrobe would be valued between £10 and £20, and would consist of three complete outfits and accessories. John Hicks, for instance, a gentleman's son apprenticed in the early 1650s, brought into service two new suits and a new cloak, a good large cloth coat and a good old suit, a frieze short coat, two felt hats, two pairs of new worsted stockings, a pair of new waxed boots, two pairs of shoes, four shirts (two new), six new bands and eight old bands, four handkerchiefs and six caps, all of which were said to be worth at least £15. Thirty years later, John Parker, apprentice to an upholsterer, had two new cloth suits and a new serge suit, together with a campaign coat, one new caster and a felt, three pairs each of new hose and new stockings, eight shirts, a dozen and a half of bands, six handkerchiefs and other necessaries, valued at £13 'or rather more'.[26]

Not many inventories list clothing but, when they do, one can see that the basic male wardrobe of three suits and accessories was maintained into adult life, though many people accumulated much more, such as the merchant William Kersteman, who had seventeen shirts, nineteen neckclothes and five complete suits when he died in 1711. The clothing of men in this class was normally woollen or worsted for the outer garments and linen for shirts, bands, drawers and sometimes waistcoats, but most men also had some silk in their wardrobe, some silk stockings perhaps, several silk handkerchiefs, one best silk suit and very often a silk 'nightgown', a loose dressing gown worn as much in the day as at night. Many men wore a turban to cover their shaved heads when wearing their nightgowns, a piece of oriental exoticism which was reflected in the furnishing tastes of the middle classes.[27]

There is less information on the clothing of middle-class women, but what there is suggests that they, too, maintained a minimum of three complete outfits and accessories (and often much more) and that a high proportion of their outer clothing was made of silk or silk mixtures. One can take as an example Frances Gardner, the widow of a grocer, whose clothing was listed in 1665. Frances was only twenty-seven and her husband worth only £642, but her wardrobe shows why the Spitalfields silk industry was to flourish. She had one suit of mixed tabby and one of black lustring, seven petticoats, two unspecified and the others made of sky colour tabby, white dimity, crimson silk mohair, turkey mohair and cloth with gold lace, the most expensive item. She also had a riding suit, a damask cloak with silver hooks, a satin mantle with bonelace, three tufted and three smocked waistcoats, an old black gown and a grogram gown, two fans, two pairs of gloves, an old apron and a parcel of small linen, the whole lot being valued at £17 10s. Susanna Hardy, the widow of an apothecary who died in 1676 worth £652, had a similar wardrobe – 'a sute of mourning, two gowns, eight petty coats, one pair of bodyes, a silke petty coat laced with silver and gold lace, a red mantle laced with silver lace, three women's mantles and two pairs of silk stockings', valued at £16. 7s.[28]

It is difficult to generalize about the cost of clothes because so much depended on the fabric and embellishments. Table 10.6 overleaf gives some idea of the range of prices for a few common types of textile. These are drawn from stock-lists in inventories and would be wholesale prices. One could argue for ever about just what a 'yard' was or what exactly mohair, camlet or drugget were, but it can at least be seen that there was a very wide variation in price for textiles bearing the same

TABLE 10.6: Wholesale Prices of Textiles, 1671–1701

Type of Textile	Range of Prices per Yard
WOOLLENS & WORSTEDS	
Cloth, broadcloth	10s.6d., 8s.6d., 7s.6d., 6s.6d., 5s.6d., 5s.
Serge	4s.6d., 3s., 2s.6d., 2s.2d., 2s., 1s.6d.
Bays	2s.3d., 2s., 1s.8d., 1s.
Kersey	2s.7d., 2s.2d., 2s.
Calamanco	3s., 2s.6d., 2s
Frieze	3s., 1s.
Penistone	2s., 1s.8d.
MIXTURES (mainly wool/silk)	
Mohair	5s., 4s., 3s., 2s.6d., 1s.8d.
Camlet	5s., 3s.1d., 1s.6d., 1s.3d., 1s.
Drugget	3s.6d., 2s.6d., 1s.6d., 1s.3d.
Parragon	1s.8d., 1s.
Stuffs	1s.3d., 1s.
SILKS	
Gold & silver brocade	50s.
Velvets	26s., 18s., 16s.
Tabbys	9s., 5s.6d.
Wrought satin	4s., 3s.
Lustrings	4s.6d., 2s.3d.
Indian taffety	3s.6d., 1s.8d.
Indian satin	1s.6d.

Source: S.36 (1671), S.57 (1673), S.60 (1673), S.79 (1675), S.111 (1678), S.245 (1696), S.282 (1701). Where textiles are individually valued in inventories, this is by the piece, the yard or the ell, most silks being by the piece or the ell. The following are a few examples of the price per ell of silks and fine linens: white sarsnet 8s., Florence satin 8s., Dutch farrandine 7s., English farrandine 4s., Morella tabby 6s.6d., black lustring 7s., coloured lustring 5s., alamode 4s.6d., 3s.6d., Holland linen 4s., 3s.6d., 3s., 2s., cambrick 4s., lawn 4s.6d. I have relied on the *OED* for definitions, though it is clear that textiles of the same name were not always made of the same materials.

name. It can also be noted that woollen broadcloth was more expensive than all but the most expensive silks and that there was a wide range of cheap silks which overlaps all but the cheapest woollens, worsteds and mixtures. These prices make it clear why the wearing of silk could go so far down the social hierarchy.[29]

In Table 10.7 opposite, these fabrics are turned in to ready-

TABLE 10.7: Wholesale Prices of Ready-made Clothes

Type of Clothing	Prices in Stock-lists	King
MEN		
Coats:		20s.
Cloth	36s., 25., 23., 21s., 16s.8d., 10s.	
Drugget	22s.	
Frieze	12s.	
Bays	10s.	
Fustian	6s.	
Waistcoats:		15s.
'Rich'	52s.	
Cloth	22s.	
Calamanco	16s., 12s.8d.	
Silk	18s., 8s.2d., 7s.	
Breeches:		10s.
Cloth	8s.	
Silk	28s., 15s., 6s.8d.	
Calamanco	12s., 8s.6d.	
Stuff & serge	7s., 6s.	
Hats:		2s.3d.
Beavers	34s.9d.	
Narrow casters	24s., 18s., 15s., 12s., 4s.	
Felts	4s., 2s.10d., 2s., 1s., 0s.8d.	
Caps	6s., 4s.	
Shirts:	15s.2d., 10s., 8s.2d., 3s.5d.	2s.6d.
Cloaks:	53s., 50s., 33s.4d., 20s., 15s.	80s.
WOMEN		
Mantuas:		20s.
Silk	20s., 14s., 12s., 11s., 10s., 9s.7d.	
Stuffs, serge	14s., 9s., 8s.	
Calico	10s.6d.	
Petticoats:		20s.
Silk	20s., 11s., 9s., 8s.6d., 6s.3d.	
Serge	10s.	
Flannel	5s.	
Stays (bodies)	7s.6d.	8s.

Source: S.2 (1666), S.60 (1673), S.169 (1681), S.207 (1688), S.209 (1689), S.245 (1696), S.254 (1698), S.273 (1701). Gregory King in GLRO, JB/Gregory King, fo. 203.

made clothes and valuations of some types of men's and women's clothes are listed, again from stock-lists. On the right-hand side of the table are Gregory King's valuations for these articles from his table of 'Annual Consumption of Apparell, 1688'. Once again, there was a wide range of prices, depending on the textile used and the quality of the finish. These prices are, of course, the absolute minimum for new clothes, since the stock-list prices are wholesale and King's estimates were supposed to be an average for all classes. In any case, it is unlikely that many middle-class men and women bought their outer garments ready-made, though they would quite often buy shirts, smocks, bands, handkerchiefs, drawers etc. from haberdashers and milliners. Such things might also of course be made up at home by the women of the household.

Drawing on the prices in Tables 10.6 and 10.7 and other prices, it seems probable that it would cost a minimum of £6 or £7 to provide a complete ready-made outfit for a man of any quality at all.[30] Such a price would soon shoot up if one bespoke the clothes from a tailor or bought anything of even moderately high quality. Pepys, for instance, who was a snappy and ambitious dresser, laid out £17 in 1664 on 'my fine coloured cloth suit, with my cloak lined with plush' and £24 in the following year on 'my new silk camelott sute, the best that ever I wore in my life'.[31] Pepys did rather tend to overdo the luxury of his dress and was told in 1669 that his gold-lace sleeves were inappropriate to his position, but many merchants and wealthy shopkeepers would probably have spent this sort of money on their clothes, mercers in particular being renowned for their luxurious dress. However, the average man of the middle station would have been much more modest, though he would probably have paid more than the prices listed in Table 10.7 since he would have had many of his clothes made by a tailor.

One can get some idea of making prices from a tailor's account-book of the late 1690s and early 1700s. Most of his customers provided their own fabrics and his bills are for making up the material and the cost of the accessories. Coats cost between 7s. and 9s. to make up, waistcoats and breeches about 5s. or 6s., giving some idea of the labour involved since journeymen tailors got about 10s. a week wages. Accessories, such as buttons, shalloon for lining and pockets, silk thread and twist, might well cost as much again and all this takes no account of the cost of the cloth. Tailors also did maintenance and repair work on clothes: 2s. for scouring a suit, 1s. for taking spots out of a coat, similar prices for pressing, spongeing, napping and other services. Dressmakers got lower pay than journeymen tailors and costs were normally so modest that few middle-class women would have bothered to make their own clothes at home. And even a mantua-maker was paid better then the sempstress who made up shirts and smocks. Stephen Monteage, for instance, paid £3 6s.6d. for Holland linen to make six shirts in October 1733 and, in November, he paid Mrs Tomlins 9s. for making them.[32]

In order to estimate the total demand for clothes, one also needs to know something about annual turnover. How much did people need to buy each year to keep up with fashion and to replace worn articles? This would obviously vary considerably with the individual and is also something on which there is no real evidence. However, a very rough approximation can be provided by looking at Gregory King's estimates of 'annual consumption of apparell'. For instance, he thought that a million 'coats for men' would be consumed every year or rather less than one coat per man per year, assuming that men were a quarter of the population. Since he also put down a million men's waistcoats and breeches and a million each of women's 'petticoats and wastcoats' and 'bodyes and stays', he seems to have believed that most adults would buy on average a complete outfit every year, and presumably middling people would buy rather more than the average. King also allows for roughly two pairs of stockings, shoes and gloves and two shirts per head of the population every year, not to mention a huge range of other items only likely to be purchased by the middling and upper classes, such as perukes, swords, muffs, masks, fans etc.[33]

If these figures are even roughly right, one can begin to see how Jacob Vanderlint could estimate in 1734 that a middling man would spend £16 a year on his own clothes, £7 each on his four children and £16 for his wife, 'who can't wear much', a total of £60 or just over a quarter of his expenditure. By coincidence, the attorney William Moses, whose personal accounts have survived for the year 1679–80, spent exactly £60 on clothes in the year, of which just over £40 was in seven separate tailors' bills. Miss Goreing, a young lady living on her own with two servants, spent £31 on clothes in 1697–8, including tailors' bills, fabrics and accessories such as hoods, gloves and shoes, and she spent over £52 in 1703–4.[34] So, although one cannot really tell if Vanderlint's estimate was accurate, it was certainly not outrageous. People did spend a lot on clothes and it is no wonder that such a high proportion of the population was engaged in making them.

The clothes that were replaced each year still had a long life in them. Some provided the raw materials with which the tailor produced a 'new' suit; others were cut down for children, refashioned for apprentices or given to maid-servants, the fashionable embellishments being carefully removed. Others would end up in the huge second-hand market, to be worn by the poor and then to be cut down to be worn by the children of the poor. Such recycling was much greater in our period than it is today but nevertheless the regularly recurring demand for new clothes, especially by the men and women of the middle station, was one of the major factors keeping the economy going. So was the recurrent demand for furniture and furnishing materials, which is now considered.

iv Domestic Comfort

'True comfort, as we understand it, was invented by the French in the seventeenth century,' writes Peter Thornton, who singled out the 1630s as the key decade in this development and showed how the new comfort was quite quickly transferred to the homes of aristocratic Englishmen in the early Restoration period.[35] This section will look at how the homes of middling Londoners were also transformed in the course of our period.

This is much easier to document then diet or apparel, since most inventories list furniture, often in considerable detail. One can start by looking at valuations of domestic goods, though it should be noted that these are 'clearance sale' and not replacement values, and people actually spent much more than the figures listed by the valuers. Table 10.8 opposite provides average valuations broken down into five wealth groups and distinguishing between two sub-periods, before and after 1690. The table shows that there was little change over time, a rather

TABLE 10.8: Value of Domestic Goods by Wealth Groups

| Wealth Groups | Average Value of Domestic Goods | | | No. of Cases |
	Overall	Before 1690	After 1690	
Less than £500	£63	£59	£70	98
£500–£999	74	69	80	48
£1000–£1999	100	102	98	64
£2000–£4999	116	120	108	91
£5000 and over	225	250	206	71
				372
Whole sample	115	119	111	

Source: Inventories of sample. For three cases, it was impossible to separate the value of domestic goods from the other items. Valuations of plate and jewellery are not included in these totals.

TABLE 10.9: Average Valuation of Contents of Rooms

Room	Ave. value
Best bedroom	£23.3
2nd bedroom	10.6
3rd bedroom	6.9
Dining-room	12.2
Kitchen	13.1

Source: As Table 10.8. The analysis is based on 318 inventories which can be broken down to provide this information and does not include taverns, inns etc., or other cases where the rooms were not listed separately.

surprising result since, as will be seen, there was considerable qualitative change in domestic goods. As one might expect, richer people spent more than poorer people, though it is clear that demand for such goods was relatively inelastic.[36] It seems, too, that richer people were spending rather less and poorer people rather more as time went on.[37]

It was seen in Chapter 8 that the typical middle-class house had about seven rooms, comprising four or five bedrooms, one or two living rooms, the best one normally being called the dining-room and and the second best the parlour, and a kitchen. In Table 10.9 above, the average value of the contents of the main rooms is listed and it can be seen that the most valuable room was normally the best bedroom, a room which was used for entertaining as well as sleeping, as is clear from contemporary prints and descriptions as well as from the inventories. Five of the sample, all merchants, had magnificent best bedrooms valued at over £100. Another merchant, who died in 1701, had a dining-room valued at £100, and there was a tendency for this room to be upgraded as our period continues to provide an increasingly important second focus of display.[38]

What one might call class as well as wealth affected the level of domestic consumption. For example, 38 of the 162 people worth more then £2000 had best bedrooms valued at less than £15. Since these people could clearly have afforded bedrooms valued at the £20, £30 or more which was normal in this wealth group, it is interesting to see if they shared any characteristics. When one looks at their occupations, it is clear that they did, since, with few exceptions, they made their money in ways not considered very genteel by their contemporaries. There were only two merchants amongst them, for instance, and virtually none of the fashionable sort of shopkeeper. The fact is that most merchants, mercers and drapers made very sure that they would not be found dead in a bedroom worth less then £15, a fear not shared by such ungenteel tradesmen as builders, wine coopers, cheesemongers, coalmongers, soapmakers, distillers, printers and cloth finishers. Such men, although wealthy, saw no reason to lay out money on unnecessary display in their bedrooms or in any other part of their homes, a fact which helps to explain why they often managed to accumulate as much as mercers and merchants, since they were not subject to the same haemorrhage of their capital on domestic display.

One can now look at the qualitative changes in the contents of houses. These were considerable and, for the most part, followed with some delay the changes discovered by furniture historians in their studies of the court and aristocracy.[39] One striking feature was the increasing emphasis on lightness, both in terms of visibility and in the materials used for hangings, curtains, bed furniture and upholstery. The replacement of small paned windows by sash windows from the late 1680s and a much greater provision of sconces and standing candle-sticks, often backed with mirrors, did much to dispel the gloom of interiors. From the 1690s, many wealthy people were using the much larger mirror plates now available as chimney glasses above their fireplaces and pier-glasses between the windows, while, in general, one finds a much wider use of looking-glasses and their introduction to nearly every room. In 1691, Guy Miège noted the light and airiness of the London house, the 'lightsom stair-cases, fine sash-windows and lofty ceilings', the latter usually plastered, which 'make by their whiteness the rooms so much lightsomer.'[40]

The use of lighter textiles was equally marked, heavier draperies such as broadcloth and serge being replaced by lighter mixtures such as mohairs and camlets, and, increasingly, by silks and cottons. These changes in taste are especially marked in the furnishing of beds, which were normally adorned with a huge yardage of textiles in the form of curtains, valances, headcloths and testers, quite apart from the quilts, blankets, rugs and sheets which lay on top of the nearly ubiquitous and expensive feather-beds. By the reign of Queen Anne, the hangings of the best bed in the house were nearly always camlet, mohair, damask or silk and many were also lined with silk or cotton, a development which can be seen throughout the house as camlet and mohair gradually replaced serge in the second and third bedrooms too and as similar textiles were used as hangings and furniture coverings generally.[41]

The furniture itself was becoming more comfortable, curves which fitted the human body replacing the upright, angular furniture of earlier days, while improvements in upholstery led to better padded seats and a much wider use of cushions and squabs, usually stuffed with down or feathers. Sitting comfortably was now very much the thing to do and the ability to do so is indicated by the increasing appearance of couches, sofas and settees and by the 'easy chair', the high-backed, winged and well-upholstered armchair described by John Gloag as 'a national symbol of ease and comfort'. He dates the easy chair from the 1670s, but it is not common in our inventories before the reign of Queen Anne.[42] Another innovation was the replacement of the 'turkeywork' chair by the cane chair as the normal form of upright chair for sitting at table and, in general, the much wider use of light, elegant and resilient canework in other types of furniture. Cane chairs are found in aristocratic inventories of the 1660s and John Gloag has suggested that the demand for the new chairs 'was suddenly and dramatically expanded' by the Great Fire in 1666. This attractive thesis is not supported by our inventories, which show that the key decade for the adoption of the new chair was the 1680s, some twenty years after its first introduction, and it is in the same decade that anguished petitions from the turkeywork makers are found in a bid to ban the products of their competitors.[43]

The decline of serge as a furnishing material and the rise of the cane chair are just two examples of the influence of fashion on domestic interiors. There were many others, such as the introduction of the 'oval table' from the 1670s, and it is clear that fashion, often derived from French or aristocratic models and followed with a delay of a decade or two, was an imperative influence forcing Londoners to change their furniture and furnishings long before they were worn out. This was good news for manufacturers and traders in general, although there were of course losers, such as the serge-makers of Exeter and the turkeywork makers of Bradford, who had good cause to bemoan their fate, while the cane-chair makers of London were basking in the sun.

Cane-work was first introduced from the Far East from where the rattans were imported and is an example of a wide range of innovations which bore a Far Eastern, Indian or Levantine influence. Japanning was another oriental import, a technique imitated by English craftsmen from at least the 1670s. Japan work begins to appear in middling homes in the 1690s, the banker Thomas Williams, for example, having japan boxes, a chest of drawers, a table with matching candle stands and a japan cribbage board in 1697, while after 1700 references to japan work become commonplace. Japan and other lacquer-work was usually associated with high-quality cabinet-making and one sees increasing examples of this, much of it imported by the East India Company. The merchant John Barkstead, for instance, who died in 1694, had an 'Indian trunke and frame', 'a pair of India cabinets' and an 'India cabinet and frame'.[44]

Another oriental product domesticated by the English was china, examples of which can be found in the earliest of our inventories but which did not become really common until the 1690s and the reign of Queen Anne. By this time, collecting china had become a craze for many people, such as John

Sherwood, a drysalter who died in 1703 with some 200 pieces of china and 'tonquin' in his house. Following in the wake of the china boom came the dual invasion of coffee and tea-making equipment into London homes. This was rare before the 1690s but, as with so many other innovations, what was rare or unknown in the 1680s becomes commonplace in the reign of Queen Anne, when inventory after inventory has its coffee-pot and coffee-mill or the standard set of tea-kettle, lamp and stand usually kept in the dining-room.[45]

Another feature of middling homes was the huge increase in pictures, ornaments and bits and pieces as the period goes on. One finds pictures right from the beginning, but not very many of them. By the 1690s and the early eighteenth century, many people had huge collections of pictures and prints, the latter often being imported by the East India Company and thus giving a further oriental flavour to the houses. The haberdasher, Robert Fotherby, for instance, had forty-four Indian pictures in his dining-room when he died in 1709. Pictures could be found all over the house, often replacing the tapestries and wall hangings which were much commoner in the early part of the period. One is rarely told what was represented, but 'landskips', 'sea peices' and paintings of the King and Queen were quite often mentioned. Portraits of members of the family were also becoming increasingly popular, Daniel Thomas having six 'family pictures' in his hall, an indication of a growing bourgeois self-awareness which must have given a lot of work to portrait-painters from the 1690s onwards.[46]

Halls were also a common place to find a clock, as indeed was the head of the staircase, Tristram Shandy's father being unusual in 1715 neither in the ownership of a clock needing to be wound only once a month nor in the place where he chose to keep it. Clocks can be found from the beginning of our period and they had become very common, though not ubiquitous, by the reign of Queen Anne. By this date, there were often several clocks scattered through the rooms of houses, the dining-room being the commonest place to keep one, apart from halls and passages. Perhaps surprisingly, there were very few clocks in servants' rooms and workshops, despite E. P. Thompson's insistence on the connection between the development of the clock and labour discipline, the only two examples being Adrian

Vanderpost, sugar-refiner of Vauxhall, who had an 'old' clock in the men's garret and Richard Walford, a metalworker, who kept a clock in his workshop and only an hourglass in his dining-room.[47]

Bric-à-brac and ornaments, such as 'images' made of alabaster and marble, stags' heads, bird-cages, chess, draughts and backgammon tables and pieces and anything else which might be captured by the catchall word 'toys', all became increasingly prominent and must, together with too much furniture, have made a terrible clutter in many homes. The impact of the collecting fever can perhaps best be seen in the inventory of Daniel Thomas, a mercer who died in 1704. In his closet, he had, amongst other things, 740 books, two models of churches, three telescopes, a globe, several maps, two hourglasses, a sailing compass, a draughts board and some fishing tackle. In other rooms, he had another 150 books and atlases, some 200 pieces of china, getting on for 100 pictures, more maps, a Noah's ark and a small organ, as well as a collection of weapons which included 18 hand-guns.[48]

Pepys's observation that one in three families in the City had a pair of virginals amongst their goods when they fled from the Fire, and the emphasis on music-making at home in his diary, has led music historians to believe that middling Londoners were a very musical lot indeed, constantly engaged in entertaining each other in impromptu domestic concerts. This, however, is not borne out by our inventories, in which one finds only thirty-three men, less than a tenth of the sample, with any musical instruments in their house and six of these had only an instrument described as 'old' stored in the garret, suggesting that if their household had once been musical it was so no longer. The data give some substance to the view that growing access to professional music in concert rooms from the 1680s had a dampening effect on domestic music, the proportion of men with musical instruments falling from one in seven to one in seventeen before and after 1680.[49]

The room which saw the least change was the kitchen, with its extensions into buttery and pantry, most of the change that there was consisting of an improvement of amenities in the kitchens of the less wealthy. This development meant that, by the late seventeenth century, the kitchen was the room with the narrowest range of valuations, the great majority being valued at between £10 and £20, whatever the wealth of the house-holder. Kitchens were used not just for the preparation, cooking and serving of food but also for washing dishes and for making, mending, washing and ironing clothes, and their contents reflect these various functions. They were also the place where servants, apprentices and younger children ate their meals and relaxed, so that all kitchens contained one or more tables and several chairs and stools, the furnishings becoming increasingly attractive over time, with better quality chairs, curtains, perhaps a canary or a parrot in a cage, a clock, some pictures and a screen to protect the occupants from the heat of the fire.[50]

Heat was provided by an open fire, either in a grate or a range, the latter presumably being what we understand by a range, with side ovens heated from the fire. Ovens, in fact, are rarely mentioned, possibly because they were landlords' fittings but quite probably because few houses did their own baking, the Londoner being well served by professional bakers, who baked three times a day and delivered to the door as well as being prepared to bake the housewife's pies and pasties in their large ovens. Most cooking involved spit-roasting, frying, simmering and boiling, and a formidable array of equipment for this can be found in all kitchens.

Nearly everyone had at least two or three spits turned by a weight-driven jack, the grease being caught in a large dripping-pan. The battery of kettles, pots and pans, which were increasingly made of brass or copper and were becoming more specialized into saucepans, stewpans, fish-kettles, tea-kettles etc., were suspended from hooks over the fire or, from about 1700, from a swinging chimney crane, or they could be placed on the 'cheeks' of the range. All households also had frying-pans, grid-irons for grilling or broiling, long-handled skillets for boiling or stewing, each with their own little legs, and chafing dishes whose base held burning charcoal to keep food hot. Food preparation is represented by cleavers, chopping and shredding knives, flesh forks, skewers, ladles and scummers, a vast array of metalware which helps one to understand why London had so many smiths and metalworkers, the jacksmith for instance being an important and independent trade.[51]

Very few houses had less then 100 pounds weight of pewter

as well as brass, copper, iron and tinware. This was normally valued by weight but was occasionally itemized. The cheese-monger Samuel Palmer, for instance, had twenty pewter dishes including a basin, a cheese plate and a pie plate, thirty-nine plates, a dish frame, two saucers and a salt.[52] Pewter was gaining at the expense of the wooden trencher, in common use at the beginning of our period, but losing out to glass, china, copper, brass and tinware. Silver was not in common use as table-ware by the middle class but almost everyone had some 'plate', which might range from the silver cup and two silver spoons of the salesman Richard Stock, valued at £4 12s., to several hundreds of pounds worth for the richer men, objects of pride and display which would only be seen in the kitchen for cleaning. The quantity of cutlery, sometimes silver but usually steel, also grew; forks, in particular, which were hardly used at all for eating in the 1660s, had become a common item by the early eighteenth century.[53]

Most kitchens had a cistern or sink, with water pumped from the companies' mains, and most had a copper and numerous tubs for washing clothes. Ironing was done with smoothing-irons heated on the fire or with box-irons filled with charcoal, and what had to be ironed can be seen by looking into the linen cupboards, whose contents were usually listed separately, their average value being greater than that of the entire contents of the kitchen but with a similar range from about £10 to £25. These valuations represented an amazing number of separate items, an average of thirty-six sheets, eighty-nine napkins and fifteen table-cloths; linen chests also held pillow-beeres (i.e. cases), towels, childbed linen, window curtains (mainly of cotton or muslin) and yards and yards of Holland, diaper, huckaback, damask etc. which had not yet been made up.[54]

Peter Thornton writes that faces and hands were wiped after meals with a hot, damp napkin, which would help to explain the large numbers. He also claims that many people in the seventeenth century 'were a good deal less dirty than is now generally supposed'.[55] He makes a good case but it is difficult to be totally convinced. Houses, clothes, bed linen, cooking equipment and furniture certainly seem to have been kept scrupulously clean – but were people? There is not a single bath-tub, let alone a bathroom, in the 375 inventories that have been studied, though both the vessel and the name existed. Thornton says that many of the numerous tubs kept in kitchens and cellars may well have been used for personal washing, which seems a reasonable hypothesis but no more. Many houses also list ewers and bowls in bedrooms and, of course, materials for washing such as soap and perfumed washballs were easily available, though pretty expensive. Nonetheless, one must still be slightly suspicious of the personal hygiene of our period. Pepys often complained about dirtiness in other people and seems to have washed regularly every morning but whether this normally went beyond hands and face seems doubtful. Washing his feet seems to have been sufficiently rare to merit the occasional diary entry, as it does in the diary of Stephen Monteage seventy years later, whose feet were washed about once a month, normally by his maid. Whether either of them were in the habit of washing those parts of their bodies which lay between face and feet one cannot tell since they never tell one, which in the circumstances would suggest that they rarely did.[56]

Innovations in the kitchen may have been rare, except for the multiplication of relatively minor gadgets,[57] but they were widespread elsewhere in the house and even the kitchen saw the introduction of the equipment for making hot drinks. Who were the innovators? Who were the people who had already abandoned serge bed curtains before 1680, who already had cane chairs in the 1670s, china before 1690 or tea-making equipment before 1700? None of these innovations was particularly expensive; all of them were within the purchasing power of all the sample and indeed virtually everyone had adopted them by the end of the period. Nevertheless, with the exception of china, whose acquisition seems to follow no particular pattern, those who innovated were by no means a random group. They were nearly all either very wealthy men who might well have the entrée to West End houses or they were tradesmen with an aristocratic business who would see the new fashions when they delivered goods to their clients' houses and who might well think that being fashionable themselves could only enhance their business reputation.

These new fashions represent the 'true comfort', which was mentioned at the beginning of this section, and which, by the reign of Queen Anne, had been introduced to a very considerable extent into the homes of middle-class Londoners. They now lived in houses which were better lit, were hung with more attractive textiles and were furnished in a way which would have made both sitting and sleeping more of a pleasure than they had been in the 1660s. Furniture was more sophisticated, walls were decorated with pictures instead of just hangings and tapestry, and surfaces were covered, perhaps littered would be a better word, with china, glass and ornaments instead of just with table carpets. Overall, there was little difference in the total valuation of domestic possessions at the beginning and the end of the period. However, it does seem clear that the poorer members of the middle station had definitely upgraded their domestic interiors. One might take as an example Thomas Toms, a barber-surgeon of Stocks Market, who died in 1719 aged only thirty. His total assets were valued at £484, of which £49 consisted of the value of his domestic possessions, which were kept in just four rooms. Lack of space forced him to keep a press bed in his dining-room, but the rest of the furniture was very fashionable: a chimney glass, two pier glasses, a pair of glass sconces, nine cane chairs with cushions, eleven pictures and two prints, a glass case, a tea table and forty-one pieces of china. Such a room would have seemed amazingly luxurious to a similar barber-surgeon in the 1660s but, by the 1710s, it was simply in fashion and Thomas Toms was doing nothing extraordinary in furnishing his room in this manner.[59]

Such changes made houses much more comfortable, but they also have a wider significance. When one finds that men worth less than £500 were making a fairly successful attempt to furnish their homes in a way similar to those of great merchants, one can be sure that the economy as a whole was benefiting. Thomas Toms' mirrors and his forty-one pieces of china were good news for the expanding English glass and pottery industries. This deepening of the market also encouraged manufacturers and suppliers to cut costs and prices, by innovations, imitations and a successful search for cheaper sources of supply, and this could well be why what seem to be much better domestic interiors were valued in the early eighteenth century at little more or even less then those of the 1660s and 1670s.[60]

This section has concentrated on those personal possessions

which were accumulated in the house and for most people these were all the possessions that they had, apart from their investments and the tools and stock in trade connected with their business. However, some members of the middle class owned their own transport, the greatest status symbol of the age being one's own coach or carriage. This was no light matter, as readers of Pepys's diary will remember, months of planning, worry and discussion finally ending with the arrival of his coach and horses in November 1668, an acquisition which 'doth put me into the greatest condition of outward state that I ever was in, or hoped ever to be, or desired'.[61] Such glory was an immense expense, not just for the £50–£100 or more that the coach would cost, but for the very high maintenance costs and such ongoing expenses as rent of a coach house, the wages of the coachman and the cost of feeding the horses, a horse's food being about 5s. a week, very much the same as that of any other member of the household. It is not surprising, then, that only sixteen men in our sample owned a coach, nearly all of them merchants with a median fortune of £15,000.[62]

Lesser men had to content themselves with their own riding horse, though this too posed problems in the more densely populated areas and horsekeeping was likely to cost considerably more each year than the value of the horse. Nevertheless, one in five men had his own horse, this being virtually essential for some occupations, such as the apothecaries who had to be able to visit their patients. The remainder had to content themselves with hiring a coach or a horse when they needed one, while on most occasions they would have walked, this being much the commonest way of getting round London. Contemporary diaries leave us in no doubt that early modern men and women were much more active pedestrians than we are today.[63] It is clear, too, that they positively enjoyed walking for the fresh air and exercise and also for their health, though, as will be seen in the next chapter, it might take more than walking to keep a person alive in Augustan London.

11 Sickness and Death

It was seen in the last chapter that middling Londoners were living more comfortable lives in the early eighteenth century than they had been in the 1660s. They were also living rather longer lives, a fact which helped them to become richer and so better afford the comforts that have been described. However, life still remained precarious, and sickness and death, the morbid subjects of this chapter, were an ever-present reminder of the fragility of existence in Augustan London. The great plague of 1665 may have been the last outbreak of this terrible disease, but no one living in London during our period was to know this and there were in any case a host of other diseases which could strike down anyone of whatever age or class with alarming speed.

i Disease and Mortality

'Dear Brother, I was very sorry to hear of your being so bad: but rejoysed very much in your next to hear of your being like to do well again. . . .I was so bad my self that I thought I should have deighed; I was took with a violent chollick in my stomach which held me from Satterday to Thursday.' 'I have had the misfortune of losing my deare child Johney he deyd last week of a feaver and breeding his teeth which I believe was the cause of his feaver . . . it tis a great trouble to me but these misfortunes we must submit two.'[1]

These extracts are from just two of many letters written by Sarah Smyter to her brother, the tea dealer Henry Gambier, few of which have no reference at all to sickness or death. Such preoccupation was normal in a world where any cold might be the forerunner of a terminal fever and where the simplest cut could lead to a fatal infection, and it was small wonder that people constantly worried about their coughs and colds and the state of their bowels. Despite the high quality of their diet and their comparative cleanliness, middling households were far from exempt from the general unhealthiness of the age and few can have known a year pass by without at least one member suffering a serious illness. Few people were under any illusions as to where such illnesses might lead. They sent for the apothecary or physician; they submitted to the gruesome medical attention of the day, to bleeding and vomits, purges and enemas; but they also provided for the all too likely event that these would be of no avail. 'Being at present sicke and weake in body but of sound and perfect mind' was a common introductory phrase in wills and it meant exactly what it said. Four out of five of the wills left by the men in our sample were made on their deathbeds, a fact which suggests that they made a fresh will every time they were seriously sick since it is unlikely that they all succumbed the first time they were laid low. Many did, however, and it is no wonder that the survivors should acquire the habit of resignation expressed by Sarah Smyter or accept the judgment of the distinguished physician Gideon Harvey that 'diseases and death are marks of the divine justice in the punishment of sin'.[2]

Resignation and submission in the face of death did not mean that no attempt was made to avert it. The medical profession has been discussed in Chapter 2, but an interest in medicine and disease was no monopoly of the professionals. *Every Man his own Doctor* was the title of a book published by John Archer in 1673 and this seems indeed what every man was trying to be.[3] Correspondence, commonplace books, cookery books, diaries, every form of personal writing which has survived, attest to the fascination with disease. Such writing teems with the platitudes and jargon of Galenist medicine, with humours and constitutions, and above all with the discussion of possible cures, the ancient country lore of herbs and cordials handed down from mother to daughter being interspersed with the latest panacea recommended by neighbours, doctors, apothecaries and purveyors of patent medicines.[4]

Such panaceas provide an indication of just how much medical fashion has changed. The main object of John Archer's book is made clear by a large advertisement inserted as frontispiece. This proclaimed the virtues of his own particular brand of tobacco which, amongst other things, 'purifies the air from infectious malignancy by its fragrancy, sweetens the breath, strengthens the brain and memory, cures pains in the head, teeth etc . . . cures the worst of gouts, all pains in the limbs; also dropsies, scurvy, coughs, distillations, consumptions'. Dudley Ryder, whose diary is punctuated by self-diagnosis, was a great believer in purging waters but placed his main hopes in his regular visits to the cold bath, which he believed would 'strengthen my body, purge it of ill humours, fence me against cold, prevent convulsions . . . cure me these rheumatic pains . . . secure me against the gout'. Jumping into a cold bath was not everybody's taste, however, and most people stuck to various sorts of medicine to cure their ills or prevent them.[5]

Some of these seem harmless enough and the alcohol content would have made the sufferer feel better if nothing else; for example, the Queen of Hungary's water, a rosemary-flavoured brandy, was a great favourite – 'a spoonful when feeling run down, night or day, *ad libitum*'. Another popular tonic was Daffy's Elixir, which was invented by a clergyman in the Restoration period and was still being sold in this century. What it tasted like one can no longer tell, but it was probably pretty good since it contained brandy, canary wine, oranges, lemons, rhubarb and a certain amount of borax, perhaps to convince customers that it really was a medicine and not just a rather expensive sort of gin. Medicines also drew heavily on a massive increase in the import of oriental drugs. The growth in the import of opiates was particularly striking, a development owing much to the enthusiastic support of Dr Sydenham. 'Among the remedies which it has pleased Almighty God to give to man to relieve his sufferings, none is so universal and so efficacious as opium,' he wrote, and Sydenham's laudanum – 2 oz strained opium, 1 oz saffron, 1 drachm each of cinnamon and cloves in a pint of canary wine – became a very popular prescription, very much the aspirin of the period.

Opium and alcohol might be the most effective ingredients but most medicines contained at least one distinctly odd ingredient and many were very weird indeed. Treacle water, 'a universal remedy against every possible disease', contained in its simplified form thirty-two ingredients, including the horn of a stag, while one of the favourite ingredients in Dr Thomas Willis's *Pharmaceutice Rationalis* of 1679 was 'water of earthworms . . . no matter what the disease'. Others put their faith in millipedes. James Chase, apothecary to the court of William III, recommended their use in cases of difficult breathing, sixty bruised in white wine, which was then strained and flavoured with saffron and spirit of maidenhair. Nicholas Culpeper, whose pharmaceutical works were very influential, thought millipedes should be boiled in oil to 'help pain in the ears, a drop being put into them'. Then there were Goddard's Drops, which were made from powdered human bones amongst other things. Dr William Salmon tells us that if they were distilled from the bones of the skull they would be good 'for apoplexy and vertigo and megrims [migraines] etc. But if you want it for gout of any particular limb it is better to make it from the bones of that limb'. Twenty to sixty drops in a glass of canary were recommended for these drops, which were 'famed through the whole kingdom' and so admired by Charles II that he was said to have offered £5000 for the formula.[6]

Such were just a handful of the 1190 ingredients which appeared in the *London Pharmacopoeia*, the standard reference book on pharmacy, which was fully approved by the College of Physicians and included amongst 193 animals, animal parts or excrements, 'horn of a unicorn or rhinoceros, the bone from the heart of a stag, elephant tusk, bezoar stone . . . frog spawn, crayfish eyes, penis of a bull, flesh of vipers, nest of swallows, oil of foxes'. By the end of our period, this work had got into its fourth edition and Sir Hans Sloane, who presided over its publication in 1721, claimed in the preface that all remedies owing their use to superstition and false philosophy had been thrown out. There was indeed a greater simplicity 'and puppies, hedgehogs, wagtails, bread-crust plaster, lapis lazuli pills and Galen's unguentum refrigerans' had been dismissed, but many old and apparently superstitious formulas were retained. This may well have been the age of reason and Sloane, amongst many others, was certainly a reasonable man but medicine was still a fairly desperate science in thrall to desperate, dangerous and usually disgusting cures.[7]

Given the apparent absurdity of much of what was offered by

the medical establishment, and its continued dependence on a considerable amount of magical and astrological belief, it is hardly surprising that many Londoners turned to magic and astrology themselves. Charms and amulets were sold and treasured; almanacks published information to guide their readers as to the most propitious times for medical treatment. The wise doctor accepted the superstition of the layman, as John Webster pointed out in 1677 when discussing how he dealt with those who believed they were 'bewitched, forespoken, blasted, fairy-taken, or haunted with some evil spirit and the like'. 'If you indulge their fancy, and seem to concur in opinion with them, and hang any insignificant thing about their necks, assuring them that it is a most efficacious charm, you may then easily settle their imaginations, and then give them that which is proper to eradicate the cause of their disease, and so you may cure them.'[8] One cannot but applaud such a sensible approach; the only problem is that, the more one reads about contemporary medicine, the more one thinks that the charm might well be more efficacious than the physician.

The literate Londoner may have left abundant evidence that he belonged to a race of hypochondriacs but he certainly had adequate grounds for his continuous worries about his health. The sad truth was that, for the most part, the medicine of the day did not work and the numerous illnesses of middling people only too often led to their deaths at what would seem to us very unsuitable ages. The appalling mortality of infants and children has been discussed in an earlier chapter and this is a fact of the period which is well known. What is less well known is the vulnerability of young and middle-aged adults. This is illustrated in Figure 11.1, which compares the age at death of London adults between 1730 and 1749 with the situation today. The difference is quite staggering; at just those ages when we can feel most safe, our ancestors were most likely to die, in their twenties, thirties, forties and fifties, when they would be actively engaged in running a business and bringing up a family. The death of the breadwinner in his prime was thus the norm in this society, a daily disaster which left behind children and wives who had been supported in the majority of cases by earnings which required the dead man's own individual application and knowledge.[9]

FIGURE 11.1   Proportional Distribution of Adult Deaths in London
1730–49 and England & Wales 1976

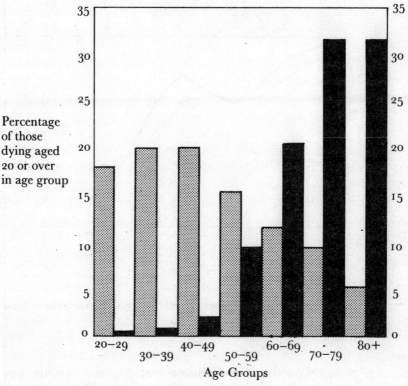

Key: ▨ London 1730–49   ■ England & Wales 1976

Source: London 1730–49 calculated from Bills of Mortality in Guildhall Library;
England and Wales 1976 from United Nations, *Demographic Yearbook* (New York,
1979) pp. 758–9. In 1730–49, 51.9% of all deaths were of people under 20 and, in
1976, only 2.4%.

The period 1730–49 was chosen for this analysis because it
was only from 1728 that age at death was recorded in the
London Bills of Mortality. Before that date there is no direct
evidence on which calculations can be based.[10] However, what
evidence there is suggests that by the 1730s there had been a
distinct improvement on the past and that the period directly
covered by this book, particularly the first thirty years of it, was
considerably worse in terms of the mortality of adults from the
London middle station. This can be illustrated from two

FIGURE 11.2   'Middle-Class' Mortality in London, 1675–1804

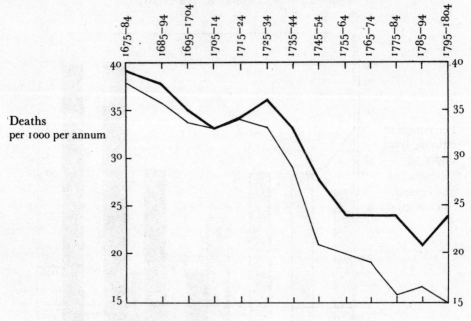

Key: ⎯⎯⎯ London Bridge group of parishes   ⎯⎯ Guildhall group of parishes

Source: See text and note 11.

sources, neither particularly reliable but together giving one some confidence that one is observing reality. Figure 11.2 is again based on the Bills of Mortality. The method used was to calculate deaths per thousand for two groups of 'middle-class' parishes clustered round the Guildhall and the northern approaches to London Bridge.[11] The analysis would hardly satisfy a historical demographer but the results are still very striking, showing as they do a virtually continuous decline in mortality in both groups of parishes from the late 1680s to the early 1780s, with the exception of a serious hiccup in the two decades 1715–34, a period which includes the well-known time of general high mortality in the late 1720s.

It is of course possible that the decline in deaths per thousand illustrated in Figure 11.2 was entirely accounted for by a fall in infant and child mortality and that there was no improvement in adult mortality, which is our main interest

FIGURE 11.3 Age at Death of London Citizens, 1620–1739

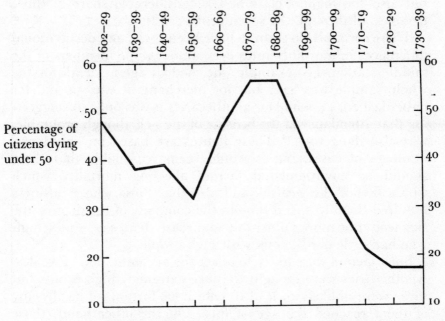

Source: See text and note 12.

here. That this is probably not the case is indicated by Figure 11.3 above, which is based on the genealogical material collected in Boyd's Index of London Citizens and shows the proportion of citizens dying under the age of fifty at decadal intervals between 1620 and 1739. This indicates that there was a considerable increase in adult mortality at early ages in the third quarter of the seventeenth century but that, after 1689, there was a continuous decline until 1739 when the data run out.[12] There is no sign here of the high mortality of the 1720s, possibly as a result of a quirk in the data but quite probably reflecting a change in the social incidence of disease. Charles Creighton explained the contemporary obsession with the high mortality of the 1670s and 1680s by the fact that it was particularly serious for adults and 'that a good many of them had been among the well-to-do', a hypothesis which is certainly illustrated in Figure 11.3. However, from 1715 onwards, there was a change. 'Our history henceforth has little to record of malignant typhus fevers, or of smallpox, in those snug houses of the middle class, although not only the middle class, but also the highest class had a considerable share of those troubles all through the seventeenth century.'[13]

There certainly do seem to have been social and occupational differences in mortality rates even amongst the members of the middle station. For example, the median age at death for the whole sample was 44½ but for merchants it was 52 and for haberdashers 43, while for apothecaries it was only 40, suggesting that attendance at the bedside of the sick, though profitable, was also dangerous.[14] These figures are based on only small numbers of cases, but it would seem reasonable that there should be environmental factors affecting mortality which would favour the wealthy and also that those whose business required them to spend time in the company of the poor or the sick would be more vulnerable to disease than, say, a merchant who had little need to mix with such people.

Such factors were likely to affect the accumulation of wealth. Apothecaries were thought to make extremely high profits but these were unlikely to lead to enormous fortunes if hardly any of them reached the age of fifty. On the other hand, those already favoured by fortune were more likely to live longer and so accumulate even more. What was true of individuals and of separate occupations was true of the middle station as a whole. Those who succumbed to the very high mortality of the early part of our period were not in a position to accumulate as much as those who survived it or who were born after it was over, a fact which is reflected in our sample, those dying before 1690 leaving a median fortune of £1353 and those dying afterwards £2076. There were other reasons for this 50 per cent increase in accumulation, but an improvement in life chances is clearly one important factor to take into account when considering why middling Londoners were able to grow richer in the reign of Queen Anne and richer still later in the eighteenth century.[15]

Richer and longer lived they may have been, but they still died appallingly young by the standards of today. This was a fact of life in Augustan London and one with which middling people had to learn to live. The sad and often sordid scene of the death-bed was soon obliterated by the pomp of the funeral, while the money so eagerly accumulated during the lifetime of the deceased was quickly distributed amongst his heirs, subjects which are discussed in the next section.

ii Funerals and the Transmission of Wealth

'I must have you to know', wrote a merchant in 1703 to his factor in Danzig, 'that I did not spare for any thing that is in fashion at funerals but had all to the height of the mode and soe as he made a good exit.' In fact he spent £125, quite a modest sum for a merchant's funeral, making a good exit being just about the most expensive single item in the affairs of the middle station. It was an expense which humbler people could ill afford at such a difficult time, but both respect for the dead and the need to maintain status in the eyes of the neighbourhood ensured that there was normally 'a very good company along with the Corps'.[16]

There was a standard form for a middling funeral which could be expanded or contracted to allow virtually any expenditure to be made, the funerals of our sample ranging in cost from £3 to £728. Generally speaking, the richer the deceased the more extravagant and lavish was the funeral, as can be seen in Table 11.1 overleaf, though there were many exceptions. The puritans had campaigned against the expense and secular pomp of funerals, and such attitudes are sometimes reflected in instructions given in wills. James Blatt, for instance, willed that he be 'decently buried but as frugally as may be'. The noncomformist threadman William Ambler, who was buried in Bunhill Fields, was more specific both as to cost and motive: 'My will is that not exceeding twelve persons be invited to my buriall because the most of what I have is in other men's handes and therefore I would not have the whole charge of my funerall exceeding tenn pounds', and that was exactly what was spent. However, modesty and frugality clearly meant different things to different people. Philip Scarth, a druggist, willed that his funeral be 'as private as conveniently may be'; the surgeon Richard Blundell wanted 'decently to be buryed without pomp and with as little charge as is consistent with that decency'; their funerals cost £200 and £176 respectively.[17]

Really lavish funerals to which hundreds of people had been invited normally started in the hall of the deceased man's livery

TABLE 11.1: Distribution of Funeral Expenses

| Cost of Funeral | Fortune at Death | | | | |
	Under £1000 %	£1000– 1999 %	£2000– 4999 %	£5000– 9999 %	£10,000 & over %
Under £50	66	26	14	4	5
£50–£99	27	53	51	17	0
£100–£199	7	15	31	55	18
£200 and over	0	6	4	24	77
	100	100	100	100	100
Average cost	£43.3	£84.3	£98.2	£152.6	£299.3
Number of cases	71	34	51	29	22

Source: Based on 207 inventories of the sample which contain this information. The cost of five funerals, all of merchants, exceeded £400.

company, from which a huge procession, sometimes with scores of coaches, would proceed to the church. Alderman James Birkin, for instance, a former master of the Clothworkers' Company, willed that his corpse be carried from the company hall to the church of St Dunstan's in the East, where he was to be buried in the chancel under the tombstone where his wife already lay. The master, wardens and assistants of the company were to be invited and 'also a considerable number of the Artillery Company of which I am a member', the poor children of Christ's Hospital and 'so many poor old men as I shall be years old . . . I being about the middle of April last at the age of fiftie and three years'.[18]

Such funerals cost £400 or £500 or more. A typical middling funeral was more modest but still expensive, as can be seen from the table. Most would begin and end at home. After the corpse had been laid out and dressed in its burial clothes, it was normally left on view in an open coffin for several days 'to give the dead man an opportunity of coming to life again if his soul had not quite left his body' and to allow time for the executors to make arrangements. Invitations were sent out, often on printed tickets, black cloth, gloves, hatbands and rings were purchased for the mourners, refreshments bought, the church and preacher booked and the grave bespoke. On the day, the mourners came to the house and 'sat down in the room where the coffin was, looking as grave and as sad as we could'. Such gravity did not prevent the consumption of a glass or two of wine before the coffin was nailed up and the company marshalled for the procession, each with a sprig of rosemary to throw into the grave.[19]

The procession through the streets to the church was a man's last opportunity to impress his neighbours and even modest funerals would have coaches for the chief mourners and scores of people on foot following the hearse. These arrangements did not cost very much compared with the total expenditure on the funeral. There is, for instance, an undertaker's bill for the 1731 funeral of John Hatfield, a Westminster tobacconist. The total cost was £47, about average for the poorer members of the middle station. Just under £18 was spent on a very handsome gilt-handled elm coffin, upholstered in silk, and on fine linen funeral clothes, the latter costing an additional £2 10s. for an exemption from the law requiring people to be buried in woollen cloth. Another £16 went on gloves, cloaks, hatbands and rings for the mourners and nearly £8 on expenses at the church and the gravedigger's fees. Compared with this, the pomp in the street to ensure a good exit in the eyes of the world was cheap. 'A neat hears and paire of horsis' was only 10s., three coaches and pairs 7s.6d. each and then there were fairly small expenses for cloaks, gloves and scarves for coachmen, porters and the parish bearers.[20]

More coaches or coaches with four or six horses cost more money, but the real expense of funerals was laid out on cloth for mourning, broadcloth for men and silk for ladies, and on such customary presents as rings. Dudley Ryder bought 5¼ yards of black cloth at 18s. per yard for his grandmother's funeral in 1716 and many people provided mourning cloth for twenty or thirty people, the price per yard often being specified in the will to suit the dignity of the recipient. Rings might add up to even more. The merchant John Barkstead willed that 'every of my kindred and relations and those also of my wife who shall be invited to my funeral' should be given a ring worth £1. Most people gave rings to friends and neighbours as well and this could soon mount up. William Paggen's executors, for instance, paid the banker Thomas Williams for 143 gold rings.

They also paid £11 15s. to a herald for painting escutcheons – armorial shields which were hung over the windows and later fixed on the hearse – and these claims to gentility seem to have been quite commonly used in the middle station, sufficiently so for some people to make a point of saying in their wills that they did not want them, such as the skinner William Sawyer, who wanted 'noe heraldry att my funeral'.[21]

After the burial, the procession made its way back to the deceased man's house and here there would be a second 'drinking'. These usually seem to have been fairly modest affairs. The 120 guests at the funeral of Pepys's brother Tom, a tailor, were served with 'six biscuits a-piece and what they pleased of burnt [i.e. mulled] claret'. Some people provided even less. Samuel Chambers, another tailor, willed that his widow 'shall give only a glasse of wine', while William Mackley wanted 'only gloves and rosemary but not a drop of wine' to be given at his funeral, a dry farewell for a man who had been a brewer.[22]

The drinking was often the occasion for the reading of the will to assembled relatives and friends, and so can fittingly lead into a discussion of the ways in which the fortunes of middling people were distributed after their deaths. In the majority of cases, this was governed by the Custom of London, which provided detailed rules for the division of the personal estates of freemen and could override the provisions of a will. The first charges on the estate after it had been inventoried and valued were the deceased man's debts and the cost of his funeral. Then a deduction was made for the 'widow's chamber', which usually worked out at some £20 to £30 and represented the value of her clothing, jewellery and the furniture of her bed-chamber. What remained, if anything, was then available for division.[23]

The rules for this were simple enough. One-third of the net estate went to the widow; one-third was divided equally between the children and one-third, 'the dead man's share', could be bequeathed by will. If the man died intestate, as 40 per cent of our sample did, then this residual share was divided half to the widow and half equally between the children.[24] A complicated formula, known as 'hotchpotch', was used to calculate a fair division between the children when one or more of them had been 'advanced' by the payment of a portion or dowry during their father's lifetime.[25]

This equitable system, fair to widow and children alike, also governed the wishes of the majority of those who died testate, being either reflected in the distribution of the 'dead man's share' or of the whole personal estate in those cases where the will did not follow the Custom of London. Widows had sometimes been provided for by jointure or other prior contract but, where this was not the case, over 40 per cent received half or more of the dead man's share and another 20 per cent received a third.[26] The children, too, were normally treated as equally by will as they were by custom. If one ignores only children and the small number of testators who left nothing from their dead man's share to the children (mostly those with very young children who left it all to the widow), then two-thirds of the remainder divided the estate equally amongst all the children. In the distribution of real estate, on the other hand, one can see a tendency to discriminate both by age and sex. Where there were both sons and daughters, in three-quarters of the cases the daughters got nothing and in nearly 40 per cent of cases all the real estate eventually went to the eldest son, often as a reversion from the widow. Middling people therefore believed in partible inheritance for their personal estate but had a strong tendency towards the gentry preference for primogeniture in the disposition of their real estate.[27]

Wills also provide an opportunity for insights into the ways in which testators viewed their friends and relations. One can start by looking at who was appointed as executor, as is set out in Table 11.2 overleaf. Here it can be seen that, even if wives did not play a very important role in their husbands' businesses, they were sufficiently trusted to be appointed as executrix in the majority of cases, less then a quarter of testators who left a widow not naming her at all. However, nearly three-quarters who named their widows did so as either one of two or more joint-executors or provided for overseers to assist her, suggesting that most middling people did not believe their wives capable of handling the business on their own.[28]

The table also shows the importance of brothers, brothers-in-law and 'friends' in the lives of the middle station and these relationships are well reflected in Table 11.3 (p. 317) which

TABLE 11.2: Executors of Wills

Relationship to Testator	Sole Executor	Joint Executors	Overseers
Widow	96	31	2
Brother	12	15(18)	21(33)
Son	8	13(15)	2
Friend	3	22(31)	58(96)
Brother-in-law	2	8	22(28)
Cousin/kinsman	2	7	5
Father	1	1	0
Daughter	0	5	0
Son-in-law	0	3	5
Uncle	0	2	7
Father-in-law	0	1	11
Aunt	0	0	2
Sister	0	0	1

Source: Based on 181 wills of members of the sample, 124 (68.5%) of which named a sole executor, 49 (27.1%) named two joint-executors and 8 (4.4%) named three. Ninety testators (49.7%) appointed overseers, of which 21 appointed one, 51 appointed two, 11 appointed three, 3 appointed four and 2 each appointed five and seven. The numbers in parentheses indicate the total number of that relationship, i.e. there was often more than one son, brother, friend etc. named as executor or overseer.

analyses the recipients of legacies, most of which appear as deductions from the dead man's third of the estate before the main division between widow and children.[29] This analysis throws some interesting light on middling society and makes clear the effects of the high mortality of the period. The very small percentage of wills which mention parents, parents-in-law, uncles, aunts or grandchildren clearly reflects the fact that such relations were rarely alive at the time of the death of adults. The middle-class world was thus largely a two-generation one, consisting of young and middle-aged adults and their children. Such conditions highlighted the importance of other young and middle-aged adults on whom one had some claim, such as brothers and sisters, cousins, brothers-in-law and, perhaps most important of all, 'friends'. Such people were remembered with gratitude and affection in wills, though they rarely received so valuable a legacy as those bequeathed to those felt to be more in need, such as nephews, grandchildren and close female relations.

One surprise in this analysis of wills was the relatively small

TABLE 11.3: Recipients of Legacies in Wills

Type of Legatee	Percentage of Wills	Type of Legatee	Percentage of Wills
No legacies	33.1	Sister-in-law	7.2
Charity	30.4	Aunt	6.6
Friend	26.5	Minister	5.0
Cousin/kinsman	23.8	Grandchild	4.4
Sister	23.2	Uncle	4.4
Nephew	18.8	Mother-in-law	3.9
Brother	18.2	Godson	3.3
Niece	17.7	Father-in-law	2.8
Maidservant	14.9	Father	1.7
Brother-in-law	13.8	Stepchild	1.7
Manservant	13.3	Son-in-law	1.1
Mother	8.3	Daughter-in-law	0.6

Source: Based on 181 wills. The figures relate to the percentage of wills with one or more of the above types of legatee. Many wills mention more than one, e.g. the average number of friends in those wills which mention them was 2.5 and of cousins or kinsman 2.3.

TABLE 11.4: Valuation of Legacies

Type of Legatee	Median Value	Percentage in Valuation Groups			No. of Cases
		£10 & less	£11–99	£100 & over	
Grandchild	£50	17	44	39	18
Sister	30	41	24	35	54
Nephew	28	39	30	31	70
Niece	20	45	32	23	62
Mother	20	33	47	20	15
Charity	11	49	31	20	55
Brother-in-law	11	48	42	10	33
Brother	10	56	33	11	45
Sister-in-law	10	75	19	6	16
Cousin/kinsman	10	73	19	8	101
Friend	10	65	30	5	120
Aunt	8	86	14	0	14
Minister	7	92	8	0	12
Manservant	5	74	26	0	43
Maidservant	5	95	5	0	41

Source: As Tables 11.2 and 11.3. Only groups with over 10 legatees have been included.

amount left by this class to charity, since historians have been led to believe from the work of W. K. Jordan that middling Londoners were very charitable indeed.[30] In fact, less than a third of testators made any charitable bequests at all and the majority of these were fairly trivial relative to the value of their estates, as can be seen from Table 11.4 (p. 317). Nearly half the charitable left £10 or less, the £5 left by James Blatt to the poor of his London parish and £5 to the poor of Sudbury in Suffolk, where he did much of his business, being typical bequests.[31] On the other hand, twenty people left over £100 and a handful of these left very large sums indeed.

Alderman Sir Jonathan Dawes left £500 'towards the relief of the poor children in Christ's Hospital' and £1000 to set up a trust to provide £50 per annum 'to be distributed amongst the poor people of Wootton-under-Edge, Gloucestershire, where he was borne', large sums but still worth less than 4 per cent of his personal estate. Such a contribution pales beside the bequests of the former sugar refiner and alderman John Hobby, who died in 1675 aged sixty-three. He left £3000 to set up a charitable trust to provide £40 per annum towards apprenticing four 'blew coat boys', £20 per annum towards setting them up when they had finished their time, £60 per annum to provide clothing for 'thirty poor ancient persons' and £50 per annum 'to be used for the discharge of 25 poor prisoners for debt'. He also left £500 'to be distributed amongst such of my poorest and nearest kindred to be chosen by my executors' and willed that the residue of his estate 'be paid by my executors to such pious and charitable acts as to them shall seem most meete and just'. In a codicil made shortly before his death, he thought of a mass of other people whom he could help, 'to the blind woman in Coleman Street – £3', 'to the filecutter's wife with five children – 40s.' and so on.[32]

However, as has been seen, Alderman Hobby was very much an exception. The wills of our sample do not reflect the charity discovered by Jordan for the period before 1660. Several reasons can be suggested for this. Our sample by definition were men who died with children under the age of twenty-one and it seems certain that it was the childless or those who had already advanced all their children who would be most likely to be charitable on a really large scale, a hypothesis supported by the fact that several men willed that legacies should go to charity at the discretion of executors if all their children died before they were of age. Our period is also one when the nature of charity was changing. Now that the poor law was well established and was operating fairly efficiently in London, there must have seemed less need for testamentary charity towards the poor. Meanwhile, charity for educational purposes, which had been an important feature of the period before the Civil War, took on a new form with the establishment of charity schools which were largely financed by subscription *inter vivos* rather than by charitable bequest. These were often said to have been supported mainly by middling people and many of our apparently non-caring sample may well have given considerable sums in this way during their lifetimes. Nevertheless, one does have to consider one last possibility, that the London middle class of our period was simply less charitable than their ancestors, a view certainly held by many.[33]

Wills are sometimes seen as windows on the soul of the past, providing an insight into the nature and strength of the religious belief of the testator, but this is in fact rarely the case. Some wills certainly do contain a statement of faith, sometimes at great length, as in that of the Huguenot merchant John Dubois. Most wills, however, merely reflect the scrivener's formula book, with a short stylized spiritual introduction before getting down to business, 'and as to my worldly goods', while a surprisingly large number are totally secular in character. Wills sometimes give other hints as to piety or belief, such as bequests to a minister, specification of the text for the funeral sermon, bequests of bibles and other religious works, sometimes with manuscript annotations made by the deceased, and quite often admonitions to widows and particularly to children as to how to live in future, such as that of William Mackley who prayed 'his deare children to observe and follow the directions given them in a paper some time ago'. Such last wishes can be a guide to attitudes but, since the great majority of wills do not contain such material, a serious analysis would have to conclude that on the evidence of this source most middling people were neither pious nor particularly interested in religion, which is almost certainly not true.[34]

One would have to come to a similar conclusion with regard to much other interesting information that one finds in wills, since one of the penalties of the quantitative bias of recent scholarship has been to force historians to appreciate that they cannot generalize about a class on the basis of two or three literary references, however striking they may be. The dying wish of the jeweller Nathaniel Ragdale 'that no Jew or Papist shall inheritt or enjoy any part of my estate whatsoever' is not sufficient evidence to state that middling Londoners were an extremely prejudiced and intolerant lot, though there is in fact much other evidence which could be adduced to support such a statement. Similarly, the fact that William Waldron left all his Hebrew, Greek and Latin books to his son William does not allow one to make general statements about the education and scholarship of cheesemongers, let alone of middling people as a whole. Neither does his desire to be buried 'soe neare my late deceased wife as conveniently can be' mean that he had preferred his first wife Mary to his current wife Judith, though it might do, and one can find plenty of other evidence in wills hinting at the stresses caused by the early deaths of spouses and subsequent remarriages of middling men and women.[35]

Wills are certainly interesting and useful sources in this respect, reflecting as they often do the multiple dangers, problems and anxieties of the lives of the middle station and their fears of what might happen to their loved ones in a world in which they were no longer present. The physical danger of the otherwise comfortable life of the merchant can be seen in the will of Samuel Tomlins, who left £100 towards the redemption from the corsairs of Algiers of his brother-in-law John Coleborn, 'a slave beyond sea'. Its commercial dangers are reflected in the will of the goldsmith-banker Thomas Williams, whose trade obliged him 'to great dealings with merchants and others, men of trade and adventure, some of which have or may meet with losses and misfortunes' and who instructed his executor and overseers 'to make such reasonable composition with such debtors as to them shall seem meet'. The collection of post-mortem debts was never an easy task and several testators made arrangements to assist the widow in this respect, such as Richard Darnelly, who appointed Mr Reynolds, a merchant, as debt-collector at £10 a quarter, 'hee being a fitt man to that purpose', or Edward Treherne, looking-glass manufacturer to the Queen and two of the King's mistresses, who provided £10 for getting in debts incurred by Nell Gwynne.[36]

Wills also provided an opportunity for reward and punishment. Only about one in six or seven testators left legacies to servants, a reflection no doubt of the high turnover, which was discussed in an earlier chapter. However, long service was noted and sometimes generously rewarded. The apothecary Peter Cully left his 'truly honest and faithful servant' Thomas Aungier 'my case of instruments that I use to carry in my pocket and also my other case of instruments in the drawer in the shoppe', together with all his medical and pharmaceutical books and manuscripts, his wearing apparel, a legacy of £10 and £5 to buy mourning. The merchant John Brookes left £30 to his nursemaid Frances Fairfield 'as an acknowledgement of her care and love to my children'. However, it has to be admitted that such generosity was very unusual. The majority of testators, as has been seen, left their servants nothing, while some of those who did remember servants and apprentices used the legacy as a means of ensuring that they would not immediately desert the widow. The builder John Wildgos, for instance, left his apprentice Thomas Thornton £10 on condition that he serve out the remainder of his time with his wife Elizabeth or if he left that it should be with her consent.[37]

Conditions were also sometimes tied to family legacies in an attempt to control the future. Some legacies to widows were to be reduced or made void if they remarried, though this was unusual, and in most cases the testator was mainly interested in protecting his children rather than punishing their mother for doing what was normal in this class. Widows who remarried might be required to give good security for the payment of legacies to the children or to deposit those legacies in the hands of overseers or trustees.[38] Attempts were also made to control the children through threats or promises in a will. In three cases, as has been mentioned earlier, this went as far as disinheriting the eldest son, a very sad breakdown in family relations, as can be seen from the words of Richard Darnelly whose son Daniel 'doth still continue his exorbitant and evil courses and wicked company . . . with griefe of heart I speake it and I beseech the Lord to forgive him'.

Most fathers did not go so far but several had serious doubts about their sons. George Carew had his portion docked by £200 because of his 'extravagant expenses' while up at Wadham

College, Oxford. George Phinnes was left some property but only 'on condition . . . he doe peaceably and quietly permitt and suffer his sister my daughter Sarah to have and enjoy her legacies', a question here of sibling rivalry between the children of two different mothers. Joseph How was only to inherit his father's distillery in White Cross Street at the age of twenty-three 'if he behaves himself', while Edward Osborne's ten-year-old son was made joint residual legatee with his mother but only 'if he be dutyfull and obedient to his mother and doe take virtuous and good courses. But if he shall happen to be disobedient to his said mother and grow idle and extravagant then I will and devise his parte . . . unto my said wife.'[39]

Once again, such comments and conditions in wills are unusual. They catch the eye, but they are not typical and it would be wrong to draw the conclusion that the men of the middle station were engaged in some generation-gap struggle with their children or that they disapproved of their wives remarrying. The fact is that most wills reflect a world of harmony in which everybody is 'deare and loving' and there seem to be no doubts in the testator's mind about the rationality, good sense and equity of the various members of his family. Some wills are so full of names and descriptions that one can get a real picture of the people who made up this harmonious middling world. The widowed apothecary, Peter Cully, for instance, mentioned over 150 people in his will, ranging out from his two 'deare' sons John and Abraham to his brothers and sisters and other relations in London and his native Berkshire, to the ministers, lecturers, clerks and sextons of the churches he attended, to thirty-three 'very loveing friends and neighbours', all named, to the eleven other 'loveing brethren' in an apothecaries' club, to herbarists and medical colleagues, to the masters of the physic gardens in Westminster and Oxford. He was quick to note the social eminence of some of his relatives, 'my much esteemed cousin the Lady Cullen', but he did not forget or despise the humble, the poor of Wantage where he was born or of St Andrew Undershaft where he plied his trade, 'my man Theophilus Davis', 'my man George Ward', his maids, his butcher, 'the porters that ply at my dore', 'Jane the herbwoman', 'my new cookmaid', 'old Henry Knox', 'Gammer Bess, Gammer Alice and Nurse Blake'.[40]

Cully's world was the world which this book has tried to describe, the world of middle-class Londoners. The method of analysis and description employed has allowed some fairly concrete statements to be made about their social and economic behaviour and to give some idea of their material existence. However, there are large areas of human behaviour where the sources available do not enable one to speak with confidence, such as was found in the discussion of relations between the sexes or between parents and children. Religion is another problem area. One could make a pretty good *prima facie* case that this class was very religious and that this would have been likely to affect their attitude to everything else, including the making of money. However, this would be virtually impossible to prove conclusively. It is easy enough to find evidence that this person or that was pious or religious, whatever such adjectives may mean, but how does one establish the intensity of religious belief of a whole class? On the other hand, there is no doubt that middle-class people were materialistic and acquisitive and that, for the most part, they behaved with the economic rationality which theorists assume, rather optimistically, to be typical of the human race. However, let us be charitable and assume that their outward piety and respectability reflected an inner faith and that they lived, as the merchant Mun Browne hoped that his family would live after his death, 'in love, peace and charity and in the feare of the Lord, Amen'.[41]

Conclusion

12 The London Middle Class

Now that the middle class has been buried and its worldy goods redistributed, an attempt can be made at some conclusions in this last chapter. A start can be made by reconsidering the social structure which was discussed in Chapter 1, where it was suggested that a tripartite division provided a useful working model of the structure of society. This division can still be seen after our survey of metropolitan society and economy. There is an upper class, 'an upper part of mankind', who have often been described in a sort of shorthand as 'West End society' or 'the aristocracy and gentry of the West End'. There is a middle class or 'middle station', commercial and industrial capitalists and professional men who work hard to make profits and improve themselves. And there is a working class, a 'mechanick part of mankind', who have been found becoming more proletarian as they became increasingly divorced from the possibilities of upwards social mobility and improvement.

However, the problem of defining the dividing points in this social stratification is no less intractable than it was in Chapter 1. Who really belongs to this upper class, a group who were defined as living 'on estates and without the mechanism of employment'? Such a definition will stretch to cover an awful lot of people, from the King living on the income from his dwindling estates and on the 'estate' provided by a reluctant and watchful parliament through great aristocrats and wealthy gentlemen to retired shopkeepers and fairly impoverished widows. Can all these people be subsumed under one head? Contemporaries of course did divide the upper class into aristocracy and gentry, a distinction which is useful if one takes the extremely loose definition of gentleman current in the early eighteenth century. However, some people living off 'estates' hardly fit even the loosest definition of gentry and one wonders if some additional label is needed, such as that very vague 'upper middle class' which the Victorians found so useful and which has survived as a way of distinguishing one sort of middle-class person from another down to our own times.

In 1794, Archenholtz noted the difference between the gentry or 'the great' and the mere 'rich', a 'difference which holds even in the hours of eating and drinking, in the kind of amusements, the dress and manner of speaking etc.', and he went on to say that the two groups held each other in mutual contempt.[1] Such a difference was probably even greater in our period and one could well label the mere rich as upper middle class, a group rather less eminent then the 'aristocracy and gentry of the West End' but fairly easily distinguished from those below them by their wealth and genteelness if not their gentility. The *Oxford English Dictionary* defines 'genteel' as 'gentlemanly or ladylike in appearance', the suffixes making a rather nice distinction between such people and true gentlemen or ladies. Into this group one could put many Londoners who fit uneasily into the middle station or middle class proper, such as the more eminent professional men and their ladies and many of the wealthier commercial men such as the richer merchants and bankers, the latter group being described by some modern writers as the 'mercantile bourgeoisie' just to confuse the issue.[2]

The expression 'lower middle class' has occasionally crept into the text of previous chapters, reflecting a need to make yet another division within the middle station. Lower middle is as anachronistic as upper middle, but it does help to describe a group who were growing in numbers and importance. These were the reasonably well educated and usually salaried people with posts in the government bureaucracy, such as customs officers and clerks, or in commerce, such as book-keepers. Once one sees these people with their low incomes but genteel pretensions as different from the middle class proper, one can soon find many others who conform to the same general type, such as schoolmasters, lesser clergy, much of the lower strata of the legal profession and, because of their income but not their education, such lowly members of the commercial middle station as small shopkeepers. All these people took a middle-class view of the world in terms of their genteelness and their desire to be thought different from the common herd, but their incomes tended to condemn them to a lesser and often fairly desperate existence. In our period, the numbers of this proto-type lower middle class were still fairly small but such people were destined to become the largest group in the middle classes as bureaucracy grew and as the expansion in the unit size of business demanded ever more 'white collar' workers.

Lower-middle-class incomes were often lower then those of many 'mechanicks' and this fact serves to emphasize the problem of treating the 'mechanick part of mankind' as a unitary group. By our period, this was becoming increasingly difficult to do as the distinction between the independent artisan with his own workshop and tools and the paid employee who hired his tools or worked in a master's shop became more apparent. There had always been journeymen and masters, of course, but what is seen in our period is the creation of a much larger class of permanent journeymen with no hope of ever acquiring their own workshop and becoming master in their turn. The numbers of semi-skilled and unskilled were also growing as the division of labour broke down former skilled jobs into their component parts and as the development of the workshop as a proto-factory created jobs for people who can only be described as labourers.

How do all these people fit into the social structure? The independent artisan who owned a workshop had most of the attributes of the middle class even if he did work with his hands. He used his own capital, hoped to make profits and had a fair chance of improving himself and his family and accumulating over his life-cycle. He might be rough and hardly genteel, but he was clearly in a totally different economic situation from the great majority of mechanicks. Such people have generally been regarded here as lowly members of the middle station, even if they did not share all the social and cultural attributes of this group. Moving down the scale, it is also clear that some distinction must be made between the skilled and the unskilled, even if both are employees rather then independent men. Most skilled men earned at least 15s. a week by the early eighteenth century; many earned a £1 or more. Even in the uncertain employment market of London, where workmen might consider themselves lucky to work for two-thirds of the year, such wages were substantial and could produce a yearly income from £25 to £40 or more, very much the same as that earned by many of the salaried people in the lower middle class.[3]

Such incomes placed artisans in a completely different world from that of the unskilled or labourers, who would be lucky to earn 10s. a week. Most would earn less and very much less if they were women. Wages at this level would produce an annual income of less that £20, quite often as low as £10 or £12, an income which could afford none of the creature comforts available to the artisan. In 1709, Defoe divided the population into seven groups, of whom two were 'the working trades who labour hard but feel no want' and 'the poor that fare hard', a good description of the difference between an artisan on £1 a week and a man who was unskilled or whose skill had become devalued by economic change and was earning only 10s. Double the income at this level meant not just a relative difference in comfort but a completely different life-style and it is doubtful if social analysis is helped by putting both men in the same class, even though they both depended on their hands for a living.[4]

'The poor that fare hard' were not the lowest group in Defoe's analysis, for beneath them were 'the miserable that really pinch and suffer want'. There were many tens of thousands of such miserable people in London, who would have thought they were in clover if they could have earned 10s. a week for half the year. Such were the casual workers, hoping for a day's work from one of the official porters, from a builder or from the rakers who cleaned the streets, running messages, cleaning shoes, washing clothes, pushing wheelbarrows, hawking food, carrying pots from taverns, doing what they could to scrape together a living. Many were elderly or sick; many were women or children; many were simply under-employed in modern terms, idle, lazy or shiftless in contemporary usage. Such were the real poor, the paupers, men and women who occasionally lived well for a day or two as a result of a windfall piece of work, who occasionally sought outdoor relief from the parish and, in between these extremes, lived a wretched scraping life which was a mockery of that enjoyed by most Londoners.

At the start, a division of society into just three groups or classes was made, and this still remains a useful division. But once this division was probed into, problems arose which were easiest to solve by expanding the number of strata in society. At the moment, these run to eight or possibly nine, starting with the aristocracy and gentry and moving down through the upper middle class, middle class proper, lower middle class, independent artisans, wage-earning artisans, 'the poor that fare hard' and 'the miserable'. Does this help one to understand the society any better? All these groups would be recognizable to contemporaries even though some of the labels are anachronistic. In practice, it is extremely difficult to distinguish from documents just who belonged to each group, though this would have been more obvious to contemporaries, who would have been able to note the speech, bearing, dress and social behaviour of their neighbours as well as having a much better idea then we have of their incomes. Even so, each group would have merged into each other and the divisions which have been drawn would have vanished in reality. Society was a continuously ascending hierarchy of people or families, each one a little better off or a little more genteel than the one below it, not a set of discrete, self-contained groups. 'Every Englishman', wrote a Swiss who knew the English well, 'constantly holds a pair of scales wherein he exactly weighs the birth, the rank and especially the fortune of those he is in company with, in order to regulate his behaviour accordingly.'[5]

It was possible for the individual to move up or down this hierarchy and many did so. Hard-working artisans saved money and became members of the middle station or, more likely, saved enough to apprentice their children to a more genteel trade. Shopkeepers worked hard so that their children might be educated and become gentlemen or at least become professionals and so ease their way into the upper middle class. Gentlemen wasted their estate and tradesmen went bankrupt and descended to the gutter. There were few barriers to such downwards mobility and a slide once started could become uncontrollable. For those moving up, however, there were barriers, some of which were virtually unclimbable. The greatest barrier and one that was getting higher was that between the poor and the middle station. With no money and no education, there were few ways over this barrier even for the artisan, for, as has been seen, the entry costs for middling occupations were rising and they were difficult to save even from a prosperous artisan income of £40 a year. Only patronage or a lucky legacy was likely to solve this problem. The other main barrier in society could be climbed, but it might take two generations to clamber over it. This was the barrier between the middle station and the gentleman. The self-made man of business 'may not always meet with respect equal to his large and acquired fortune; yet if he gives his son a liberal and accomplished education, the birth and calling of the father are sunk in the son; and the son is reputed, if his carriage is suitable, a gentleman in all companies'.[6] Josiah Tucker's comment suggests that there well may be something in the original tripartite social structure given here. Borderlines might be blurred but there really was an upper and a lower as well as a middling part of mankind.

In this book, this middling part of mankind has tended to be treated as if it were fairly homogeneous. This has been done for convenience as much as out of conviction, since it is obviously easier to generalize if one does not have to qualify every time one makes a point. Nevertheless, in some very general senses, the middle class can be treated as homogeneous. They were defined in the first place as people of capital who were interested in profit, accumulation and improvement, and there seems little need to make any qualifications about that. It has also been seen that, rich or relatively poor, they shared many common experiences: the period of training as an apprentice, the common problems of running a business, the common problems of when to marry and who to marry. Even in matters of consumption, there are striking similarities in patterns of demand between those who had accumulated a few hundred pounds and those who were worth ten times as much.

However, it would be wrong to leave the impression that a great merchant was essentially the same sort of person as the owner of a small haberdasher's shop. It has been seen that rich merchants, with their political and financial significance as well as their wealth, really belonged to what might be called the upper middle class. But one also needs to distinguish between people at lower levels in the hierarchy, between those who were worth several thousands and those who were only worth several hundreds. Wealth brought prestige and power or the possibility of power in our period, just as it has in most other periods, even if the power was only that of a common councillor and the prestige was recognized by a seat at the front of Allhallows, Bread Street. Nor was wealth the only criterion distinguishing one middle-class person from another. Age was still a source of respect, rather than a social problem, and birth was still important, even in this class. A mercer whose father was a gentleman would have the social edge over a rather richer mercer of more lowly birth.

Birth and money were probably the most important distinguishing features within the middle class, but occupation was certainly another factor defining the degree of one's genteelness, as is often noted in Campbell's *London Tradesman*.[7] Merchants were more respected then wholesalers, who, in turn, were better than retailers and manufacturers. And, within these broad groups, there were many other distinctions which could override an individual's actual wealth in determining his social position. There seems little doubt that it was smarter to be a Levant merchant than a Baltic merchant, to keep a mercer's shop rather than to be a haberdasher, to own a tavern rather than an alehouse. Such subtle differences in degree of genteelness affected behaviour and choice of friends and marriage partners; they also affected consumption, as was seen in Chapter 10 where it was possible to define a long list of ungenteel tradesmen who, despite their wealth, found it unnecessary to lay out money on a fashionable display in their homes.[8]

Finally, some comment needs to be made on the title of this book, *The Making of the English Middle Class*. It is a historical joke that the middle class is always rising, a point made many years ago in a scathing attack on his fellow historians by the American J. H. Hexter.[9] Since I have read his article, I have been able to avoid some of the pitfalls which he ridiculed. There is no suggestion here that either the king or the aristocracy were middle class; nor do I arrive at 'the *ne plus ultra*, a conception of the middle class that includes the whole human race from time immemorial'. Indeed, my middle class is very much the middle class defined by Professor Hexter, though he might not approve of the inclusion of small shopkeepers and manufacturers in the group. He might also not approve of the implication in this book that the middle class had finally arrived, since he seems to think that the key dates in such an arrival were the French Revolution and the 1832 Reform Act.[10]

However, I am not interested here in political power, nor indeed in that struggle between classes which dominates much discussion on the subject. The intention in this book has really only been to claim that the period 1660–1730 saw fundamental changes in the lives of the middle class and of the way in which such people were perceived both by themselves and by the rest of society, changes which have never been reversed and lead inexorably to the even more middle-class middle class of the nineteenth century and today. Nor do I claim that the middle class only appeared in the late seventeenth century, despite the desire of any historian to have anything that is important happen in his period.

In this respect, it was salutory to re-read Sylvia Thrupp's excellent book, *The Merchant Class of Medieval London*.[11] This covers very much the same ground as is covered here, her 'merchants' being rather wider in definition than mine and including wholesalers and the wealthier retailers. And, of course, one finds that such people did very much the same sort of thing in late medieval London as they did in Augustan London. They bought and sold, made profits and accumulated, but they also had a 'love of ease and comfort and good living' and acquired 'all the modern conveniences of their age', many of these being the same conveniences as my middling people acquired. In the late fourteenth century, as in the late seventeenth century, fashion was tending to obscure class distinctions, so much so that in 1390 Bishop Brunton was distressed that he could not tell the difference between a countess and the wife of a citizen. In the 1720s, Defoe was also worried about fashion and class, and was distressed that he could not tell the difference between a housemaid and a fine lady, much to the amusement of his contemporaries.[12]

Plus ça change? Well, I certainly would not deny that Sylvia Thrupp was writing about a group who were recognizably middle class in the sense adopted in this book. Nevertheless, there are important qualitative and quantitative differences which have to be stressed. Her merchants are certainly interested in making money, but the world in which they made it was a very different place from the London of Queen Anne. One is struck particularly by the choking blanket of corporatism and fraternalism, of guilds and companies, of petty regulations and petty authority, which smothered the business lives of these late medieval merchants. Nowadays, one is told that English-men have been individualists since they crawled out of the Saxon forests in the mists of time, but to my mind there is little doubt that the Londoners of 1700 were much more individual-istic than their ancestors of 1500.[13] They were much more secular too, no longer bound by the endless round of civic ceremony and religious pageant which circumscribed the lives of the medieval merchants, and indeed their deaths. As Thrupp noted, 'the custom of setting aside at least one third of a man's movables . . . as a kind of voluntary death duty for pious and charitable purposes considerably hindered the accumulation of capital'.[14] No such problem in our age, where such charity as still existed was designed to create an obedient and subservient working class rather than to ensure the immortality of the collective middle-class soul.

One should note too that Thrupp was writing about a very small city, less than a tenth of the size of the London of 1700. In the long run, it is likely to be sheer numbers that change attitudes and the numbers of the middle class were becoming quite large by our period. It was guessed earlier that about a quarter of the population of London belonged to the middle class and it seems a reasonable guess that there were a similar proportion of middling people in other English towns. Professor Wrigley has recently told us that the proportion of the English population living in towns with over 5000 people rose from 8¼ to 21 per cent between 1600 and 1750, and it must be assumed that the urban middle class rose at least as fast, probably faster, since, as has been seen, the second part of this period saw an acceleration of growth in manufacturing, inland trade and professional services.[15] Such figures suggest that at least 5 per cent of England's population belonged to the urban middle class by 1700, a figure which would have at least to be doubled to allow for people of similar life-style and social attitudes who lived in the countryside – the better off farmers, inland traders and food processors, such as millers and maltsters, and manu-facturers, such as clothiers and ironmasters. All these members of the provincial middle class took their lead from the Londoners who have been described in this book.

So the actual numbers of the middle class were beginning to be quite important in our period and it seems hardly surprising that this should affect attitudes. Nevertheless, it is not the impact of numbers which I have principally stressed in this book. What seems really important about the period is the qualitative rather than the quantitative changes in the lives of middle-class Londoners.

I do not want to try to define what exactly is the essence of a middle-class existence. However, it is almost impossible not to notice the vast number of vaguely middle-class things which either originated in our period or, if they originated earlier, became common in the late seventeenth and early eighteenth centuries, such as clocks, laudanum, fire insurance, street-lighting, novels, newspapers, tea-drinking and the three-piece suit. Or, how about eating too much sugar, statistics, economics, hobbies, clubs, the national debt, undertakers, accountants, workhouses and the Society for the Propagation of Christian Knowledge? One sees the same sorts of development in the mental attitudes of the age as the world became more middle-class – the craze for reason and the study of mathematics, indeed the earnest pursuit of almost any form of knowledge, sentiment in literature and the theatre and a sensibility that sees the beginnings of 'Victorian' attitudes to the 'home' and to the place of middle-class women within it, the beginnings too of that middle-class compassion for animals which was to restrict the brutal tastes of the poor for what were now increasingly seen as cruel sports. 'By the eighteenth century', writes Keith Thomas, 'this outlook had become the orthodoxy of the educated middle classes and all those who, like Steele and Addison, upheld an ideal of cultivated refinement.'[16]

One should remember too that most of these cultivated and refined middle-class people were also capitalists. It was once a common historical belief that the middle class as we know them were created by something called the Industrial Revolution which happened in the late eighteenth and early nineteenth centuries. Historians nowadays are none too sure whether there ever was an Industrial Revolution and are even less sure when it happened if it ever did. This is not the place to enter into that debate but, if the Industrial Revolution was something to do with innovation, machines, factories and the increasing impact of capital on the economic life of the country, then it may well have started in the London that has been studied here. All those labour-saving innovations that were mentioned in Chapter 2, those new industries and workshops, the growing financial sophistication, the increasing separation between the capitalists and a wage-earning working class: this may all seem small beer compared with what was to happen in Lancashire later in the eighteenth century, but it was certainly a beginning. As a contemporary noted in relation to the weavers' riots against the multiple spindle ribbon looms in 1675: 'That by the same reason the single loom weavers complaine of the engin looms, many self interest and envious people will complaine of the engins for water mills, saw mills, and engins for spliting of iron ... and many other injenious, usefull and profitable inventions now in England, but we doubt not but injenuity will find encouragement in England.'[17]

Ingenuity did find encouragement in England, unhindered as elsewhere in Europe by conservative attitudes towards economic or indeed social change. Such encouragement created an environment in which the London middle class could make money with no fear that it would be arbitrarily taken away from them and in which they could use that money to improve themselves. They used their wealth and their new-found social confidence to develop a new type of society which has proved to be a model, not just for the developing middle class of provincial England but for Europeans and Americans and indeed for the whole world.

Notes

Abbreviations

Add.   Additional Manuscript, British Library
AgHR   *Agricultural History Review*
Antiq. Jnl   *Antiquaries' Journal*
BL   British Library
Burl. Mag.   *Burlington Magazine*
CJ   House of Commons, Journals
CLRO   Corporation of London Records Office
CSB   Common Sergeant's Books, CLRO
CSPD   *Calendar of State Papers, Domestic*
CTB   *Calendar of Treasury Books*
ELP   *East London Papers*
EcHR   *Economic History Review*
EngHR   *English Historical Review*
FurnH   *Furniture History*
GHMS   Guildhall Library Manuscript
GLRO   Greater London Record Office
GM   *Guildhall Miscellany*
GSLH   *Guildhall Studies in London History*
HMC   Historical Manuscripts Commission
JBS   *Journal of British Studies*
JEGP   *Journal of English and German Philology*
JEH   *Journal of Economic History*
JFamH   *Journal of Family History*
JHI   *Journal of the History of Ideas*
JHMed   *Journal of the History of Medicine*
JMH   *Journal of Modern History*
Journals   Journals of the Court of Common Council, CLRO
JPE   *Journal of Political Economy*
JTptH   *Journal of Transport History*
LJ   *London Journal*

LRS   London Record Society
L.S.E.   London School of Economics
MCE   Mayor's Court, Equity, CLRO
MCI   Mayor's Court, Interrogatories, CLRO
MedH   *Medical History*
OED   *Oxford English Dictionary*
Orphans   Orphans' Inventories, CLRO
P&P   Past and Present
PMA   Post-Medieval Archeology
PRO   Public Record Office
Review   (see Bibliography p. 432)
S.   Sample, see Appendix A, p. 394
SocH   *Social History*
Sun   Sun Fire Office, Policy Register Numbers, GHMS
             11936
TextH   *Textile History*
TRHS   *Royal Historical Society, Transactions*

The notes normally refer only to the surname of the author, or the first word or words of the titles of anonymous works, and the date of publication. For full details of references, see the Bibliography. For abbreviations see above.

1 The Middle Station

1. E.g. Defoe (1726–7) ii, pt ii, 106; Defoe (1719) p. 6; Misson (1719) pp. 69, 92, 314. For a discussion of the vocabulary of social classification in the eighteenth century, see Corfield (1987). See also Wrightson (1986) for a general discussion of the social order of early modern England.
2. *Review*, 22 January 1709.
3. *Review*, 22 January 1709.
4. Wagner (1972) pp. 130–3, 371–7; Styles (1953).
5. T. Smith (1583) pp. 39–40, quoted in Coleman (1973) p. 97; Miège (1703) p. 264; Bailey (1730) s.v. 'Gentleman'.
6. Grant (1962) pp. 197–9.
7. Grant loc. cit.
8. Everitt (1966) pp. 67–8; cf. Styles (1953) for a similar analysis of the Warwickshire gentry.
9. S. R. Smith (1973) p. 200; cf. Kahl (1956).
10. Stone (1966) pp. 27–8; and see Hughes (1926) pp. 366–8 for the problems faced by the conservative analyst of English society, Edward Chamberlayne.

11. Crouzet (1981) p. 71.

12. Stone (1984) pp. 287–8.

13. Miège (1703) p. 266; Steele, Act IV, Scene 2.

14. Schuyler (1931) p. 264, quoted in Andrew (1981) pp. 367–8.

15. See Campbell (1747) for examples of this grading; Richardson (1741), Letter I.

16. *Discourse* (1678) p. 5; cf. the views of Perkin (1969); Crouzet (1981) p. 68.

17. Defoe (1726–7) i, 138.

18. Watt (1957) p. 41; for literacy, see Cressy (1980); the best way to find out what was being published is to look at the *Term Catalogues* produced by the Stationers' Company. See Arber (1903–6).

19. Hughes (1926) p. 364.

20. Burnet (1969) vi, 215; Fielding (1751) p. 156. For a general discussion of changing literary attitudes to merchants and business in our period, see McVeagh (1981), whose chapter titles indicate the growing acceptance of the 'capitalist': Ch. 2 'Commerce approved, 1650–1700', Ch. 3 'The merchant as hero, 1700–1750'.

21. Crouzet (1981) p. 71.

22. Shadwell, *The Scowrers*, Act II, Scene 1; Defoe (1722) p. 52.

23. *Tatler* No. 25 (7 June 1709); Baxter (1673); Brown (1715) iv, 122.

24. Butler (1896) pp. 296–7.

25. See, for example, 3 W&M c. 6 (1692 Poll Tax) and 6 & 7 W&M c. 6 (1694 'Marriage Duties Tax').

26. The main gap in the coverage is that there are hardly any professional people in the sample, except apothecaries. For more detail on the sample and a list of those included, see Appendix A. The inventories and related documents are in CLRO.

2 The Metropolitan Economy

1. Brett-James (1935) pp. 495–513; Finlay & Shearer (1986).

2. Norwich, the second biggest city, had only some 30,000 inhabitants and Bristol, the third, only 20,000. London's population was over twice that of all the other 30 towns with populations over 5000 put together. Corfield (1982) p. 8, Table I, and see in general pp. 6–16. For a recent survey of provincial towns in our period, see Borsay (1987).

3. E.g. Defoe (1726–7) ii, pt ii, 122. For the uniqueness of London, see Wrigley (1967) and Wrigley (1985), where the rapid growth of London is contrasted to the comparative stagnation of other large European cities in the century after 1650.

4. *Review*, 18 February 1706/7.

5. Beier (1986). Other problems with this study include the problematical definition of production and the complete omission of some non-production occupations, such as domestic service which probably provided work for some 7 to 8 per cent of the entire population and a much higher proportion of the labour force – see pp. 76, 218–19, 357 (note 187).

6. This percentage, which is only meant to be very approximate, is based on a very wide range of modern specialist studies and contemporary literature, references to which appear in the remaining notes to this chapter.

7. On women in the labour force, see Earle (1989).

8. In general on the silk industry, see Warner (1921), Rothstein (1961); for a discussion of many of the subsidiary textile industries, see Wadsworth & Mann (1931).

9. On silk-throwing, see Wadsworth & Mann (1931) pp. 106–7; Rothstein (1961) pp. 131–2; Stern (1956); for contemporary estimates of numbers employed (ludicrously high), see Macpherson (1805) ii, 497; *CJ* xiii, 42; xvii, 393b. For inventories of silk-throwers, see PRO PROB 4/3500, /6878, /8075, /13885. The industry probably reached its peak size in the late seventeenth century when masters began to seek out cheaper rural labour.

10. Campbell (1747) pp. 147–50; *Case* (1743) claims that, in 1743, there were in the parish of St Giles Cripplegate 118 masters who owned '85 sheds for the spinning gilt and silver thread in which were 255 pair of wheels'; for two inventories of gold and silver threadmakers in the sample, see S. 151 & 194; for the chequered early history of the industry, see Stewart (1891).

11. On stockings and framework-knitting, see Thirsk (1973) and Chapman (1972), although both these articles and indeed nearly all the literature on this subject concentrate on the provincial rather than the London industry, which collapsed rapidly in the face of provincial competition after 1730. For numbers of frames, see D. M. Smith (1963) p. 129. For inventories of London framework-knitting workshops, see PRO PROB 4/3306 & /7878,

12. *Brief History* (1702) pp. 165–6; *Case* (1712); Wadsworth & Mann (1931) pp. 126–8, 171–3. S. 323 is the inventory of a weaver of silk, silk/wool and worsted fabrics.

13. Corfield (1982) p. 74 estimates 10–12,000 silk-weavers in the 1740s and 1750s; Warner (1921) suggests 15–18,000 looms in the early eighteenth century.

14. E.g. in 1697–8, London paid 66 per cent of the duty on exported cloth (*CJ* xiii, 152–4). See also Ramsay (1982) for generalizations about changes over time and discussion of London's function as a cloth-finishing centre. London's percentage of cloth exports was slowly declining over our period.

15. Kerridge (1985) pp. 150, 157.

16. For calico-printing, see Campbell (1747) pp. 116–19; Wadsworth & Mann (1931) pp. 130–40; Clayton & Oakes (1954). An Act of 1721 prohibited the use of all printed, stained and dyed calicoes, though this still left linens to be printed and also cotton-linen mixtures, which were exempted from the prohibition. An inquiry at this time showed that there were 31 calico-printers in the country employing 600–800 people, all but one in and around London.

17. There were said to be 7000 journeymen tailors in London and Westminster in 1721 (Galton (1896) p. 1). Over 20 per cent of all employed women in London were engaged in making clothes in the early eighteenth century – see Earle (1989).

18. Lemire (1984) emphasizes the second half of the eighteenth century as the key period in the development of ready-made clothing. However, Ginsburg (1972) p. 67 traces the industry back to the sixteenth century but thinks that it proliferated in the late seventeenth century because of the development 'of the more easily fitting simply cut suit', a very reasonable hypothesis which is supported by a writer in 1681 who stated that 'many remember when there were no new garments sold in London as now there are, only old garments at second hand'. (*Trade* (1681) quoted by Galton (1896) p. xvii.) For stock-lists demonstrating the sale of ready-made clothes, see S.169, 245, 252, 273.

19. For King's figures, see GLRO JB/Gregory King and see pp. 269–72 for more on the distribution of expenditure between various items.

20. Figures for the rebuilding are given in Reddaway (1940) p. 24 and Bell (1923) p. 224. On the building industry, see Colvin (1954), Chs 1 & 2, and Knoop & Jones (1936). On the expansion of the built-up area, see Summerson (1962).

21. Beier (1986) p. 148, Table 13, suggests that metalworking and leather were rather bigger employers than building, but these were certainly the next three biggest industries. The numbers are little more than an educated guess.

22. For the leather industry, see Clarkson (1960) (1) & (1960) (2); Campbell (1747) pp. 216–23. See also Mayer (1968) on the curriers and *Case* (n.d.) (1) for some valuable insights into shoemaking, the biggest employer in the leather industry.

23. Birmingham and Sheffield were just beginning to challenge London's dominance in brass and copperware and cutlery, but were still only very small cities, with populations of 7000 and 10,000 respectively in 1700. Hand-gun manufacture began in Birmingham after the Civil War but did not really challenge the London industry, which was concentrated in the area round the Tower, until the eighteenth century. On brass and copper, see Hamilton (1926) and Gentle & Feild (1975), though both books concentrate on Birmingham rather than London; on pewter, see Hatcher & Barker (1974); on clockmakers, see Loomes (1981) and on watchmakers for a rather later period, see Weiss (1982), who suggests that there were some 8000 in this industry in London in 1798; on gunmaking, see Stern (1954) (1). Much information can also be gleaned from the various entries in Campbell (1747).

24. Campbell (1747) pp. 24, 144, 177–80, 250–1.

25. Bailey & Barker (1969); B. M. D. Smith (1967) p. 139.

26. The main exports were cabinets, chairs, chests of drawers, clock cases, desks and looking-glasses – Joy (1965) pp. 3–4. For a list of 115 upholsterers and 55 cabinet makers active between 1660 and 1720, see Heal (1952). There were certainly many more who between them provided work for several thousand in woodworking and ancillary trades, such as sawyers and glue-makers.

27. On coachmaking, see Straus (1912). By the mid-eighteenth century, there were nearly 9000 four-wheel carriages in England, 4000 in London,

and there were also over 2000 two-wheel chaises in the metropolis (PRO T47/2). The industry employed a host of specialists for such things as wheels, door glasses, leather bodies, harness, silk linings and upholstery, metal fittings and locks, gilding, carving and coach-painting.

28. The hat-making industry grew very rapidly as more and more people at home and abroad wore felt and beaver hats, exports rising from 68,000 hats in 1700 to a peak of 700,000 in 1736, mostly made in London. Later in the eighteenth century the metropolis was to lose its pre-eminence to the hatters of Stockport and Manchester. I have relied mainly on an excellent paper by Corner (1985), from which the export figures are drawn.

29. Maitland estimated the number of bakers in 1730 at 1072, who would each employ some 4 or 5 journeymen or women and apprentices (Maitland (1739) p. 531). In general on baking, see Thrupp (1933).

30. Defoe (1724–6) i, 347.

31. On shipbuilding, see Banbury (1971) and Green & Wigram (1881). Twelve of the private yards were big enough to produce fourth-rate and even third-rate men-of-war for the navy during time of war. See Ehrman (1953) pp. 71–5 & App. I (E); Pool (1966); PRO ADM 106/2178 p. 101. On the royal dockyards, see Ehrman (1953) pp. 70–108 and Coleman (1953–4).

32. R. Davis (1962) p. 33. This proportion was to decline fairly continuously through the eighteenth century and was only 29.9 per cent in 1788. The absolute total of London shipping kept rising. By the later eighteenth century only about one-fifth of the city's foreign-going shipping was being built on the Thames. Jarvis (1969) pp. 407–8.

33. For three excellent inventories of ropemakers, all with assets valued from £4000 to £7000, see PRO PROB 4/5453, /14701, /20130.

34. For the brewing industry, see Mathias (1959), figures for the trade in 1700 on p. 6. It seems probable that, including draymen, each common brewer employed an average of somewhere between 5 and 10 men.

35. Mitchell & Deane (1962) pp. 251, 254–5. On the Gin Age in general, see George (1925) pp. 27–42.

36. For some contrasting inventories of distillers, see S.251 (a big malt distiller); S.287 (a big compound distiller); S.46 (a very small compound distiller). In 1703, there were 298 distilleries on the rounds of the London excisemen, a number which is likely to have grown considerably as the Gin Age continued (PRO CUST 48/10 p. 39).

37. For statistics of glassmakers, see Houghton (1727–8) ii, 48 and PRO CUST 48/6 p. 36. There were 90 glass-houses altogether in England, the other main centres being Stourbridge, Bristol and Newcastle, the last specializing in window glass which was carried to London on the colliers. London specialized on the high-quality end of the trade – mirror glass, crystal and the more expensive 'crown' or Normandy window glass – though the metropolis was also a major producer of cheaper window glass and bottles, one London house claiming a stock of 144,000 bottles in 1698. London was to lose most of its glass industry later in the eighteenth century and, by 1833, there were only three glasshouses left. In general on the glass

industry, see Godfrey (1975), Polak (1975) and Buckley (1915), and on looking-glasses, see Wills (1965).

38. There were said to be some 30 soapmakers in London in 1683 (CLRO MCI 413A) and 1107 in England and Wales in 1712 (*CTB* xxvi, pt ii, 56, 378; PRO CUST 48/11 pp. 62–3). However, since 28 of the 39 extra excise officers taken on to survey the new soap tax were in London, it is clear that the London works were very large compared to their provincial counterparts and none of the five soapmakers in our sample had a fortune of less than £1000. Londoners also produced nearly all the high-quality 'Castile' soap which was made from imported raw materials such as Baltic potash and olive oil.

In 1710, the excise officers found 436 wax and tallow candlemakers in London and some 3000 in the provinces. The Londoners were much the biggest operators, producing nearly a third of total national production and nearly all of the more expensive wax candles (PRO CUST 48/10 p. 320; PRO AO1/1078/729A; *CTB* xxiv, pt ii, 253).

Between 1660 and 1750, the number of British sugar refineries grew from about 50 to 120, there being 80 in London at the later date (Deerr (1950) ii, 458; *CJ* xxvi, 703). The refineries were nearly all fairly big businesses and getting bigger over time. The average valuation of utensils and stock in 14 sugar-houses insured by the Sun Fire Office in 1730 was about £3000 and, by the end of the century, refiners rarely insured their stocks for less than £5000 (GHMS 11936; Stern (1954) (2)).

Between 1668 and 1724, the number of master-printers in London increased from 26, employing an average of 6–7 men, to 75, employing over 10 men (Plant (1974) pp. 64, 85–6; Maxted (1977) p. xxx); for a list of the printers in 1724, see Nichols (1812–15) i, 288–312. Provincial competition was growing but there were still only 28 printing-houses outside London in 1724. There were also 200 or more bookseller/publishers and booksellers in London (Plant (1974) p. 64).

39. On this, see pp. 120–22.

40. There is evidence of 25 pottery sites in London before 1750, most of them on the south bank of the river. See Weatherill & Edwards (1971) and Edwards (1974).

41. On this, for the late sixteenth century, see Rappaport (1983–4).

42. On the problems of credit, see Chapter 4.

43. Hatcher & Barker (1974) p. 246.

44. See, for example, S.112, the inventory of John Skipper of Cornhill, who dealt in every sort of brass, copper and iron product, selling his goods to such prodigious wholesale customers as the Royal African Company or great merchants trading overseas. He produced nothing on his own premises but the £48 he owed 'several men for wages' suggests that some production was under his control.

45. S.116 (Rainer); S.86 (Treherne); for a useful discussion of the functions of the upholsterers, see Thornton (1978) pp. 97–106 and for some inventories of upholsterers, see S.144, 186, 367.

46. This trend was a major factor encouraging the progressive flight of

London's industries to the provinces, since the big hosiers, ironmongers, etc. did not care where the products they sold were made as long as they were made well and cheaply. On the relationship of the London hosiers to the Midlands stocking knitting industry, see Chapman (1972) and for a description of the 'Hardware-men' in the middle of the eighteenth century, see Collyer (1761) pp. 160–1. By then, they dealt mainly in goods made in Sheffield and Birmingham and some had a turnover of over £50,000 a year.

47. For the development of the building contractor, see Knoop & Jones (1936); for Barbon, see North (1890) iii, 53–60; on the riskiness of building speculation, see Campbell (1747) p. 161 and for some successful builders, see S.49, 115, 152.

48. The knitting-frame was invented in 1589 but not much used till the second half of the seventeenth century, especially from the 1670s when flamboyant fashions which were difficult to knit by machine were replaced by a vogue for silk hose in plain colours (Thirsk (1973), Chapman (1972)). The ribbon or Dutch loom was introduced from Holland in 1616 and was said to do the work of from 4 to 7 hand-weavers. It was banned in England, as in many continental countries, but the English ban proved ineffective, especially after the failure of the weavers' riots of 1675 (Wadsworth & Mann (1931) pp. 99–105; Dunn (1973)). Silk-throwers used multi-spindle mills, which are described in Chambers (1728) s.v. 'Milling, or throwing of silk'. Other examples include wheel-cutting machines in watchmaking, horse-powered saw-mills and cranes, a machine for cutting, grinding and polishing plate glass for mirrors, 'outdoing the operation by the hands, almost a thousand fold' (Salmon (1701) quoted by Wills (1965) p. 146)), and a tobacco-shredding machine (Cary (1695) p. 146 and compare S.179 (1682) with S.309 and 319 of the early eighteenth century, both of which had shredding machines). A different type of innovation can be seen in many metal trades, where casting and foundry work were becoming more important. The moulds required were too expensive for poor craftsmen, who found themselves degraded to mere performers of repetitive tasks using moulds 'furnished' by wealthier men. See Campbell (1747) p. 179 and S.50, a pewterer who had 31 cwt of brass moulds worth £146, over 40 per cent of his assets. There were no doubt many other innovations, individually fairly trivial but cumulatively important in increasing labour productivity.

49. Many efforts were made, both by the workers and the guilds, to halt the growth of the big masters. In 1675, there were riots directed at those ribbon-weaving masters with large numbers of ribbon looms on their premises (see Dunn (1973)). In 1710, there were riots aimed at framework knitting masters with large numbers of apprentices (Wells (1935) pp. 39–40). The Company of Silk Throwers passed an unsuccessful ordinance to limit the extent of manufacture by any one master (Stern (1956)). In 1667, counsel considered this ordinance as against the law and liberty of the subject, i.e. a restraint against trade, and this legal principle was to mean that most attempts by guilds or livery companies to prevent the growth of big business would be unsuccessful. On the general collapse of the authority of the livery companies, see pp. 250–3. For the inventory of a wealthy master silk-throwster, see PRO PROB 4/8075, Robert Godard, who left £9000.

50. A good example is the Quaker Thomas Hall, who died in 1722 worth £16,000 (Corner (1985)).

51. For the huge yard at Blackwall of Sir Henry Johnson, the biggest private shipbuilder in England, see Green & Wigram (1881). For some smaller but still impressive yards, see PRO PROB 4/6037 and 5/2035. Ropewalks also needed plenty of space – see the inventories in note 33 above.

52. The value of fixed capital is difficult to assess, since it was normally valued at scrap or very cheap second-hand prices in inventories and was also probably undervalued in insurance contracts, which in any case do not often distinguish the value of stocks from fixed equipment. As a result of such valuation policies, no one in the sample had as much as £1000 of fixed equipment but a few hundred pounds would be sufficient to keep small men out of these industries, which is the main point here.

53. Mathias (1959).

54. S.115 (Marshall) – see also Colvin (1954) p. 378; S.229; on the Blackwell Hall Factors, see Westerfield (1915) pp. 296–302; Ramsay (1943) Ch. 8; Mann (1971) Ch. 3; D.W. Jones (1972) (2); R. Davis (1967) pp. 107–15; Price (1980) pp. 102–7 and Ramsay (1982) Ch. 5.

55. S.251.

56. S.184.

57. Chamberlayne (4th ed. 1670) p. 470.

58. Roberts (1641) pp. 1–3; Defoe (1697) p. 8.

59. This figure was suggested to me by James Alexander, who is analysing the London poll-tax records of the 1690s. D. W. Jones (1972) (1) p. 350, fn. 30, gives 2000, based on port-book records, but these entries would contain many people who were not full-time merchants and would not have been considered merchants by their contemporaries. For wholesalers and retailers engaging in foreign trade, see S.17, 23, 31, 41, 81, 171, 182, 184, 193, 221.

60. S.315.

61. Many merchants, and very often very rich ones, were not Citizens of London and so would not appear in the Orphans' Court records which I have used, so it is possible that these figures underestimate merchant wealth. The records also underestimate the wealth of all groups to a certain extent, since the average age at death was likely to be lower for those leaving orphans than for all middle-class Londoners and survival was a major influence on accumulation (see pp. 141–2). However, this does not affect the relative wealth of different groups in the middle class, which is what I am interested in here. I owe these points to a discussion with Henry Horwitz.

62. Rates of commission varied from 1½ to 2 per cent in Holland or Hamburg to 3 per cent in the Levant and 5 per cent in the West Indies, though most trades offered various types of extra perks for factors on top of these. Much higher rates of accumulation could be earned by the supercargoes or travelling factors in the China trade, where a single voyage might yield several thousand pounds. Westerfield (1915) p. 356 fn. 1; Gill (1961) p. 32; Morse (1921).

63. For these two companies, see Chaudhuri (1978) and K. G. Davies (1957).

64. Wood (1935); Hinton (1959) and in general, see Scott (1910–12).

65. Price & Clemens (1987) discuss the huge reduction in the numbers of firms importing tobacco, despite an increase in the amount imported, and a similar though lesser reduction in the number of sugar importers. See also R. Davis (1967) p. 61 for the Levant trade.

66. For 'basic' Levant traders, see S.11, 224, 285; for 'diversified' businesses, see S.42 (Dawes), 43, 71, 99, 107, 292. On the Levant trade in general, see Wood (1935), R. Davis (1967).

67. S.52 (Ferney); S.19, 107 (clandestine traders – on this subject see Zahedieh (1986)); S.315 (Vansittart), cf. S.107 for a similar business combining very large Danzig and Levantine trades with an impressive trade to North America and the West Indies. The Baltic trade took three main forms: the timber trade from Norway, the trade in pitch, tar and iron from Sweden and the trade in hemp, flax and potash form Danzig and Riga.

68. For data on overseas trade, showing the rapid growth of trade with America, see R. Davis (1954) and R. Davis (1962) (2), both republished in Minchinton (1969). The other main growth areas were the trade with India and the Far East, the slave trade from Africa to America and the trade to Spain and the Mediterranean, the last especially in the later seventeenth century.

69. Defoe (1726–7) i, 102.

70. A good example of both these trades is William Paggen, a tobacco merchant, who owned shares in several slave ships and imported negro boys to sell as servants in Europe, one of whom, 'Black Jack', was to play a prominent part in his funeral procession. He also re-exported tobacco to Holland and Hamburg and had invested in storage space in the Isle of Wight in order to satisfy the requirements of the Navigation Acts that tobacco be landed in England before being shipped to its final market. However, his re-export business was modest compared to that of John Cary, who in 1695 re-exported a million pounds of tobacco, one-third of that year's total, to Holland, Germany and the Baltic. S.212 (Paggen), S.279 (Cary) and see D. W. Jones (1972) (1) pp. 331–2.

71. Campbell (1747) p. 288; for the commission business, see K. G. Davies (1952); Price (1980); Donnan (1931).

72. On shipping shares, see R. Davis (1962) pp. 81–100; Price (1980) pp. 40–2 and Jarvis (1969) pp. 414–61. The average of 114 ships valued in the inventories of the sample was just over £2000 and the median just over £1000, with a range from under £100 for small coasters to over £11,000 for East Indiamen. Only about one ship in ten was owned by an individual and these were mainly small, averaging about £170 in value. The biggest shipowner was Sir Jonathan Dawes (S.42), with shares in 15 ships worth £5532, but this was only 10 per cent of his assets. For an example of suppliers with shipping shares, see the inventories of the three ropemakers in note 33 above, who had shares in 61 ships between them.

73. For examples of merchants with domestic business interests, see S.65 (copperas manufacturer); S.167 (property development); S.259 (lead mines); S.292 (dye-works). For a merchant who kept a shop to sell goods acquired in his Mediterranean trade, see S.309.

74. Fire insurance policies give a good idea of the vast numbers of warehouses and of the vaults and cellars with which London was honeycombed, especially the area near the waterside (GHMS 11936 *passim*). For descriptions of counting-houses, see, for example, S.42, 52, 71.

75. Magalotti (1821) p. 295. See also Roger North on his brother Dudley, who found that he had to move from the West End to the City because 'his business, which was very considerable, made it needful for him to have warehouses and to converse near the Exchange and in a mercantile way, so that he might readily carry persons to see his goods' (North (1890) ii, 173).

76. The two most useful modern books which I have found are Westerfield (1915) and Price (1980) but best of all are the contemporary works, especially those by Defoe, e.g. Defoe (1724–6), (1726–7) and (1730).

77. *Review*, 18 February 1706/7.

78. The main exception to the general specialization were the so-called 'warehousemen', a sort of super-wholesaler who bought up goods of all kinds to sell to the merchants, especially to those in the American trades (Defoe (1726–7) i, 4; Defoe (1730) p. 22; Price (1980) pp. 101–17).

79. On the Blackwell Hall Factors, see references in note 54 above. The London-based Norwich Factors provided similar services for cloth made in that city.

80. Quoted by R. Davis (1967) p. 115.

81. Rothstein (1961) pp. 131–2; for the inventory of a silkman, see S.136, Samuel Tomlins, who sold mainly to the lacemakers of Buckinghamshire, his native county.

82. See, for example, S.132. For other inventories of leather-sellers, see S.221 and 348.

83. Westerfield (1915) pp. 314–18; for the linen industry and the rise of the drapers, see Harte (1973). By the early eighteenth century, many of the bigger linen-drapers did their own importing.

84. S.317 is the inventory of the junior partner. See also Jones (1972) (1) p. 332 and Price (1980) p. 98. Other wholesale dealers in imported goods include oilmen, drysalters (dye-stuffs), mercers (silks), timber-merchants and the dealers in tea, coffee, china and other goods imported by the East India Company (for a good example, see the papers of Henry Gambier in PRO C108/132). Wine merchants were unusual in selling direct to the tavern-keepers and gentlemen who were their main customers, but there were also intermediaries in this trade called wine-coopers, whose main function was as tasters and mixers of wine but who also used their expertise to deal in wine themselves.

85. For general discussion of the grain trade, see Defoe (1726–7), ii, ii, 31–46; Westerfield (1915) pp. 130–86; Gras (1915); McGrath (1948); Fisher (1935); Baker (1970); Chartres (1986); Chartres (1977) (1).

86. Defoe (1726–7) ii, ii, 36.

87. *Essay* (1718) pp. 17–18.

88. Houghton (1727–8) i, 301, 313–14. His estimate was based on information from 'an ingenious butcher'. The retailers were known as cutting-butchers. On London as a meat market, see Chartres (1977) (1) pp. 19–24; Westerfield (1915) pp. 187–201; McGrath (1948) and P. E. Jones (1976).

89. Maitland (1756) ii, 758. For inventories of rather smaller but still wealthy wholesale cheesemongers, see S.17, 193, 274, 335. About 20 to 25 cheesemongers dominated the wholesale distribution of cheese in the late seventeenth century, while there were some 250 retail and wholesale cheesemongers altogether (Stern (1979) p. 231). In general, see Stern (1973); Stern (1979); Chartres (1977) (1) pp. 28–30; Westerfield (1915) pp. 204–8.

90. Clay (1984) ii, 47. For the London coal trade, see Westerfield (1915) pp. 218–39; R. Smith (1961) and Flinn (1984).

91. The coal-heavers who unloaded the coal in the river and the lightermen who brought it to the shore at Billingsgate controlled a bottleneck in the supply of the fuel and so were able to hold the market to ransom, a power which they used to exact commissions when the coal was sold on the London market. See R. Smith (1961) pp. 34–46, *CJ* xxi, 369–73, 516–18 and George (1927). For some inventories of coalmongers, see S.48, 311, 360 and see also the daybook of John Martin for 1734–5, which gives a very good idea of the way the trade within London operated, showing especially the advantage of having enough space and money to buy coal in the summer when it was some 15 per cent cheaper, big customers getting a discount of 12½ per cent on top of this (PRO C108/82).

92. Deering (1751) pp. 91–2. For a description of a provincial shopkeeper buying his stock in London, see Marshall (1974) pp. 89–90. For a wholesale haberdasher with a factor in Manchester, see S.358.

93. Defoe (1724–6) i, 80–1; S.317.

94. Defoe (1726–7) ii, ii, 142; bankruptcy data from PRO B4/1–2. For a more detailed analysis of this material, see Appendix C. For some big wholesale haberdashers, mercers and linen-drapers, see S.171, 202, 206, 338, 358.

95. Chamberlayne (4th ed. 1670) pp. 469–70; N.H. (1684) pp. 70–1. There is no estimate of the numbers of shopkeepers in our period but by extrapolating from Schwarz's analysis of the tax assessments of the 1790s I would guess that there were some 2000 or 3000 shops not selling food and drink in our period (Schwarz (1979) pp. 256–8; Schwarz (1982) pp. 176–8, 183–5). The best discussion of the development of retailing is D. Davis (1966), esp. Chs 3–9.

96. 'Haberdashers' here includes milliners and yarn-dealers, etc. Drapers, mercers, grocers and salters were usually much better off than haberdashers, who were near the bottom of the retailing fraternity, only chandlers of the main groups coming beneath them. For the general pattern of shopkeeping fortunes, see Table 2.2 on p. 36.

97. S.141.

98. For a fine collection of trade cards, see Heal (1925). These cards were used for advertisement and for making out invoices. They became much commoner after the end of our period.

99. *Brief History* (1702) p. 152; Sun 34864. A rather different sort of shop could be found in the Royal Exchange (built 1568) and the New Exchange in the Strand (1609), both of which had galleries with a large number of small shops or booths mainly selling mercers', haberdashers' and milliners' goods. See D. Davis (1966) pp. 104–7, 122–6 and for inventories of such shops, see S.3 and S.60.

100. *OED* s.v. 'Haberdasher'; S.146.

101. S.53; cf. John Adam of Fenchurch Street (S.283), who sold 'cizars', razors, 'tobacco, snuff and ink boxes of silver, tortoiseshell, shagreen, brass, ivory and leather', canes, whips, coffee mills, powder horns and '467 brass, ivory, steele and wooden toys'.

102. On the markets, see Defoe (1724–6) i, 343–5; D. Davis (1966) pp. 74–81; Robertson (1958) and Robertson (1961).

103. Campbell (1747) p. 280.

104. S. 271; cf. S.1, 85, 150, 153, 257, 280.

105. E.g. S.138, 157, 214, 230, 334.

106. S.316 (Pott). For a hardware shop specializing in turnery ware, see S.116; for a fishermen's supply shop, see S.139 and S.343, who also dealt in seeds and gardening equipment. S.89 was a specialist garden supply shop. All these shops stocked household goods as well.

107. On the financial revolution, see Dickson (1967).

108. For details, see Vernon (1678) p. 128; on scriveners, see Tawney (1925) pp. 96–101; Coleman (1951–2) and, on Sir Robert Clayton, the greatest scrivener-banker of the late seventeenth century, see Melton (1986). Another group of financial intermediaries were the brokers, whose original function was to introduce potential buyers and sellers on the Exchange. Many began to specialize in the market for bills of exchange, bringing buyers and sellers together and discounting bills themselves (Vernon (1678) p. 109; Scarlett (1682) p. 8).

109. PRO C107/70–72, 113.

110. See 'The Mystery of the New Fashioned Goldsmiths or Bankers' (1676), reprinted in Martin (1892). For bankers in general, see Richards (1958); Hilton Price (1890–91); Joslin (1954) and Martin (1892).

111. *Collection* (1677); there is a copy of the list of goldsmith-bankers in Hilton Price (1890–91) pp. 158–9; for 1725, see Joslin (1954). The development of banking suffered a serious check in 1672 by the 'Stop of the Exchequer', when the Crown reneged on money lent by the bankers (see Horsefield (1982)). The bankers' papers that survive suggest that the assets of banks ranged from £50,000 or less up to about £200,000, equivalent to the assets of very wealthy merchants but not huge businesses. They were all completely dwarfed by the Bank of England. For studies of various bankers, see Joslin (1954); Hoare (1932); Shelton (1956); Clay (1984) ii, 275 and, for a banker in our sample, see S.246, Thomas Williams, who had gross assets of £70,000 and net of £55,000.

112. Judging from inventories, few middling people borrowed from banks, whose main customers were the gentlemen of the West End.

113. *Proposals* (1706) p. 9; *CJ* xxv, 45–8. The maximum legal rate of interest was 6 per cent until 1713 and then 5 per cent for the rest of our period.

114. S.45. Cf. S.84, 149, 196.

115. For more on investment, see Ch. 5, pp. 143–57.

116. It is unfortunately impossible to separate wholesalers from retailers in Table 2.2, since inventories do not always provide sufficient information for this purpose. Some give the addresses of debtors of the business, which can indicate a widespread inland trade; some have warehouses but no shop, which suggests a wholesale business; in other cases, a large number of individual trade debts in scores or hundreds of pounds is a fair indication of a wholesale business, since few retail debts ran this high. However, such indications are not really sufficient to place all the people listed in the table as either retailers or wholesalers, especially as many were both. Nevertheless, it is a reasonable assumption that anyone who left over £2000 was either a wholesaler or at least had a large wholesale component in his business, while few wholesalers would have left less than £1000.

117. There were altogether 34 men in the sample (9 per cent) who left more than £10,000 – 16 merchants, 1 banker and 8 wholesalers, the 4 manufacturers in Table 2.1 (p. 32) and 5 rentiers, most of whom were probably retired merchants.

118. In 1739, Maitland counted nearly 16,000 victualling establishments in London, a figure which was swollen by the rapid increase in dramshops from the 1720s. Somewhere around 10,000 or 12,000 would probably have been more normal for our period. Turning such numbers into employment poses the usual problems but, at a guess, one might suggest an average employment of 10 for an inn, 7 for a tavern, 3 for coffee-houses and alehouses and 1 for dram-shops and brandy-shops. If these multipliers are applied to Maitland's estimates of 207 inns, 447 taverns, 551 coffee-houses, 5975 alehouses and 8659 brandy-shops, one would get 33,000 people, which does not seem too unrealistic, though the true figure might lie anywhere between 20,000 and 40,000 (Maitland (1739) p. 531).

119. Maitland (1739) p. 531 has 207 inns; Chartres (1977) (3) p. 27 states that there were about 150 inns engaged in the transport trades in 1715. Chartres is the best authority on London inns in this period. See also his thesis, Chartres (1973).

120. Chapman (1972) pp. 20–1.

121. Pepys 10 May 1663; Swift (1948) i, 48; Ward (1924) p. 206. See also Pepys vol. x, s.v. 'Taverns'; Simon (1906–9) iii, 192–252 and J. Paul de Castro, 'Dictionary of the principal London taverns', GHMS 3110.

122. This description is based on the 20 taverns in the sample, which had an average of 10 private drinking-rooms each. S.192 is the Crown in Threadneedle Street; see also Pepys x, 420 and Lyons (1944) p. 270.

123. French wines were legally available as prize-goods during the wars between 1689 and 1713, and much was also smuggled. During periods of prohibition, inventories often list large quantities of very highly priced

wines simply described as 'red' or 'white', which one suspects were French wines imported from northern Italian, Spanish or even Irish ports to defraud the customs. For some examples for the period after 1689, see S.238, 248, 325, 350, 352.

124. Quoted by Ellis (1956) p. 52; Macaulay (1850) i, 367; on coffee-houses, see Ellis (1956); Lillywhite (1963) and Pelzer (1982). Most coffee-houses were small businesses, unlike taverns, which would have been unlikely to produce a fortune of much over £100 for their proprietors. For a derogatory description of coffee-house keepers, see *Case* (1729) pp. 8–9.

125. Ward (1924) p. 11.

126. S.327; Maitland (1739) p. 531; the authority on alehouses is Clark (1983), see, especially, pp. 195–249. Most alehouses operated at an artisan level of fortune, although some were becoming respectable from the late seventeenth century, and this top sector of the trade would have attracted middle-class investment.

127. I have relied heavily on the unpublished dissertation of Hopkin (1980) for this section on cook-shops.

128. Misson (1719) pp. 145–6; Smollett (1748) pp. 102–3.

129. Maitland (1739) p. 531. This incredible figure seems fairly accurate. Cf. the count of 3835 dram-shops in the metropolitan districts of Middlesex in 1736, a much smaller area than Maitland's (Clark (1983) p. 239).

130. Altick (1978) p. 37. This delightful book on the shows of London is highly recommended.

131. Defoe (1725) p. 33; cf. MCI 534, a case relating to the apprentice Edward Day, who was addicted to playing at 'shoffel board', 'rolley polley' and 'playing with dice at wheel barrows in the street'; *Account* (1722).

132. Chancellor (1925) pp. 151–4; Malcolm (1808) pp. 309, 321; Pepys 21 December 1663. For a good description of a cock-fight, see Uffenbach (1934) pp. 48–9.

133. Pepys 14 August 1666; Evelyn (1955) 16 June 1670; both quoted by Chancellor (1925) in his section on bull and bear baiting, pp. 144–51; Malcolm (1808) pp. 327, 329; for opera prices, see Avery (1960) p. lx.

134. *Foreigners* (1729) p. 120.

135. Tilmouth (1957–8) pp. 15–19; Young (1965) p. 39; see also Harley (1968) on the social history of music.

136. Ward (1699); Malcolm (1810) p. 310; for some insights into the London dancing world, see Ryder (1939), esp. pp. 127–8, 192.

137. On the theatre, see Nicoll (1923); Nicoll (1925); Van Lennep (1965); Hotson (1928); Avery (1960) and Pedicord (1954). After the Licensing Act of 1737, London was again restricted to two theatres, Drury Lane and Covent Garden.

138. Opera stars could earn staggering salaries. The top opera singers for the 1708 season got over £400 while, in the 1720s, the castrato Senesino and the *prima donna* Francesca Cuzzoni both earned over £2000 for a single season.

139. Fisher (1948).

140. Gregory King thought that there were 10,000 'persons in the law' in

1688, a figure which Professor Holmes does not consider to be too far over the mark (Holmes (1982) p. 154), and there would certainly have been 10,000 by 1730. It seems a reasonable guess that at least half of these were resident in London. King also thought there were 10,000 clergymen, which Holmes thinks was probably too low (Holmes (1982) pp. 94–5). At least 1000 of these must have lived in London. Holmes estimates 10,000–15,000 teachers of all sorts in England and Wales, and leans towards the higher number (Holmes (1982) p. 52). It seems probable that London would have been unequally represented in the profession, considering the concentration of schools and the wide range of specialist teaching. So, at a guess, there were 2000 or 2500 teachers. Finally, there were about 100 physicians (Roberts (1964) (2) p. 381; Holmes (1982) pp. 170–1), 100–200 surgeons (Roberts (1964) (2) p. 381; *A List of the names of surgeons etc.*, BL 777.1.3/1) and some 400, or possibly up to 1000, apothecaries (Roberts (1964) (2) pp. 277, 381; Holmes (1982) p. 310; *Tentamen* (1704) p. 49 and see successive lists prepared by the Society of Apothecaries, BL 777.1.3/4, 4*, 7, 9 etc.). Such estimates add up to nearly 10,000, although many people at the bottom of the legal and teaching professions were hardly middle-class – one might hazard a figure of between 5000 and 7000 middle-class professionals in London altogether, compared to some 20,000 to 25,000 householders in the whole of the middle station (see, pp. 80–1).

141. Holmes (1982) p. 124. This book and Prest (1987) (1) have been my main guides for this section on the professions. On lawyers, see Holmes (1982) pp. 115–65; Robson (1959); Duman (1981); Prest (1981) (2); Prest (1987) (2) and Birks (1960).

142. Quoted by Prest (1981) (2) p. 77. The income of the typical member of the commercial middle class with a fortune of about £2000 would have been about £200–300 (see pp. 269–70). The number of barristers reached a peak in the 1660s and was to fall in our period (Prest (1987) (2) p. 76).

143. *Compleat* (1683) p. 13; John Evelyn, quoted by Holmes (1982) p. 152. The numbers of attorneys and, especially, solicitors continued to grow during our period but at a slower rate than in the half century before the Civil War (Prest (1987) (2) pp. 72–9).

144. Details of the legal bureaucracy are normally included in the guidebooks of the period, e.g. Chamberlayne, Miège, Hatton.

145. Details of fees can be found in legal textbooks, e.g. the various editions of *The Compleat Solicitor* or *Practick* (1681). See also the records of the enquiry into legal fees in 1731–2 in House of Commons, *Sessions Papers* vol. xiii; the Doorkeeper's fees are on p. 309.

146. Chamberlayne (22nd ed. 1707) pp. 193–4; House of Commons, *Sessions Papers* xiii, 442–3.

147. In general on the Church, see Overton (1885); Sykes (1934); Wickham Legg (1914); Cragg (1951); Holmes (1982) pp. 83–114; O'Day (1987). For biographies of two important Bishops of London, see Sykes (1926) and Carpenter (1956).

148. Burnet (1969 ed.) vi, 190–7, quotation on p. 192; Chamberlayne quoted in Overton (1885) p. 303.

149. For clerical incomes see Burnet (1969 ed.) v, 121; Overton (1885) pp. 303–5 and for a general discussion see Holmes (1982) pp. 92–107. Incomes were to grow both absolutely and in relation to other incomes in the century following our period (O'Day (1987) pp. 54–6).

150. *Spectator*, 24 March 1710/11. As early as the 1620s, recruitment throughout the diocese of London was wholly graduate (O'Day (1987) p. 46).

151. There were, however, less churches after the Fire than there had been before, 35 of the 87 which were burned not being rebuilt. Nevertheless, new churches and chapels were being built in the suburbs, their numbers increasing after 1711 when an Act of Parliament provided for the building of 50 new churches, 12 of which were actually built in our period. For surveys of London churches, see *Pietas* (1714) and Parish Clerks (1732), which describes 111 in the metropolis, and there were also at least 60 chapels.

152. Hatton (1708) vol. i, p. xxxvii. See also Wickham Legg (1914) pp. 88–110.

153. *The Contempt of the Clergy Consider'd* (1739), quoted by Sykes (1934) p. 221; Burnet (1969 ed.) vi, 215. See also Sykes (1934) p. 227.

154. Parish Clerks (1732).

155. Stackhouse (1722) pp. 83, 86; Sykes (1934) pp. 206–9.

156. Quoted by Overton (1885) p. 298. The vestry minutes of St Katherine Cree provide a good example of clerical competition. In 1691, the Vestry drew up a short-list of eight curates and made arrangements for each to preach, one in the morning, one in the afternoon, over the next four Sundays, after which the Vestry chose the successful candidate (GHMS 1196/1, 20 June & 13 July 1691).

157. Estimates of the numbers of dissenters in London vary but they were probably about 10–15 per cent of the population. See below, note 41 of Ch. 9.

158. Watts (1978) p. 342; Holmes (1982) pp. 111–14.

159. On literacy in London, see Cressy (1980) pp. 73–5, where he analyses the proportion in various parishes who either signed or made a mark on nationally collected loyalty declarations in the early 1640s. The national average was for 70 per cent to leave a mark, while the four London parishes included had figures of 33, 21, 17 and 9 per cent. See also, on the literacy of London women, Earle (1989). On elementary schools in London, see Anglin (1980); Wide & Morris (1969). Much information can also be gleaned from such publications as Hatton (1708); Parish Clerks (1732); Maitland (1739).

160. On the charity schools, see M. G. Jones (1938) and for the estimate of cost per head, see Maitland (1739) p. 639.

161. Castle Street Free School (see Hatton (1708)). The standard work on grammar schools is Vincent (1969). See also Wallis (1952).

162. Quoted by Holmes (1982) p. 47.

163. Dare (1963); Pearce (1982) p. 84.

164. Heal (1931) has biographical information on writing-masters and many details on the schools. On mathematics teachers and schools, see Taylor (1954) and Taylor (1966).

165. Vincent (1969) pp. 199–202; Hans (1951) pp. 82–7.

166. For Newington Green Academy, see Girdler (1953) and J. W. A. Smith (1954) pp. 56–61. Good dissenting academies attracted Anglicans as well as dissenters.

167. *Collection*, 27 July 1694; three at Hackney, two at Chelsea, one each at Greenwich, Mile End, Bethnal Green and Kensington. On Westminster and St Paul's, which were well on the way to becoming what we now call public schools, see Sargeaunt (1898) and McDonnell (1909).

168. Sargeaunt (1898) p. 101; Heal (1931) p. 7; Hans (1951) pp. 70–7.

169. Dare (1963) pp. 15, 34; Hatton (1708) provides a good idea of the range of grammar school salaries. The salaries of grammar school teachers could go as low as 5s. a week (Cressy (1987) p. 144). For charity school teachers, see M. G. Jones (1938) pp. 96–109.

170. There were some 40 physicians in London in the 1620s, 136 in 1695 and 78 in 1719, about one doctor for every 10,000 people at the worst and one for every 4000 at the best (Roberts (1964) (2) p. 381; Holmes (1982) pp. 170–1). On the education of physicians, see Allen (1946); Poynter & Bishop (1951), introduction. In general on the medical profession, see Hamilton (1951), Roberts (1964) (1); Roberts (1964) (2); Poynter (1961) (2), Holmes (1982) pp. 166–205 and Cook (1986). It should be noted that, in addition to the representatives of 'official' medicine discussed here, there were large numbers of empirics, quacks, astrologers and women learned in herbal lore, who practised an 'alternative' medicine which was often just as effective (or otherwise) as that provided by the 'professionals'.

171. Hone (1950) p. 34; Wall et al. (1963) p. 125.

172. Sydenham quoted by Holmes (1982) p. 182; Hone (1950) pp. 113–14.

173. On the education of surgeons, see Peachey (1924) Ch. 1. Not much work has been done on the wealth of surgeons but see Holmes (1982) p. 232 and Poynter (1965) (1) pp. 208–9 for some suggestive data. The one surgeon in the sample, Richard Blundell, left nearly £10,000 in 1718 (S.371).

174. *Tentamen* (1704) pp. 69–70. For more on the training of apothecaries, see Wall et al. (1963) pp. 76–90. On numbers, see note 140 above.

175. S.33; *Fair Play* (?1708) quoted by Hamilton (1951) p. 161 fn. 2; Pittis (1715) p. 13; Wall et al. (1963) p. 82.

176. Pittis (1715). Holmes (1982) pp. 218–26 has data on physicians' earnings and investments.

177. For change in the civil service, see Holmes (1982) pp. 239–61; Aylmer (1980).

178. Holmes (1982) p. 256 suggests about 3000 permanent posts in London by 1725, to which might be added about 1000 for the royal household and maybe another 1000 for the latter's servants and for part-time employment in the customs service. Hoon (1968) pp. 92–166 suggests a regular customs establishment in London of 1200–1500, which could be doubled in busy times by part-time employment. R.E. (1877) pp. 17–19 suggests 700 in the London excise service by 1750. For the royal household, see Beattie (1967). Holmes (1982) p. 256 states that 'the overwhelming bulk of the

government's office staff and 95 per cent of its local revenue men earned between £40 and £80 a year'.

179. On the growth of the army as a profession, see Holmes (1982) pp. 262–74. See also Scouller (1966), esp. pp. 81–96.

180. On the trade in art, see Haskell (1959). For painters at work in London during this period, see Walpole (1888).

181. Croft-Murray (1962) i, 43–8. Taverns were another lucrative source of demand for decorative art. For pictures in middle-class homes, see p. 295.

182. Lely left an estate in land worth £900 p.a. and a picture collection which was auctioned for £26,000; Kneller left an estate worth nearly £2000 p.a., despite losing £20,000 in South Sea stocks (Walpole (1888) ii, 99, 133, 202–11; Whitley (1928) i, 4–5). On Stevenson, see Redgrave (1878) p. 413 and S.131.

183. P. Rogers (1978) pp. 17–18 makes the point that most writers were drawn from those with a learned and usually university background. See also his *Grub Street* (1972) for the world of the hack.

184. Van Lennep (1965) pp. liii, lxxxii-iii; Avery (1960) p. ci; Collins (1927) p. 34.

185. Jacob Tonson, one of the most successful publishers of his day, who left over £40,000 in 1739, was considered a fair dealer with authors but, as his fortune indicates, he was even fairer to himself (Lynch (1971)). For some bad bargains by writers, see Nichols (1812–15) ii, 458.

186. P. Rogers (1978) pp. 53–4; Holmes (1982) p. 33.

187. The only near-contemporary estimate of the number of servants in London which I have found is Hanway (1767) ii, 158, where he reckoned that they were 1 in 13 of the population, i.e. 50,000 of his estimated population of 650,000. This proportion is about the same as that in mid-Victorian London (McBride (1976) p. 36; Mitchell & Deane (1962) p. 19) and there seems no reason why the proportion would have been any less in our period when the population of London was about 500,000, giving a servant population of, say, 35,000 to 40,000. Maitland (1739) pp. 618–21 says that there were 22,000 sailors in London's merchant fleet in 1732; a House of Commons committee report stated that there were 9717 freemen of the Watermen's Company in 1724, while apprenticeship was at the rate of about 450 a year between 1700 and 1730 (Humpherus (1887–89) ii, 122–3, 214). On land, there were some 5000 official porters and coalheavers, 672 carts, each with at least one carter, 800 hackney coaches and unknown numbers of wheelbarrowmen, all engaged in carriage within the city, while there were many hundreds more residents who engaged in inland carriage outside the city (Stern (1960) pp. 50–1, 85; R. Smith (1961) p. 49; Maitland (1739) pp. 625, 800). Adding all these together and a few more for luck, the total numbers engaged in carriage would certainly have been 30,000 at any time in our period and much more by 1730.

188. For more on domestic servants, see pp. 218–19. Little work has been done on the lives of London servants but it is interesting to note that, in Paris, the large numbers of male domestics were generally better off than other wage-earners and were often able to accumulate quite respectable fortunes (Roche (1987)).

189. On seamen's wages, see R. Davis (1962) p. 84; Ehrman (1953) p. 129. Ships' captains were often the managing agents of shipowning syndicates and indeed it was often the captain who created the ship by organizing its building and selling shares to his suppliers and to members of the mercantile community.
190. GHMS 6308/1A, Thomas Walker & Co. of Whitechapel owned 90 lighters; Chartres (1973) pp. 176–210; GHMS 12833/1; on the carmen, see Bennett (1952).
191. Dowdell (1932) p. 105 & fn. 10.
192. Hatton (1708) pp. 791–8; see also Strype (1720) i, 26–7; *Foreigners* (1729) pp. 10–12, 50; Maitland (1739) pp. 622–30; Scott (1910–12) iii, 3–33 & 418–22.
193. Falkus (1976). On urban improvement, see also Jones & Falkus (1979).
194. On the development of insurance generally and particularly fire insurance, see the first chapters of Dickson (1960) and Supple (1970). See also Scott (1910–12) iii, 372–88 for details of the companies and Blackstone (1957) on fire-fighting.
195. S.341; cf. S.372. See, in general, Gittings (1984) and Taylor (1983). For more on funerals, see pp. 311–14.
196. Labrousse & Braudel (1970) pp. 601–50; Rudé (1971) pp. 52–63; Schwarz (1979) and Schwarz (1982). I have assumed there were about 100,000 households in London, based on a population of just over 500,000 and a household size of about five persons. See estimates by Gregory King in Thirsk & Cooper (1972) p. 772 and by Jones & Judges (1935) pp. 58–62.

3 Apprenticeship

1. Burton (1681) p. 2; in a lawsuit of 1654 a linen-draper claimed that, although an apprentice might be of little value to his master in the first part of his time, 'in the latter parte he could be worth £20 a year or more' and other witnesses put the value at £30 or £40 (MCI 68).
2. Many such apprentices never bothered to take up their freedom, as can be seen by the very great difference between the numbers who became apprentices and the numbers who became freemen. For some data in the middle of the seventeenth century, see S. R. Smith (1973) pp. 197–8.
3. See, for example, Campbell (1747) pp. 127, 195–6, 283.
4. In general on the decline in apprenticeship, see Kellett (1957–8) pp. 388–9, Kahl (1956), Glass (1969) p. 385. The freedom of the Companies was increasingly acquired by redemption (a flat fee) and by patrimony (because one's father had been a freeman). See p. 256, for examples of the Distillers' Company selling the freedom to interlopers who wished to trade in the City.
5. On the need for immigration to maintain the population, let alone increase it, see Wrigley (1967) and Finlay (1981) pp. 8–9.
6. For what follows on the geographical and social origins of apprentices,

see Stone (1966), Glass (1969), Kahl (1956), S. R. Smith (1973), Kitch (1986) and Wareing (1980). The main source for analysis of both social and geographical origins are the records of the Livery Companies, especially the apprentice binding books, which normally give the place of origin and the occupation and/or status of the father of the apprentice. Comments on the geographical origins of the sample are based on 236 out of 375 cases for which this information is available and on social origins on 211 cases.
7. See pp. 7–13.
8. Stone (1984) pp. 233–4.
9. Fletcher (1975) p. 37; GHMS 10823/1 p. 38; North (1890) ii, 2–3.
10. North (1890) i, 21; ii, 46; GHMS 10823/1 p. 35.
11. Apprentices in London were supposed to be 14 before they were bound (see *Laws* (1765) p. 112). We can calculate the ages at apprenticeship of just over half the sample: 30 per cent were 16 and 81 per cent were between 15 and 18 inclusive. These ages are much lower than those discovered by Rappaport for the middle of the sixteenth century; he found that most men in London did not start their apprenticeship until they were 20 or older (Rappaport (1983) p. 115). These are surprising findings and one wonders what these young men did between leaving school and taking up their apprenticeships.
12. Wadsworth (1712) p. 58, quoted by Morgan (1944) p. 39; Campbell (1747) pp. 2–3.
13. E.g. Burton (1681); Trenchfield (1671).
14. For Purcell, see the apprenticeship bindings of the Drapers' Company and notes attached to them; for Randall, S.93 and Drapers' Company records; Williams, S.114, Meredith, S.270; Stationers' Company records.
15. MCE 1679, Sturges v. Compeere; *Collection*, 10 February 1693.
16. MCI 385, 57.
17. CLRO Small Ms. Box 40, No. 14. Contract between Richard Robinson and Isaac Terry, ironmonger, 9 August 1682.
18. For those members of the sample for whom information is available, the terms were 113 at 7 years, 74 at 8 years and 5 at 9 years.
19. Clothes were often a point at issue in disputes between masters and apprentices, and many witnesses provide valuations (MCI & MCE *passim*). See also p. 284.
20. Defoe (1726–7) i, 183; Wood (1935) p. 215; Kirkman (1673) p. 34; Beloff (1942) p. 39; MCI 379, 411 (and several other cases, e.g. 371, 377).
21. These figures are all gleaned from cases in MCI and MCE. For the rise in premiums, see Defoe (1715) pp. 260–1; Defoe (1724) pp. 10–11; Dunlop (1912) pp. 199–204 suggests that premiums were relatively new but see Thrupp (1948) p. 214 for premiums being paid in the fourteenth century.
22. Jordan (1960) pp. 166–72; MCE 1678–9 Maslyn v. Phipps; 1680–1 Parsons v. Royce.
23. Dunton (1705) pp. 34–9; cf. Beloff (1942) p. 39; MCE 1680–1 Gawden v. Harris.
24. Campbell (1747) p. 304; see also Dunlop (1912) p. 54, Miège (1691) iii, 112; *Laws* (1765) p. 112. It seems clear that some masters failed to enrol

apprentices for reasons of deliberate fraud, using this loophole to get rid of their apprentices after a few years and then take on a new lad with a new premium. See, for instance, MCI 377 (1680). Contracts were broken by sueing in the Common Law side of the Mayor's Court – see the cases in MCE – and attempts to recover premiums were normally made on the Equity side of the same court – see MCI.

25. GHMS 12017 pp. 19–20; MCI 413; MCI 444.
26. MCI 441; MCI 420.
27. Defoe (1724) pp. 12–13.
28. Kirkman (1673) pp. 35–6; MCI 358.
29. MCI 358; on the work done by merchants' apprentices, see Vernon (1678), MCI 358, 391 etc.
30. Campbell (1747) p. 283; cf. pp. 195–6; MCI 377; MCI 379; MCI 373.
31. On the education of surgeons, see Peachey (1924) Ch. 1; on apothecaries, Wall et al (1963) pp. 76–90; on masterpieces, Dunlop (1912) Ch. 13.
32. Mason (1754) pp. 14–19; North (1890) ii, 37; Kirkman (1673) pp. 46–7; MCI 70; MCI 419.
33. Dunlop (1912) pp. 196–7; Nichols (1812–15) i, 307; MCI 427.
34. On service in general, see Kussmaul (1981).
35. MCI 413B.
36. For some complaints about food, see MCI 67, 391, 461. On diet in general, see pp. 279–80; for some violence, see MCE 1680–1 Parsons v. Foyce; MCI 66.
37. MCI 62, 368, 370, 377, 382, 385.
38. Defoe (1726–7) i, 129; MCE 1680–1; GHMS 12017 p. 20; the only figures for pocket money which I have come across are fairly low, £2 p.a. for a linen-draper's apprentice (MCI 382), £4 p.a. for a goldsmith-banker's son (S.246), but it is clear from the evidence in lawsuits that many apprentices had far more than this to spend.
39. MCI 358 (1678).
40. MCI 382, 390; cf. 358, 369, 378, 391 etc.
41. MCI 371, 377, 379, 390 etc.
42. Miège (1691) iii, 112; MCI 42, 48, 66, 368, 371, 386 etc.
43. Glass (1969) p. 386; S. R. Smith (1973) p. 196; Finlay (1981) p. 67, drawing on work by Elliott, estimates that there were 32,000–40,000 apprentices in 1600 and 27,200–32,640 in 1700, a huge relative fall from 13.6–17.0 per cent of total population to 4.0–4.8 per cent; for a study of the apprentices as 'adolescents', see S. R. Smith (1973) (2).

4 Business

1. This was probably true in Elizabethan London. Rappaport (1984) pp. 115–23 shows that about half of all masters opened their first shops more than 18 months after freedom and that the average delay was three years. His data also indicate that nearly half of all freemen eventually became

masters. Such figures suggest that many masters were financing themselves at least partly by saving wages.

2. Young merchants could built up capital from commissions earned abroad (see p. 35). Some young men also received salaries or commissions as managers or factors in domestic businesses and these earnings were likely to be far higher than those of a book-keeper.

3. Campbell (1747) pp. 337ff; Collyer (1761) *passim*.

4. Campbell (1747) p. 64.

5. S.113; PRO C105/15, Herne v. Barber. Letters from John to James Hudson dated 2 February 1732 and 25 February 1733.

6. 90 out of 275 whose age at marriage is known married at these ages and another 33 married under 24. See pp. 180–5 for a general discussion of age at marriage – the median for the whole sample was 27.

7. GLRO DL/C/247 fos 149–50 (Tarry); for examples of apprentices marrying their masters' daughters, see note 31 of Chapter 7 below.

8. Jordan (1960) pp. 68, 172–7; James (1948) pp. 158–9; Johnson (1922) iv, 323, shows that the Drapers' Company lent 42 legacy parcels to young men in 1687–8, a total of £6900 or about £165 per man. Other examples include the Grocers, who had 30 different legacies totalling £3660 lent out to 81 people in 1635–6 (average £45) (GHMS 11732), and the Fishmongers, who had 35 legacies totalling £2755 lent out to 77 men in 1690 (average £36) (GHMS 6248).

9. Defoe (1726–7) i, 258–74; 34 of the sample were in partnerships and 341 were not, as far as one can tell from the inventories. In analysing the bankruptcy data for 1711–15, lower percentages of partners were found, 8.8 per cent of creditors and 5.8 per cent of debtors. The commonest occupations amongst these 110 partnerships were merchants (32), linen-drapers (19), haberdashers (7), warehousemen (6), mercers (5) woollen-drapers (5), silkmen (4). PRO B4/1–2. For the analysis of this data, see Appendix C, p. 409. These figures understate the proportion of partnerships, since on occasion individuals both sued and were sued without reference to their partnerships, so that the 10 per cent derived from the sample is probably fairly accurate.

10. Defoe (1726–7) i, 312–15; Marshall (1974) pp. 89–90; Barbon (1690) pp. 27–8; cf. William Petty, who stated that traders should not rise 'into debt above halfe the stocke they set up with' (quoted by Hoppit (1986) (2) p. 66).

11. North (1890) i, 53. The story relates to the 1660s.

12. Defoe (1726–7) i, 345–6, quoted by Yamey (1949) p. 104.

13. *Review* vi, 129–32; cf. iii, 21–7, 33–5; v, 519–20; Defoe (1726–7) i, 412–13; Defoe (1729) p. 19.

14. S.25.

15. Brown (1760) iv, 156; PRO C108/30, letter dated 4 November 1763; Knatchbull quoted by Federer (1980) p. 10; GHMS 205/2; PRO C108/353, Greening v. Greening, Thomas Greening to his father, 19 February 1740.

16. GHMS 11892A, Mitford to George Mallabar, 1 February 1704. As an example of slow payment, one might take the group of Board of Works

tradesmen, who in 1719 claimed to be owed about £40,000 for work performed in George I's reign (from 1714), £20,294 from Queen Anne's reign (1702–14) and £54,910 from the reign of William III (1689–1702). Quoted in Federer (1980) p. 8.

17. Defoe (1726–7) i, 433–4; price quotations from GHMS 11892A, 19017/1, PRO C105/5, C104/44; *CJ* xxv, 46; see also Price (1980) pp. 97, 100, 108–9 for discounts of 6 and 10 per cent per annum granted to merchants in the later eighteenth century who paid in advance of the time for which they had been given credit.

18. The extent of liabilities and the range of their proportion to assets (from 0 to well over 100 per cent), together with fact that virtually all occupations can be found amongst those with both high and low liabilities, suggest that attempts to deduce net wealth from probate inventories, which only very rarely list liabilities, must be very suspect.

19. Most of the sub-groups of assets distinguished in Table 4.6 are simple enough to identify in inventories. The main problem lies in the distinction between 'trade credit' and 'personal loans'. Loans made on real security, such as pawns or mortgages, are easy to identify but those made on personal security can easily be confused with normal trade credit. To get round this problem, an assumption has been made. All debts owing to the deceased in round figures and secured by bond or other formal instrument (or round figures plus interest at the normal rate of 6 per cent) have been identified as loans and all other debts have been treated as trade credit. In most cases, this is realistic enough. Many lists of debts start with figures such as £500, £100, £103, £101 10s., £50, £53 etc., all secured by bonds, and then continue with non-rounded and unsecured figures. But, in some cases, there is ambiguity and one must accept that there is a measure of uncertainty in the distinction between the two types of debt. However, the distinction is worth trying to make, especially for the analysis of investment in the next chapter.

20. S.126 and S.303. The value of equipment cannot always be distinguished from stock in trade but other largish valuations were two printers with £388 and £400 and a sugar refiner with about £300 (S.37, 66, 355). Valuations of such items do, however, pose a problem since they are likely to be old and may well be valued at 'scrap' prices, while stock-in-trade was normally fairly new and would be valued at wholesale prices.

21. In the 81 inventories which give this information, the median proportion of doubtful and desperate debts to all debts was 31 per cent. These figures are likely to exaggerate bad debts since the really good debts might well have been called in before the inventory was drawn up. The mercers, Alexander and Bostock, had cumulated bad debts equal to 13 per cent of all debts in 1714 and 10 per cent in 1721, figures which may better represent a general pattern (PRO C110/43). Carlton (1974) p. 44 makes the point that, by setting down good debts as doubtful debts, executors were in a position to cheat legatees entitled to a fixed proportion of the estate, especially children.

22. Vanderlint (1734) p. 142.

23. Some good examples of such letters can be found in the letter-book of a London tailor, PRO C108/30.

24. Vernon (1678) p. 184. On the custom of London relating to 'foreign attachment' see *Laws* (1765) pp. 113 ff.

25. *CJ* xlvii, 645. See Innes (1983) pp. 251–61 for a clear summary of the legal process for collecting debts in the late eighteenth century, which was very much the same as in our period. See also Francis (1986), who, in a very detailed study, emphasizes the attractiveness of common law litigation for the creditor. So long as the creditor could prove the debt, he had a very high probability of complete recovery, whilst the convicted debtor had to pay all costs, making debt collection through the courts a very cheap operation. The very predictability of the legal process provided the creditor with the means effectively to threaten the debtor by the issue of a writ and the pre-trial process. He concludes (p. 905) that 'the promotion of strict, objective attitudes towards debtor performance displaced more lenient social attitudes towards debtors', one more instance of the increasingly capitalist world portrayed in this book. See also Francis (1983) for the development of a more 'certain' contract law in the seventeenth century, a development which he sees as a result of a mutual interest between common lawyers seeking maximum income and businessmen seeking maximum certainty in recovering their debts. My thanks to Henry Horwitz for these two references.

26. Numbers would depend on whether there had recently been an Act to clear the gaols of poor prisoners. In 1791, there were 1957 prisoners for debt in English gaols, of whom 1251 were on mesne process (i.e. awaiting trial), 570 in the King's Bench and 260 in the Fleet Prison, the two main debtors' prisons in London. There would probably have been at least as many in our period since, despite the smaller population, the prisons were cleared less frequently and charitable organizations to free poor prisoners were not so prominent. Defoe claimed that there were 5000 prisoners for debt, but this is almost certainly an exaggeration. *CJ* xlvii, 646; *Review* iii, 90; v, 579–83; for a summary of Defoe's views on imprisonment for debt, see Owens & Furbank (1986).

27. *Parliamentary History* viii, 711, 723.

28. Defoe (1729) pp. 17–21.

29. Vernon (1678) pp. 183–4; *CSPD* 1675–6, p. 86; *CJ* xiii, 36b, 92, 126, 414; and for an excellent general discussion of Courts of Conscience, see Winder (1936).

30. Vernon (1678) pp. 173–7.

31. On private compositions, see Vernon (1678) pp. 167–72; Defoe (1726–7) i, 204–24; Philips (1731) pp. 8–9. All lay writers stress the advantages of compositions over formal bankruptcies.

32. Vernon (1678) pp. 185–6; for a clear summary of the laws of bankruptcy, see Duffy (1980). See also Holdsworth (1903–72) viii, 229–45; xi, 445–6; W. R. Jones (1979). The standard contemporary textbook was Goodinge (1713). Only 'traders' could become bankrupt, a rather vague description which covers virtually everyone who is the subject of this book except such professionals as doctors and lawyers and some people in artisan

trades. Gentlemen could not become bankrupts, unless they were also
traders, and therefore could only be sued on a first come first served basis
for insolvency, though it was of course open to their creditors to agree to a
private composition.

33. *Essay* (1707) p. iv; for a spirited defence of the new laws, see Defoe
(1706). The Acts are 4, 5 Anne c.17 and 6 Anne c.22. Further small
changes in the law were embodied in a codifying Act of 1732 (5 Geo. II
c.30) which fixed the law until the end of the eighteenth century. Quotation
from *Review* vi, 551.

34. Defoe (1726–7) i, 84; *Essay* (1707) p. 2.

35. Hoppit (1986) (1) pp. 45–7 and W. R. Jones (1979) p. 5 for overall
rates of bankruptcy; numbers of cheesemongers (411) and taverns (447)
from Maitland (1739) p. 531; for the number of apothecaries, see Ch. 2,
note 140, above; numbers of bankrupts from PRO B4/1–2, the tavern-
keepers were described as vintners. Other high numbers of bankrupts
relative to likely total numbers include merchants (133), mercers (27),
linen-drapers (26), brewers (14), dyers (13) and shipwrights (7). Other
vulnerable businesses were probably normally too small to merit a
commission of bankruptcy. There were, for instance, only 11 distillers, 9
haberdashers and 18 victuallers amongst the bankrupts in these years,
while the building industry, often cited as very prone to bankruptcy, hardly
shows up at all, just 8 carpenters and 1 bricklayer.

36. See the rough calculation of the numbers of middle station households
on p. 80–1. The 20 years is calculated on the basis that most careers started
at about 25 and the average age at death of the sample was 45.

37. Barbon (1690) p. 2.

38. For an example of a man who had adopted this strategy, see S.39,
Moses Ingram. He had zero liabilities and his capital was invested in 11
loans secured by bonds and some tenements in Leadenhall Street. There
are many others in the sample. Older men tended progressively to shift
their capital into this sort of investment portfolio.

39. Defoe (1726–7) i, 75–6; PRO C108/284.

40. Marshall (1974) pp. 95–6; GHMS 18760/1, Boughey to Dr Humphrey
Babington, 9 March 1675.

41. Matthews (1906) pp. 22–3. The maximum rate was lowered to 5 per
cent in 1714. Very secure borrowers like the East India Company could
borrow well below the maximum, but most of the bonds held by men in our
sample carried interest at the maximum.

42. Ashton (1959) pp. 86–7; CLRO MCI 375; Orchard & May (1933) pp.
35–7; Sybil Campbell (1933); Price (1980) p. 60.

43. Goodinge (1713) p. A3; Defoe (1726–7) i, p. viii.

44. On renting and leasing shops and houses, see pp. 207–9. Price (1980)
p. 100 gives an example of a merchant in the 1770s borrowing on bond at 5
per cent to earn discounts of 10 per cent for early payment. This must have
been very common. Federer (1980); PRO C108/353, Greening v. Greening.

45. Barbon (1690) p. 19; Defoe (1726–7) ii, 133–4.

46. PRO C107/140, Ashton v. Harbin. The wharfingers provide another

example. These were the men who ran the 19 'legal quays' between London Bridge and the Tower where all overseas trade had to be unloaded. For much of our period, the wharfingers combined in 'an offensive and illegal monopoly', as their opponents termed it, sharing the profits from the wharves pro rata of their investment (PRO C110/181, Smith v. Ashton; *The Case of the Wharfingers* (1704)). In general on the wharfingers, see Chartres (1980) and for the copperas industry, see Bettey (1982). On the Virginia merchants, see Olson (1983).

47. *Case* (1711) (1); *Case* (n.d.) (1); PRO C108/132, undated but probably 1720s.

48. PRO C114/56 pt 2 (Palmer); GHMS 15892A (Mitford).

49. For examples of correspondence in wholesale trades, see PRO C108/132 (letters to Henry Gambier, tea and china dealer), C105/15 (letters to James Hudson, mainly a linen trader but also hats, butter and a host of other things). See Margaret Evans (1977) for the wholesale apothecaries Estwick & Coningsby, nearly all of whose provincial correspondents were kin or in-laws of one or other of the partners, a fact which determined the regional concentration of their business. Nearly all James Hudson's English business was with his native north country and his brother was his chief correspondent and all his correspondents were brother Quakers (PRO C105/15, Herne v. Barber). Inventories which give addresses of debtors also often demonstrate a regional concentration (e.g. S.171, Peter Short, whose wholesale haberdashery business was concentrated in the east Midlands and Yorkshire). A hint of regional concentration can also often be seen in the addresses of the debtors of those London wholesalers who sued more than one provincial bankrupt. The salter Thomas Constable sued three bankrupts in the period 1711–15, one each in Bury St Edmunds, Cambridge and Norwich; the mercers Lane & Harrison sued three mercers in Frome, Wellington (Somerset) and Devizes, while the two mercers sued by Shewell & Allen lived in Staffordshire and Shropshire. One should not exaggerate such concentration, however, since such easy patterns do not emerge in every case. PRO B4/1–2. For the analysis of these docket-books, see Appendix C, p. 409.

50. These examples are all from the correspondence of James Hudson in PRO C105/15, Herne v. Barber, letters of 10 October 1731, 2 February 1732 & 19 April 1733 from his brother John and a letter of 18 March 1732 from Anthony Wilson. For a book on the influence of seasonability generally, see E. L. Jones (1964).

51. PRO C105/15, Herne v. Barber, John to James Hudson, 2 February 1732.

52. On the history of negotiable instruments, see, in particular, Holden (1951) and Holden (1955). Promissory notes, which had formerly been known as 'writings obligatory' or 'bills of debt', were simply writings in some such form as 'I promise to pay A or order so much at such and such a time for value received'. They had no standing at law in the early seventeenth century but were indorsable and negotiable by the end. The inland or foreign bill was similar to a post-dated cheque. 'Pay A or order so

much at such and such a time and place to my account.' Although principally a method of remitting money, the bill incorporated credit till the due date and, in foreign bills, a speculation in the movement of exchange rates since the sum mentioned would be worth more or less in other currencies by the time the bill was presented. There were normally four names on a bill, the 'drawer', who instructed the 'drawee' to pay the 'payee', and the 'deliverer' who had given value to the 'drawer' in the first place. 'Drawer' and 'drawee' and 'deliverer' and 'payee' were often two sets of business associates. Indorsement simply meant that the 'payee' wrote on the back of the bill or note, 'Pay the contents on the other side to B', thus making it negotiable. The legal problem had been to determine just what rights B had, since his name did not appear on the original bill. Normal practice was for the drawer to advise the drawee by letter that he had drawn the bill. The drawee then 'accepted' it and made payment at the due date. If the drawee refused to pay an accepted bill, he was liable in law. If he refused to accept the bill (perhaps because he had been given no advice or because the drawer had made no prior arrangements), then the payee could sue the drawer for the money.

53. On the butchers and graziers, see M. G. Davies (1971), who discusses the dominant role assumed by Smithfield as a source of cash in London for the country gentry who used their rents to buy claims to funds in London. In the late seventeenth century, simple instructions in the form of a letter were being replaced by bills and non-commercial people had to be carefully instructed in the conventions surrounding the use of bills. For some nice examples, see the correspondence of the merchant Thomas Boughey with Dr Humphrey Babington of Trinity College, Cambridge (GHMS 18760/1, letters of 9 & 16 March 1675). For Compigne and Gambier, see a mass of letters in C108/132. The quotation is dated Winton, 29 June 1730.

54. Yamey (1969) pp. 109–10.

55. GLRO DL/C/245 fos 79–80, 349–58; /247 fos 149–50.

56. Grassby (1969) pp. 728–9.

57. Grassby (1969) p. 733 and see pp. 728–36 for examples of profits from our period; Barbon (1690) p. 32.

58. PRO C110/185, Unwin v. Unwin; C110/43, Alexander & Bostock; C103/160, Burgess & Taylor; C110/167, Herne v. Humphreys; C110/179, Staunton & Thorne.

59. *CJ* xxv, 46–7; purchase of food was obviously income inelastic; so was the purchase of more durable domestic goods, as is shown on pp. 120–1, 291.

60. Marshall (1920) p. 228.

61. Grassby (1969) p. 734; see also pp. 728, 732; North (1890) ii, 409–10; for rates of interest on loans in Syria, see the account book kept by Thomas Palmer as a young factor in Aleppo, PRO C114/56 pt 2; on marriage contracts and dowries, see pp. 194–8.

62. For mortality, see pp. 306–9 and see Earle (1986) pp. 55–63 for a development of this argument about the effects of mortality on accumulation. For the growing tendency for sons to follow their fathers into business, see N. Rogers (1979) and Horwitz (1987) (1).

5 Investment

1. The breakdown was investment assets (35 per cent), business assets and cash (61.7 per cent) and domestic goods, plate and jewellery (3.3 per cent). The percentages for investments are calculated by adding together the two figures for 'personal loans' and 'other investments' in Table 4.6 (p. 121). For the method used to distinguish 'personal loans' from 'trade credits', see note 19 of Chapter 4, above.

2. This investment cycle is not as simple as suggested in Morris (1979). Morris analysed three sets of business papers to demonstrate a regular progression from business to rentier activity as businessmen got older. Our sample supports his general hypothesis, but the data suggest that the timing and degree of rentier activity varied very considerably.

3. For the changing life expectancy of the London middle class, see pp. 306–9.

4. Mortgages formed only 7 per cent of the total of loans and mortgages, confirming the view of D. W. Jones that lending on mortgage was not an important part of the investment activities of the London business community (D. W. Jones (1972) (1) pp. 338, 353). For the view that ruining gentlemen by lending to them on the security of mortgages was one of the main activities of London tradesmen, see Tawney (1925) pp. 35–42.

5. On this subject see, in particular, Dickson (1967).

6. For an alternative view that it was money diverted from trade by wartime dislocations which provided this finance, see D. W. Jones (1972) (1).

7. For books providing guides to valuations, see Leybourn (1668), Primatt (1667), Phillips (1719). See also Grassby (1969) pp. 739–40.

8. See S.44, 49, 73, 115, 152 for builders as developers; for a scrivener who handled many mortgages, see PRO C107/70–72, 113.

9. On shipowning, see pp. 40, 76 and R. Davis (1962) pp. 81–100. On earnings from capital invested in shipping, see R. Davis (1957).

10. For a full description of the different forms of government debt and an analysis of those who held the debt in sample years, see Dickson (1967).

11. On the government lotteries, see Ewen (1932) pp. 127–63.

12. Ewen (1932) pp. 137–9. PRO E401/2599–2600 has the names of the beneficiaries of the First and Second Classis Lotteries.

13. It should be noted that the men in our sample were virtually all dead by the time of the excitement surrounding the South Sea Bubble in 1720. This no doubt tempted more small men to dabble in the stock market but, as has been recently shown, the Bubble year was not a bad one for commercial bankruptcies and most of those who burned their fingers were either gentlemen with little experience or rather foolish members of the 'mercantile bourgeoisie'. See Hoppit (1986) (1) pp. 47–8 and in general on the Bubble, see Carswell (1960).

14. S.354.

15. Coventry quoted by Stone (1984) p. 18; de Muralt (1726) p. 9; Defoe (1726–7) ii, i, 159–82.

16. Lindsay (1978) p. 194. For a general discussion of the return on landed property, see Clay (1974) and for a recent revisionist approach, see Allen

(1988), who puts the net return on land rather higher than Lord Hervey (p. 34).

17. Three main sources have been used to get information on real estate holdings – unpaid rents in inventories where these are specifically described as rents for freehold or copyhold property or where there is no corresponding leasehold property listed; memoranda in the Common Serjeants' Books, which often mention real property; wills, which nearly always mention real property if there was any. Altogether, 181 wills (48 per cent of the whole sample and 80 per cent of those described as testate) have been found. It seems probable that, using all three sources, not much real property has been missed.

18. S.61, 89, 218; S.157.

19. For descriptions of such property, see Defoe (1724–6) i, 168–9 and ii, 2–3. For an analysis of the Middlesex villa market, see Martindale (1968).

20. S.157, 171, 276; Defoe (1724–6) i, 168–9.

21. Stone (1984).

22. Habakkuk (1940); Habakkuk (1960); Holden (1955).

6 Women and Business

1. Kenny (1879) p. 13.

2. Defoe (1724) (2) p. 148.

3. Quoted by Stone (1977) p. 331. There is a huge literature on the common law status of married women; for valuable studies, see Kenny (1879) and Holdsworth (1903–72) iii, 520–33. See also the contemporary legal texts, e.g. *Baron & Feme* (1719) and *Treatise* (1732). For a general book, see Reiss (1934).

4. *Treatise* (1732) p. 91.

5. Quoted by Kenny (1879) p. 100. On the doctrine of separate estate and the associated 'equity to a settlement', see Kenny (1879) pp. 98–115; Holdsworth (1903–72) v, 310–14; vi, 644–6, xii, 275–6; Okin (1983).

6. For the custom and legal decisions relating to it, see Holdsworth (1903–72) ii, 387; iii, 323; Bohun (1702) pp. 124–5; *Baron & Feme* (1719) p. 304; *Treatise* (1732) pp. 91, 104; *Laws* (1765) p. 111. For the *feme sole* in later medieval London, see Lacey (1985) pp. 42–5.

7. Defoe (1726–7) i, 348–68; for an interesting recent article on women in business in this period, see Prior (1985).

8. Defoe loc. cit; *Advice* (1678), see advertisement in Vernon (1678).

9. Literacy rates show a remarkable rise during our period. See Cressy (1980) p. 144, Table 7.2, which shows a fall in female illiteracy in London and Middlesex from 80–90 per cent of a sample drawn from the period 1580–1640 to under 50 per cent in the early eighteenth century. See also Earle (1989) for the literacy of London women and, in general, on the female labour market in the London of our period.

10. Campbell (1747) p. 189.

11. Clark (1919).

12. Defoe (1726–7) i, 355; Clark (1919) pp. 35–6; Stone (1977) pp. 350–1.

13. Mandeville (1709) p. 128; Child (1694) pp. 4–5.
14. Defoe (1724) (2) pp. 148–9; social comment on idle women can be found scattered through the pages of the *Tatler* and *Spectator*. Some of the most savage invective came from the pen of Swift, e.g. *The Progress of Marriage* (1722); *The Journal of a Modern Lady* (1729).
15. MCI.
16. Alice Clark claimed that one indication of a decline in the role of wives in business was a growing reluctance of husbands to appoint them as sole executrixes (Clark (1919) p. 39). She gave no evidence for this assertion but it was tested against our sample. From 164 wills (excluding those of widowers), it was found that 21 per cent of men appointed their widow as sole executrix with no overseers, 57 per cent appointed the widow as joint-executrix or sole executrix with (normally male) overseers to assist her and 22 per cent did not name the widow as executrix at all. However, when the figures are broken down for those who died before and after 1690, there was an increase in widows as sole executrixes from 12.5 to 36.7 per cent and a decrease in widows not named at all from 25 to 16.6 per cent, the opposite trend to that posited by Alice Clark.
17. Gregory King estimated that there were 98,000 husbands, 10,600 widowers and 37,100 widows in late seventeenth-century London, making widows about a quarter of the combined total (Thirsk & Cooper (1972) p. 773)). In David Glass's analysis of the 1692 Poll Tax, he found that widows were just over 10 per cent of the total of the above three categories (Glass (1969)). Female heads of households should lie somewhere between these two figures, since many of King's widows would be dependants, while many female householders would be too poor to pay the Poll Tax. Many of these widows were probably not heads of households for very long since, contrary to rural English experience, London widows of the middle station were quick to re-marry (Brodsky (1986) pp. 122–34).
18. PRO B4/1–2. See Appendix C for more on these records. Since writing this chapter, I have done much more work on the women's labour market in London. See Earle (1989).
19. Glass (1969) p. 580, Table 5 (52 women and 622 men).
20. This sample was drawn from GHMS 11936/23–29 (1726–29); 281 (89 per cent) of the policies were held by a woman on her own, 16 (5 per cent) by two women and 20 (6 per cent) by a woman together with a man.
21. This assumption does not ignore the possibility that women in the second group also had wages or paper securities and that women in the third group lived off all the various types of income.
22. Sun 39146, 40120.
23. These inventories are in PRO PROB 4/1/1–1300. Since there are about 25,000 inventories in the whole series, this is probably about a 5 per cent sample of all inventories of London widows in this series.
24. PRO PROB 4/1/107 and 171.
25. CLRO Orphans 1049; cf. 331 for another pawnbroker and 414, 473, 492, 516, 639, 664, 699, 706, 788, 933, 940, 960, 1037, 1281, 1428, 1631, 1962, 2041, 2055, 2130, 2746, 2826 for other businesses run by women.

26. For the later period, see Johnson (1985).

27. CLRO Orphans 1032, 1086, 964. Cf. 347B, 451, 713, 1026, 1151, 1278, 1293, 1351, 1894 for other widows living on rentier investments.

28. The bargain was not all on one side. Vivien Brodsky has recently shown that the literary emphasis on the lusty remarrying widow who very often married a younger man was by no means the fiction that some historians have suggested (Brodsky (1986)).

7 Marriage

1. Stone (1977), especially p. 274. Trumbach (1978) has a similar thesis to that of Stone, but confines himself explicitly to the aristocracy. For some critics of Stone, see Wrightson (1982) pp. 66–118, Houlbrooke (1984) and Macfarlane (1986). For a good general introduction to modern historical studies of the family, see Anderson (1980).

2. *Treatise* (1732) p. 25; example from GLRO DL/C/165 fo. 233v; in general on this subject, see Swinburne (1686) and Helmholz (1974).

3. Salmon (1724) p. 180; see also Swinburne (1686) p.2.

4. R. L. Brown (1981) pp. 117–36. Much the commonest occupations of London-based grooms given in Fleet registers are those of craftsmen, but 'tradesmen and innkeepers' account for 9 per cent of the occupations recorded between 1700 and 1750 (ibid. p. 126). Brown's figures are probably too high since nearly a quarter of entries in Fleet registers are duplicates. The numbers are also swollen in the early eighteenth century by the marriages of soldiers and sailors (information from Amanda Copley via Jeremy Boulton).

5. Quoted by ibid. p. 124.

6. Misson (1719) p. 183; see also Jeaffreson (1872) p. 134, R. L. Brown (1981) p. 124; Frith (1954), introduction, has a discussion of the licence system.

7. Misson (1719) pp. 351–3.

8. Elliott (1981) p. 82.

9. Hajnal (1965); Macfarlane (1986); Wrigley & Schofield (1983) pp. 157–84.

10. Elliott (1981) pp. 84–6. Her analysis was based on GHMS 10091/1–7. Nothing much seems to have changed by our period, judging from my analysis of a small sample of licence applications for the years 1667, 1696, 1715 and 1730 in GHMS 10091. The early age at marriage for women in London is confirmed by Finlay in his reconstitution study of four parishes, which had average ages for women at first marriage of 23.0, 19.7, 21.5 and 23.0 (Finlay (1979) pp. 31–2). There were far more immigrants than London-born in the metropolis so the average age at marriage in London would be nearer the immigrant average but still considerably younger than elsewhere in the country.

11. Closeness in age between marriage partners is sometimes seen as a *prima facie* case for assuming that love has played a more important part in the choice of partners than other considerations such as money or dynastic

strategy. Such assumptions are impossible to prove but, if they were true, then our results would throw considerable doubt on Stone's thesis that it was the upper bourgeoisie who pioneered the marriage based on affection and companionship, since it is this group which have the biggest age difference between bride and groom (Stone (1977) pp. 274–81, 294, 362 etc.). It is possible that this pattern of men marrying much younger wives may have been reversed in the common circumstances of the remarriage of widows. From a reconstruction of late sixteenth-century data, Vivien Brodsky found more than half of widows remarrying single men of whom a large proportion were younger than their brides (Brodsky (1986) pp. 122–34, esp. p. 127).

12. For a discussion of age at marriage in terms of such strategies, see Wrigley (1983) and see also Macfarlane (1986), where a basic reason why Westerners got married later than other people was because they saw marriage and children as something economically costly which would be unlikely to bring about the economic benefits assumed in most other parts of the world, where marriage created no new expense in the form of a separate household and children were regarded as an economic asset.

13. Tryon (1691) p. 463; Dunton (1705) p. 70. One should note too that merchants often spent most of their early years in business overseas and so would not be in a position to start their courtships until they were 30 or so.

14. Thirsk & Cooper (1972) p. 773.

15. Defoe (1722) p. 18.

16. Laslett (1965) pp. 81–9 worries that we get the wrong idea about the age at marriage of girls from the creative literature of the past. However, playwrights would be quite realistic to produce drama for an upper- and middle-class London audience in terms of girls thinking it normal to be married by the age of 21 and not all that unusual to be married at 18.

17. Defoe (1722) p. 58.

18. Stone (1977) pp. 274–81 discusses the gradual victory of more liberal views on this subject in the late seventeenth and eighteenth centuries; Macfarlane (1986) pp. 120–47 and Wrightson (1982) p. 78 find liberal views at an earlier date, though Macfarlane emphasizes the greater importance of parents' advice in the middling ranks (p. 132). Gillis (1985), on the other hand, emphasizes the continuing importance of family, friends and community, though he does not suggest that such influence prevented individual choice, just that it made it very difficult to fly in the face of contrary advice.

19. Dunton (1703–8) p. 148; for a rather more liberal approach, see Taylor (1650) p. 201; Defoe in *Review* i, 272 distinguished between those over 21 who should regard their father's advice 'with the utmost deference' and those under age 'who ought not to disobey him, nor ask his reasons'.

20. In the period March 1667 to March 1668, there were 30 London spinsters over 21 whose parental consent was recorded and 49 where it was not; in January to September 1696, the figures are 28 and 47. In both periods, the median age of those with consent was 22 and without was 26 (GHMS 10091/27 & 33). In the early eighteenth century, recorded parental

consent for over age girls declines very considerably, possibly reflecting a change of attitude but quite likely merely a change of recording practice (GHMS 10091/51 & 70 for 1715 and 1730).

21. GHMS 10823/1 pp. 59–64.

22. *Laws* (1765) p. 68.

23. GHMS 10823/1 pp. 63–4; CLRO, Common Serjeants' Books. These record the division of estates and have memoranda which would surely have mentioned the disinheritance of daughters if this had occurred.

24. S.246 (Williams); cf. S.177 and 303; S.13, 93, 99, 101, 212 (if she married without consent her £500 legacy to his other daughter), 250 (with consent a legacy of £2000, without consent an annuity of £100 p.a.), 319, 337; S.85, S.347 (Sellers), S.279 (Cary).

25. E.g. DL/C/246 fos 129, 132 – Greenell v. Tucker (1699).

26. Ryder (1939) pp. 309–10; Dunton (1705) p. 90; GLRO DL/C246 fo. 129; DL/C/247 fo. 92. For discussions of contemporary literature, see Stone (1977) pp. 275–6; Macfarlane (1986) pp. 174–6, who claims that this stress on a companionate marriage was peculiarly English and surprised foreigners, e.g. the French.

27. See Earle (1976) pp. 252–60 for Defoe's views on this subject.

28. Ryder (1939) p. 310.

29. Defoe (1722) (2) p. 6; for an interesting analysis of the stress caused by courtship problems, very often the result of parents, friends or employers forbidding marriage to loved ones, see MacDonald (1981) pp. 72–111.

30. Tryon (1691) p. 452; Baxter (1673) p. 481; Ryder (1939) p. 224.

31. S.27 (Pocock); S.281 (Melmoth); cf. S.146, 203, 228, 253, 265 for others in the sample who married their master's daughter and S.270 for Luke Meredith who married his master's grand-daughter.

32. S.14, 37, 115, 77.

33. Miège (1691) p. 262.

34. Quotations from a defamation case, Fawden v. Wilkins, in GLRO DL/C/245 fo. 215. Large numbers of these cases were brought annually during our period, nearly always by women who had been called whore, harlot etc. in public.

35. Dunton (1705) p. 48; Mason (1754) p. 17.

36. This paragraph is based on the general impression gained from evidence in a number of court cases, mainly in GLRO DL/C/245–8.

37. PRO C5/92/13; C5/594/22; Brown (1760) iii, 54; cf. Defoe on marriage broking in *Review* ix, 82.

38. PRO C5/631/107; C5/436/151.

39. For estimates of the return on land, see Clay (1974) and Allen (1988). There is a huge literature on upper-class marriage contracts; for a recent contribution with many references, see Outhwaite (1986). A settlement by jointure was made by a minimum of 30 of our sample; there may have been a few more amongst those whose wills have not been found but the total is unlikely to be more than 10 per cent of the sample. References to jointures can be found in wills, in memoranda of the Common Serjeants' Books and occasionally in inventories. S.250 (March); cf. S.304, 329, 354; PRO C5/

183/76; C5/417/25; the mercer Joshua Monger sold the lands which he had with his wife Rebecca as her portion and which were supposed to secure her jointure, 'by her consent'. He then provided in his will that the sale price of £420 'be taken out of the estate and bestowed and laid out by the executrix on the purchase of lands . . . to be settled on my wife for life' (S.67, PRO PROB 11/344 fo. 48).

40. GHMS 12017 p. 23 (Fryer); S.57 (Ewens); cf. S.8 (marriage covenant £1000, estate £1216), S.346 (£2000, £1053); PRO C5/189/26 (Tandin); S.170 (Skrine).

41. There were 18 men who had pre-contracted by bond in the sample; since the sum appears as a debt in the inventory, it is unlikely that any have been missed. For jointures, see note 39 above; Mandeville (1709) p. 112; Defoe (1722) p. 58. On separate estate, see p. 159. On pin-money, see Kenny (1879) pp. 116–17. It seems to have been quite common amongst the landed classes in our period. For an example of an agreement for the wife to will part of her dowry, see PRO C5/60/6, Berry v. Skinner, where John Berry received £700 portion with Thomasin Skinner 'but prior to marriage Thomasin got his agreement that £200 of her portion be hers to will as she thought fit'. Such agreements were often made by widows to protect the children of previous marriages.

42. For a summary of the debate on this subject, see Outhwaite (1986).

43. GHMS 10823/1 p. 42. For some examples of the effects of the high mortality of husbands and wives in their prime, see Brodsky (1986) pp. 137–40.

44. PRO C5/181/84, Robinson v. Allen (Mackernes), C5/273/44, Tysoe v. Harman (Thomas Robinson).

45. See note 1 above for references.

46. On the legal position, see pp. 158–60; for the double standard, see Thomas 1959); for conduct books, see Powell (1917).

47. Ryder (1939) p. 274.

48. On divorce, see Macfarlane (1986) esp. pp. 227–33 and the references he cites; for examples of deeds of separation, see PRO C107/176, Walker v. Bevis and C110/147, Attorney-General v. Whittington, though both of these relate to gentry marriages. The main court dealing with divorce in London was the Consistory Court, whose records are kept in GLRO. The discussion of alimony is based on eight cases recorded in GLRO DL/C/98, covering the period 1696/97. The weekly payments were 4s., 5s., 6s., 6s.3d., 7s.6d., 10s., 10s., 10s. On alimony and maintenance, see *Treatise* (1732) pp. 171–2.

49. *Treatise* (1732) pp. 91–2.

50. GLRO DL/C/245 fo.93; Defoe (1724) pp. 6–7; GLRO DL/C/245 fo. 196.

51. Particular references are not given for all the quotations in the rest of the chapter. They all come from GLRO DL/C/165 and /245–248.

8 The Household

1. E. Jones (1980) p. 126.
2. For studies on the social topography of seventeenth-century London, see

E. Jones (1980); Finlay (1981) pp. 77–81 based on data for the City in the 1630s; Jones & Judges (1935–6); Glass (1966) p.xxiii based on data for the City in the 1690s; Power (1986) based on data for the whole metropolis in the 1660s.

3. Nothing much had changed by the 1790s, when L. D. Schwarz found a distribution of rich and poor very similar to that found by Power for the 1660s. He also found the middling people spread 'remarkably evenly across London, forming about a tenth of the population everywhere, irrespective of the wealth or poverty of their parish' (Schwarz (1982) p. 174).

4. Defoe (1724–6) ii, 2. Another 29 men in the sample had a residence in London and a second country residence which was normally not far from the outskirts of the metropolis. Other people used to rent houses or apartments in the country for the summer.

5. Simond (1817) i, 64 quoted by Summerson (1962) p. 67; Chs 4 and 5 of the latter provide a good introduction to the London house of our period.

6. Descriptions of houses in this section rely largely on inventories. These give a good idea of numbers and location of rooms and mention yards, cellars, garrets etc., but give no description of external appearance, measurements etc.

7. Maitland (1739) pp. 294–6; Reddaway (1940) pp. 129–30. In general on the rebuilding, see Reddaway (1940), Bell (1923) and P. E. Jones (1966).

8. At least 138 (37 per cent) of the sample owned a lease of their dwelling-house; others owned leases which are not specifically described as their dwelling-house but which might have been or might just be an investment. In their fullest form, inventories state the number of years to come on a lease, the quit rent, the clear rent if the property is let to a third party, the number of years' purchase and the valuation. Only a minority include all this information. For books on valuation and building costs, see Leybourn (1668), Primatt (1667), Phillips (1719).

9. Average length of lease remaining was 27 years; median 20; range 2½ to 73 years; based on 55 inventories which provide this information. Reddaway (1940) Chs 3 and 4; P. E. Jones (1966) for details of the bargains struck.

10. For examples of valuations with low quit-rents, see S.23, tobacconist in Walbrook (59-year lease, £2 p.a. quit-rent, valued at £374); S.44, builder in Spitalfields for his house, garden and yard (74, £6 p.a., £180); S.77, soapmaker in Bread Street Hill (50, £15 p.a., £340); S.91, merchant in Bevis Marks (41, £5 p.a., £640).

11. A. Smith (1961) i, 131–2; rents can be calculated if unpaid rent for a specific time is listed in inventories. See S.340 (jeweller in Cheapside, £80); for £60, see S.13 (linen-draper in Leadenhall Street); for £50 to £55, see S.40 (rentier in Adam Court, Broad St), S.52 (merchant in St Dunstan's Hill, S.83 (mercer in Milk St), S.224 (merchant in Aldermanbury). For some lower rents, see S.4 (£20, apothecary of St Andrew Undershaft), S.54 (£12, carter in Thames St), S.161 (£30, working goldsmith in Foster Lane), S.164 (£20, comb-maker in Rosemary Lane, Whitechapel). A more comprehensive source for rents can be found in the assessments for the

parliamentary aids from 1689 onwards, later known as the Land Tax (Ward (1953) pp. 6–10). For example, the 1694 aid (5 W&M c.1) was assessed in two parts: 4s. in the £ of one year's value of lands, messuages etc. and 24s. for every £100 of personal estate (i.e. 4s. in the £, assuming that the return on such estate was 6 per cent). In the City, the 'real' part of this assessment was made on the actual or computed rack rents paid by occupiers. It is clear from appeals (CLRO Ass. Box 2, No. 1) that this tax very accurately reflects actual rents, which ranged for those in our sample from £200 p.a. for the merchant John Cary to £12 p.a. for the haberdasher George Fryer. The most seriously affected by this tax were tavern-keepers. John Carter (S.248), for instance, was paying one-fifth of £140 (£28) p.a. as tax on a tavern in King Street, near Guildhall, which since he died in 1697 worth only £484 must have been a very serious drain on his income. The second part of the tax, on personal estate, was grossly underestimated and very regressive. To take two examples, the wine merchant John Newton, who died in 1697, was rated at £200 personal estate and was actually worth £14,402 when he died, while the tavern-keeper mentioned above, John Carter, was also rated at £200 but was actually worth only £484 when he died in 1697. Despite the regressive assessment of this tax, it provides a fairly good indication of the rank order of personal wealth – people who died wealthy generally paying the most and people who died relatively poor the least, despite the particular example above.

12. A. Smith loc. cit; Swift (1948) i, 34; Derbyshire Record Office, Gell Papers, 258/68/11 i, j, l; de Saussure (1902) p. 165; cf. Misson (1719) p. 145. Both the last two foreigners were impressed by the ease with which lodgings could be found.

13. Not all inventories give sufficient detail to determine lay-out. However, many specify that rooms were up one, two or three pair of stairs or in the garret, were at the back, front, middle, east, west etc. The greatest difficulty is with kitchens and dining-rooms, which did not really need any further description since it would be obvious which room was meant. However, position is often clear from the order in which rooms were listed.

14. S.164 (Justice); S.115 (Marshall); see S.259 and 296 for merchants with houses laid out like this.

15. S.94 (Edwards); for examples of 'missing' rooms, see S.95 (only one room on second floor), S.113 (only one room on first and third floors), S.133 (either first or second floor missing).

16. S.272 (Pinder); S.107 (Birkin). Numbers of rooms here and below include bedrooms (inc. garret bedrooms), living rooms and kitchens but do not include such additions to living rooms as closets or to kitchens as wash-houses and butteries; nor do they include cellars or rooms used for work such as shops, workshops or warehouses.

17. For a detailed description of the tax, see Glass (1966).

18. Thirsk & Cooper (1972), p. 772; Jones & Judges (1935) pp. 58–62. See also Glass (1969) for analysis of a sample of parishes within the Walls; in Table 1 (p. 375) he presents figures of 6.03 persons per house (inc. 1.38 children and 1.43 servants and apprentices) for his sample of 40 parishes.

19. London (1966).

20. S.274 (Assessment 4.6); cf. John Hicks (S.309, Ass. 44.31), who left £2370 in 1704; Edward Osborne (S.307, Ass. 9.35), who left £2197 in 1704; Thomas Penford (S.278, Ass. 77.12), who left £1832 in 1701 and Luke Meredith (S.270, Ass. 35.27), who left £1501 in 1700 – all non-payers of surtax who seem unlikely to have accumulated this rapidly. Meredith, for example, would have had to make compound clear profits over all his household expenses of 25 per cent p.a. to have turned £500 into £1500 in just five years. On rates of profit, see pp. 137–42.

21. Wigfall (S.259, Ass. 34.2); Levett (S.317, Ass. 59.24); cf. the banker Thomas Williams (wife and 3 children missing), who had a house at Stratford (S.246, Ass. 71.18) and the merchant Francis March (S.250, Ass. 29.17), who had 3 sons missing, all under the age of apprenticeship, as is known from his will; they were probably at boarding school. For other examples, see the source note at the end of Table 8.3, p. 217.

22. A. Smith (1961) i, 132. 'A tradesman in London is obliged to hire a whole house. . . . His shop is upon the ground-floor, and he and his family sleep in the garret; and he endeavours to pay a part of his house-rent by letting the two middle stories to lodgers.' Very few members of our sample conform to this specification. The 1695 assessments suggest that there were far more lodgers in poorer quarters of the town and in the houses of poorer people and widows.

23. The two people who have been put down as lodgers, a man and a woman of the same surname but not married, were not specified as either lodgers or servants.

24. One can get a fairly good idea of who did or did not employ servants from the schedules drawn up for the Poll Tax and Marriage Duties Tax in the CLRO. Very few people can be said not to belong to the servant employing class simply on the grounds of their occupation.

25. Defoe (1724) p. 139.

26. Defoe (1725) pp. 4, 8. For general comment, see that book and Defoe (1724), and for a wider sampling of contemporary criticism, see Hecht (1956). Our inventories suggest that Defoe exaggerated a little, but correctly discerned the trend, the wages of maids in the 1670s being about £3–3½ a year and in the 1710s about £5–5½.

27. *London Chronicle* (1758) iii, 327c; Defoe (1725) pp. 18–19. Job specification seems to have been the normal pattern, as can be seen from the assessment for St Michael Bassishaw (CLRO Marriage Duties No. 73), which has very detailed information on occupations. See also pp. 220–9 for Pepys's household, where the jobs were always specified.

28. All these epithets are from *The Compleat Servant-Maid* (1677). Wishful thinking did not change much. See *The Servant's Calling* (1725).

29. For Pepys's household, see Pepys vol. x, 193–7; in the same volume there are brief biographical notes on some of his servants. References to servants can be found in the index, vol. xi and detailed references are not given here, except for full quotations.

30. Pepys's clerk, Will Hewer, also lived in the household till November

1663, when he went into lodgings, and his duties also combined personal service and government work.

31. GLRO DL/C/246, Chambers v. Chambers, fos 61–89. See also Earle (1989), where it is estimated that median time in one place was about one year.

32. De Saussure (1902) p. 157; Houghton (1727–8) i, 349. For an interesting discussion of household tasks, see Davidson (1983).

33. Pepys 4/4/1663 and 29/7/1663.

34. E.g. GLRO DL/C/245, Fell v. Fell, fo. 91.

35. I may have missed some of Pepys's groping but, as far as I can see, the chosen girls were the companions Mary Mercer (after 17 months in Pepys's household) and Deb Willet (after 6 months) and the maids Susan (after nearly 2 years' service), Nell Payne (after one month) and Jane Birch (after Pepys had known her for 10 years).

36. Pepys 3/11/1663, 21/2/1664 and 29/8/1664.

37. Pepys 7/1/1663.

38. Pepys 19/2/1665; GLRO DL/C/245 fo. 215; Pepys 20 and 21/8/1663.

39. Pepys 12/11/1662; 8/10/1666; 8/12/1662; 3/9/1666; 12/3/1663; 10/6/1663; 13/5/1667.

40. Pepys 2/4/1661; 26/8/1661; 9/4/1663; 27/4/1663; 27/3/1664; 27/5/1664; 23/4/1666.

41. GLRO DL/C/246 fos 43, 74–5 and see these depositions generally for servant life.

42. Brodsky (1986) pp. 134–7.

43. Defoe (1727) (2) p. 133; on contraception, see Stone (1977) pp. 261–7; Earle (1976) pp. 266–8; on fertility, see Finlay (1979) pp. 26–38, who suggests that the higher fertility in wealthier parishes might be explained by a greater use of wet-nurses so that mothers did not have the partial protection from conception that breast-feeding provides.

44. See, in particular, Stone (1977) p. 82 and Ch. 9 and Plumb (1975); for a summary and critique of this school of historians, see Pollock (1983) pp. 1–67.

45. Pollock (1983) esp. pp. 144–56. This book contains the most devastating critique of the harsh childhood thesis but see also Wrightson (1982) pp. 104–18 and Macfarlane (1979).

46. Pollock (1983) *passim*. For her critique of her sources, see pp. 68–95.

47. Pollock (1983) p. 145.

48. Wadsworth (1712) p. 58 quoted in Morgan (1944) p. 39; Ryerson (1961); Stone (1977) pp. 113–16, 267–73; Mechling (1975).

49. Generalizations from depositions in GLRO DL/C/245–248.

50. This paragraph is based on the inventories of the sample. One inventory (S.304) lists a 'Noah's ark' but this seems to have been for the delectation of the father, an inveterate collector, rather than for his children. See Plumb (1975) for the increase in spending on children. Most children's toys, if they had them, would probably have been too cheap and battered to merit valuation, but once again there is the problem of silence.

51. Disinherited – S.12 (PROB 11/324 fo. 91), Richard Darnelly; S.116

(PROB 11/357 fo. 68), John Rayner; S.216 (PROB 11/400 fo. 12), William
Ambler; see also for obedience, duty etc. to the mother, S.246, 280, 285,
307, 316, 354 etc. Most wills give no clue to feelings on these subjects, one
way or the other. For Stone's views, see Stone (1977) Ch. 9.
52. For some examples of 'mixed' families, see Nos 7, 15, 18, 24, 30, 35 and
36 in Table 8.3 (p. 214), all of which were headed by a man living with his
second wife and most of which had children from at least two marriages.
Recent work has shown that widows did not remarry as often as once
thought (see Carlton (1978), Todd (1985)). However, widows in our class
would have been financially attractive to suitors and it seems probable that
their remarriage rate would have been much higher than the average, as
has recently been shown by Brodsky (1986) in her study of late Elizabethan
London. For a case involving refusal to let children of a previous marriage
into the house, see GLRO DL/C/246, Chambers v. Chambers. For a will
expressing fears about the children of a first marriage, see PRO PROB 11/
363 fo. 78 (Richard Davis).
53. On the feeding of infants, see Pollock (1983) pp. 212–18. For a
contemporary critic of wet-nursing, see Tillotson (1694) pp. 104–11. See
also Finlay (1979), esp. pp. 34–5 where he indicates that the practice was a
common one.
54. Misson (1719) p. 33.
55. GHMS 10823/1 p. 36; cf. GHMS 12017 pp. 11–14. A rather good idea
of the atmosphere in a middle-class household can be obtained from the
dialogues in Defoe (1715).
56. Will of Sir John Robinson, PRO PROB 11/362 fo. 28; this was a
common formula. On worries about money, see Pollock (1983) p. 115. For
a good example, see BL Add. 4454, the commonplace book of Katherine
Austin, a propertied London widow who saw her main duty in life to insure
that the estate created by her father and by her husband and his father
should be handed on intact to her children.
57. Campbell (1747) p. 4; on middle-class schools, see pp. 65–8.
58. The diary and letters of the Quaker hop-merchant Peter Briggins
provide a good example of relations between parents and children at
boarding school (see Howard (1894) pp. 46, 54, 67, 73).
59. GHMS 10823/1 p. 38; Hedges (No. 35) and Cary (36) in Table 8.3
(p. 214). On ages that children left home, see Wall (1978).

9 Civic Life

1. *Spectator* No. 9, i, 29. On London clubs, see Clark (1986).
2. CLRO MCI 370.
3. Thomas (1971) p. 528, quoted by MacDonald (1981) p. 102; Pearl
(1979) pp. 25–6 for changes in the ward inquest and see Pearl (1961) pp.
45–68 for a description of the government of the City; good examples of
ward inquest records for our period can be found in GHMS 60 (Cheap)
and 4069/2 (Cornhill); GLRO DL/C/245 fo. 207 for the coffee-house, but
see the depositions from Consistory Court cases generally for masses of this

sort of material; it was also part of the duties of churchwardens and sidesmen to enquire 'into the lives of inordinate livers' (Miège (1691) ii, 257).

4. GLRO DL/C/245 fo. 204 (Gentry v. Gentry) see /246 fo. 90 (Johnson v. Cooper) for a mention of a skimmington ride; see also Misson (1698) p. 70 where he refers to 'charivari' processions in the streets of London which he was told were set up when 'a woman of the neighbourhood has beaten her husband, because he has accused her of making him a cuckold'; in general on 'skimmingtons', 'rough music' etc., see Thompson (1972); Shoemaker (1987) pp. 274–8 found that by 1720 there was something that could be called a riot every other day in the metropolis. Similar situations are often described in the numerous defamation cases in the Consistory Court records in GLRO. Although they were not particularly interested in adultery, mention should also be made of the moral policing of the Societies for Reformation of Manners, which sprang up in the metropolis and elsewhere from the 1690s. Many of these were local societies, inaugurated by Anglicans and dissenters alike, who employed an army of informers to bring convictions for such moral offences as drunkenness, swearing and, particularly, the non-observance of the Sabbath. See Bahlman (1957).

5. S.123. For general discussion of the methods of prosecuting crime in the early modern period, see Sharpe (1984) and Beattie (1986). See also Howson (1970) pp. 24–6 and Tobias (1979) Ch. 2 for discussions of the policing available in the metropolis.

6. For information on the parish life of the sixteenth century, see Pendrill (1937) and Brigden (1984). See also Burke (1977) for a general discussion of popular culture in seventeenth-century London. On ward or precinct dinners and breakfasts organized by the questmen, see Webbs (1908) ii, 597–8. This seems to have been the main function of the inquest. See, for instance, the accounts of Cheap Wardmote Inquest for 1701 (GHMS 60). Their receipts were £132, of which £38.10.0 was contributed by members of the inquest themselves and £84 'of the severall inhabitants of this ward in the house box'. Their disbursements included about £100 in such items as the Steward's Bill (£22), Vintner's Bill (£52), sugar and spice, ale and beer, ' brawne', coffeeman and baker. Cf. Cornhill Ward (GHMS 4069/2) where the main disbursements were also the steward's, butler's and cook's bills.

7. This section on Allhallows is based mainly on the Vestry Minutes (GHMS 5039/1), the Churchwardens' Accounts (GHMS 5038/1–2), Hatton (1708) i, 103–6 and Birch (1896) pp. 101–2. The most important local officials were the churchwardens, who were in charge of policy towards the poor. A wealthy parish like Allhallows attracted a fair number of orphans dumped on its doorsteps. See the parish register GHMS 5031 for their baptisms and a brief description of their discovery. These seem to have been well treated, put out to nurses who were paid 10s. a month, fed, clothed, educated and eventually placed as apprentices. The rather thoughtless paternalism of the day led to virtually all parish orphans being given the surname Allhallows. One suspects that one of the parish nurses, Rebecca Somerset, was herself a former parish child from St Mary Somerset. For this practice, see Pearl (1981) p. 128.

8. GHMS 5039/1, 1 April 1698; on the separation of the sexes in the church, see Wickham Legg (1914) p. 150 and Wheler (1698) pp. 99–100, who complained about the abuse of a 'promiscuous mixture' creeping in. Pepys's ideal of a good church service was 'a good sermon, a fine church [in this case Greenwich] and a great company of handsome women' (Pepys, 13 January 1661).

9. Seating from GHMS 5039/1 22 July 1701; poor rates for 1701 from GHMS 5038/2. On Buckingham, see de Krey (1985) p. 149 and Woodhead (1965) p. 40. In one year, 1673, the women of the parish were also seated, quite separately, from the men.

10. Seating from list of 1694; occupations from 1692 Poll Tax (CLRO Assessment Box 56.1) and from the parish register (GHMS 5031); tax ratings from the Poll Tax and the Marriage Duties (CLRO Marriage Duties 2); that the back rows seated newcomers and the peripatetic can be seen from the fact that the clerk quite often did not know the christian names of those seated there and also by an analysis of turnover. If those known from the parish register to have died in the interim are left out, then 58 per cent of those seated in 1694 were also seated in 1701. However, the figures are almost exactly two-thirds of those in the first four rows and one-third of those in the last two rows.

11. The seating places are all in the Vestry Minutes (GHMS 5039/1). For the 1678 Poll Tax, see CLRO Assessment Box 67.2. For Keeling and Buckingham, see Woodhead (1965) pp. 40, 101. One assumes that Bristow had already served the local offices before the records begin.

12. Other parishes had rules for the same purpose, e.g. St Bride Fleet Street where, on 8 April 1697, a committee was chosen 'for ye regulating ye seating of ye people in ye pews in ye church' and produced a set of rules for seating men and women on the basis of seniority, past and present office-holding etc. (GHMS 6554/2).

13. Webbs (1906) pp. 62–3; for St Giles, see *Account* (1725) pp. 21–2 for the situation in 1724 before the workhouse was built; for Allhallows Bread Street, see references in note 7 above; for a general discussion of poor relief in late seventeenth-century City parishes, see S. Macfarlane (1986) pp. 254–7.

14. Webbs (1908) pp. 626–7. In two places, G. S. De Krey ((1983) p. 607, Table 1 and (1985) p. 198, Table 5.1) has also suggested that a fair number of common councilmen, particularly Tories, 'were of unpretentious social status' on the basis of what he calls their 'real wealth'. His analysis is based on 151 new common councilmen in the years 1695–1703 whom he has traced in the second quarter assessments of the 1694 parliamentary aid in CLRO. (On this tax, see note 11 of Chapter 8.) De Krey has used the tax on rent as an indication of 'real wealth' and has divided his common councilmen into three groups, 'over £80 p.a.', '£41 – £80 p.a.' and '£40 p.a. or less', the implication being that those in the last group are quite poor, though in fact rentals are not a very good proxy for wealth.

15. The occupations of the 46 common councillors were as follows: 16 merchants, 3 wholesale haberdashers (the poorest worth just under £4000),

3 apothecaries (ave. wealth £3874), 2 wholesale and 1 retail grocers, 2 woollen-drapers (worth £12,000 and £4000), 2 linen-drapers (1 insolvent, 1 worth £10,000), 2 builders (worth £5000 & £13,000), 2 wholesale tobacconists, a very rich rentier, a cloth finisher, a printer, a publisher/bookseller, a leather-seller, a silkman, a coal merchant, a wholesale distiller (worth £12,000), a druggist, a dyer, a hop merchant, a carman and a dealer in turnery ware. By a freak of the sample, all nine aldermen were merchants, which was certainly the commonest but by no means the only occupation of this City élite; 6 of the 9 paid fines to escape the office, either immediately or after a year or two's service.

16. There is a very large body of literature on the history of individual livery companies, most of it of little more than antiquarian interest, though there are honourable exceptions. The standard work on the problems of the companies in our period is Kellett (1957–8).

17. Kellett (1957–8) p. 385; for successful prosecutions of the Pewterers' Company for trespass, see Hatcher & Barker (1974) pp. 205–6; for worries about the cost and legality of searches in the Tallow-Chandlers' Company, see Monier-Williams (1977) pp. 185–6. A prosecution brought in 1709 by a Piccadilly candle-maker for damage done to his property by a company search cost the company £200 in legal fees and costs, and made them even more reluctant to attempt to enforce their former powers (p. 196).

18. Kellett (1957–8) p. 384 re the decision in the case of J. Tolley, quoting Bohun (1702) p. 115; for the diversity of trades amongst members of the Drapers' Company, see Johnson (1922) iv, 98–102, 161–2, 368–71.

19. See Kellett (1957–8) pp. 388–9 for numbers of new freedoms.

20. GHMS 11589/1 (Grocers' committee meeting of 18 March 1691).

21. For example, the average length of time between the date of freedom and the date of becoming assistant for 71 members of the court of the Fishmongers between 1641 and 1700 was just under 28 years, suggesting that the average age of new assistants was in their early fifties (calculated from the initial letters A–M in GHMS 5587/1). For 14 members of the sample on whom this information is available, the average age was exactly 50. Since assistants normally served for life, the average age of the court would of course be much older.

22. This section on the Apothecaries is based on GHMS 8202/2 (Warden's accounts, 1668–1692), 8200/4 (Court minutes, 1694–1716), 8202/2 (Quarterage Book) and Wall et al (1963).

23. GHMS 6208/4, 21 February 1694. This section is based on this volume of Court minutes, 6207/1 (Court minutes, 1714–30) and 6203/1 (Renter warden's account book, 1671–1735).

24. On the Vintners' Company in general, see Crawford (1977). The section which follows is based on GHMS 15201/6 (Court minutes, 1703–21) and 15333/6 (Accounts, 1687–1712).

25. Unwin (1938) pp. 37–8. The section that follows is based on GHMS 5571/2 (Court minutes, 1683–1708), 5561/3 (Prime warden's accounts, 1682–1706), 5563/6 (Renter warden's accounts, 1690–1700).

26. Rees (1923) pp. 169–76.

27. Ravenhill (1689) introduction n.p.; this book has a good summary of the financial position of the Grocers. Otherwise, this section is based on GHMS 11588/6 (Court minutes, 1692–1738), 11571/18 (Warden's accounts, 1692–1701) and 11589/1 (Committee book, 1683–1719).
28. Quoted by Fisher (1968) p. 77.
29. Dunn (1973); Rothstein (1964).
30. De Krey (1985) p. 247; cf. ibid., pp. 57–8 when the descent of Spitalfields weavers on parliament in August 1689 confused an already confused situation.
31. On 1641–2, see Pearl (1961) and Manning (1976). On the other riots, see Beloff (1938), Sachse (1964), Holmes (1976) and N. Rogers (1978).
32. Furley (1959), quote from p. 17; N. Rogers (1978).
33. Quoted by Allen (1976) p. 570.
34. For a general discussion of the electorate and voting in the constituencies during this period, see Speck (1970) and for an analysis of the proportion of the City electorate who voted in elections from 1690 to 1715, see de Krey (1985) p. 249. The proportion ranged from a low of 62 per cent in 1695 to a high of 92 per cent in 1713.
35. Quoted by Speck (1970) p. 95. See also pp. 76–7, 95, where he emphasizes the importance nationally of the London elections, and App. E on pp. 128–30, where he estimates the numbers of electors. The members for the City of London were elected by the liverymen, whose numbers had been swollen by the companies' thirst for livery fines to 7500–8000 by the early eighteenth century; 3200 freeholders voted in Middlesex, 5900 householders in Westminster and 3500 in Southwark, a total of over 20,000 voters for the metropolis or about 1 in 5 of the householders. The national electorate rose from about 200,000 in the 1690s to over 250,000 in 1715, which probably represented about the same proportion of householders.
36. The following section draws on all the writers mentioned in notes 30 to 35 above, together with Horwitz (1987) (2), Plumb (1967), Holmes (1967), Brenner (1973), J. R. Jones (1961), de Krey (1983), N. Rogers (1977), Colley (1981) and Sutherland (1956).
37. Fisher (1968) pp. 80–1; cf. Brenner (1973) p. 92; de Krey (1985) pp. 167–76; N. Rogers (1977) p. 3; Colley (1981).
38. For the details of the change in politics from the mid-1690s, see de Krey (1985). Prior to the Revolution of 1688, it was the Whigs who were the radical party but by the late 1690s the Tories had taken over this role, while the rich Whigs abandoned populism and concentrated on making money as the City élite.
39. N. Rogers (1978) pp. 84–6.
40. De Krey (1985).
41. Estimates of the numbers of dissenters and whether they were increasing or decreasing vary considerably between different historians. Watts (1978) suggests that there were 338,000 dissenters in England in 1715–18, of whom 33,220 were in London (pp. 270, 509) and he also argues that the numbers had been falling since the late seventeenth century. Holmes (1976) argues that they had been increasing and that there were

about 500,000 in England and 100,000 in London in the reign of Queen Anne (p. 63), and he is followed by de Krey (1985) p. 75 and, in general, pp. 74–120, though he seems to have a very elastic view of what constitutes a dissenter. It is not clear whether Watts' figure, which relates to 'hearers', includes children but in any case it certainly does seem rather low, while those of Holmes and de Krey are probably too high, and one might plump for somewhere in the middle, say 10–15 per cent of the population of London, a very sizeable number.

42. Defoe (1726–7) i, 47; Defoe (1724–6) i, 72.

10 Expenditure and Consumption

1. Thirsk & Cooper (1972) pp. 780–1; for an excellent criticism of King's figures, see Holmes (1977), who suggests that King seriously underestimated the incomes of many groups in his table. Massie (1761); for a discussion of Massie's work, see Mathias (1957).

2. Massie (1760).

3. For the profits of merchants, see p. 139. Grassby (1969) p. 733 suggests a rate of 6 to 12 per cent.

4. Some confirmation that such estimates are approximately right can be obtained from partnership agreements, which usually stated what individual partners could draw for their 'housekeeping, dyett and other particular expenses'. Not many such agreements survive, but those which have been seen have average annual drawings of £200 and a range from £78 to £312 (PRO C110/43, Alexander v. Alexander; C110/85, Unwin v. Unwin; C110/179, Price v. Stanton; C110/167, Herne v. Humphreys; C103/160, Burgess v. Taylor).

5. I am grateful to Negley Harte and Nicholas Rogers for these two references. Vanderlint's other expenditure was household maintenance (soap, sewing and haberdashery materials, repairs of household goods, scouring and cleaning equipment) – £32 6s.8d; coal and candles – £9 15s; shaving and shoe-cleaning – £2; schooling (at 10s. per quarter per child) – £8; lying-in expenses (£10 once every two years) – £5; maid's wages – £4 10s.; pocket-money (4s. a week for the master, 2s. for the wife and children together 'to buy fruit and toys') – £15 12s.; entertainments – £4; medical expenses – £6; holidays ('a country lodging sometimes for the health and recreation of the family') – £8.

6. On a weekly basis, King's estimate works out at 3s. to 6s. per head and Vanderlint's at just over 4s., figures which fit in well with other data that has been found, e.g. 4s. a week for apprentices and maids and 5s. a week for a man and his wife in a 1619 master baker's household (Thrupp (1933) p. 17) and figures of 3s.10d., 4s., 5s., 5s.4d. and 5s.6d. from accounts attached to inventories (S. 135, 139, 254 and 312). See also *Brief History* pp. 83–4, where the author suggests an expenditure per head from 4s. to 6s. or 7s. a week.

7. Boswell (1950) p. 34. In 1734, Vanderlint estimated that his middling family would spend a penny a head a day on tea and sugar, about one

seventh of total expenditure on food and drink. The habit had not yet penetrated much below the middle classes, as tea continued to be very expensive. Tea was normally drunk sweet without milk and was an important factor in the huge increase in sugar consumption. A recent estimate of English per capita sugar consumption suggests a fourfold increase from a low base between 1660 and 1700 and a further doubling between 1700 and 1725 (Galenson (1986) p. 6).

8. On mealtimes, see Rees & Fenby (1931).

9. Quoted by Ashton (1897) p. 141.

10. For a case involving the supply of meat to a middling household, see CLRO MCI 49; see also Table 10.5 (p. 281) for the difference in meat consumption between middling and labouring families.

11. E.g. Drummond & Wilbraham (1939) pp. 133–4.

12. Thick (1985) p. 507 and, in general, pp. 503–32 provides an excellent survey of the growth of market-gardening in our period. Much of these vegetables would have been eaten by the poor since they were very cheap once the season was under way.

13. Misson (1719) p. 314. Cf. de Muralt (1726) p. 11: 'they eat much flesh and little bread, which is another bad custom.' On tomatoes, see Wilson (1973) p. 346.

14. Swift (1948) i, 328; Ryder (1939) pp. 49, 190. In *Compleat* (1729) there are 100 recipes for preserving and 50 for pickles, while fruit would also have found its way into many of the 'made wines' and cordials. For estimates of the quantities of imported fruit, see McGrath (1948) pp. 208–9.

15. Misson (1719) p. 315; Wilson (1973) p. 182.

16. E.S. (1729) end-cover; Pepys 26 January 1660, cf. 26 March 1662, 13 January 1663, 4 April 1663 for some other impressive meals. For food in Pepys, see the essay in the *Companion*, vol. x, s.v. 'Food' and the *Index*, vol. xi.

17. On the mackerel fishermen of Folkestone see Defoe (1724–6) i, 123; Pepys 31 August 1664; Ashton (1897) p. 145.

18. MCI 391, evidence of Jeremiah Hamond, a schoolmaster lodging in the house of William Coles. For other complaints, see MCI 49, 318, 429, 461, 502, 508 and 535, usually complaining of insufficient or unwholesome food, but these are a small number relative to the total of apprentice cases. MCI 461 makes the same complaint as Hamond about the bread and cheese being locked up.

19. Pepys 7 July 1665; some of the men in the sample had as many as 20 dozen glass bottles (e.g. S.259) but in only a few cases were their contents, if any, valued – e.g. S.80, the apothecary Richard Tomlinson, who had a parcel of bottles, some filled with cider and some with claret valued at £8.

20. De Muralt (1726) p. 10.

21. The following section on dress draws mainly on Arnold (1970), Brooke (1958), Buck (1971), Buck (1979), Cumming (1984), Cunnington (1951), Cunnington (1955), Ewing (1984), Ribeiro (1983), Ribeiro (1984).

22. For many delightful definitions of articles of dress, see Holme (1688). See, for example, iii, 15 – a band, 'an ornament for the neck which is of the

finest white linnen cloth . . . made by the art of the seamster, and washed and starched, slickened and smoothed by the care of the laundress', and iii, 17 – 'a cravatt is another kind of adornment for the neck, being nothing else but a long towel put around the collar and so tyed with a bow knott'.

23. Buck (1971) p. 12; Riberio (1984) p. 118; Cunnington (1955) p. 163.

24. Mandeville quoted by Ribeiro (1984) p. 116; see also Ch. 5 of her book for many other examples of social criticism of dress.

25. Buck (1971) p. 5 & *passim*; inventory of Anne Deacon, Orphans 1049.

26. MCI 48 and 385. Cf. 49, 54, 55, 57, 66, 67, 370 etc. The range of value in the cases I have looked at was from £6 to £50, but most apprentices had at least the basic outfit of three suits and accessories.

27. PRO C107/172 (Kersteman); for inventories from the sample which list men's clothing in more or less detail, see S.4, 10, 33, 66, 82, 168, 254, 318, 319. On the nightgown, see Ashton (1897) pp. 122–3.

28. S.1 and Orphans 1151. Women's clothes were normally worth more than those of men because of the greater proportion of silk and lace and the high yardages needed to make gowns and petticoats. Neither men's nor women's clothing are realistically valued in post-mortem inventories, but one can see what they were worth to their wearers from insurance valuations. The clothes of middle-class women, insured separately by the Sun in the late 1720s, were valued from £20 to £200, with £40 or £50 being typical. GHMS 11936/23–29.

29. Ribeiro (1984) pp. 48–9 gives a range of silk prices later in the eighteenth century from 70s. or more a yard for a rich flowered silk brocaded in gold through 20s. for a figured silk to a plain taffeta at about 8s. Her textiles are for the upper classes and cheap silks went lower than this. See also Arnold (1970) p. 27 for prices of ready-made silk nightgowns from the *Spectator* of 1711, 'from rich brocades of 6 guineas a gown to thread sattins of 37s. . . . the cheapest to be had in Town'. S.282 (1701) has silk nightgowns at a wholesale price of £4 and stuff ones at 22s., while S.15 (1667) has 'small and greate India gowns' at 21s.

30. This is a very rough and ready estimate based on a cloak or campaign coat at 30s., hat 10s., peruke 20s., coat 20s., waistcoat 15s., breeches 10s., shirt 10s., stockings 5s., shoes 5s. and drawers 2s.6d. (dimity and kersey drawers for men were valued in 1672 at 2s.3d. a pair in CLRO Orphans 699).

31. Pepys 30 October 1664, 1 June 1665. For comment on Pepys's extravagance, see Ashton (1985) p. 78. For some really expensive clothes, see PRO C113/31 pt 2, which has tailors' bills for the Duke of Monmouth, among others. He paid £108 for one outfit.

32. PRO C114/182. Unnamed tailor's day-book. Cf. C113/31 for the accounts of William Watts, tailor in the 1660s, and C108/30 for the much fuller papers of Mark Sayers in the early 1760s. Monteage in GHMS 205/1.

33. GLRO JB/Gregory King fo. 203.

34. Vanderlint (1734) pp. 141–2; cf. p. 75 where the London labourer and his wife are estimated to spend £2 10s. each on their clothes and £1 for each of the four children; BL Add. 26057; PRO C114/182.

35. Thornton (1978) p. 10 and *passim*.

36. The general point of inelasticity can be illustrated further by looking at linen and pewter, two items which were in every household. The average value of linen only ranges from £9 to £26 and the average weight of pewter from 135 to 264lb for the wealth groups in Table 10.8, despite the fact that the richest group were at least ten times as rich as the poorest.

37. Further indication that the poorer members of the sample were upgrading their houses can be seen by a decline in the number of rooms with relatively low valuations. For example, 48 per cent and 35 per cent of best bedrooms were valued at less than £15 before and after 1700, 64 per cent and 39 per cent of dining-rooms were valued at less than £10, and 30 per cent and 15 per cent of kitchens were valued at less than £10 in the same two sub-periods.

38. S. 42, 43, 65, 71, 224 and 279 for men with a room valued at over £100. The number of cases where the contents of the dining-room were worth more than those in the best bedroom doubles after 1700 from 12 to 24 per cent of the sample.

39. For background on the history of furniture and interior design I have relied mainly on Edwards (1964), Fowler & Cornworth (1974), Gloag (1964), Thornton (1978), Thornton & Tomlin (1980) and Wills (1971). There is of course a huge literature on these subjects, but addressed mainly to art historians, collectors and restorers rather than to social historians.

40. Thornton (1978) pp. 9–10; Miège (1691) ii, 31–2; on looking-glasses, see Wills (1965).

41. In the period 1665–79, the main textiles used for best bed hangings in the 78 inventories which provide this information were old draperies (13), serge and perpetuana (48), camlets, mohairs, stuffs and other mixtures (13), silks (2) and others (2). In 1700–20, there are also 78 inventories and the breakdown is old draperies (5), serge and perpetuana (5), camlets (23), mohairs (17), damasks (8), cheneys (7), stuffs (3), pure silks (4) and others (6). Silk and cotton were also the main lining materials.

42. Gloag (1964) p. 82. Only four inventories have an easy chair before 1700.

43. Turkeywork was an imitation of Turkish rug design made mainly in Norwich and Bradford and used in panels for upholstering the backs of chairs. Gloag (1964) pp. 77–8; Thornton (1978) p. 202; see *CJ* x, 282, 313 for petitions in the late 1680s from Bradford in favour of the unsuccessful bill to ban cane chairs and Walton (1973) p. 48 for a similar petitioning campaign by the London Upholders' Company. In the 1660s, 7 inventories mention turkeywork chairs and none mentions cane chairs; the figures for succeeding decades are: 1670s (59/6), 1680s (32/31) 1690s (13/53), 1700s (14/53) and 1710s (1/22).

44. Williams (S.246); Barkstead (S.236). The Indian competition aroused much resentment from, among others, the London Joiners' Company, which claimed in 1700 that in the previous four years there had been imported from India 6582 tea-tables, 4120 dressing, comb and powder boxes, 818 lacquered boards, 597 sconces, 589 looking-glass frames, 428

chests, 244 cabinets, 70 trunks and 52 screens. The Indians made these 'after the English fashion, by our models' and all these articles can be found in our inventories. (*Case* (1700), in BL 816.m.13(2), ibid (1) is a similar petition from the japanners); see also *CJ* xiii, 553. The petitioning was successful and, in 1701, parliament imposed added duties on East Indian goods (Joy (1965) p. 2).

45. Sherwood (S.295), cf. S.304, 313, both of which have over 100 pieces of china. Only one inventory listed equipment specifically for making or serving hot drinks before 1690 but, in the 1690s, 12 per cent did and 48 per cent did between 1700 and 1709. The preference for tea at home is shown by the fact that tea equipment outnumbered coffee equipment by over two to one in the inventories, while the chocolate pot came a very poor third.

46. S.239, 304, 338. De Saussure (1902) p. 69 noted the lack of hangings in London houses at the end of our period, which he attributed to the coal smoke.

47. Thompson (1967); Vanderpost (S.66); Walford (S.332); most clocks were simply described as a clock, a small clock or a clock and case, except in the earlier part of the period when 'pendulum clock', 'clock with weights' etc. is more common. In the early eighteenth century, one finds a few 'month' clocks (e.g. S.326, 343) but, when such things are mentioned, 7- and 8-day clocks are much commoner. There were also repeating and alarm clocks (e.g. S.279, 304, 314).

48. S.304.

49. Pepys 2 September 1666. Our material may understate the true position since the inventories list 14 virginals, 11 harpsichords, 3 spinets, 2 organs, 7 viols, 3 violins and a lute and not a single woodwind instrument. It seems possible that, like other small personal possessions, such instruments as recorders might well have been overlooked by the assessors.

50. Cf. Priestley & Corfield (1982) p. 107 for similar developments in Norwich kitchens during the same period.

51. For the description of articles in the kitchen I have relied mainly on the *OED* and on Lindsay (1927). I would recommend anyone interested in the history of kitchen equipment to look at some of these inventories, which contain a huge amount of detail that means little to me as a non-specialist. On the jacksmith, see Campbell (1747) pp. 179–80. Most houses had plenty of brass and copper implements in other rooms as well as the kitchen, fire furniture for instance, while a dozen or so brass candle-sticks and at least one warming-pan were normally listed in kitchen inventories. Further demand for metal goods came from the large number of weapons kept in many houses. (See above, p. 243.)

52. S. 274. Incidentally, my sources do not support the estimates of late seventeenth-century pewter stocks in Hatcher & Barker (1974) pp. 129–30. They estimate that those with incomes of £200–500 would have 350–550 lb, £100–200 would have 200–350 lb and £50–100 would have 100–150 lb. I do not have income figures but by wealth groups the figures are as follows, average pewter weights in pounds in brackets: over £5000 (265), £2000–5000 (183), £1000–2000 (168), £500–1000 (153) and under £500 (135) – in other words they seem to exaggerate the stocks of the wealthy.

53. Stock (S.252); for a good listing of plate, see S.374, John Goodlad, whose dressing-table set alone was worth nearly £60.

54. The average valuation of linen was nearly £16 and of the contents of kitchens, including pewter and brass but not of course linen, just over £13. A sub-sample of 1 in 5 of the 375 inventories was used for listing the details of domestic life and of these 75 inventories, 50 listed linen in sufficient detail to provide these averages. For an insight into the types and uses of cottons and linens, see J.F. (1696).

55. Thornton (1978) pp. 315–21.

56. Pepys vol. x, 103 and see 30 May 1663, 20 June 1666 etc. for washing feet. Monteage in GHMS 205, e.g. 1 in 1733 when his feet were washed on 14 January, 4 February, 11 March etc. Bugs and lice were a major problem; for an entertaining article on the subject, see Boynton (1965) and for contemporary advice on how to deal with them, see Southall (1730). London had many public bathhouses, also Turkish baths or hummums, there being at least 10 by the reign of Queen Anne. See the list in Lillywhite (1963) p. 95.

57. Things which one finds in inventories at the end of the period but not at the beginning include chimney cranes, trivets, toasting-irons or toasters, plate warmers, extinguishers (for candles rather than fires I think), brass savealls (contrivances to hold candle-ends so that they burn to the end), voyders (trays to sweep crumbs into after a meal) and clothes horses.

58. The median fortune of the first ten people with bed hangings of camlet, mohair, damask or silk was over £5000. Similar figures were found for the first people with cane chairs and over £10,000 for the first ten people with tea-making equipment. Most of those less wealthy were tradesmen with an almost exclusively West End clientèle.

59. S.373.

60. This cannot be proved since inventories rarely put a value on individual objects but value rooms or parts of rooms in a lump. In any case, it is difficult to compare the value of pieces of furniture over time since it is almost impossible to be sure that one is comparing like with like.

61. Pepys 30 November 1668.

62. In 1727/28, there was one person keeping a coach for every 42 houses in the City and one for every 15 houses in wealthy and more spacious Westminster, where houses were often built with stables or mews attached, as in St George's Hanover Square, which had one coach for every 4.3 houses (Maitland (1739) pp. 354ff.).

63. Both Swift (1948) and Pepys demonstrate that they were energetic walkers, but the most enthusiastic of all that I have come across was the accountant Stephen Monteage (GHMS 208).

11 Sickness and Death

1. PRO C108/132. Sarah Smyter to her brother Henry Gambier, 15 May 1717 and 12 April 1716.

2. The time that elapsed between the date of signing a will and the date of

proving it was less than a year in 78 per cent of 167 cases and less than three months in 59 per cent; Harvey (1678), introduction, A2; Gregory King thought that, on average, each person had four serious illnesses, the last one being mortal. In the same paper, he has an interesting analysis of expenditure on 'physick and chirurgery'. He thought that the nation as a whole spent just under £¼m a year, of which 61 per cent was spent on apothecaries, 17 per cent on doctors and quacks, 13 per cent on 'kitchen physick' (i.e. self-treatment) and 9 per cent on surgeons. GLRO JB/ Gregory King fo. 206.

3. Archer (1673).

4. Most of these books seem to have concentrated on the need for 'a steddy and regular course of living'. See, for example, Maynwaring (1683) p. 16 where he emphasized the virtue of the golden mean, not too much and not too little of sleep, meat, drink, exercise etc. Cf. Tryon (1691).

5. Archer (1673); he was not alone in his belief in the curative virtues of tobacco; cf. Dr Everard, *Panacea, or a Universal Medicine, being a discovery of the wonderful virtues of tobacco* (1659); Ryder (1939) p. 196.

6. Matthews (1978) pp. 164, 170; Brockbank (1964) pp. 2, 8; Wootton (1910) ii, 117, 143–4, 172–3, 179–82; Culpeper (1953) p. 30; all these works have a mass of fascinating material on the pharmacy of the period. For a collection of recipes designed to assist those who wished to undercut the apothecaries, see Harvey (1678). See also PRO C114/59, a daybook kept by Anthony Daffy between 1675 and 1680 which records the sales of thousands of ½-pint and pint bottles of the elixir to customers all over the country and as far afield as the coast of Coromandel. On the drug trade, see Roberts (1965).

7. Brockbank (1964).

8. Clarkson (1975) pp. 103–5; Webster quoted in Hunter & Macalpine (1963) pp. 209–10. He was actually referring to his own practice in Clitheroe, Lancashire, 'where ignorance, popery, and superstition doth much abound', but there seems little doubt that such attitudes could be found amongst middling Londoners as well, despite their veneer of sophistication.

9. See Blauner (1966) for an interesting discussion of the problems of a society in which people often 'die with unfinished business'.

10. A few earlier parish registers give age at death. See Figure 3 in Forbes (1976) p. 403 which shows a similar picture to the one in our figure. Finlay (1981) Ch. 5 was unable to calculate adult mortality rates by the methods of family reconstitution, since few people stayed in the same parish for long enough to provide him with data, and he was forced to match his observed infant and child mortality rates to modern life tables, a hazardous exercise as he himself admits.

11. These are parishes which had high proportions of their householders assessed for personal estate valued over £600 in the Marriage Duties assessments of 1695, as analysed by Jones & Judges (1935) pp. 45–63. The parishes in the London Bridge group were St Andrew Hubbard, St Benet Gracechurch, St Botolph Billingsgate, St Dionis Backchurch, St Dunstan in

East, St Gabriel Fenchurch, St George Botolph Lane, St Leonard Eastcheap, St Magnus, St Margaret Pattens, St Mary at Hill; and in the Guildhall group were Allhallows Bread Street, Allhallows Honey Lane, St John Evangelist, St Lawrence Jewry, St Martin Ironmonger Lane, St Mary le Bow, St Mary Magdalen Milk Street, St Matthew Friday Street, St Michael Bassishaw. Populations are taken as those provided by the assessments of 1695 for the period 1676 to 1704 and then are assumed to have changed evenly decade by decade until they reached the figures given in the 1801 census. The deaths are from the Bills of Mortality. The method used here is crude, but one is given confidence by the fact that the experience of both groups of parishes moves very much in tandem and that the larger individual parishes within the groups consistently mirror the experience of the group as a whole. One would be reluctant to put much reliance on the exact figures of deaths per thousand but can be reasonably confident that the trend is accurate.

12. The method used was simply to collect from the Boyd data all those cases (2744) where it was possible to find a date of birth or baptism and a date of death, burial, probate or post-mortem inventory, the assumption being that any bias in Boyd's data was consistent throughout the period. It should be noted that no one should be able to enter the Boyd data unless they were already 24, the minimum age of citizenship, though in fact there are a few people in their earlier twenties.

13. Creighton (1891) ii, 22–25, 61. The high mortality of the third quarter of the seventeenth century shows up throughout the country. Creighton thought it was due to smallpox, typhus and a particularly virulent form of influenza.

14. Based on 43 merchants, 34 haberdashers and 16 apothecaries. See also Earle (1986) p. 55, Table 3.12. Across the whole period of the Boyd data used in Figure 11.3, the average percentage of citizens dying under 50 was 38.7 per cent but for members of 'artisan' livery companies it was 45.6 per cent and for Clothworkers and Mercers, the two companies with the wealthiest members, it was 34.4 per cent.

15. For a development of this argument, see Earle (1986).

16. GHMS 11892A, Michael Mitford to John Lowther, 21 December 1703, with reference to the latter's brother's funeral; Pepys, 18 March 1664, his brother Tom's funeral. On the rise of the undertaking profession, see p. 79 and Gittings (1984).

17. S.56, 216, 239, 371. A few people were very specific about the costs of their funeral; Sir John Smith (S.65) willed that £600 be spent and John Dubois (S.191) £400, the actual cost being just over £398.

18. S.107; cf. S.65, Alderman Sir John Smith and S.97, Edward Darling, landlord of the Three Tuns at Charing Cross, obviously an officer in the Trained Bands who wished 'to be interred with part of my company marching before my corps'. However, very few wills do spell such things out, though some make it clear that they did not wish their funeral to be a public spectacle, e.g. Sir Nicholas Butler (S.269) who wanted 'none to be at my funeral but my owne family'. For some idea of numbers at funerals, see

Pepys x, 152–3. Two city halls were needed to hold the gathering for the funeral of the goldsmith-banker Sir Thomas Vyner; 400 or 500 people attended the funeral of Anthony Joyce and 100 to 200 coaches carried Sir William Batten's mourners from London to his burial at Walthamstow.
19. Quotations from Misson (1719) p. 90, a good description of a middling funeral, and Ryder (1939) p. 91, his grandmother's funeral. Not many people left instructions in their wills, normally restricting themselves to willing that they be buried at the discretion of the executor or 'in a decent manner'. Some specify the church and the preacher and a few are more detailed, willing that they be buried near their former wife, father, children etc. or in a particular vault. By our period, some of the City churches were getting very full. See Pepys, 18 March 1664, where he arranges for the burial of his brother Tom in the middle aisle of St Bride's Fleet Street. The gravemaker told him that it was very full but for sixpence and his father's sake he would 'justle them together' to make room for him.
20. PRO C105/15, Hatfield v. Holmes, bill dated 13 May 1731.
21. Ryder (1939) p. 340; S.236; S.212; PRO PROB 11/368/147 fo. 45v, will of William Sawyer; cf. S.91, 269.
22. Misson (1719) p. 91 wrote that everyone drank two or three cups; only six bottles of wine were provided at the funeral of John Hatfield in 1731 (PRO C105/15). Pepys 18 March 1664; S.232; S.289, Mackley made a rather odd request in the codicil to his will: 'I pray let the stone that was taken out of my body be layd upon my corps while it stands in the room to show the Lord's goodness to me in sparing my life.' Readers of Pepys's diary will be familiar with his gratitude at having survived the operation for cutting for a stone.
23. On the Custom, see *Laws* (1765) pp. 80–3, 99–100, 105–9 etc; Carlton (1974) pp. 45–50; for a case where it was claimed that the Custom overrode a will, see MCE 1680–1, Stockdale v. Butler; *Laws* (1765) p. 99 says that where an estate exceeded £2000, the widow's chamber should be £50 but this does not seem to have happened in practice. There is also confusion between the chamber and the 'widow's paraphernalia', which normally meant her jewellery.
24. Since the sample is drawn specifically from people whose estates were divided by the Court of Orphans there is clearly a bias towards those who accepted the Custom and were quite happy to die intestate and allow its rules to govern the division of their estate. The Court of Orphans had a chequered history in our period, which caused fewer and fewer people to use its services, and a random sample of middling people would certainly have a much lower proportion of intestates. On the Court, see Carlton (1974), esp. Ch. 6. Horwitz (1984) has analysed a sample of wills made by wealthy Londoners between 1660 and 1754 and found that a high proportion did not follow the Custom of London, though this did not mean that they necessarily treated their children inequitably. Those who were least likely to follow the Custom were the elderly and/or those with relatively few surviving children, i.e. just the sort of people who were least likely to appear in our sample.

25. For details, see Carlton (1974) pp. 48–50. Orphanage portions were due to be paid at 21 or marriage and could be retained by widows or guardians if recognizances and sureties were found, could be lent out to third parties on the same conditions or deposited in the Chamber of London. Interest, called 'finding money', was paid to the guardian for the maintenance and education of the children. The City government regularly borrowed money from the orphans' fund in the Chamber and, when the City went bankrupt in 1682, the orphans were the main losers, a scandal which naturally made the whole system very much less attractive to executors and testators. The orphans' rights were eventually secured by new taxes on coal and, although the numbers of people using the Court declined quite rapidly from the 1680s, there were still sufficient to maintain our sample up to 1720. After this date, there are very few and the Custom of London itself was abolished in 1725. See Carlton (1974) Ch. 6 and Kellett (1963).

26. About 25 per cent received nothing from the dead man's share, often because they were given a life interest in real property.

27. Wills are very complicated to analyse. A coding system was devised for personal estate as follows: a) equal division between all children – 64 per cent; b) eldest son more than the rest – 13 per cent; c) son(s) more than daughter(s) – 9 per cent; d) eldest of either sex more than younger – 9 per cent; e) daughter(s) more than son(s) – 4 per cent; f) younger children more than older – 1 per cent. For real estate the raw figures were: a) to sons but only had sons – 4; b) to eldest son only – 21; c) to eldest sons only – 7; d) to sons, nothing to daughters – 13; e) to sons and daughters – 13; f) to daughters but only had daughters – 5; g) not left to children – 7; h) sold and added to personal estate – 6.

28. Of those who died testate and left a widow, 21.3 per cent appointed her sole executrix with no overseers, 56.7 per cent appointed her joint-executrix or sole executrix with one or more overseers and 22 per cent did not name her at all.

29. Two-thirds of wills mention legacies apart from what was left to widows and children: 73 testators (40.3 per cent) named 1–5 legatees; 32 (17.7 per cent) named 6–10; 13 (7.2 per cent) named 11–20 and 3 (1.7 per cent) named over 20, the greatest number being the 72 named by John Hobby (S.91 and see p. 318). Mourning bequests are also mentioned in 57 per cent of wills, the recipients showing similar patterns to those in Table 11.3 but most wills only name a small proportion of those who received cloth, gloves, rings etc. and that much of the distribution was left to the discretion of executors.

30. See Jordan (1960).

31. S.56 (0.2 per cent of his net estate). Altogether, 50 testators left 97 separate bequests to the poor worth a total capital value of £5242, 10 left 11 bequests for religious purposes worth £484, 4 left 6 bequests for education worth £273, 3 left 4 bequests to help with apprenticeship premiums or give loans to young beginners worth £1318 and 3 left 1 bequest each for poor prisoners worth a total of £1055. Miscellaneous bequests worth £400 were also left to the Artillery Company, Bedlam Hospital, the Salters' Company and 'charity'.

32. S.42, S.91.

33. For a general work on charity after 1660, see Owen (1964) pp. 11–88.

34. S.191 (Dubois); S.289 (Mackley); cf. S.12, Richard Darnelly, who willed that 'four ministers of God's word' should be at his funeral; S.13, Richard Bridges, who willed that the 8th and 9th verses of Psalm 16 should be the text at his funeral sermon, and several others with such hints of piety or the nature of their belief, e.g. S.96 who left £2 to 'a poor pious nonconforming minister' to be chosen after consultation with the minister of his own congregation.

35. S.340 (Ragdale); S.193 (Waldron).

36. S.136; S.246; S.12; S.86.

37. S.4; S.354; S.49, cf. S.91 – £2 to all those servants 'who shall live a year after with my wife'.

38. Reduction or voiding of widows' legacies on remarriage in S.14, 31, 67, 152, 365; new arrangements for children in S.5, 30, 187, 208, 231 etc.

39. S.12, cf. 116 and 216 and see p. 235; S.285; S.82; S.303; S.307; for some comments in wills relating to daughters' marriages, see pp. 187–8.

40. S.4.

41. S.71; for an insight into just how much religious belief could affect behaviour and lifestyle, see Seaver (1985).

12 The London Middle Class

1. Archenholtz (1794) p. 122, quoted by Rudé (1971) pp. 55–6.

2. E.g. Dickson (1967) pp. 279, 302; Rudé (1971) p. 52. The confusion is made worse by the fact that many writers treat this 'upper middle class' group as the whole of the middle class and do not really acknowledge the existence of the bulk of the people discussed in this book.

3. For wages, see Gilboy (1934) and Tucker (1936). Some idea of incomes is given in King's table, see Thirsk & Cooper (1972) pp. 780–1.

4. *Review* vi, 142.

5. Rouquet (1755) quoted by Wagner (1972) p. 96.

6. Schuyler (1931) p. 264 quoted by Andrew (1981) pp. 367–8.

7. Campbell (1747) *passim*.

8. See p. 292.

9. Hexter (1961).

10. Hexter (1961) pp. 75, 112–16.

11. Thrupp (1948).

12. Thrupp (1948) pp. 139, 143, 148; see the comment of Robert Dodsley on Defoe quoted in Earle (1976) p. 174.

13. Macfarlane (1978).

14. Thrupp (1948) p. 312.

15. Wrigley (1985) Table 7.2. For an estimate of the size of the middle class in London, see p. 80–1.

16. Thomas (1983) p. 159 and see this book generally for changing attitudes to the natural world. For a discussion of changing attitudes towards women in literature, see Utter & Needham (1937).

17. Quoted by Wadsworth & Mann (1931) p. 103.

Appendix A: The Sample

The sample of middle-class people used in this book is not a random sample in the statistical sense. It has been created by linking together material from three different sources: the 'Orphans' Inventories' drawn up after a citizen's decease by the Court of Orphans, the Common Serjeants' Books kept by the same institution, in which the value of citizens' estates was summarized and the details of division between the children listed, and, thirdly, the genealogical material contained in Boyd's Index of London Citizens, which is kept in the library of the Society of Genealogists.

There are over 3000 inventories in the collection in the Corporation of London Records Office. These are stored in rolls, some of which are several yards long. I found that I could get through about eight or ten in a day, so, life being short, it was necessary to derive some way of sampling them. The method used was to select all inventories for which Boyd had a date of birth or baptism, enabling an age at death to be calculated. This has proved a useful tool in analysing such things as fortune at death, investment and household structure. A total of 450 citizens who died between 1665 and 1720 satisfied these requirements and this number was eventually whittled down to 375 to eliminate cases where linkages were doubtful or where the inventory was not drawn up in the normal format.

These two sources provide a mass of information on the genealogical and material conditions of the deceased citizens. Further material was recovered by searching the records of Livery Companies for information on apprenticeship and freedom, data which provide amongst other things the name of the master and date of apprenticeship, the name and status or occupation of the apprentice's father or guardian and his place of origin. Many of these records have been lost and others are very difficult to search but, in all, information was recovered for about 200 members of the sample. A final further linkage was made for those described as testate in the Common Serjeants' Books. A search in the PROB 11 section of the Public Record Office produced wills for just under half of the whole sample and about 80 per cent of those who died testate.

The nature of the sources used means that the sample contains few very old men, since 'orphans' were defined as children under twenty-one when their citizen fathers died. It also contains no bachelors or childless men and, perhaps more seriously, no men who were not citizens of London. This means that such important middling people as lawyers and physicians are not represented (though apothecaries are) and neither are commercial people who declined to take up the freedom of the City of London, a growing proportion of the middle station as the period continues. Another problem of coverage derives from the fact that the Court of Orphans itself had serious problems in our period (see notes 24 and 25 of Chapter 11), with the result that fewer and fewer citizens made use of its services. This may have produced a bias in the material used, though it is difficult to determine what form it would have taken.

Despite these shortcomings, the sample has a very wide coverage of different occupations and of men who died at different ages (e.g. 22 per cent in their fifties and 10 per cent over sixty) and with different fortunes. Another sample would probably have produced rather different figures in the tables but would be unlikely to upset the trends and conclusions which have been reached in the book. The men included in the sample are listed in the following pages, the order being by date of death from 1665 to 1720.

List of Sample

References in the notes to people from the sample start with S., followed by the number, and may include material from any of the sources used.

Boyd = Boyd's Index of London Citizens; CSB = Common Serjeants' Books, CLRO; Orphans = Orphans' Inventories, CLRO; Will references are to PRO PROB 11 with the / followed by the folio number; TEST = Testate, but no will found; INT = Intestate; Coy = Livery Company (for abbreviations, see p. 404); x means that information relating to apprenticeship and/or freedom has been found.

No.	Name	Boyd	CSB	Orphans	Will	Coy
1	Gardner, John	20027	ii,23	273	317/82	T/C
2	Locky, John	19676	ii,22	270	INT	M/Tx
3	Eardly, Richard	24963	ii,24	276	319/43	HABx
4	Cully, Peter	19753	ii,30	292	321/96	APOTx
5	Higgins, Herbert	19822	ii,41	317	321/129	JOINx
6	Wise, William	19687	ii,44	326	322/152	VINTx
7	Eales, Bernard	6683	ii,42	322	INT	MERC
8	Vyner, James	25469	ii,210	555	323/31	GOLDx
9	Harrison, Edmund	9602	ii,86	432	324/80	EMBR
10	Partridge, Andrew	25258	ii,72	398	324/112	T/C
11	Stonehouse, Thomas	12185	ii,43	324	324/98	APOTx
12	Darnelly, Richard	24927	ii,261	719	324/91	HABx
13	Bridges, Richard	2049	ii,61	601	324/89	MERCx
14	Hopkins, Thomas	15706	ii,197	519	324/93	CUT
15	Cole, Thomas	20363	ii,35	301	INT	P/S

No.	Name	Boyd	CSB	Orphans	Will	Coy
16	Poyner, George	20961	ii,193	510	INT	IRON
17	Swale, John	17038	ii,102	465	INT	CLOTx
18	Porter, Steven	25282	ii,65	386	INT	VINTx
19	Orme, Robert	17262	ii,216	1021	330/107	HABx
20	Sampson, Thomas	20541	ii,226	603	329/44	UPH
21	Kirk, Edmund	25152	ii,198	523	329/34	HAB
22	Milford, Gervase	25219	ii,205	542	INT	GROC
23	Hodilow, George	16514	ii,276	758	INT	M/Tx
24	Felton, John	24983	ii,233	630	332/4	CLOTx
25	Crane, Owen	24911	ii,234	636	334/133	APOTx
26	Stevens, Richard	25409	ii,247	681	INT	DRAPx
27	Pocock, Roger	25276	ii,354	1002	333/114	MERCx
28	Bagnall, John	13276	ii,245	672	334/130	CUT
29	Bedford, Henry	24771	ii,232	623	334/131	COOK
30	Brett, Thomas	24804	ii,215	571	332/4	VINT
31	Clark, William	19884	ii,224	599	333/72	SALT
32	Wallis, Richard	5509	ii,274	751	333/126	COOP
33	Rigby, Hamnett	25309	ii,314	865	INT	APOTx
34	Boddington, George	24790	ii,287	784	337/119	CLOTx
35	Marsh, John	25199	ii,277	762	INT	GIRD
36	Michelborn, Richard	25214	ii,264	727	336/65	CLOTx
37	Flesher, James	19697	ii,257	709	335/4	STATx
38	Medgate, Joseph	17593	ii,272	744	336/80	HAB
39	Ingram, Moses	25130	ii,303	827	INT	M/Tx
40	Clutterbuck, James	18197	ii,302	825	INT	DRAPx
41	Sawyer, Thomas	17326	ii,301	819	INT	CLOTx
42	Dawes, Sir Jonathan	14645	ii,298	809	INT	FISHx
43	Bonfoy, Nicholas	4088	ii,281	975	INT	CLOTx
44	King, Michael	25149	ii,275	757	INT	CARP
45	Axtell, Nathaniel	24736	ii,269	738	338/10	VINTx
46	Grove, William	17460	ii,267	732	INT	BREW
47	Godsalve, Richard	25023	ii,274	752	TEST	APOTx
48	Baldwin, Thomas	24745	ii,275	278	338/48	WOOD
49	Wildgos, John	20450	ii,279	767	339/68	CARP
50	Hartwell, Henry	25068	ii,281	775	339/61	PEWT
51	Franklin, Joseph	369	ii,281	774	INT	PLUM
52	Ferney, John	20407	ii,306	839	339/99	DRAPx
53	Oldham, Thomas	25247	ii,308	847	TEST	GIRD
54	Powney, William	25290	ii,317	871	339/79	CAR
55	Richardson, William	25308	ii,322	888	339/65	WEAV
56	Blatt, James	5636	ii,337	941	343/120	DRAPx
57	Ewens, John	16760	ii,334	931	INT	VINTx
58	Bolton, Ambrose	17081	ii,330	917	TEST	MERCx
59	Claggett, Edward	10504	ii,318	874	342/34	DRAPx
60	Gresham, Seyliard	25038	ii,323	890	INT	P/S

No.	Name	Boyd	CSB	Orphans	Will	Coy
61	Aspinall, John	24732	ii,309	849	342/68	INN
62	Budden, George	24823	ii,324	895	342/99	BLAC
63	Driver, Thomas	20707	ii,331	922	343/145	COOP
64	Rosemary, Henry	20716	ii,331	921	INT	FRUT
65	Smith, Sir John	10619	ii,328	910	342/105	SALTx
66	Vanderpost, Adrian	25463	ii,370	1057	341/48	MERCx
67	Monger, Joshua	10705	ii,338	944	344/48	MERCx
68	Steedman, William	19995	ii,372	1062	345/91	FISHx
69	Crooke, Andrew	24913	ii,367	1047	INT	STATx
70	Butler, John jr	16969	ii,364	1036	347/11	FLET
71	Browne, Mun	13813	ii,351	993	346/122	MERCx
72	Marten, John	20529	ii,343	966	TEST	HABx
73	Wood, William	17409	ii,331	923	INT	TYLE
74	Howes, Robert	23281	ii,335	937	TEST	FELT
75	Adderly, Hugh	4003	ii,344	966	INT	VINT
76	Writor, Harloe	16766	ii,351	991	INT	DRAPx
77	Wharton, James	25512	ii,354	1000	345/79	SALT
78	Golding, Richard	23005	ii,383	1095	INT	IRON
79	Langton, Edward	23384	ii,364	1033	347/49	DYER
80	Tomlinson, Richard	25446	ii,389	1111	348/94	APOTx
81	Lambert, William	19618	ii,400	1147	TEST	APOTx
82	Phinnes, George	20579	ii,413	1224	349/115	CLOTx
83	Shipman, Gervase	19722	ii,412	1219	348/87	M/Tx
84	Bradshaw, Henry	24801	ii,410	1205	349/106	M/Tx
85	Darby, Richard	24924	ii,406	1186	348/83	GROCx
86	Trehern, Edward	19903	ii,405	1177	INT	JOIN
87	Bourchier, Anthony	9130	ii,402	1157	INT	MERCx
88	Appletree, John	24723	ii,392	1123	348/96	HABx
89	Dixon, Thomas	19755	ii,392	1121	348/98	GROCx
90	Tucker, Humphrey	24557	ii,391	1117	INT	DRAPx
91	Hobby, John	17813	ii,374	1070	347/35	HAB
92	Stone, Joseph	20095	ii,414	1353	INT	HABx
93	Randall, John	8578	ii,414	1320	352/132	DRAPx
94	Edwards, William	18387	ii,410	1204	350/49	CLOTx
95	Grant, William	25032	ii,409	1200	TEST	GOLDx
96	Hayward, William	20690	ii,408	1196	351/101	FISHx
97	Darling, Edward	24926	ii,404	1171	350/37	VINTx
98	Sell, Richard	21051	ii,391	1119	INT	M/Tx
99	Hampton, Walter	13024	ii,426	1298	352/140	MERCx
100	Winch, Robert	17832	iv,3	1322	351/96	HAB
101	Wombwell, Steven	25542	ii,385	1100	INT	DIST
102	Sleymaker, Edward	25371	ii,401	1154	TEST	FREE
103	Edmonds, William	20107	ii,404	1170	350/38	M/T
104	Waggorne, John	25473	ii,419	1260	351/107	DIST
105	Clay, Edmond	23436	ii,429	1308	350/2	HABx

No.	Name	Boyd	CSB	Orphans	Will	Coy
106	Tull, Samuel	22567	ii,423	1285	353/9	GIRD
107	Birkin, James	19247	iv,1	1314	354/70	CLOTx
108	Casberd, Joseph	25624	iv,151	1762	354/73	T/Cx
109	Lewis, Edmond	25848	iv,47	1465	INT	HABx
110	Leech, Robert	16911	iv,26	1392	INT	CLOTx
111	Heath, Roger	11749	iv,34	1419	INT	HABx
112	Skepper, John	2922	iv,36	1423	INT	T/C
113	Hunlock, Osbaston	25815	iv,37	1426	TEST	APOTx
114	Williams, Thomas	20778	iv,54	1489	358/118	STATx
115	Marshall, Joshua	9884	iv,60	1503	356/36	FREE
116	Rayner, John	25947	iv,23	1378	357/68	SALT
117	Dryden, Henry	25698	iv,26	1735	INT	GROC
118	Copping, Samuel	25661	iv,29	1400	INT	L/S
119	Neesum, John	20997	iv,39	1437	356/36	JOIN
120	Richardson, Francis	17910	iv,47	1466	INT	SALTx
121	Boden, John	21377	iv,48	1470	INT	FOUN
122	Preston, John	17364	iv,75	1536	361/134	SKINx
123	Kingsley, Edward	20826	iv,78	1548	359/47	CARP
124	Sawbridge, Isaac	21722	iv,92	1579	360/121	COOP
125	Came, Thomas	188	iv,120	1648	359/54	CLOTx
126	Coles, Thomas	16963	iv,77	1540	360/115	M/Tx
127	Gawden, Charles	20274	iv,102	1603	361/161	SKINx
128	Marsh, Ralph	19763	iv,42	1564	359/35	PEWT
129	Packer, Steven	16968	iv,46	1460	TEST	VINTx
130	Ansell, Thomas	17204	iv,48	1632	INT	SALTx
131	Stevenson, Thomas	20624	iv,51	1480	INT	P/S
132	Hood, Robert	20264	iv,67	1519	360/70	SALT
133	Gopp, Ichabod	21165	iv,87	1562	TEST	M/T
134	Guy, William	25768	iv,90	1574	TEST	HATB
135	Flory, James	25725	iv,170	1819	359/56	FREE
136	Tomlins, Samuel	26035	iv,120	1649	363/100	SADD
137	Moody, Thomas	20437	iv,126	1668	INT	GLAZ
138	Tasker, Edward	26021	iv,140	1712	364/135	SALTx
139	Davis, Richard	17398	iv,152	1763	363/78	PEWT
140	Warren, Samuel	21043	iv,175	1834	364/176	SADD
141	Floyd, Joseph	18619	iv,95	1587	362/19	MERCx
142	Dilkes, Fisher	2537	iv,107	1613	INT	SKINx
143	Dodson, William	25691	iv,117	1641	INT	VINTx
144	Coke, Richard	25654	iv,121	1652	INT	SKINx
145	Impy, John	16773	iv,123	1657	INT	DRAPx
146	Pead, Thomas	17325	iv,133	1685	362/27	HABx
147	Rainsford, Edward	25941	iv,141	1714	363/65	DRAP
148	Carleton, Matthew	25621	iv,147	1745	363/104	MERCx
149	Keech, John	25828	iv,147	1744	INT	GOLDx
150	Newton, Richard	25893	iv,148	1858	362/39	GROCx

No.	Name	Boyd	CSB	Orphans	Will	Coy
151	Sheppard, John	25986	iv,160	1786	INT	HABx
152	Knight, Thomas	17609	iv,183	1855	363/81	FREE
153	Prestwood, Abraham	21199	iv,136	1694	INT	SALT
154	Day, Thomas	17510	iv,146	1735	INT	GROC
155	Holroid, Nathan	17568	iv,161	1792	365/45	LOR
156	Plummer, William	25926	iv,162	1794	INT	HABx
157	Langhorne, Richard	19674	iv,165	1801	365/46	SALT
158	Loadman, Robert	17786	iv,169	1814	INT	ARM
159	Savill, Gilbert	17710	iv,170	1817	INT	WEAV
160	Harris, Joseph	17078	iv,129	1675	INT	GOLDx
161	King, Thomas	25833	iv,138	1704	TEST	GOLDx
162	Buggins, Edward	21305	iv,146	1739	INT	VINTx
163	Lee, Lancelot	17559	iv,155	1772	366/60	FISHx
164	Justice, William	25827	iv,165	1946	366/73	L/S
165	Berriffe, Thomas	13425	iv,166	1806	INT	M/Tx
166	Rawlinson, William	17235	iv,176	1837	INT	MERCx
167	White, Steven	26075	iv,181	1849	TEST	GROCx
168	Loveday, Thomas	17904	iv,186	1863	368/143	GOLDx
169	Walker, Thomas	21313	iv,193	1885	INT	M/Tx
170	Skrine, John	20933	iv,195	1892	368/173	IRON
171	Short, Peter	13014	iv,217	1968	367/135	M/Tx
172	Elkins, Thomas	25704	iv,186	1862	367/128	CLOTx
173	Hotchkis, Richard	25806	iv,186	1865	369/5	SCRI
174	Warren, Lawrence	26061	iv,180	1846	INT	PEWT
175	Archer, Richard	17791	iv,176	1836	INT	HAB
176	Stileman, Samuel	17374	iv,205	1928	371/151	APOTx
177	Wallis, Daniel	26054	iv,207	1935	371/114	CLOTx
178	Pearce, Edward	25916	iv,193	1886	INT	DIST
179	Wymondsold, Richard	26084	iv,203	1919	370/78	BOWY
180	Ride, Thomas	21373	iv,205	1926	INT	COOP
181	Fell, John	25710	iv,209	1938	372/4	DIST
182	Pratt, Thomas	25935	iv,211	1947	372/38	P/S
183	Thomas, John	17582	iv,216	1965	372/50	CLOTx
184	Ladds, William	13607	iv,220	1980	374/105	DRAPx
185	Gawthorne, Nathaniel	3639	iv,226	1991	373/56	SKINx
186	Avery, Henry	13251	iv,246	2047	TEST	DRAPx
187	Dios, Joseph	14686	iv,222	1983	375/14	L/S
188	Walford, Robert	26052	iv,223	1985	377/120	TURN
189	Redshaw, Christopher	17562	iv,233	2011	INT	FISHx
190	Chapman, John	20987	iv,229	2001	INT	MERCx
191	Dubois, John	10771	iv,235	2015	378/169	WEAV
192	Mason, George	854	iv,229	2002	380/61	VINTx
193	Waldron, William	20037	iv,232	2169	375/24	SALT
194	Yardley, Thomas	17950	iv,240	2029	INT	LBSM
195	Bass, Francis	21391	iv,249	2057	INT	VINTx

No.	Name	Boyd	CSB	Orphans	Will	Coy
196	Thorn, Andrew	26030	iv,242	2034	382/7	HABx
197	Davis, Thomas	25682	iv,238	2021	INT	TYLE
198	Ellis, John	14248	iv,239	2026	INT	GIRD
199	Wood, Richard	26086	iv,248	2054	TEST	HAB
200	Crooke, Robert	25670	iv,259	2080	INT	SALT
201	Brearcliffe, Mark	21615	iv,254	2069	TEST	HABx
202	Jenks, Francis	2724	iv,292	2153	INT	FISHx
203	Dowse, John	284	iv,294	2159	INT	VINTx
204	Green, Robert	19772	iv,255	2070	TEST	M/T
205	Lawrey, Jeremiah	20764	iv,260	2082	INT	APOTx
206	Mingay, Roger	14091	iv,264	2117	INT	DRAPx
207	Sealey, Richard	25970	iv,273	2114	INT	MERCx
208	Dent, Richard	18156	iv,290	2147	390/31	SALT
209	Rosagan, Robert	25955	iv,270	2105	INT	HABx
210	Rookes, Richard	25954	iv,262	2088	394/24	VINTx
211	Whiston, Nicholas	26073	iv,286	2139	397/168	HAB
212	Paggen, William	21281	iv,278	2124	398/29	CLOTx
213	Stanley, John	20989	iv,289	2146	INT	GROC
214	Head, Joseph	25786	iv,296	2164	INT	SALT
215	Hunlock, Philip	25814	iv,275	2118	400/124	VINTx
216	Ambler, William	16684	iv,275	2119	400/120	HABx
217	Flowerden, John	17956	iv,281	2129	401/136	GROCx
218	Kendrick, Andrew	13667	iv,315	2208	TEST	MERCx
219	Ireland, Edward	29577	v,30	2282	TEST	L/S
220	Fickis, Benjamin	25713	iv,276	2120	TEST	POUL
221	Wotton, Henry	26096	iv,290	2148	TEST	L/S
222	Douglas, Richard	25699	iv,294	2158	INT	VINT
223	Russell, Roger	25963	iv,278	2123	INT	APOTx
224	Balam, Anthony	21518	v,23	2264	INT	FISHx
225	Jellings, John	25823	iv,302	2175	409/88	T/C
226	Baugh, Nicholas	21063	iv,300	2172	408/21	M/Tx
227	Rudd, Robert	25960	iv,302	2178	INT	COOP
228	Stokes, Humphrey	26011	iv,305	2185	410/135	GOLDx
229	Andrews, Joel	3016	iv,307	2189	408/1	CLOTx
230	Norris, Philip	21341	iv,306	2186	409/53	FISHx
231	Allen, Thomas	17072	iv,310	2199	414/61	VINTx
232	Chambers, Samuel	25633	iv,315	2207	415/122	DRAPx
233	Brown, Joseph	21603	v,7	2226	415/106	CUT
234	Portress, John	25931	iv,314	2205	414/68	L/S
235	Biddle, Edward	21087	v,10	2234	INT	CURR
236	Barkstead, John	4048	v,21	2261	420/93	MERCx
237	Dring, Thomas	27293	v,22	2263	421/152	STATx
238	Smith, Simon	542	v,11	2236	INT	VINTx
239	Scarth, Philip	2384	v,23	2514	427/160	GROCx
240	Dighton, James	27288	v,6	2225	INT	POUL

No.	Name	Boyd	CSB	Orphans	Will	Coy
241	Baily, Robert	26136	v,8	2228	429/204	STAT
242	Filewood, John	21122	v,18	2252	INT	POUL
243	Moore, Hector	29638	v,15	2245	INT	GOLDx
244	Wise, Thomas	29821	v,15	2246	TEST	CLOC
245	Broadhurst, John	21595	v,21	2262	430/29	M/Tx
246	Williams, Thomas	2481	v,32	2288	439/152	GOLDx
247	Kniveton, James	29601	v,36	2298	INT	HABx
248	Carter, John	26235	v,19	2256	INT	VINTx
249	Newton, John	20139	v,85	2501	444/45	HABx
250	March, Francis	18166	v,39	2306	441/246	SKINx
251	Maddox, Robert	29624	v,37	2343	INT	DIST
252	Stock, Richard	29749	v,31	2285	INT	M/Tx
253	Brooke, Philip	1048	v,47	2324	TEST	CLOTx
254	Scatliffe, Henry	29723	v,81	2434	INT	M/Tx
255	Hastings, John	27961	v,83	2441	INT	T/C
256	Seabrook, Robert	29718	v,35	2297	INT	LOR
257	Hackshall, Allan	17977	v,39	2307	449/41	FISHx
258	Waldo, Samuel	28248	v,42	2313	INT	CLOTx
259	Wigfall, Daniel	29810	v,44	2318	450/51	VINTx
260	Fryer, George	22150	v,38	2304	INT	LOR
261	Adams, John	26106	v,44	2317	INT	IRON
262	Winston, Henry	23115	v,62	2361	INT	COOP
263	Barber, Thomas	26129	v,80	2429	453/186	COOK
264	Fitzhugh, William	21308	v,65	2371	INT	STAT
265	Newcome, John	29648	v,51	2333	INT	APOT
266	Shuter, James	18230	v,57	2348	456/105	DYER
267	Lancaster, Gilbert	29602	v,58	2350	TEST	INN
268	Jones, Thomas	29592	v,45	2319	INT	APOTx
269	Butler, Sir Nicholas	4134	v,53	2338	457/125	SKINx
270	Meredith, Luke	14179	v,61	2356	456/116	STATx
271	Hayward, Samuel	3666	v,66	2375	455/49	ARM
272	Pinder, Lawrence	21818	v,85	2449	INT	FOUN
273	Bowell, William	22156	v,71	2394	INT	M/Tx
274	Palmer, Samuel	29655	v,72	2398	TEST	FISHx
275	Baker, Lancelot	26125	v,76	2411	INT	GOLDx
276	Hedges, Sir William	15801	v,80	2432	461/113	MERCx
277	Scott, Thomas	29724	v,81	2435	INT	CLOTx
278	Penford, Thomas	29671	v,84	2445	462/173	STATx
279	Cary, John	13856	v,86	2503	460/58	SALT
280	Thornbury, Thomas	608	v,87	2653	465/105	SALTx
281	Melmoth, William	19960	v,89	2512	INT	APOTx
282	Leman, Neville	29613	v,77	2417	461/114	DYER
283	Adams, John	26105	v,79	2425	TEST	CUT
284	Greening, John	11559	v,85	2447	461/114	CORD
285	Carew, George	26913	v,91	2513	463/18	IRON

No.	Name	Boyd	CSB	Orphans	Will	Coy
286	Stevenson, Lawrence	21205	v,76	2414	INT	IRON
287	Philips, Edward	29674	v,88	2509	464/83	DIST
288	Harrison, Richard	21895	v,89	2511	TEST	CLOT
289	Macklin, William	29622	v,98	2546	466/138	DIST
290	Clark, George	18215	v,85	2446	INT	VINTx
291	Cullen, Abraham	27275	v,102	2558	TEST	HABx
292	Treadway, George	29767	v,182	2812	TEST	MERCx
293	Grevill, Francis	429	v,110	2587	471/154	GOLDx
294	Lawrence, Thomas	29607	v,111	2594	TEST	DRAPx
295	Sherwood, John	29729	v,121	2627	INT	DYER
296	Richardson, William	11049	v,141	2692	INT	FISHx
297	Cooke, Miles	27263	v,96	2538	INT	ARM
298	Bucknell, Emanuel	26903	v,102	2560	469/62	WEAV
299	Griffith, William	27945	v,103	2562	TEST	INN
300	Boultby, Benjamin	17739	v,108	2579	TEST	SALT
301	Aldersley, John	26108	v,112	2597	INT	L/S
302	Sayer, Richard	29717	v,121	2625	INT	SALT
303	How, Joseph	27992	v,138	2679	470/92	DIST
304	Thomas, Daniel	29762	v,111	2593	INT	MERCx
305	Pead, Thomas	5227	v,125	2638	INT	GROCx
306	Minshall, Francis	29636	v,126	2641	INT	VINTx
307	Osborne, Edward	29650	v,117	2614	477/134	VINTx
308	Woolley, Adam	17292	v,123	2634	476/121	GOLDx
309	Hicks, John	27976	v,131	2657	477/164	CLOTx
310	Hiett, Richard	27980	v,111	2591	TEST	BUTC
311	Lillie, Richard	21817	v,124	2636	INT	WEAV
312	Parnell, Thomas	29660	v,131	2658	477/153	COOK
313	Cheslin, John	26919	v,139	2684	INT	GROCx
314	Gouge, Thomas	27939	v,144	2702	INT	DRAPX
315	Vansittart, Peter	29781	v,150	2718	INT	FISHx
316	Potts, John	23015	v,155	2733	484/185	GROCx
317	Levett, Francis	10933	v,185	2817	INT	MERC
318	King, Jonathan	29599	v,172	2783	TEST	CLOCx
319	Winn, John	29819	v,181	2810	487/53	MERCx
320	Waller, Henry	29790	v,152	2876	INT	VINTx
321	Woodgate, Thomas	13008	v,153	2729	INT	IRON
322	Knapp, George	14038	v,163	2756	490/195	HABx
323	Sabin, Joshua	29712	v,170	2779	INT	WEAV
324	Munford, John	21045	v,197	2860	INT	GROCx
325	Barrow, John	26134	v,161	2752	494/98	VINTx
326	Whichcot, Benjamin	29804	v,204	2882	497/240	M/Tx
327	Crooke, Thomas	27273	v,165	2762	TEST	WEAV
328	Eborn, John	27907	v,168	2772	493/83	DIST
329	Wintle, William	19610	v,172	2784	INT	DYER
330	Caldecott, George	21554	v,209	2893	TEST	MERCx

No.	Name	Boyd	CSB	Orphans	Will	Coy
331	Main, Edward	29625	v,177	2796	502/135	MERC
332	Walford, Richard	29785	v,181	2807	INT	TURN
333	Reynolds, Richard	29694	v,181	2809	INT	APOTx
334	Comport, Robert	17725	v,185	2819	INT	GROCx
335	Rouse, John	28127	v,188	2828	INT	CLOTx
336	Breese, Underhill	26891	v,186	2821	TEST	HABx
337	Swanwick, Major	10167	v,195	2851	512/299	DRAPx
338	Fotherby, Robert	27922	v,213	2902	INT	SALT
339	Seakins, Matthew	29719	v,194	2850	INT	T/C
340	Ragdale, Nathaniel	29688	v,204	2881	512/296	T/C
341	Phipps, Richard	17899	v,202	2873	INT	JOINx
342	Booth, John	21567	v,202	2875	INT	GROCx
343	Ford, Samuel	27921	v,200	2869	TEST	TYLE
344	Hancock, Edward	11719	v,208	2891	INT	MERC
345	Brice, Shadrach	26893	v,220	2920	INT	SALTx
346	Crouch, Peter	21596	v,221	2921	INT	APOTx
347	Seller, Robert	29720	v,217	2911	524/246	COOK
348	Heriot, Thomas	28030	vi,1	2965	INT	HABx
349	Dugdale, Thomas	14139	v,218	2913	INT	SKINx
350	Ayloffe, Richard	26122	v,219	2916	521/119	VINTx
351	Dorrington, Francis	27290	v,219	2917	INT	M/Tx
352	Bretten, Thomas	26892	v,230	2946	529/204	COOP
353	Micklethwait, Jonathan	29879	vi,21	3012	529/216	MERCx
354	Brookes, John	26959	vi,13	2995	527/108	EMBR
355	Collins, Freeman	27257	v,228	2940	531/5	STATx
356	Grace, Richard	27940	v,231	2947	TEST	SALTx
357	Watts, Samuel	29800	v,233	2955	TEST	HABx
358	Ashby, George	26165	vi,11	2991	531/1	HABx
359	Booth, Caleb	26943	vi,8	2982	538/2	SOAP
360	Gibbs, Francis	17862	vi,5	2975	INT	DYER
361	Fawdrey, Robert	28002	vi,7	2981	INT	COAC
362	Clack, Thomas	26975	vi,8	2983	INT	CURR
363	Dennett, Robert	27320	vi,15	3000	INT	B/Sx
364	Lamb, Arthur	29855	vi,26	3024	547/142	DRAPx
365	Hawes, Thomas	28021	vi,16	3003	548/176	T/C
366	Bates, Charles	26937	vi,34	3044	INT	STATx
367	Staples, John	29959	vi,43	3066	TEST	UPH
368	Mansfield, Lewis	29868	vi,36	3050	554/195	DIST
369	Mason, William	29871	vi,44	3069	564/108	GROC
370	Borlase, Henry	13513	vi,50	3083	INT	COOP
371	Blundell, Richard	26941	vi,37	3052	564/124	B/Sx
372	Leaper, John	29859	vi,44	3070	INT	JOINx
373	Toms, Thomas	29968	vi,52	3088	INT	B/Sx
374	Goodlad, John	11696	vi,71	3150	TEST	M/Tx
375	Blackall, John	11551	vi,79	3176	TEST	CLOTx

Abbreviations of Livery Companies

APOT	Apothecary	FELT	Feltmaker	M/T	Merchant-taylor
ARM	Armourer	FISH	Fishmonger	P/S	Painter-stainer
B/S	Barber-surgeon	FLET	Fletcher	PEWT	Pewterer
BLAC	Blacksmith	FOUN	Founder	PLUM	Plumber
BOWY	Bowyer	FREE	Freemason	POUL	Poulterer
BREW	Brewer	FRUT	Fruiterer	SADD	Saddler
BUTC	Butcher	GIRD	Girdler	SALT	Salter
CAR	Carman	GLAZ	Glazier	SCRI	Scrivener
CARP	Carpenter	GOLD	Goldsmith	SKIN	Skinner
CLOC	Clockmaker	GROC	Grocer	SOAP	Soapmaker
CLOT	Clothworker	HAB	Haberdasher	STAT	Stationer
COAC	Coachmaker	HATB	Hatband-maker	T/C	Tallow-chandler
COOP	Cooper	INN	Innholder	TURN	Turner
CORD	Cordwainer	IRON	Ironmonger	TYLE	Tyler/Bricklayer
CURR	Currier	JOIN	Joiner	UPH	Upholder
CUT	Cutler	L/S	Leather-seller	VINT	Vintner
DIST	Distiller	LBSM	Longbowstringmaker	WEAV	Weaver
DRAP	Draper	LOR	Loriner	WOOD	Woodmonger
EMBR	Embroiderer	MERC	Mercer		

Appendix B: Real Estate Holdings of Sample

In Section ii of Chapter 5, the real estate holdings of the sample were discussed. Information on these was acquired from three main sources: the listing of unpaid rents in inventories which were not backed by the listing of leasehold property, memoranda in the Common Serjeants' Books and information from the wills of the sample. Altogether, 181 wills have been found (48 per cent of the whole sample and 80 per cent of those who were testate) and it seems probable that, using all three sources, not many men with real estate will have been missed, since it is a reasonable assumption that most men who possessed real estate would have made a will. Only a minority of references contain valuations or a statement of the rental of property, and the valuations in the list below are therefore mainly guesstimates. Where property has been valued, this has been used as a guide to the value of what seems a similar sort of property which has not been valued. Rentals have been multiplied by 20 to provide valuations.

The properties have been graded for value on a five point scale for value as follows: 1 = less than £300; 2 = £300–£999; 3 = £1000–£1999; 4 = £2000–£5000; 5 = over £5000.

They have also been classified by type as follows: A = London property; B = suburban or villa property; C = provincial urban property; D = one or two farms; E = larger country estate.

Sample	Description of Real Estate Holdings	Grade	Type
S. 4	Unpaid rents @ £65 p.a; no leases	3	A
S. 9	Tenements @ £100 p.a. in St Giles Cripplegate; tenement on Tower Hill; land in Essex & Ireland	5	A,E
S. 10	3 houses in Monkwell St; houses in Dunnings Alley; dwelling-house in Bishopsgate Street	3	A
S. 12	Messuage with land in Tottenham	2	B

Sample	Description of Real Estate Holdings	Grade	Type
S. 14	Two houses in Botolph Lane; half of Cox Key	3	A
S. 15	Three messuages in Trinity Court, Aldersgate Street, worth less than one-third of personal estate of £600	1	A
S. 16	Farm in Herts, 43 acres of wheat growing, say 100 acres @ 5/- to 7/6 an acre	2	D
S. 21	Farm and other property in Surrey	2	D
S. 23	House in Southwark	1	A
S. 24	Foreclosed lands and tenements in Kent = £1400	3	E
S. 25	Dog and Bear Inn, Southwark	1	A
S. 27	Lands in Berks, his home county	4	E
S. 31	Copyhold estate in Somerset = £100	1	D
S. 37	Lands and tenements in West Ham = c.£1500; lands in Berks = c.£1190; in Herts = £300; land in Yorkshire; land in Kent @ £35 p.a.; house in Southwark; some of this mortgaged	4	A,B,E
S. 45	Dwelling-house, other houses and land at Cow Cross; house in Twickenham	3	A,B
S. 48	Tenements in Southwark	1	A
S. 56	Messuages and lands in Suffolk, less than £1000	2	D
S. 59	Three houses in City; houses and land in Greenwich; property in Canterbury	4	A,C
S. 61	House with some land in Lancashire	1	D
S. 65	London houses; land in Surrey and Essex; copyhold and freehold land in Isleworth; in all over £380 p.a.	5	A,B,E
S. 69	Copyhold lands in Middlesex (fine = £150); house in Kensington	3	B,E
S. 70	Two houses in Leadenhall Street; copyhold in Surrey	3	A,D
S. 82	Three messuages in Staying Lane	1	A
S. 89	House in Stratford and 7 small houses in Greenwich	2	A,B
S. 93	Eight houses in City; 6 houses and copyhold land in Tottenham	5	A,B
S. 97	Freehold and copyhold property in Hampstead	2	B
S. 99	House and ground in Gloucestershire	2	D
S.100	Freehold messuages and lands	3	?
S.105	Urban estate in Nottingham; lands and tenements in Cow Cross	3	A,C
S.108	Messuage at Slough	1	D
S.114	Three houses in Hosier Lane	2	A
S.115	Several houses in Whitefriars; lands in Surrey and Cambridgeshire	5	A,E
S.125	Copyhold messuages, tenements and land in Mortlake	2	D

Sample	Description of Real Estate Holdings	Grade	Type
S.127	Farm at Leyton	2	B
S.136	Freehold farms and lands in Bucks and Herts; houses in London	4	A,E
S.138	Lands and tenements in Gloucs; also in Leyton	3	B,E
S.139	House near Temple Bar	2	A
S.147	Three copyhold messuages in Suffolk	2	E
S.150	Freehold and copyhold land in Essex	2	D
S.157	Manor of Somersby, Lincs @ £100 p.a.; five farms in Lincs = at least £1200	4	E
S.164	Lands in Kent @ £57 p.a.; copyhold in Dagenham	3	E
S.167	Copyhold lands in Manor of Hackney; land in Ireland; in all at least £385 p.a.	5	A,E
S.168	Two houses in Warwicks; land in Berks & Oxfordshire	3	E
S.171	Manor and lordship of Claythorpe & Bellew, Lincs; other freehold and copyhold land in Lincs; estate at West Ham	5	B,E
S.183	Freehold messuages and lands in Surrey	2	D
S.191	Property in Wales, Surrey and Kent, the last valued @ £1680	5	E
S.193	Freehold and copyhold in Norfolk and Suffolk	3	E
S.196	Messuage and land in Bristol, more than £100 p.a.; messuages and lands in Edmonton and Gravesend, more than £80 p.a.	4	B,C
S.208	Four houses in St Dunstans in the East	3	A
S.210	Messuage in Westminster	1	A
S.218	Farm in Herts	2	D
S.219	Six freehold tenements in Lambeth	2	A
S.225	Farmland and meadows in Hunts and Bucks	2	D
S.231	Freehold lands in Surrey and Yorkshire, £240 p.a.	4	E
S.234	Four houses in London; freehold estate in Herts and Bucks @ £40 p.a.	4	A,D
S.237	Six houses in London @ £164 p.a	4	A
S.239	Lands in Yorks and Essex; copyhold in Isle of Wight, the last valued at £500	4	E
S.241	Houses in Southwark	2	A
S.247	Farm in Kent @ £36 p.a.	2	D
S.249	Land in Essex = £550; land in Notts = £450	3	E
S.253	Manor of Levenhall, Suffolk and two houses in London, in all worth at least £2000	4	A,E
S.257	Two messuages with orchards in Tooting; 8 cottages in Lambeth	3	A,D
S.259	Lands in Yorks @ £120 p.a.	4	E
S.265	Land in Bedfordshire @ £90 p.a.	3	E
S.269	Several messuages, farms and lands	3	E

Sample	Description of Real Estate Holdings	Grade	Type
S.271	Farm in Essex	2	D
S.275	Property in Suffolk	2	D
S.276	Signiorie of Inchequine, Ireland & other Irish lands	4	E
S.277	Property in Walthamstow @ £29 p.a.	2	B
S.282	Tenements and land in Yorkshire	2	D
S.285	Messuages and lands	3	E
S.288	Rents due @ £19 p.a., no leases	2	?
S.289	Farms in Suffolk, Wilts, Essex and Sussex	3	E
S.303	Land in Bucks @ £20 p.a.; farm in Middlesex	2	D
S.308	Five farms, 3 cottages and other lands in Derbyshire; copyholds in Highgate and Stepney; 6 houses in City	5	A,B,E
S.313	Property in Clerkenwell	2	A
S.314	Rents @ £185 p.a., no leases	4	?
S.316	Land in Wales = £200; in Warwickshire = £250	2	D
S.319	Land in Derbyshire @ £20 p.a.	2	D
S.322	Land in Bucks = £1500; half the manor of Symeons in Chilton, Bucks	4	E
S.325	Messuages in West Ham; messuages in Penrith	2	B,D
S.326	Farms in Suffolk, Essex & Cambridgeshire @ £123 p.a.; houses in Southwark	4	A,E
S.331	Freehold houses in Wood Street	3	A
S.340	Freehold houses in Blackfriars	2	A
S.345	House in Kingston @ £18 p.a.	2	B
S.347	Three houses in Whitechapel and Shoreditch	2	A
S.348	Land in Hants @ £55 p.a.	3	E
S.353	Copyhold lands in Herts @ £41 p.a.	2	D
S.354	House and land in Hackney = £650	2	A
S.355	Freehold houses in Wapping	2	A
S.358	Farms in Northants and Hunts @ c.£50 p.a.; house in Coleman St, in Fleet St, 4 in Blackfriars; one in Bermondsey	4	A,E
S.364	Estate in Colchester	2	C
S.365	Freehold estate in Berks	3	E
S.375	Lands and tenements in Writtle and Chignell, Essex	4	E

Appendix C: Credit Patterns from Bankruptcy Records

The table below is based on the bankruptcy docket-books for the calendar years 1711–15 (PRO B4/1–2). The first stage in bankruptcy proceedings was for a creditor to establish a claim against an alleged bankrupt and for a docket of bankruptcy to be struck. These were recorded in the docket-books which, from 1710, give the name, address and occupation of the debtor and of the creditor, normally just one creditor owed at least £100 but sometimes two or more. There were more dockets than bankruptcies since they were often struck as a measure of insurance and a creditor would not necessarily push the matter any further if he could find a better method of proceeding (Pressnell (1956) p. 445; Ashton (1959) pp. 113–14). There are also other problems, such as duplication, renewed commissions and partners who were named as individuals as well as partners. In the analysis, all duplications and renewed commissions (very common in 1715) have been removed and partners treated as one debtor, not counting the individuals separately. Occupations cause problems too. Many people described as gentlemen were actually merchants or wholesalers, as can be seen when they sued more than one person and were given a different description. Livery Companies are also sometimes given as occupations, sometimes accurately, sometimes obviously not, such as the mercer who sued two bankrupts, one a copper merchant and the other a brazier. In all, there were 1094 debtors recorded in the docket-books for these five years, 637 from the metropolis, and there were 825 separate London creditors. Of the latter, 76 sued two different bankrupts, 17 sued three, 2 sued four and 1 each sued five, seven and nine different bankrupts. The last five super-creditors were the linen-draper Robert Macmorran (4), the hosier Christopher Topham (4), the Blackwell Hall factors Smith & Wallington (5), the linen-drapers Yonge & Lloyd (7) and finally the great wine merchant Manasses Whitehead, who sued eight London tavern-keepers and a merchant in these five years.

The source is an attractive one for fairly impressionistic insights into the credit relationships existing in various occupations and can also be used as a general data bank on business. It has been used on several occasions in the book, in Chapter 2 in an analysis of the credit relationships between London and the provinces, in Chapter 4 to provide some indication of the proportional importance of partnership in business and in Chapter 6 to provide one way of trying to estimate the relative significance of women in business. Insights from the data have also been used in the general discussion of occupations in Chapter 2. Analysis of the pairs, of bankrupt and creditor, provides some idea of the direction of credit in business and indeed, as one first flicks through the docket-books, one's eye immediately picks out some delightful examples of economic logic, such as the whalebone-cutter who sued a whalebone-seller or the diamond-cutter who sued a Westminster jeweller (B4/1 pp. 35 & 89). In the table below are set out the occupations of the creditors of some of the commonest London debtor groups. There are lots of oddities, some of them no doubt due to the problems of occupational labels mentioned above and some of them certainly because the creditor who sued out the commission of bankruptcy was a person who had loaned money to the debtor rather than given him trade credit. Nevertheless, there are sufficient patterns apparent to justify such conclusions as silkmen normally gave credit to silk weavers and weavers to mercers, rather than the other way round.

See pp. 127–30 for a further discussion of bankruptcy.

TABLE C.1: Creditors of Selected London Debtor Groups by Occupations

Debtors	Creditors
Brewers	Gentleman(4), cooper(2), maltster(2), brewer, factor, widow, apothecary, merchant, peruke-maker, linen-draper
Butchers	Butcher(5), gentleman(2), tallow-chandler(2), victualler(2), merchant, tripeman, leather-seller, cordwainer, glazier, vintner, coffeeman, silkman
Chapman	Linen-draper(3), weaver(3), apothecary(2), butcher(2), inn-holder(2), merchant(2), gentleman, grocer, mariner, Blackwell Hall factor, chapman, yarn-seller, cowkeeper, tallow-chandler, widow, brewer
Cheesemongers	Cheesemonger(2), widow(2), cheesefactor, merchant, tallow-chandler, gentleman, merchant-taylor

Debtors	*Creditors*
Distillers	Distiller(3), widow(3), goldsmith(2), corn-factor(2), salter, tobacconist, gentleman, clothworker, merchant, mealman
Dyers	(Dry)salter(7), gentleman(2), brewer, hosier, dyer, merchant
Goldsmiths	Gentleman(9), merchant, mercer
Grocers	Grocer(2), salter(2), merchant(2), distiller, haberdasher, gentleman, apothecary
Haberdashers	Merchant(5), pinmaker, feltmaker, tailor, yeoman, salter, mariner
Linen-drapers	Linen-draper(10), merchant(7), widow(4), gentleman(4), jeweller, haberdasher, druggist, upholder
Mercers	Weaver(15), merchant(7), warehouseman(3), mercer(3), gentleman(2), linen-draper(2), haberdasher(2), dyer, draper, cutler, factor, carpenter, chapman, goldsmith
Merchants	Merchant(71), gentleman(20), packer (6), linen-draper(5), (Blackwell Hall) factor(4), warehouseman(3), weaver(3), glover (2), clothier(2), widow(2), hosier(2), grocer(2), apothecary(2), ropemaker(2), haberdasher(2), skinner(2), goldsmith(2), yeoman, druggist, surgeon, carrier, vintner, mason, joiner, pewterer, silkman, victualler, silk-thrower, tinplate-worker, grazier, tailor, felt-maker, peruke-maker
Victuallers	Brewer(9), gardener(2), cook(2), plasterer, widow, haberdasher of hats, cooper, slopseller, cordwainer, anchorsmith
Vintners	(Wine) merchant(22), (wine) cooper(11), gentleman(5), vintner(4), widow(4), cook, drysalter, plasterer
Warehousemen	Merchant(7), clothier(2), weaver(2), mariner, apothecary, inn-holder, goldsmith
Weavers	Silkman(6), merchant(4), weaver(3), mercer, widow, silk-thrower, embroiderer, wool-comber, woollen-draper
Woollen-drapers	Clothier(14), Blackwell Hall factor(6), gentleman(2), widow, grocer, draper

Source: See introduction above. The numbers in brackets are the number of times that a person from each creditor occupation sued a person in the debtor occupation in the left-hand column. No number means once.

London and the Provinces

In Tables c.2–4 below, the same material has been analysed in order to examine the credit relationship between London and the provinces.

London creditors were named for just over a third of the 457 provincial debtors in 1711–15, while the only two provincial centres which really show up as sources of credit from this analysis were Bristol and Exeter, whose citizens sued 36 and 24 provincial debtors respectively. Both cities had well-defined geographical regions of credit. Exeter's influence was confined almost entirely to Devon and Cornwall but with a few debtors to the east, as far as Portsmouth. Bristol had a much larger hinterland, mainly in the counties of the Severn Valley and on both sides of the Bristol Channel, but stretching as far as Chester to the north and Oxford to the east. Few other cities had any debtors outside their own counties, though one can see the beginnings of northern distributing centres which were soon to be very important, such as Manchester and Leeds.

Londoners sued debtors from 41 English and Welsh counties and Tables C.2 and C.3 show clearly what function the metropolis played in the provision of credit to the provinces, a function which was dominated by the provision of trade credit to textile retailers and to a lesser extent retail food and drink outlets. Other functions which one might have expected to have been important, such as the provision of credit to provincial industry and to the wholesale distribution of agricultural products, make a very poor showing in the figures.

TABLE C.2: Occupations of Provincial Bankrupts Sued by Londoners

Occupations	Nos	%
Mainly textile retailing	97	63
Food and drink retailing	24	16
Geneal wholesaling & distribution	13	8
Industry	9	6
Agricultural wholesaling	8	5
Miscellaneous	3	2
	154	100

Key: *Mainly textile wholesaling* – mercer(39), chapman(37), linen-draper(6), milliner(3), haberdasher(3), draper(2), tailor(2), button-seller, hosier, salesman, shopkeeper, upholder (1 each). *Food & drink* – grocer(7), vintner(4), victualler(3), distiller(3), butcher(2), fruiterer(2), chandler, cheesemonger, confectioner (1 each). *General wholesaling* – merchant(11), bargemaster, warehousekeeper (1 each). *Industry* – clothier(4), carpenter, currier, fuller, leather-dresser, powder-maker (1 each). *Agricultural* – timber-merchant(3), corn-factor, fellmonger, maltster, mealman, yeoman (1 each). *Miscellaneous* – bookseller, painter, goldsmith (1 each).

TABLE C.3: Occupations of Londoners Sueing Provincial Bankrupts

Occupations	Nos	%
Mainly textile wholesalers	112	54
Food, drink & tobacco wholesalers	42	20
General wholesalers & distributors	21	10
Genlemen, widows & scriveners	17	8
Leather trades	5	2
Other specific trades	12	6
	209	100

Key: *Mainly textile wholesalers* – linen-drapers(34), mercers(25), haberdashers(24), woollen-drapers(8), hatmakers(4), chapmen(3), silkmen(3), 'merchant-taylors'(2), haberdasher of hats, hosier, milliner, tailor, salesman, silk-dyer, weaver, upholder, whalebone-seller (1 each). *Food, drink etc.* – grocer(11), cheesemonger(7), distiller(5), salter(4), corn-factor(3), tobacconist(3), cooper(2), vintner(2), baker, butcher, brewer, inn-holder, victualler (1 each). *General wholesale* – merchant(15), warehouse-man(4), carrier, mariner (1 each). *Leather* – cordwainer, currier, glover, leather-seller, skinner (1 each). *Other trades* – soapmaker(6), oilman(2), timber-merchant(2), combmaker, stationer (1 each).

TABLE C.4: Occupations of Non-Londoners Sueing Londoners

Occupations	Nos	%
'Investors'	33	41
Provincial wholesalers & shopkeepers	13	16
Food & timber trades	12	15
Industry	12	15
Carrying	6	8
Merchants overseas	4	5
	80	100

Key: *Investors* – esquires & gentlemen(16), widows & spinsters(10), no logical pattern between creditor & debtor(3), professionals(2), yeomen not sueing food traders(2). *Wholesalers & shopkeepers* – merchants(7), grocers(3), chapmen(2), mercer(1). *Food & timber* – maltsters(4), grazier, gardiner, farmer, cheesefactor, wool-merchant, meal-man, corn-merchant, timber-merchant (1 each). *Industry* – clothiers(6), ironmon-gers(2), lacemen(2), hosier(1), button-maker(1). *Carrying* – mariners(2), bargemaster, carrier, hostman, wharfinger (1 each). *Merchants overseas* – 1 each from Amsterdam, Antwerp, New York and Oporto.

When the reverse flow of credit is looked at, a very different picture emerges. In all, 94 non-Londoners sued 73 London debtors, but the number of creditors was swollen by the 14 separate clothiers who sued the Covent Garden woollen-draper James Douxsaints in 1715. If they are left out, then the occupations of the other 80 creditors were as in Table c.4. Here one can see that the direction of credit in agriculture and provincial industry tended to be more from the provinces to London than the other way round, several of the provincial merchants being also probably concerned with the flow of industrial products to London such as the nine from Leeds, Manchester, Exeter and Norwich. However, what is most striking about the table is that over 40 per cent of the provincial creditors could be described as investors, this injection of country funds being a vital fuel for the London business machine.

Bibliography

Manuscript sources

The list only includes the main sources used. For detailed references and other sources, see Notes.

1. *Corporation of London Records Office*
Assessments for 1694 4s. Aid
Common Serjeants' Books
Marriage Duties Assessments
Mayor's Court, Equity and Interrogatories
Orphans' Inventories
Poll Tax Assessments for 1692

2. *Greater London Record Office*
Consistory Court Records (DL/C), allegations, libels, deposition books

3. *Guildhall Library*
Business and family papers
Livery Company records: freedom registers, apprenticeship binding books, court minutes and wardens' accounts
Marriage licence applications (GHMS 10091)
Parish and ward records: vestry minutes and churchwardens' accounts
Sun Fire Office policy registers (GHMS 11936)

4. *Livery Company Halls*
The archives of the Clothworkers, Drapers, Goldsmiths, Mercers, Salters, Skinners and Stationers were searched for the apprenticeship and freedom records of the sample.

5. *Society of Genealogists' Library*
Boyd's Index of London Citizens

6. *Public Record Office, Chancery Lane*
Bankruptcy Docket-Books (B.4)
Chancery Proceedings (C.5) sampled, using index for apprenticeship and marriage contract cases
Chancery Masters' Exhibits (C.103–C.114) searched for London family and business papers
Copy Wills (PROB 11)
Probate Inventories (PROB 4 & 5)

Bibliography

The works listed are those which have been referred to in the Notes. References in the Notes are given by author and date of publication or first word of anonymous works and date of publication. Place of publication is London unless otherwise stated. Where there is a second publication date in parentheses, the second one has been consulted. For abbreviations of journals etc., see p. 339.

Account (1722): *An Account of an endeavour to suppress gaming houses*
Account (1725): *An Account of Several Workhouses*
Advice (1678): *Advice to the Women and Maidens of London*
Allen (1976): David F. Allen, 'Political clubs in Restoration London', *HJ* xix
Allen (1946): Phyllis Allen, 'Medical education in seventeenth-century England', *JHMed* i
Allen (1988): R. C. Allen, 'The price of freehold land and the interest rate in the seventeenth and eighteenth centuries', *EcHR* 2nd ser. xli
Altick (1978): R. D. Altick, *The Shows of London, 1600–1862* (Cambridge, Mass.)
Anderson (1980): Michael Anderson, *Approaches to the History of the Western Family, 1500–1914*
Andrew (1981): Donna T. Andrew, 'Aldermen and big bourgeoisie of London reconsidered', *SocH* vi
Anglin (1980): J. P. Anglin, 'The expansion of literacy: opportunities for the study of the three Rs in the London diocese of Elizabeth I' *GSLH* iv
Arber (1903–6): Edward Arber, *The Term Catalogues, 1668–1709* 3 vols
Archenholtz (1794): J. W. Archenholtz, *A View of the British Constitution and of the Manners and Customs of the People of England*
Archer (1673): John Archer, *Every Man his own Doctor*
Arnold (1970): Janet Arnold, 'A mantua c. 1709–10', *Costume* iv
Ashton (1897): John Ashton, *Social Life in the Reign of Queen Anne*
Ashton (1959): T. S. Ashton, *Economic Fluctuations in England, 1700–1800*
Ashton (1985): Robert Ashton, 'Samuel Pepys's London', *LJ* xi
Avery (1960): Emmett L. Avery, *The London Stage, 1700–1729* (Carbondale, Ill.)

Aylmer (1980): G. E. Aylmer, 'From office-holding to civil service: the genesis of the modern bureaucracy', *TRHS* 5th ser. xxx

Bahlman (1957): Dudley W. R. Bahlman, *The Moral Revolution of 1688* (New Haven)

Bailey (1730): Nathaniel Bailey, *Dictionarium Britannicum*

Bailey & Barker (1969): F. A. Bailey & T. C. Barker, 'The seventeenth-century origins of watchmaking in south-west Lancashire', in J. R. Harris (ed.), *Liverpool and Merseyside*

Baker (1970): Dennis Baker, 'The marketing of corn in the first half of the eighteenth century: North-east Kent', *AgHR* xviii

Banbury (1971): Philip Banbury, *Shipbuilders of the Thames and Medway* (Newton Abbot)

Barbon (1690): Nicolas Barbon, *A Discourse of Trade*

Baron & Feme (1719): *Baron & Feme: a Treatise of the Common Law concerning husbands and wives*

Baxter (1673): Richard Baxter, *A Christian Directory*

Beattie (1986): J. M. Beattie, *Crime and the Courts in England, 1660–1800* (Oxford)

Beattie (1967): J. M. Beattie, *The English Court in the reign of George I* (Cambridge)

Beaven (1908, 1913): Alfred B. Beaven, *The Aldermen of the City of London*

Beier (1986): A. L. Beier, 'Engine of manufacture: the trades of London', in Beier & Finlay (1986)

Beier & Finlay (1986): A. L. Beier & Roger Finlay, *The Making of the Metropolis: London, 1500–1700*

Bell (1923): W. G. Bell, *The Great Fire of London in 1666*

Beloff (1938): Max Beloff, *Public Order and Popular Disturbances, 1660–1714* (Oxford)

Beloff (1942): Max Beloff, 'A London apprentice's notebook', *History* xxvii

Bennett (1952): E. Bennett, *The Worshipful Company of Carmen*

Bettey (1982): J. H. Bettey, 'The production of alum and copperas in southern England', *TextH* xiii

Birch (1896): George H. Birch, *London churches of the seventeenth and eighteenth centuries*

Birks (1960): M. Birks, *Gentlemen of the Law*

Blackstone (1957): G. V. Blackstone, *A History of the British Fire Service*

Blauner (1966): Robert Blauner, 'Death and Social Structure', *Psychiatry* xxix

Bohun (1702): William Bohun, *Privilegia Londini: or, the laws, customs, and privileges of the City of London*

Bonfield et al. (1986): L. Bonfield, R. M. Smith & K. Wrightson (eds), *The World We Have Gained* (Oxford)

Borsay (1987): Peter Borsay, 'Urban development in the age of Defoe', in Clyve Jones (ed.), *Britain in the First Age of Party, 1680–1750*

Boswell (1950): James Boswell, *London Journal, 1762–63* (ed. F. A. Pottle)

Boynton (1965): L. O. J. Boynton, 'The Bed-Bug and the "Age of Elegance"', *Furniture History* i

Brenner (1973): Robert Brenner, 'The Civil War politics of London's merchant community', *P & P* 58

Brett-James (1935): N. G. Brett-James, *The Growth of Stuart London*

Brief History (1702): *A Brief History of Trade in England*

Brigden (1984): S. Brigden, 'Religion and social obligation in early sixteenth-century London', *P & P* 103

Brockbank (1964): William Brockbank, 'Sovereign remedies: a critical depreciation of the seventeenth-century London Pharmacopoeia', *MedH* viii

Brodsky (1986): V. Brodsky, 'Widows in Late Elizabethan London: remarriage, economic opportunity and family orientations', in Bonfield et al.

Brooke (1958): Iris Brooke, *Dress and undress: the Restoration and the Eighteenth Century*

Brown (1981): Roger Lee Brown, 'The rise and fall of the Fleet marriages', in Outhwaite (1981)

Brown (1715): Tom Brown, *Works* 4th ed.

Brown (1760): Tom Brown, *Works* 9th ed.

Buck (1979): Anne Buck, *Dress in Eighteenth-century England*

Buck (1971): Anne Buck, 'Variations in English women's dress in the eighteenth century', *Folk Life* ix

Buckley (1915): Francis Buckley, *Old London Glasshouses*

Burke (1977): P. Burke, 'Popular culture in seventeenth-century London', *LJ* iii

Burnet (1969): Gilbert Burnet, *History of my Own Times*

Burton (1681): Richard Burton (pseud. for Nathaniel Crouch), *The Apprentices Companion*

Butler (1896): Joseph Butler, *Works* (ed. Gladstone) (Oxford)

Byrd (1958): William Byrd the Younger, *The London Diary, 1717–1721* (ed. Louis B. Wright & Marion Tinling) (New York)

Campbell (1747): R. Campbell, *The London Tradesman*

Campbell (1933): Sybil Campbell, 'The economic and social effects of the usury laws in the eighteenth century', *TRHS* 4th ser. xvi

Carlton (1974): Charles Carlton, *The Court of Orphans* (Leicester)

Carlton (1978): Charles Carlton, 'The widow's tale: male myths and female reality in 16th and 17th-century England', *Albion* x

Carpenter (1956): E Carpenter, *The Protestant Bishop* [Henry Compton]

Carswell (1960): J. Carswell, *The South Sea Bubble*

Cary (1695): John Cary, *An Essay on the state of England* (Bristol)

Case (1711) (1): *The Case and Petition of the Licensed Hackney Chairmen*

Case (1729): *The case between the proprietors of newspapers, and the coffee-men of London and Westminster*

Case (1700): *The Case of the Joyners Company against the importation of manufactured cabinet-work from the East-Indies*

Case (n.d.) (1): *The Case of the Midling and Poorer Sort of Master Shoemakers*

Case (1743): *The Case of the Parish of St Giles Cripplegate*

Case (1712): *The Case of the Poor People employed in weaving silk-handkerchiefs*

Case (1704): *The Case of the Wharfingers*

Chamberlayne (1670, 1684 etc): Edward Chamberlayne, *Angliae Notitia or the Present State of England*

Chamberlayne (1707): John Chamberlayne, *Angliae Notitia* 22nd ed.

Chambers (1728): Ephraim Chambers, *Cyclopaedia*

Chancellor (1925): E. B. Chancellor, *The Pleasure Haunts of London*

Chapman (1972): S. D. Chapman, 'The genesis of the British hosiery industry, 1600–1750', *TextH* iii

Charles & Duffin (1985): L. Charles & L. Duffin (eds), *Women's Work in Pre-industrial England*

Chartres (1977) (3): J. A. Chartres, 'The capital's provincial eyes: London's inns in the early eighteenth century', *LJ* iii

Chartres (1986): J. A. Chartres, 'Food consumption and internal trade', in Beier & Finlay (1986)

Chartres (1977) (1): J. A. Chartres, *Internal Trade in England, 1500–1700*

Chartres (1977) (2): J. A. Chartres, 'Road carrying in England in the seventeenth century: myth and reality', *EcHR* 2nd ser. xxx

Chartres (1973): J. A. Chartres, 'The place of inns in the commercial life of London and western England, 1660–1760', D. Phil. Oxford

Chartres (1980): J. A. Chartres, 'Trade and shipping in the Port of London: Wiggins Key in the later seventeenth century', *JTptH* 3rd ser. i

Chaudhuri (1978): K. N. Chaudhuri, *The Trading World of Asia and the English East India Company, 1660–1760* (Cambridge)

Child (1694): Sir Josiah Child, *A New Discourse of Trade*

Clark (1919): Alice Clark, *The working life of women in the seventeenth century*

Clark (1983): Peter Clark, *The English Alehouse: a social history, 1200–1830*

Clark (1986): Peter Clark, *Sociability and urbanity: clubs and societies in the eighteenth-century city* (Leicester)

Clarkson (1975): L. A. Clarkson, *Death, Disease and Famine in Pre-Industrial England* (Dublin)

Clarkson (1960) (1) L. A. Clarkson 'The leather crafts in Tudor and Stuart England', *AgHR* xiv

Clarkson (1960) (2): L. A. Clarkson, 'The organization of the English leather industry in the late sixteenth and seventeenth centuries', *EcHR* 2nd ser. xiii

Clay (1984): C. Clay, *Economic Expansion and Social Change in England, 1500–1700* 2 vols (Cambridge)

Clay (1974): C. Clay, 'The price of freehold land in the later seventeenth and eighteenth centuries', *EcHR* 2nd ser. xxvii

Clayton & Oakes (1954): M. Clayton & A. Oakes, 'Early calico-printers around London', *Burl. Mag* xcvi

Coleman (1977): D. C. Coleman, *Economy of England, 1450–1750* (Oxford)

Coleman (1973): D. C. Coleman, 'Gentlemen and Players', *EcHR* 2nd xxvi

Coleman (1951–2): D. C. Coleman, 'London scriveners and the estate market in the later seventeenth century', *EcHR* 2nd ser. iv

Coleman (1953–4): D. C. Coleman, 'Naval dockyards under the later Stuarts', *EcHR* 2nd ser. vi

Coleman & John (1976): D. C. Coleman & A. H. John, *Trade, Government and Economy in Pre-industrial England*

Collection: *A Collection for the Improvement of Industry and Trade* (ed. John Houghton, 1692–1703)

Collection(1677): *A Collection of the names of the Merchants living in and about the City of London*

Colley (1981): Linda Colley, 'Eighteenth-century English radicalism before Wilkes', *TRHS* 5th ser. xxxi

Collier (1720): Jeremy Collier, *Essays upon several moral subjects*

Collins (1927): A. S. Collins, *Authorship in the Days of Johnson*

Collyer (1761): J. Collyer, *Parents and Guardians Directory*

Colman (1760): George Colman the Elder, *Polly Honeycombe*

Colvin (1954): H. M. Colvin, *A Biographical Dictionary of English Architects, 1660–1840*

Compleat (1729): *The Compleat Housewife*

Compleat (1677): *The Compleat Servant-Maid*

Compleat (1683): *The Compleat Solicitor, Entring-Clerk and Attorney*

Contempt (1739): *The Contempt of the Clergy Consider'd*

Cook (1986): H. J. Cook, *The decline of the old medical regime in Stuart London* (Cornell)

Corfield (1982): P. Corfield, *The Impact of English Towns*

Corfield (1987): P. Corfield, 'Class by name and number in eighteenth-century Britain', *History* lxxii

Corner (1985): David Corner, 'The London hatting trade, 1660–1800', paper given at the Pasold Conference on the Economic and Social History of Dress, 18 September 1985

Cragg (1951): G. R. Cragg, *Puritanism in the period of the great persecution*

Crawford (1977): Anne Crawford, *A History of the Vintners' Company*

Creighton (1891): Charles Creighton, *A History of Epidemics in Britain* 2 vols (Cambridge)

Cressy (1987): David Cressy, 'A Drudgery of Schoolmasters: the teaching profession in Elizabethan and Stuart England', in Prest (1987) (1)

Cressy (1980): David Cressy, *Literacy and the Social Order: reading and writing in Tudor and Stuart England* (Cambridge)

Croft-Murray (1962): Edward Croft-Murray, *Decorative Painting in England* i

Crouzet (1981): F. Crouzet, 'The sources of England's wealth: some French views in the eighteenth century', in P. L. Cottrell & D. H. Aldcroft (eds), *Shipping, Trade and Commerce*

Culpeper (1653): Nicholas Culpeper, *Pharmacopoeia Londinensis, or the London Dispensatory*

Cumming (1984): Valerie Cumming, *A Visual History of Costume: the seventeenth century*

Cunnington (1955): C. W. & P. Cunnington, *Handbook of English Costume in the seventeenth century*

Cunnington (1951): C. W. & P. Cunnington, *The History of Underclothes*

Dare (1963): R. A. Dare, *A History of Owen's School*

Davidson (1983): C. A. Davidson, *A Woman's Work is Never Done: a history of housework in the British Isles, 1650–1950*

K. G. Davies (1952) (2): K. G. Davies, 'Joint-stock investment in the later seventeenth century', *EcHR* 2nd ser. iv

K. G. Davies (1957): K. G. Davies, *The Royal African Company*

K. G. Davies (1952): K. G. Davies, 'The origins of the commission system in the West India trade', *TRHS* 5th ser. ii

M. G. Davies (1971): Margaret Gay Davies, 'Country gentry and payments to London, 1650–1714', *EcHR* 2nd ser. xxiv

D. Davis (1966): Dorothy Davis, *A History of Shopping*

R. Davis (1967): Ralph Davis, *Aleppo and Devonshire Square: English traders in the Levant in the eighteenth century*

R. Davis (1957): Ralph Davis, 'Earnings on capital in the English shipping industry', *JEH* xvii

R. Davis (1954): Ralph Davis, 'English foreign trade, 1660–1700', *EcHR* 2nd ser. vii, reprinted in Minchinton (1969)

R. Davis (1962) (2): Ralph Davis, 'English foreign trade, 1700–1774', *EcHR* 2nd ser. xv, reprinted in Minchinton (1969)

R. Davis (1956–7): Ralph Davis, 'Merchant shipping in the economy of the late seventeenth century', *EcHR* 2nd ser. ix

R. Davies (1962): Ralph Davis, *The Rise of the English Shipping Industry in the seventeenth and eighteenth centuries*

Deering (1751): G. C. Deering, *Nottinghamia Vetus et Nova*

Deerr (1950): Noel Deerr, *The History of Sugar* 2 vols

Defoe (1730): Daniel Defoe, *A Brief State of the Inland or Home Trade of England*

Defoe (1726–7): Daniel Defoe, *The Complete English Tradesman* 2 vols

Defoe (1727) (2): Daniel Defoe, *Conjugal Lewdness: or, Matrimonial Whoredom*

Defoe (1725): Daniel Defoe, *Every-Body's Business is No-Body's Business: or, Private Abuses, Publick Grievances*

Defoe (1697): Daniel Defoe, *An Essay upon Projects*

Defoe (1715): Daniel Defoe, *The Family Instructor*

Defoe (1722): Daniel Defoe, *The Fortunes and Misfortunes of the Famous Moll Flanders* (1972)

Defoe (1724): Daniel Defoe, *The Great Law of Subordination consider'd; or, the Insolence and Unsufferable Behaviour of Servants*

Defoe (1722) (2): Daniel Defoe, *Religious Courtship*

Defoe (1706): Daniel Defoe, *Remarks on the Bill to Prevent Frauds Committed by Bankrupts*

Defoe (1719): Daniel Defoe, *Robinson Crusoe* (1906)

Defoe (1724) (2): Daniel Defoe, *Roxana, the Fortunate Mistress* (1969)

Defoe (1729): Daniel Defoe, *Some Objections . . . relating to the present intended relief of prisoners*

Defoe (1724–6): Daniel Defoe, *A Tour through the Whole Island of Great Britain* (1962)

De Krey (1985): G. S. De Krey, *A Fractured Society: the politics of London in the first age of party, 1688–1715* (Oxford)

De Krey (1983): G. S. De Krey, 'Political radicalism in London after the Glorious Revolution', *JMH* lv

De Laune (1681): Thomas de Laune, *The Present State of London*

De Muralt (1726): B. L. de Muralt, *Letters describing the Characters and Customs of the English and French Nations*

De Saussure (1902): C. de Saussure, *A Foreign View of England in the reigns of George I and II*

Dickson (1967): P. G. M. Dickson, *The Financial Revolution in England*

Dickson (1960): P. G. M. Dickson, *The Sun Insurance Office, 1710–1960*

Discourse (1678): *A Discourse shewing the Great Advantages that New-Buildings, and the enlarging of Towns and Cities do bring to a Nation*

Donnan (1931): E. M. Donnan, 'Eighteenth-century merchants: Micajah Perry', *Journal of Economic and Business History* iv

Dowdell (1932): E. G. Dowdell, *A Hundred Years of Quarter Sessions: the Government of Middlesex from 1660 to 1760* (Cambridge)

Drummond & Wilbraham (1939): J. C. Drummond & Anne Wilbraham, *The Englishman's Food: a history of five centuries of English diet*

Duffy (1980): I. P. H. Duffy, 'English bankrupts, 1571–1861', *American Journal of Legal History* xxiv

Duman (1981): Daniel Duman, 'The English Bar in the Georgian Era', in Prest (1981)

Dunlop (1912): O. Jocelyn Dunlop, *English Apprenticeship and Child Labour*

Dunn (1973): Richard Dunn, 'The London weavers' riot of 1675', *GSLH* i

Dunton (1703–8): John Dunton, *The Athenian Oracle* 4 vols

Dunton (1705): John Dunton, *Life and Errors*

R. E. (1877): R. E., *Choice Chips of Revenue Lore: being papers relating to the establishment of the excise* (Portsmouth)

Earle (1986): Peter Earle, 'Age and accumulation in the London business community', in McKendrick & Outhwaite (1986)

Earle (1989): Peter Earle, 'The female labour force in late seventeenth and early eighteenth century London', *EcHR* (forthcoming)

Earle (1976): Peter Earle, *The World of Defoe*

Edwards (1964): Ralph Edwards, *The Shorter Dictionary of English Furniture from the Middle Ages to the late Georgian period*

Edwards (1974): Rhoda Edwards, 'London Potters, c.1570–1710', *Journal of Ceramic History* vi

Ehrman (1953): John Ehrman, *The Navy in the War of William III, 1689–1697* (Cambridge)

Elliott (1981): Vivien Brodsky Elliott, 'Single women in the London marriage market: age, status and mobility, 1598–1619', in Outhwaite (1981)

Elliss (1956): Aytoun Ellis, *The Penny Universities: a history of the coffee-houses*

Essay (1718): *An Essay against Forestallers*

Essay (1707): *An Essay on Credit and the Bankrupt Act*

Evans (1977): Margaret Evans, 'Francis Estwick & John Coningsby: a seventeenth-century business partnership', M.Sc. dissertation, L.S.E.

Evelyn (1955): John Evelyn, *Diary* 6 vols (ed. E. S. de Beer) (Oxford)

Everitt (1966): A. Everitt, 'Social mobility in early modern England', *P & P* 33

Ewen (1932): C. L. Ewen, *Lotteries and Sweepstakes in the British Isles*

Ewing (1984): E Ewing, *Everyday Dress, 1650–1900*

J. F. (1696): J. F., *The Merchant's Warehouse Laid Open: or, the Plain Dealing Linnen Draper*

Fair Play (1708): *Fair Play for One's Life*

Falkus (1976): M. E. Falkus, 'Lighting in the Dark Ages of English Economic History: town streets before the Industrial Revolution', in Coleman & John (1976)

Federer (1980): Andrew Federer, 'Payment, credit and the organization of work in eighteenth-century Westminster', paper given at the SSRC Conference on Manufacture in Town and Country before the Factory, Balliol College, Oxford, September 1980

Fielding (1751): Henry Fielding, *An Enquiry into the causes of the late increase of robbers with some proposals for remedying this growing evil*

Finlay (1979): R. A. P. Finlay, 'Population and fertility in London, 1580–1650', *JFamH* iv

Finlay (1981): R. A. P. Finlay, *Population and Metropolis: the demography of London, 1580–1650* (Cambridge)

Finlay & Shearer (1986): Roger Finlay & Beatrice Shearer, 'Population growth and suburban expansion', in Beier & Finlay (1986)

Fisher (1948): F. J. Fisher, 'The development of London as a centre of conspicuous consumption in the 16th and 17th centuries', *TRHS* 4th ser. xxx

Fisher (1935): F. J. Fisher, 'The development of the London food market, 1540–1640', *EcHR* v

Fisher (1968): F. J. Fisher, 'The growth of London', in E. W. Ives (ed.), *The English Revolution, 1600–1660*

Fisher (1971): F. J. Fisher, 'London as an engine of economic growth', in J. S. Bromley & E. H. Kossman (eds), *Britain and the Netherlands*

Fletcher (1975): Anthony Fletcher, *A County Community in Peace and War; Sussex, 1600–1660*

Flinn (1984): M. W. Flinn, *The History of the British Coal Industry: vol. ii, 1700–1830: the Industrial Revolution* (Oxford)

Forbes (1976): T. R. Forbes, 'By what disease or casualty: the changing face of death in London', *JHMed* xxxi

Foreigner's (1729): *A Foreigner's Guide to London*

Fowler & Cornforth (1974): John Fowler & John Cornforth, *English Decoration in the eighteenth century*

Francis (1986): Clinton W. Francis, 'Practice, strategy and institution: debt collection in the English common-law courts, 1740–1840', *Northwestern University Law Review* lxxx

Francis (1983): Clinton W. Francis, 'The structure of juridical administration and the development of contract law in seventeenth-century England', *Columbia Law Review* lxxxiii

Frith (1954): Brian Frith (ed.), *Gloucestershire Marriage Allegations, 1637–80; Publications of Bristol & Gloucs Arch. Soc.* ii

Furley (1959): O. W. Furley, 'The pope-burning processions of the late seventeenth century', *History* xliv

Galenson (1986): David W. Galenson, *Traders, Planters and Slaves: Market Behaviour in early English America* (Cambridge)

Galton (1896): F. W. Galton, *Select documents illustrating the history of trade unionism: 1. The Tailoring Trades*

Gentle & Feild (1975): Rupert Gentle & Rachel Feild, *English Domestic Brass, 1680–1810*

George (1927): M. D. George, 'London coalheavers', *Economic History* i

George (1925): M. D. George, *London Life in the Eighteenth Century*

Gilboy (1934): Elizabeth W. Gilboy, *Wages in Eighteenth-century England* (Cambridge, Mass.)

Gill (1961): Conrad Gill, *Merchants and mariners of the eighteenth century*

Gillis (1983): John R. Gillis, 'Conjugal settlements: resort to clandestine common law marriages in England and Wales, 1650–1850', in J. Bossy (ed.), *Disputes and Settlements* (Cambridge)

Gillis (1985): John R. Gillis, *For Better, for Worse: British marriages, 1600 to the present* (Oxford)

Ginsburg (1980): Madeleine Ginsburg, 'Rags to riches: the second-hand clothes trade, 1700–1978', *Costume* xiv

Ginsburg (1972): Madeleine Ginsburg, 'The Tailoring and Dressmaking Trades, 1700–1850', *Costume* vi

Girdler (1953): Lew Girdler, 'Defoe's education at Newington Green Academy', *Studies in Philology* i

Gittings (1984): C. Gittings, *Death, Burial and the Individual in early modern England*

Glass (1966): D. V. Glass, 'Introduction to London (1966)

Glass (1968): D. V. Glass, 'Notes on the demography of London at the end of the seventeenth century', *Daedalus* xcvii

Glass (1969): D. V. Glass, 'Socio-economic status and occupations in the City of London at the end of the seventeenth century', in A. E. J. Hollaender & William Kellaway (eds), *Studies in London History*

Gloag (1964): John Gloag, *The Englishman's Chair*

Godfrey (1975): Eleanor S. Godfrey, *The Development of English Glassmaking, 1560–1640* (Oxford)

Goodinge (1713): Thomas Goodinge, *The Law against Bankrupts* 3rd ed.

Grant (1962): J. Grant, 'The gentry of London in the reign of Charles I', *University of Birmingham Historical Journal* viii

Gras (1915): N. S. B. Gras, *The Evolution of the English Corn Market* (Cambridge, Mass.)

Grassby (1970) (1): Richard Grassby, 'English merchant capitalism in the late seventeenth century: the composition of business fortunes', *P&P* 46

Grassby (1970) (2): Richard Grassby, 'The personal wealth of the business community in seventeenth-century England', *EcHR* 2nd ser. xxiii

Grassby (1969): Richard Grassby, 'The rate of profit in the seventeenth century', *EngHR* lxxxiii

Grassby (1978): Richard Grassby, 'Social mobility and business enterprise in seventeenth-century England', in D. Pennington & K. Thomas, *Puritans and Revolutionaries* (Oxford)

Graunt (1661): John Graunt, *Natural and Political Observations upon the Bills of Mortality* (reprinted & edited by W. F. Willcox) (Baltimore, 1939)

Green & Wigram (1881): H. Green & R. Wigram, *Chronicles of Blackwall Yard*

Guildhall (1981): Guildhall Library, *The A to Z of Georgian London*

N. H. (1684): N. H., *The Compleat Tradesman: or, the exact dealer's daily companion*

Habakkuk (1960): H. J. Habakkuk, 'The English land market in the eighteenth century', in J. S. Bromley & E. H. Kossmann, *Britain and the Netherlands*

Habakkuk (1940): H. J. Habakkuk, 'English landownership, 1680–1740', *EcHR* x

Hajnal (1965): J. Hajnal, 'European marriage patterns in perspective', in D. V. Glass & D. E. C. Eversley (eds), *Population in History*

Hamilton (1951): Bernice Hamilton, 'The medical professions in the eighteenth century', *EcHR* 2nd ser. iv

Hamilton (1926): H. Hamilton, *The English Brass and Copper Industries to 1880*

Hans (1951): N. Hans, *New Trends in Education in the Eighteenth Century*

Hanway (1767): Jonas Hanway, *Letters on the Importance of Preserving the Rising Generation of the Labouring Part of Our Fellow Subjects*

Harley (1968): J. Harley, *Music in Purcell's London*

Harte (1973): N. B. Harte, 'The rise of protection and the English linen trade, 1690–1790', in N. B. Harte & K. G. Ponting, *Textile History and Economic History* (Manchester)

Harvey (1678): Sir Gideon Harvey, *The Family-Physician and the House-Apothecary*

Haskell (1959): Francis Haskell, 'The market for Italian art in the seventeenth century', *P&P* 15

Hatcher & Barker (1974): John Hatcher & T. C. Barker, *A History of British Pewter*

Hatton (1708): Edward Hatton, *A New View of London*

Heal (1931): Ambrose Heal, *The English writing masters and their copy books* (Cambridge)

Heal (1952): Ambrose Heal, *The London Furniture Makers*

Heal (1925): Ambrose Heal, *London Tradesmen's Cards of the Eighteenth Century*

Hecht (1956): J. J. Hecht, *The Domestic Servant Class in Eighteenth-century England*

Helmholz (1974): R. M. Helmholz, *Marriage litigation in medieval England*

Herbert (1837): William Herbert, *The History of the Twelve Great Livery Companies of London*

Hexter (1961): J. H. Hexter, 'The myth of the middle class', in ibid., *Reappraisals in History*

Hilton Price (1890–1): F. G. Hilton Price, *A Handbook of London Bankers*

Hinton (1959): R. W. K. Hinton, *The Eastland Trade and the Common Weal in the Seventeenth Century* (Cambridge)

Hoare (1932): P. R. Hoare, *Hoare's Bank: A Record, 1673–1932*

Holden (1951): J. Milnes Holden, 'Bills of exchange during the seventeenth century', *Law Quarterly Review* lxvii

Holden (1955): J. Milnes Holden, *The History of Negotiable Instruments in English Law*

Holdsworth (1903–72): Sir W. Holdsworth, *History of English Law* 17 vols

Holme (1688): Randle Holme, *The Academy of Armory*

Holmes (1982): Geoffrey Holmes, *Augustan England: Professions, State and Society, 1680–1730*

Holmes (1967): G. Holmes, *British Politics in the Age of Anne*

Holmes (1977): G. Holmes, 'Gregory King and the social structure of pre-industrial England', *TRHS* 5th ser. xxvii

Holmes (1976): G. Holmes, 'The Sacheverell Riots: the crowd and the Church in early eighteenth-century London', *P&P* 72

Hone (1950): C. R. Hone, *Life of Dr John Radcliffe, 1652–1714*

Hoon (1968): E. E. Hoon, *Organization of the English Customs System, 1696–1786*

Hopkin (1980): Karen Hopkin, 'The victualling trades of London, 1666 to 1720, with special reference to cookshops', M.Sc. dissertation, L.S.E.

Hoppit (1986) (1): Julian Hoppit, 'Financial crises in eighteenth-century England', *EcHR* 2nd ser. xxxix

Hoppit (1986) (2): Julian Hoppit, 'The use and abuse of credit in eighteenth-century England', in McKendrick & Outhwaite (1986)

Horsefield (1922): J. Keith Horsefield, 'The "Stop of the Exchequer" Revisited', *EcHR* 2nd ser. xxxv

Horwitz (1987) (1): Henry Horwitz, '"The mess of the middle class" revisited: the case of the "big bourgeoisie" of Augustan London', *Continuity and Change* ii

Horwitz (1987) (2); Henry Horwitz, 'Party in a civic context: London from the Exclusion Crisis to the Fall of Walpole', in Clyve Jones (ed.), *Britain in the First Age of Party, 1680–1750*

Horwitz (1984): Henry Horwitz, 'Testamentary practice, family strategies, and the last phases of the Custom of London, 1660–1725', *Law and History Review* ii

Hotson (1928): Leslie Hotson, *The Commonwealth and Restoration Stage* (Cambridge, Mass.)

Houghton (1727–8): John Houghton, *A Collection for the Improvement of Husbandry and Trade* 4 vols (ed. R. Bradley)

Houlbrooke (1984): Ralph Houlbrooke, *The English Family, 1450–1700*

Howard (1894): Eliot Howard (ed.), *The Eliot Papers* vol. 2 [diary of Peter Briggins] (Gloucester)

Howson (1970): Gerald Howson, *Thief-Taker General: the rise and fall of Jonathan Wild*

Hughes (1926): Helen Sard Hughes, 'The middle-class reader and the English novel', *JEGP* xxv

Humpherus (1887–9): H. Humpherus, *History of the origin and progress of the Company of Watermen and Lightermen of the River Thames* 3 vols

Hunter & Macalpine (1963): Richard Hunter & Ida Macalpine (eds), *Three Hundred Years of Psychiatry, 1535–1860*

Innes (1980): J. Innes, 'The King's Bench prison in the later eighteenth century', in J. Brewer & J. Styles (eds), *An Ungovernable People: the English and their law in the seventeenth and eighteenth centuries*

James (1948): F. G. James, 'Charity endowments as a source of local credit in seventeenth and eighteenth-century England', *JEH* viii

Jarvis (1969): R. C. Jarvis, 'Eighteenth-century London shipping', in A. E. J. Hollaender & W. Kellaway (eds), *Studies in London History*

Jeaffreson (1872): John C. Jeaffreson, *Brides and Bridals*

Johnson (1922): A. H. Johnson, *The History of the Worshipful Company of the Drapers of London* vol. iv (Oxford)

Johnson (1985): Paul Johnson, *Saving and Spending: the working-class economy in Britain, 1870–1939* (Oxford)

D. W. Jones (1972) (2): D. W. Jones, 'The "Hallage" receipts of the London cloth markets, 1562–c.1720', *EcHR* 2nd ser. xxv

D. W. Jones (1972) (1): D. W. Jones, 'London merchants and the crisis of the 1690s', in Peter Clark & Paul Slack (eds), *Crisis and Order in English Towns, 1500–1700*

D. W. Jones (1971): D. W. Jones, 'London overseas merchant groups at the end of the seventeenth century', D.Phil. Oxford

E. Jones (1980): Emrys Jones, 'London in the early seventeenth century: an ecological approach', *LJ* vi

E. L. Jones (1964): E. L. Jones, *Seasons and Prices: the role of the weather in English agricultural history*

Jones & Falkus (1979): E. L. Jones & M. E. Falkus, 'Urban improvement and the English economy in the seventeenth and eighteenth centuries', *Research in Economic History* iv

J. R. Jones (1961): J. R. Jones, *The First Whigs: the politics of the Exclusion Crisis, 1678–1683*

M. G. Jones (1938): M. G. Jones, *The Charity School Movement of the 18th Century*

P. E. Jones (1976): P. E. Jones, *The Butchers of London*

P. E. Jones (1966): P. E. Jones (ed.), *The Fire Court* 2 vols

Jones & Judges (1935): P. E. Jones & A. V. Judges, 'London population in the late seventeenth century', *EcHR* vi

W. R. Jones (1979): W. R. Jones, 'The foundations of English bankruptcy. Statutes and commissions in the early modern period', *Trans. American Philosophical Society* 69 pt 3

Jordan (1960): W. K. Jordan, *The Charities of London, 1480–1660*

Joslin (1954): D. M. Joslin, 'London private bankers, 1720–85', *EcHR* 2nd ser. vii

Joy (1965): E. T. Joy, 'The overseas trade in furniture in the eighteenth century', *FurnH* i

Kahl (1956): William F. Kahl, 'Apprenticeship and the freedom of the London Livery Companies, 1690–1750', *GM* vii

Kellett (1957–8): J. R. Kellett, 'The breakdown of Guild and Corporation control over the handicraft and retail trades of London', *EcHR* 2nd ser. x

Kellett (1963): J. R. Kellett, 'The Financial Crisis of the Corporation of London and the Orphans' Act, 1694', *GM* ii

Kenny (1879): C. S. Kenny, *The History of the Law of England as to the effects of marriage on property and on the wife's legal capacity*

Kerridge (1985): Eric Kerridge, *Textile Manufacture in Early Modern England* (Manchester)

King (1936): Gregory King, *Two Tracts* (ed. Barnett) (Baltimore)

Kirkman (1673): Francis Kirkman, *The Unlucky Citizen experimentally described in the various misfortunes of an unlucky Londoner*

Kitch (1986): M. J. Kitch, 'Capital and Kingdom: migration to later Stuart London', in Beier & Finlay (1986)

Knoop & Jones (1936): D. Knoop & G. P. Jones, *The Rise of the Mason Contractor*

Kussmaul (1981): Anne Kussmaul, *Servants in Husbandry*

Labrousse & Braudel (1970): Ernest Labrousse & Fernand Braudel (eds), *Histoire économique et sociale de la France* t.2 (Paris)

Lacey (1985): Kay E. Lacey, 'Women and work in fourteenth and fifteenth-century London', in Charles & Duffin (1985)

Lang (1974): R. G. Lang, 'Social origins and social aspirations of Jacobean London merchants', *EcHR* 2nd ser. xxvii

Laslett (1965): Peter Laslett, *The World We Have Lost*

Laws (1765): *The Laws and Customs, Rights, Liberties and Privileges of the City of London*

Lemire (1984): Beverly Lemire, 'Developing consumerism and the ready-made clothing trade in Britain, 1750–1800', *TextH* xv

Leybourn (1668): William Leybourn, *A Platform for Purchasers, a Guide for Builders, a Mate for Measurers*

Lillywhite (1963): B. Lillywhite, *London Coffee-houses*

Lindsay (1927): J. Seymour Lindsay, *Iron and brass implements of the English home*

Lindsay (1978): Jack Lindsay, *The Monster City: Defoe's London, 1688–1730*

List (1747): *A List of the names of surgeons etc.*

Littleton & Yamey (1956): A. C. Littleton & B. S. Yamey, *Studies in the History of Accounting*

London (1966): London Record Society, *London Inhabitants within the Walls, 1694*, LRS ii

Loomes (1981): Brian Loomes, *The Early Clockmakers of Great Britain*

Lynch (1971): Kathleen M. Lynch, *Jacob Tonson: Kit-Cat Publisher* (Knoxville)

Lyons (1944): Sir Henry Lyons, *The Royal Society, 1660–1940* (Cambridge)

Macaulay (1850): T. B. Macaulay, *The History of England from the accession of James the Second* vol.i, 7th ed.

McBride (1976): Theresa McBride, *The Domestic Revolution: the modernization of household service in England and France, 1820–1920*

MacDonald (1981): Michael MacDonald, *Mystical Bedlam*

McDonnell (1909): M. F. J. McDonnell, *History of St Paul's School*

A. Macfarlane (1979): Alan Macfarlane, 'The family, sex and marriage in England, 1500–1800', *History and Theory* xviii

A. Macfarlane (1986): Alan Macfarlane, *Marriage and Love in England: modes of reproduction, 1300–1840* (Oxford)

A. Macfarlane (1978): Alan Macfarlane, *The Origin of English Individualism: the family, property and social transition* (Oxford)

S. Macfarlane (1986): Stephen Macfarlane, 'Social policy and the poor in the later seventeenth century', in Beier & Finlay (1986)

McGrath (1948): P. V. McGrath, 'The marketing of food, fodder and livestock in the London area in the seventeenth century', London M.A.

McKendrick et al. (1982): Neil McKendrick, John Brewer & J. H. Plumb, *The Birth of a Consumer Society; the commercialization of 18th century England*

McKendrick & Outhwaite (1986): Neil McKendrick & R. B. Outhwaite (eds), *Business Life and Public Policy* (Cambridge)

Macpherson (1805): D. Macpherson, *Annals of commerce, manufactures, fisheries and navigation etc.*

McVeagh (1981): John McVeagh, *Tradefull Merchants; the portrayal of the capitalist in literature*

Magalotti (1821): L. Magalotti, *Travels of Cosmo the Third, Grand Duke of Tuscany, through England*

Maitland (1739): W. H. Maitland, *History and survey of London*

Maitland (1756): W. H. Maitland, *The History of London* 2 vols

Malcolm (1808) & (1810): J. P. Malcolm, *Anecdotes of the Manners and Customs of London* 1st & 2nd eds

Mandeville (1709): Bernard de Mandeville, *The Virgin Unmask'd*

Mann (1971): Julia de Lacy Mann, *The Cloth Industry in the West of England from 1640 to 1880*

Manning (1976): B. Manning, *The English People and the English Revolution*

Marshall (1920): Alfred Marshall, *Principles of Economics* 8th ed.

Marshall (1974): J. D. Marshall (ed.), *Autobiography of William Stout*

Martin (1892): J. B. Martin, *The Grasshopper in Lombard Street*

Martindale (1968): L. Martindale, 'Demography and land use in late seventeenth and eighteenth-century Middlesex', Ph.D. London

Mason (1754): Simon Mason, *Narrative*

Massie (1761): Joseph Massie, *Calculations of the Present Taxes*

Massie (1760): Joseph Massie, *To the Printer of the Gazetteer*

Mathias (1959): Peter Mathias, *The Brewing Industry in England, 1700–1830* (Cambridge)

Mathias (1957): Peter Mathias, 'The social structure in the eighteenth century: a calculation by Joseph Massie', *EcHR* 2nd ser. x, reprinted in Mathias (1979)

Mathias (1979): Peter Mathias, *The Transformation of England: essays in the economic and social history of England in the eighteenth century*

Matthews (1906): Joseph B. Matthews, *The Law of Moneylending, Past and Present*

Matthews (1978): Leslie G. Matthews, 'Day Book of the Court Apothecary in the time of William and Mary, 1691', *MedH* xxii

Maxted (1977): I. Maxted, *The London Book Trade, 1775–1800*

Mayer (1968): Edward Mayer, *The Curriers and the City of London*

Maynwaring (1683): Edward Maynwaring, *The Method and Means of Enjoying Health, Vigour and Long Life*

Mechling (1975): Jay Mechling, 'Advice to historians on advice to mothers', *Journal of Social History* ix

Melton (1986): Frank Melton, *Sir Robert Clayton and the Origins of English Deposit Banking, 1658–1685* (Cambridge)

Miège (1691): Guy Miège, *The New State of England*

Miège (1703): Guy Miège, *New State of England under our sovereign Queen Anne*

Minchinton (1969): W. E. Minchton (ed.), *The Growth of English Overseas Trade*

Misson (1698): Henri Misson, *Mémoires et observations faites par un voyageur en Angleterre*

Misson (1719): Henri Misson, *Memoirs and Observations in his travels over England* (trans Ozells)

Mitchell & Deane (1962): B. R. Mitchell & P. Deane, *Abstract of British Historical Statistics* (Cambridge)

Monier-Williams (1977): Randall Monier-Williams, *The Tallow-chandlers of London* vol. iv

Morgan (1944): Edmund S. Morgan, *The Puritan Family*

Morris (1979): R. J. Morris, 'The middle class and the property cycle during the Industrial Revolution', in T. Smout (ed.). *The Search for Wealth and Stability*

Morse (1921): H. B. Morse, 'Supercargoes in the China trade', *EngHR* xxxvi

Newman (1924): Sir George Newman, *Thomas Sydenham: reformer of English medicine*

Nichols (1812–15): John Nichols, *Literary Anecdotes of the Eighteenth Century* 8 vols

Nicoll (1925): Allardyce Nicoll, *A history of early eighteenth-century drama, 1700–1750* (Cambridge)

Nicoll (1923): Allardyce Nicoll, *A history of Restoration drama* (Cambridge)

North (1890): Roger North, *Lives of the North* 3 vols (ed. Jessopp)

O'Day (1987): Rosemary O'Day, 'The Anatomy of a Profession: the Clergy of the Church of England', in Prest (1987) (1)

Okin (1983): S. M. Okin, 'Patriarchy and married women's property in England: questions on some current views', *Eighteenth-century Studies* 17

Olson (1983): Alison G. Olson, 'The Virginia merchants of London: a study in eighteenth-century interest-group politics', *William & Mary Quarterly* xl

Orchard & May (1933): Dorothy J. Orchard & Geoffrey May, *Moneylending in Great Britain*

Outhwaite (1981): R. B. Outhwaite, *Marriage and Society: studies in the social history of marriage*

Outhwaite (1986): R. B. Outhwaite, 'Marriage as business: opinions on the rise in aristocratic bridal portions in early modern England', in McKendrick & Outhwaite (1986)

Overton (1885): J. H. Overton, *Life in the English Church, 1660–1714*

Owen (1964): David Owen, *English Philanthropy, 1660–1960* (Harvard)

Owens & Furbank (1986): W. R. Owens & P. N. Furbank, 'Defoe and imprisonment for debt', *Review of English Studies* n.s. xxxvii

Parish Clerks (1732): *New Remarks of London . . . collected by the Company of Parish Clerks*

Parliamentary History: *Cobbett's Parliamentary History of England* 12 vols (1806–12)

Peachey (1924): G. C. Peachey, *Memoirs of William and John Hunter* (Plymouth)

Pearce (1901): E. H. Pearce, *Annals of Christ's Hospital*

Pearl (1979): V. Pearl, 'Change and stability in seventeenth-century London', *LJ* v

Pearl (1961): V. Pearl, *London and the Outbreak of the Puritan Revolution* (Oxford)

Pearl (1981): V. Pearl, 'Social policy in early modern London', in H. Lloyd-Jones et al. (eds), *History and Imagination*

Pedicord (1954): H. W. Pedicord, *The Theatrical Public in the Time of Garrick* (New York)

Pelzer (1982): John & Linda Pelzer, 'The coffee-houses of Augustan London', *History Today* xxxii

Pendrill (1937): Charles Pendrill, *Old Parish Life in London* (Oxford)

Pepys: *The Diary of Samuel Pepys* 11 vols (1970–83) (ed. Latham & Matthews)

Perkin (1969): Harold Perkin, *The Origins of Modern English Society, 1780–1880*

Philips (1731): Erasmus Philips, *The Creditor's Advocate and Debtor's Friend*

Phillips (1719): Henry Phillips, *The Purchaser's Pattern* 6th ed.

Pietas (1714): *Pietas Londinensis*

Pittis (1715): W. Pittis, *Some Memoirs of the Life of J. Radcliffe*

Plant (1974): Marjorie Plant, *The English Book Trade* 3rd ed.

Plumb (1967): J. H. Plumb, *The Growth of Political Stability in England, 1675–1725*

Plumb (1975): J. H. Plumb, 'The new world of children in eighteenth-century England', *P & P* 67

Polak (1975): Ada Polak, *Glass, its makers and its public*

Pollock (1983): Linda A. Pollock, *Forgotten Children: parent-child relations from 1500 to 1900* (Cambridge)

Pool (1966): Bernard Pool, *The Navy Board Contracts, 1600–1832*

Powell (1917): Chilton Latham Powell, *English Domestic Relations, 1487–1653*

Power (1986): M. J. Power, 'The social topography of Restoration London', in Beier & Finlay (1986)

Poynter (1961) (2): F. N. L. Poynter (ed.), *The Evolution of Medical Practice in Britain*

Poynter (1961): F. N. L. Poynter, 'Influence of Government legislation', in Poynter (1961) (2)

Poynter (1965): F. N. L. Poynter, *The Journal of James Yonge, Plymouth Surgeon*

Poynter & Bishop (1951): F. N. L. Poynter & W. L. Bishop, *A Seventeenth-century Doctor and his patients: John Symcotts, 1592?–1662*

Pracktick (1681): *The Pracktick Part of the Law*

Pressnell (1956): Leslie Pressnell, *English Country Banking in the Industrial Revolution*

Prest (1981) (2): Wilfrid Prest, 'The English Bar, 1550–1700', in Prest (1981)

Prest (1981): Wilfrid Prest (ed.), *Lawyers in Early Modern Europe and America*

Prest (1987) (2): Wilfrid Prest, 'Lawyers', in Prest (1987) (1)

Prest (1987) (1): Wilfrid Prest (ed.), *The Professions in early modern England*

Price (1980): J. M. Price, *Capital and Credit in British Overseas Trade: the view from the Chesapeake, 1700–1776*

Price & Clemens (1987): J. M. Price & Paul G. E. Clemens, 'A revolution of scale in overseas trade: British firms in the Chesapeake trade, 1675–1775', *JEH* xlvii

Priestley & Corfield (1982): Ursula Priestley & P. J. Corfield, 'Rooms and room use in Norwich housing, 1580–1730', *PMA* xvi

Primatt (1667): S[tephen] P[rimatt], *The City and Country Purchaser and Builder*

Prior (1985): Mary Prior, 'Women and the urban economy: Oxford, 1500–1800', in ibid. (ed.), *Women in English Society, 1500–1800*

Proposals (1706): *Proposals for Establishing a Charitable Fund in the City of London*

Ramsay (1982): G. D. Ramsay, *The English Woollen Industry, 1500–1700*

Ramsay (1943): G. D. Ramsay, *The Wiltshire Woollen Industry in the sixteenth and seventeenth centuries*

Rappaport (1983–4): S. Rappaport, 'Social structure and mobility in sixteenth-century London', *LJ* ix & x

Ravenhill (1689): William Ravenhill, *A Short Account of the Company of Grocers*

Ravenscroft (1672): Edward Ravenscroft, *The Citizen Turn'd Gentleman*

Reddaway (1940): T. F. Reddaway, *The Rebuilding of London after the Great Fire*

Redgrave (1878): Samuel Redgrave, *A Dictionary of Artists of the English School*

Rees (1923): J. Aubrey Rees, *The Worshipful Company of Grocers*

Rees & Fenby (1931): R. N. K. Rees & Charles Fenby, 'Meals and meal-times', in Reginald Lennard (ed.), *Englishmen at Rest and Play* (Oxford)

Reiss (1934): Erna Reiss, *The Rights and Duties of Englishwomen: a study in law and public opinion* (Manchester)

Review: A Weekly Review of the Affairs of France and various similar titles (9 vols, 1704–13) (facsimile edition, 1938)

Ribeiro (1984): Aileen Ribeiro, *Dress in Eighteenth-century Europe, 1715–89*

Ribeiro (1983): Aileen Ribeiro, *A Visual History of Dress: the eighteenth century*

Richards (1958): R. D. Richards, *The Early History of Banking in England*

Richardson (1741): Samuel Richardson, *Familiar Letters on Important Occasions* (1928)

Roberts (1641): Lewes Roberts, *The Treasure of Traffike*

Roberts (1965): R. S. Roberts, 'The early history of the import of drugs into Britain', in F. N. L. Poynter (ed.), *The Evolution of Pharmacy in Britain*

Roberts (1964) (2): R. S. Roberts, 'The London apothecaries and medical practice in Tudor and Stuart England', Ph.D. London

Roberts (1964) (1): R. S. Roberts, 'The personnel and practice of medicine in Tudor and Stuart England: Part II – London', *MedH* viii

Robertson (1958): A. B. Robertson, 'Open market in London in the eighteenth century', *ELP* i

Robertson (1961): A. B. Robertson, 'Smithfield cattle market', *ELP* iv

Robson (1959): R. Robson, *The Attorney in Eighteenth-century England* (Cambridge)

Roche (1987): Daniel Roche, *The People of Paris: an essay in popular culture in the eighteenth century*

N. Rogers (1979): N. Rogers, 'Money, land and lineage: the big bourgeoisie of Hanoverian London', *SocH* iv

N. Rogers (1978): N. Rogers, 'Popular protest in early Hanoverian London', *P&P* lxxix

N. Rogers (1977): N. Rogers, 'Resistance to Oligarchy: the City Opposition to Walpole and his successors, 1725–47', in J. Stevenson, *London in the Age of Reform* (Oxford)

P. Rogers (1972): Pat Rogers, *Grub Street: studies in a sub-culture*

P. Rogers (1978): Pat Rogers, 'The writer and society', in Pat Rogers (ed.), *The Eighteenth Century*

Rothstein (1964): N. K. A. Rothstein, 'The calico campaign of 1719–21', *ELP* vii

Rothstein (1961): N. K. A. Rothstein, 'The silk industry in London, 1702–66', London M.A.

Rouquet (1755): Jean Rouquet, *The Present State of the Arts in England*

Rudé (1971): George Rudé, *Hanoverian London, 1714–1808*

Ryder (1939): Dudley Ryder, *Diary* (ed. W. Matthews)

Ryerson (1961): Alice Ryerson, 'Medical advice on child rearing, 1500–1900', *Harvard Educational Review* xxxi

E.S. (1929): E.S., *The Compleat Housewife*

Sachse (1964): William L. Sachse, 'The Mob and the Revolution of 1688', *JBS* iv

Salmon (1724): Thomas Salmon, *Critical essay concerning marriage*

Salmon (1693): William Salmon, *The Compleat English Physician: or, the Druggist's Shop Opened*

Salmon (1682): William Salmon, *Pharmacopoeia Londinensis: or, the New London Dispensatory* 2nd ed.

Salmon (1701): William Salmon, *Polygraphice*

Sargeaunt (1898): J. Sargeaunt, *Annals of Westminster School*

Scarlett (1682): John Scarlett, *The Stile of Exchanges*

Schuyler (1931): R. L. Schuyler (ed.), *Joseph Tucker: a selection from his economic and political writings* (New York)

Schwarz (1979): L. D. Schwarz, 'Income distribution and social structure in London in the late eighteenth century', *EcHR* 2nd ser. xxxii

Schwarz (1982): L. D. Schwarz, 'Social class and social geography: the middle classes in London at the end of the eighteenth century', *SocH* vii

Scott (1910–12): W. R. Scott, *The Constitution and Finance of English, Scottish and Irish Joint-Stock Companies to 1720* 3 vols

Scouller (1966): R. E. Scouller, *The Armies of Queen Anne* (Oxford)

Seaver (1985): Paul S. Seaver, *Wallington's World: a Puritan Artisan in seventeenth-century London*

Servant's (1725): *The Servant's Calling: with some advice to the apprentice*
Shadwell (1691): Thomas Shadwell, *The Scowrers*
Shadwell (1720): Thomas Shadwell, *Works* 2 vols (Dublin)
Sharpe (1984): J. A. Sharpe, *Crime in Early Modern England, 1550–1700*
Shelton (1956): S. W. Shelton, 'The Goldsmith Banker', in Littleton & Yamey (1956)
Shoemaker (1987): R. B. Shoemaker, 'The London "Mob" in the early eighteenth century', *Journal of British Studies* xxvi
Simon (1906–9): A. L. Simon, *History of the Wine Trade in England* 3 vols
Simond (1817): Louis Simond, *Journal of a Tour and Residence in Great Britain*
A. Smith (1961): Adam Smith, *The Wealth of Nations* (Cannan paperback, 2 vols)
B. M. D. Smith (1967): Barbara M. D. Smith, 'The Galtons of Birmingham: Quaker gun merchants and bankers, 1702–1831', *Business History* ix
D. M. Smith (1963): D. M. Smith, 'The British hosiery industry at the middle of the nineteenth century', *Transactions of the Institute of British Geographers* xxxii
J. W. A. Smith (1954): Joe W. A. Smith, *The Birth of Modern Education*
R. Smith (1961): R. Smith, *Sea Coal for London: history of the coal factors in the London market*
S. R. Smith (1973) (2): S. R. Smith, 'The London apprentices as seventeenth-century adolescents', *P&P* 67
S. R. Smith (1973): S. R. Smith, 'The social and geographical origins of the London apprentices, 1630–1660', *GM* iv
T. Smith (1583): Sir Thomas Smith, *The Commonwealth of England*
Smollett (1748): T. Smollett, *Roderick Random*
Southall (1730): J. Southall, *A Treatise of Buggs*
Speck (1970): W. A. Speck, *Tory and Whig: the struggle in the constituencies, 1701–1715*
Speck & Gray (1975): W. A. Speck & W. A. Gray, 'Londoners at the Polls under Anne and George I', *GSLH* i
Spectator: Joseph Addison, Richard Steele and others, *The Spectator* (ed. Gregory Smith, 1907)
Stackhouse (1722): Thomas Stackhouse, *The Miseries and Great Hardships of the inferiour clergy, in and about London*
Steele (1722): Sir Richard Steele, *The Conscious Lovers*
Stern (1973): W. M. Stern, 'Cheese shipped coastwise to London towards the middle of the eighteenth century', *GM* iv
Stern (1954) (1): W. M. Stern, 'Gunmaking in seventeenth-century London', *Journal of the Arms and Armour Society* i
Stern (1954) (2): W. M. Stern, 'The London sugar refiners around 1800', *GM* iii
Stern (1960): W. M. Stern, *The Porters of London*
Stern (1956): W. M. Stern, 'The trade, art or misery of silk throwers of the City of London in the seventeenth century', *GM* vi
Stern (1979): W. M. Stern, 'Where, Oh where, are the Cheesemongers of London?', *LJ* v

Stewart (1891): Horace Stewart, *History of the Worshipful Company of Gold and Silver Wire-Drawers*

Stone (1977): L. Stone, *The Family, Sex and Marriage in England, 1500–1800*

Stone (1984): L. & J. C. Stone, *An Open Élite? England, 1540–1880*

Stone (1980): L. Stone, 'The residential development of the West End of London in the seventeenth century', in B. C. Malament (ed.) *After the Reformation* (Philadelphia)

Stone (1966): L. Stone, 'Social mobility in England, 1500–1700', *P&P* 33

Straus (1912): Ralph Straus, *Carriages and Coaches*

Straus (1927): Ralph Straus (ed.), *Tricks of the Town: eighteenth-century diversions*

Strype (1720): John Strype, *A Survey of the Cities of London and Westminster*

Styles (1953): P. Styles, 'The Heralds' Visitation of Warwickshire in 1682–3', *Birmingham Archaeological Society Transactions* lxxi

Summerson (1962): Sir John Summerson, *Georgian London* 2nd ed.

Supple (1970): Barry Supple, *The Royal Exchange Assurance*

Sutherland (1956): L. S. Sutherland, 'The City of London in eighteenth-century politics', in Richard Pares & A. J. P. Taylor (eds), *Essays presented to Sir Lewis Namier*

Swift (1948): Jonathan Swift, *Journal to Stella* 2 vols (ed. Williams)

Swinburne (1686): Henry Swinburne, *A Treatise of Spousals or Matrimonial Contracts*

Sykes (1934): N. Sykes, *Church and State in England in the Eighteenth century* (Cambridge)

Sykes (1926): N. Sykes, *Edmund Gibson, Bishop of London* (Oxford)

Tatler: Richard Steele, *The Tatler* (ed. Lewis Gibbs, 1953)

Tawney (1925): R. H. Tawney, 'Introduction' to Thomas Wilson, *A Discourse upon Usury* (1572)

Taylor (1966): E. G. R. Taylor, *The Mathematical Practitioners of Hanoverian England* (Cambridge)

Taylor (1954): E. G. R. Taylor, *The Mathematical Practitioners of Tudor and Stuart England* (Cambridge)

Taylor (1650): Jeremy Taylor, *The Rule and Exercises of Holy Living*

Taylor (1983): Lou Taylor, *Mourning dress: a costume and social history*

Tentamen (1704): *Tentamen Medicinale*

Thick (1985): Malcolm Thick, 'Market Gardening in England and Wales', in Joan Thirsk (ed.), *The Agrarian History of England and Wales* vol. v (Cambridge)

Thirsk (1973): Joan Thirsk, 'The fantastical folly of fashion: the English stocking knitting industry, 1500–1700', in N. B. Harte and K. G. Ponting, *Textile History and Economic History* (Manchester)

Thirsk & Cooper (1972): Joan Thirsk & J. P. Cooper, *Seventeenth-century Economic Documents* (Oxford)

Thomas (1959): Keith Thomas, 'The Double Standard', *JHI* xx

Thomas (1983): Keith Thomas, *Man and the Natural World : changing attitudes in England, 1500–1800*

Thomas (1971): Keith Thomas, *Religion and the Decline of Magic*

Thompson (1972): E. P. Thompson, 'Rough Music: le charivari anglais', *Annales* xxvii

Thompson (1967): E. P. Thompson, 'Time, work-discipline and industrial capitalism', *P&P* 38

Thornton (1978): Peter Thornton, *Seventeenth-century Interior Decoration in England, France and Holland*

Thornton & Tomlin (1980): Peter Thornton & Maurice Tomlin, *The Furnishing and Decoration of Ham House*

Thrupp (1948): Sylvia Thrupp, *The Merchant Class of Medieval London*

Thrupp (1933): Sylvia Thrupp, *A Short History of the Worshipful Company of Bakers of London*

Tillotson (1694): Archbishop John Tillotson, *Six Sermons on Education etc*

Tilmouth (1957–8): Michael Tilmouth, 'Some early London concerts and music clubs, 1670–1720', *Royal Musical Association Proceedings* lxxxiv

Tobias (1979): J. J. Tobias, *Crime and Police in England, 1700–1900* (Dublin)

Todd (1985): Barbara J. Todd, 'The remarrying widow: a stereotype reconsidered', in Prior (1985)

Trade (1681): *The Trade of England Revived and the Abuses thereof Rectified*

Treatise (1732): *A Treatise of Feme Coverts: or the Lady's Law*

Trenchfield (1671): Caleb Trenchfield, *A Cap of Gray Hairs for a Green Head*

Trip (1735): *A Trip through the Town*, in Straus (1927)

Trumbach (1978): Randolph Trumbach, *The rise of the egalitarian family: aristocratic kinship and domestic relations in eighteenth-century England* (New York)

Tryon (1691): Thomas Tryon, *The Way to Health, Long Life and Happiness*

Tucker (1936): R. F. Tucker, 'Real wages of artisans in London, 1729–1935', *Journal of the American Statistical Association* xxxi

Uffenbach (1934): Z. C. von Uffenbach, *London in 1710*

Unwin (1938): George Unwin, *The Gilds and Companies of London* 3rd ed.

Unwin (1904): George Unwin, *Industrial Organization in the Sixteenth and Seventeenth Centuries* (Oxford)

Utter & Needham (1937): R. P. Utter & G. B. Needham, *Pamela's Daughters*

Vanderlint (1734): Jacob Vanderlint, *Money Answers all Things*

Van Lennep (1965): William van Lennep, *The London Stage, 1660–1700* (Carbondale, Ill.)

Vernon (1678): John Vernon, *The Compleat Compting-house*

Vincent (1969): W. A. L. Vincent, *The Grammar Schools: their continuing tradition, 1660–1714*

Wadsworth (1712): Benjamin Wadsworth, *The well-ordered family* (Boston)

Wadsworth & Mann (1931): A. P. Wadsworth & J. de L. Mann, *The Cotton Trade and Industrial Lancashire, 1600–1780* (Manchester)

Wagner (1972): A. R. Wagner, *English Genealogy* 2nd ed. (Oxford)

Wall et al. (1963): C. Wall, H. C. Cameron & E. A. Underwood, *A History of the Worshipful Society of Apothecaries of London* (Oxford)

Wall (1978): Richard Wall, 'The age at leaving home', *JFamH*

Wallis (1952): P. J. Wallis, 'The Wase School Collection', *Bodleian Library Record* iv

Walpole (1888): Horace Walpole, *Anecdotes of Painting* (ed. Dallaway & Wornum)

Walton (1973): Karin M. Walton, 'The Worshipful Company of Upholders of the City of London', *FurnH* ix

Ward (1924): Edward Ward, *The London Spy* (ed. Ralph Straus)

Ward (1699): Edward Ward, *A Walk to Islington with a Description of New Tunbridge-Wells and Sadler's Musick-House*

Wareing (1980): J. Wareing, 'Changes in the geographical distribution of the recruitment of apprentices to the London Companies, 1486–1750', *Journal of Historical Geography* vi

Warner (1921): Sir Frank Warner, *The Silk Industry of the United Kingdom*

Watson (1963): J. Steven Watson, *A History of the Salters' Company*

Watt (1957): Ian Watt, *The Rise of the Novel*

Watts (1978): M. R. Watts, *The Dissenters* vol. i (Oxford)

Weatherill & Edwards (1971): L. Weatherill & Rhoda Edwards, 'Pottery making in London and Whitehaven in the late seventeenth century', *PMA* v

Webbs (1908): S. & B. Webb, *The Manor and the Borough* 2 vols

Webbs (1906): S. & B. Webb, *The Parish and the County*

Weiss (1982): Leonard Weiss, *Watch-making in England, 1760–1820*

Wells (1935): F. A. Wells, *The British Hosiery Knitwear Industry*

Westerfield (1915): R. B. Westerfield, *Middlemen in English Business, particularly between 1660 and 1760*, Transactions of the Connecticut Academy of Arts and Sciences xix (Yale)

Wheler (1698): Sir George Wheler, *The Protestant Monastery*

Whitley (1928): W. T. Whitley, *Artists and their Friends in England, 1700–1799*

Wickham Legg (1914): J. Wickham Legg, *English Church Life from the Restoration to the Tractarian Movement*

Wide & Morris (1969): S. M. Wide & J. A. Morris, 'The episcopal licensing of schoolmasters in the diocese of London., 1627–1685', *GM*

Wills (1971): Geoffrey Wills, *English Furniture, 1550–1760*

Wills (1965): Geoffrey Wills, *English Looking-glasses: a study of the glass, frames and makers, 1670–1820*

Wilson (1973): Constance A. Wilson, *Food and Drink in Britain*

Winder (1936): W. H. D. Winder, 'The Courts of Requests', *Law Quarterly Review* lii

Wisdom (1706): *The Wisdom of the Nation is Foolishness*

Wood (1935): A. C. Wood, *History of the Levant Company*

Woodhead (1965): J. R. Woodhead, *The Rulers of London, 1660–1689*

Wootton (1910): A. C. Wootton, *Chronicles of Pharmacy* 2 vols

Wrightson (1982): Keith Wrightson, *English Society, 1580–1680*

Wrightson (1986): 'The social order of early modern England: three approaches', in Bonfield et al. (1986)

Wrigley (1983): E. A. Wrigley, 'Growth of population in eighteenth-century England: a conundrum resolved', *P&P* 98

Wrigley (1967): E. A. Wrigley, 'A simple model of London's importance in changing English society and economy, 1650–1750', *P&P* 37

Wrigley (1985): E. A. Wrigley, 'Urban growth and agricultural change: England and the continent in the early modern period', *Journal of Interdisciplinary History* xv

Wrigley & Schofield (1983): E. A. Wrigley & R. S. Schofield, 'English population history from family reconstitution: summary results, 1600–1799', *Population Studies* xxxvii

Wrigley & Schofield (1981): E. A. Wrigley & R. S. Schofield, *The Population History of England, 1541–1871* (Cambridge)

Wroth (1896): W. W. Wroth, *The London Pleasure Gardens of the 18th century*

Yamey (1949): B. S. Yamey, 'Scientific book-keeping and the rise of capitalism', *EcHR* 2nd ser. i

Yamey et al. (1963): B. S. Yamey, H. C. Edey & H. W. Thomson, *Accounting in England and Scotland, 1543–1800*

Young (1965): Percy M. Young, *The Concert Tradition*

Zahedieh (1986): Nuala Zahedieh, 'The merchants of Port Royal, Jamaica, and the Spanish contraband trade, 1655–1692', *William & Mary Quarterly*, 3rd ser., xliii

Index

In order to keep the index to a reasonable length, most names of people used as examples or quoted in the text have been omitted. The figures in parentheses refer to the numbers of Notes.